Great Cities Through Travellers' Eyes

EDITED BY

PETER FURTADO

Great Cities Through Travellers' Eyes

39 ILLUSTRATIONS

First published in 2019 in the United States of
America by Thames & Hudson Inc., 500 Fifth Avenue,
New York, New York 10110

www.thamesandhudsonusa.com

Library of Congress Control Number 2019932276

ISBN 978-0-500-02165-1

Printed and bound in the UK by CPI (UK) Ltd

To find out about all our publications, please visit
www.thamesandhudson.com. There you can subscribe
to our e-newsletter, browse or download our current
catalogue, and buy any titles that are in print.

CONTENTS

INTRODUCTION

A city can be all things to all people. One person will find myriad opportunities for profit and advancement where another sees nothing but a crowded cacophony of pressing humanity. One person sees the city as a seat of government and law, the opportunity to display unchallengeable power, while another sees it as a place of freedom and anonymity. A city can be the location for cultural or spiritual expression, a destination for people seeking meaning in their lives, or a place of crass and oppressive materialism; a playground for those with spectacular wealth, or a prison for those suffering unimaginable poverty and pain. Cities are sites of decisive conflict: wars and revolutions are decided by whether key cities fall or resist attack.

It has ever been thus. Today, almost half of us live in cities, and the rest of us rely on them to some degree. But cities have been with us for thousands of years, and they have nurtured civilization itself. Places like Ur and Sumer in Mesopotamia, Damascus and Jericho in the Levant, Mohenjo-daro and Harappa in the Indus Valley, Erlitou and Luoyang in China and Tres Zapotes and Chavín de Huántar in the Americas – the growth of these towns marks the development of a complex society with its own identity and organization that dominated the region around and led to the emergence of the world's first civilizations. Our very word 'civilization' derives from *civis*, the Latin word for a citizen or inhabitant of a city.

Cities cannot exist in isolation from the world around them. Every day, people from the surrounding countryside have come and gone through the city's gates, bringing raw materials, produce or labour, and returning with cash or goods, perhaps luxuries that can only be found where craftspeople and traders congregate. Cities send out soldiers to dominate surrounding regions or conquer other cities, traders to bring back precious goods, emissaries to seek knowledge or build connections with others. Cities attract visitors, sometimes from distant lands; and even if some cities have been devastated or even eradicated by the attentions of enemy armies from afar, others are endowed with sights distinctive enough to make a special journey worthwhile and can thrive on peaceful pilgrims or tourists enduring long and arduous journeys to see them.

And many cities – Damascus, Rome, Athens come to mind – are among the most truly enduring – the most *alive* – of all historical artefacts, not only preserved as museum pieces but remaining vital for thousands of years, each with a unique identity and appeal that has changed and grown with the vicissitudes of the centuries. The cultural and physical edifices of such cities are a palimpsest or patchwork of historical legacy and modern need. Over the centuries, they have seen all kinds of visitor – sometimes welcome, sometimes less so.

But whether a city is predominantly antique or entirely modern, travellers are frequently impressed and amazed by what they find. Whoever has made a long and difficult journey to a city will arrive full of expectation and attention, alert to whatever is impressive, strange or new. And what the visitor sees depends not just on what exists there to be seen, but on their own expectations and interests. Some will experience a direct assault on the senses, a riot of colour, texture and sound, a barrage of smells; but others, arriving in the self-same place, may come so laden with preconceived ideas and associations that what they see exists almost entirely in their imagination. Some visitors arrive in an unknown city and notice its buildings and streets, its government, its organization and the way that it treats the new arrival; a different visitor will be struck by the faces, voices and gestures of the men and women who live there, and note glimpses of unfamiliar ways of life, mysterious, alluring or even frightening.

Some of those travellers who see and feel this heightened excitement, this novelty, this danger that only the city can bring, have captured their experience in words and pictures. When set down immediately in diaries and letters, the urgency can burn off the page; even when written down months or years later in memoirs or reports, the picture can have greater polish, yet be all the more vivid for that. Then there are the travellers whose personal experiences and insights are transmuted into the universality of poetry or fiction.

The earliest accounts of travellers encountering alien cities are found in religious and epic texts: Joshua outside the walls of Jericho, the Achaeans at Troy. But memorable though the verses of the Bible and Homer may be, they are not the words of Joshua and Achilles themselves. And even in the Classical world, there are rather few descriptions of cities and visits to them, and those that do exist tend to be brief – for example, the earliest mention of Paris comes from the Roman soldier Julian, who was proclaimed emperor there in AD 361; his comment, though memorable, used just two words, '*cara* [sweet] *Lutetia*', using the name the Romans gave to their settlement by the Seine. Herodotus, who was a great traveller, tended to write about the peoples he encountered, not the places he went. Conversely, geographers like Strabo gave more detailed though often dry factual accounts of cities, and it is rare to find indications they had personally visited the places in question.

It was only in Europe's Middle Ages that a genre of writing akin to travel literature arose, initially with books written by and for pilgrims to the great religious sites, especially Jerusalem and Rome. But at the same time, Muslim writers wrote about their travels, among them the greatest pre-modern traveller of all, the Moroccan Ibn Battuta, who covered more than 70,000 miles over thirty years in the mid-14th century, and who gave detailed and personal accounts of the people he met, the places he went and the hardships of getting to them. These centuries, when the Silk Road was at its height, also saw a steady trickle of travellers from Europe to China (most famously Marco Polo, whose account of his travels became Europe's first-ever bestselling book), as well as in the other direction, including the Chinese Christian monk Rabban Bar Sauma, who wrote vividly about his visit to western Europe in the 13th century.

Travel literature as we know it – whether we mean books written to assist the prospective traveller, self-aware accounts of travelling or reports of significant journeys – became more common from the 16th century. Whether it was the European exploration and colonization of the world, the increasing scope of commercial and military activities in distant climes, the advent of the Grand Tour and other cultural or intellectual journeying, the dispersal of imperial personnel to their postings around the world or the development of mass tourism, all these and many more personal motives made travelling, and writing about travelling, a rich seam for writers and readers to mine.

In this book, several dozen of the world's greatest cities are portrayed through almost two hundred extracts from writers who visited them over the centuries. To ensure the sense of change through time, the cities included here all still flourish: ancient cities that survive purely as archaeological sites – places such as Knossos or Machu Picchu – attract a very different kind of writing. The mix of period, reasons for travel, experiences and encounters, sights and insights provide a series of illuminating shafts that add up to a surprisingly complex sketch of each city over its history, while the reactions of the writers – many of them household names – reveal as much about their own characters and interests as about the cities themselves.

So far as possible, there is a mix of not only period, cultural background and reason for their journeys and for recording them, but also ethnicity, country of origin and gender. Each extract, though, is vivid, accessible, well written and more or less self-explanatory – although some may be misleading or inaccurate in the information they offer; no one should treat this book as an entirely reliable guide to the modern city and its sights.

Many of our contributors grumble. They dislike muddy streets, bad drivers, dishonest taxi drivers, officious border guards, surly shopkeepers, importunate beggars, irritating tourists, storms, rain, sun and wind – though they can be fairly sanguine about surviving earthquakes. Some stick to the tourist trail and cling to the sanctuary of the hotel with its familiar food and creature comforts. Many others, however, just plunge into the back streets. But whether timid or bold, the travellers celebrate a great deal of what they see – a grand vista, a bustling market, a generous gesture, an alluring glance, a gracious grandee, a death-defying acrobat – and use vivid and immediate language to convey it.

Some extracts are of letters or diaries, others come from memoirs or reports; a few are taken from novels but are closely based on the author's own experience of travel. Some writers visited for a few weeks, days or even hours before moving on, others never left – but in the extracts chosen they behave as hosts showing a newly arrived guest around their adopted town. Natives or those who arrived as children are not travellers to their home cities, though, and their insights are not included. Thus, we learn about what Charles Dickens saw and felt on his brief visits to New York and Rome, but not London, which he knew far too well from the inside.

All human life – and prejudice – is here: some writers experience the places they visit as 'other' and fail to understand the people they meet on their own terms, but instead project fantasies of exoticism, mystery or depravity on them. A few reveal their racial or religious prejudices, others embrace the opportunity to experiment with drugs or indulge sexual fantasies. It should go without saying that all this says more about the author and the prejudices of his or her day, than about the places they purport to describe. This is one undoubted aspect of, and sometimes motivation for, travel in the past, especially perhaps to Middle and Far Eastern ('oriental') locations – and for this reason it is represented here. Reassuringly often, however, contributors express genuine sympathy towards and interest in their subjects, and many demonstrate admirable traits, including anger at cruelty, or compassion for the suffering they encountered, as well as exhibiting real bravery in perilous circumstances as lone travellers far from home.

Travel literature as a genre flourishes today, but it has changed. Since the 1980s the experience of travel has become very different, for two great reasons: the cut-price airlines have made city breaks – even to cities on another continent – almost commonplace; and the rise of Google and review sites like TripAdvisor means that nowhere on Earth today need be truly remote or even surprising. Additionally, the prevalence of social media and blogging has changed the experience of both reading and writing about travel to such an extent that travelling to the great cities of the world today has become a very different experience from even half a century ago. The latest entries in this book, therefore, date to the 1980s.

Of course, not every traveller thrills to cities: some prefer solitude and silence, to wander remote fastnesses, cross oceans and deserts, climb mountains, plunge through forests, or visit people whose way of life has survived unchanged for millennia, but even these explorers will pass through cities en route to the wilderness, and will eventually return to cities and city-based civilization. Yearn to escape them as you may, everyone – the traveller no less than the rest of us – needs, and in many ways loves, cities. Perhaps, through this book, we can learn to experience them afresh.

Peter Furtado

NOTE TO THE READER

The extracts in this volume date from many periods and places. Some are translated, others written in an English that seems more or less archaic to us now. Where possible, we have sought to present the translated texts in reasonably modern idiom, whereas archaic English has been left intact in most respects, except for some spelling and punctuation.

Even so, there are marked inconsistencies in spelling between the different extracts. This can be irritating when it is a question of American or British English spellings, but is far worse with regard to the spelling of place names and the transliteration of foreign words into English. Do Muslims undertake the Haj or Hajj, to visit the Kaaba, Kaba or Kabah, the sacred stone in the heart of Mecca or Mekkah? Are they, indeed, Muslims, Moslems or Mussulmans, followers of the Prophet Muhammad, Mahomet or Mohammed?

Some of the archaic forms used are seen as disrespectful, ignorant or worse by modern sensibilities. Nevertheless, this is a work of history, and the choices of our mostly long-dead authors are the ones we have reproduced without comment – even when a British traveller was disrespectful enough to visit an American president in the White House and then misspell his name (page 345).

Further, many places have changed their names through history. We probably all know that Byzantium, Constantinople and Istanbul refer to the same city on the Bosphorus. But fewer are aware that the Chinese cities of Yan, Zhongdu, Khanbaliq, Cambaluc, Dadu, Tatu and Beiping all once flourished on the site we now know as Beijing (though older readers may occasionally still use the older forms of transliteration, such as Peking or Pekin). For clarity, this book lists cities under their familiar modern names, even if their visitors knew them under different designations. Historic regions like Mesopotamia or Persia no longer have any reality and these names may be obscure to new generations of reader. Again, we cannot force consistency onto the genuine diversity of history – but we have tried to clarify these confusions for the reader wherever it seems helpful.

ALEXANDRIA

Alexandria, on the mouth of the Nile, was founded by Alexander the Great in 332 BC and was the capital for Ptolemaic and Roman Egypt. Famous in antiquity both for its Pharos, or Great Lighthouse, and for its Museum and Library, it fell to the Arabs in AD 642 and lost much of its cultural glory. Nevertheless, Islamic Alexandria thrived as a trading post, linking North Africa with the Middle East, and was an increasingly important naval base for the Arabs.

Alexandria's fortunes were revived by the appointment of Muhammad Ali as Ottoman viceroy and pasha in 1805; he began the modernization of the Egyptian economy and made Alexandria a banking centre. It was also the point of departure for many European visitors to Egypt and travellers to India, a role that became increasingly important — first with the opening of the Suez Canal in 1869, then under British control from 1882 — until after the Second World War. It remained a Levantine cultural and linguistic melting pot through the 20th century, although after Egypt's nationalist revolution led by Gamal Abdel Nasser in 1952 it became increasingly dominated by Arabic-speaking Egyptians.

20 BC STRABO

The Greek geographer Strabo (64 BC–AD 24) travelled widely in Africa and the Middle East, and based his encyclopaedic and influential Geographica *(c. AD 17) on what he saw on his travels. The work proved a highly influential source of knowledge during the Renaissance.*

Pharos is a small oblong island, quite close to the continent, forming towards it a harbour with a double entrance. The coast has two promontories projecting into the sea; the island is situated between these, and shuts in the bay.

Of the extremities of the Pharos, the eastern is nearest to the continent and to the promontory in that direction, called Lochias, which is the cause of the entrance to the port being narrow. Besides the narrowness of the passage, there are rocks, some under water, others above it, which increase the violence of the waves rolling in from the sea. This extremity itself of the island is a rock, washed by the sea on all sides, with a tower upon it of the same name as the island, constructed of white marble, with several storeys. Sostratus of Cnidus erected it for the safety of mariners, as the inscription imports....

When Alexander arrived, and perceived the advantages of the situation, he determined to build the city on the harbour.... The advantages of the city are of various kinds. The site is washed by two seas; on the north, by what is called the Egyptian Sea, and on the south, by the sea of the lake Mareia. This is filled by canals from the Nile, through which more merchandise is imported than by those communicating with the sea. Hence the harbour on the lake is richer than the maritime harbour. The exports by sea from Alexandria exceed the imports, as any person may ascertain by watching the arrival and departure of the merchant vessels, and observing how much heavier or lighter their cargoes are when they depart or when they return....

The city is the shape of a *chlamys* or military cloak. The sides are surrounded by water, and are about thirty stadia in extent; but the isthmuses, which determine the breadth of the sides, are each of seven or eight stadia, bounded on one side by the sea, and on the other by the lake. The whole city is intersected by roads; two of these are very broad and cut one another at right angles. It contains also very beautiful public grounds and royal palaces, which occupy a quarter or even a third of its whole extent.

A part belonging to the palaces consists of that called Sema, an enclosure, which contained the tombs of the kings and that of Alexander the Great. For Ptolemy the son of Lagus took the body of Alexander from Perdiccas, as he was conveying it down from Babylon.... Ptolemy deposited the body at Alexandria in the place where it now lies; not indeed in the same coffin, for the present one is of alabaster whereas Ptolemy had deposited it in one of gold: it was plundered by Ptolemy Cocce's son and Pareisactus. The Museum is also a part of the palaces. It has a public walk and a place furnished with seats, and a large hall, in which the men of learning, who belong to the Museum, take their common meal....

Above this is the theatre, then the Poseidium, a kind of elbow projecting from the Emporium, as it is called, with a temple of Neptune upon it. To this Antony added a mound, projecting into the middle of the harbour, and built at the extremity a royal mansion, which he called Timonium. This was his last act, when, deserted by his partisans, he retired to Alexandria after his defeat at Actium, and intended, being forsaken by so many friends, to lead the solitary life for the rest of his days.

c.1150 AL-IDRISI

Muhammad al-Idrisi (1100–1165) was a North African-born geographer and map-maker who lived in Norman Sicily. His Book of Pleasant Journeys into Faraway Lands *was a compilation of his academic knowledge with information from his personal travels.*

Alexandria was built by Alexander, who gave his name to it. It is situated on the Mediterranean coast, and there are a remarkable number of monuments and remains surviving which bear witness to the authority and power of him who raised them, and to his foresight and wisdom. This town is surrounded by strong walls and fine orchards. It is large, very populous, commercial and full of high buildings; its streets are wide and its buildings solid; the houses are of marble and the vaults supported by strong columns. Its markets are large and its surrounding countryside productive.

The waters of the western branch of the Nile, which run to this city, pass below the vaults of its houses, and these vaults are cheek by jowl with one another. The town itself is light and finely built. Here we find the famous lighthouse which has not equal in the entire world for its structure and its solidity; for as well as that which is made in fine stones called *caddzan*, the beddings of these stones are sealed together with lead and other adhesive materials such that it is unmovable, despite the waves that crash onto it continually from the north…. There is a wide interior staircase like those one ordinarily sees in the towers of mosques. The first staircase ends around the middle of the lighthouse, where the structure becomes narrower on all four sides…. From this gallery one continues to the top by means of a smaller staircase. On all sides it is pierced by windows that light the way to those inside and help them place their feet safely.

This building is unique, as much for its height as its solidity; it is very useful for the fire that burns day and night to serve as a signal for navigators; it is visible 100 miles away. At night it seems like a bright star; by day one can see the plume of smoke. Alexandria is surrounded by plains and great deserts, where there are no mountains or any other object that can be used for reconnaissance. Were it not for the lighthouse, most of the vessels that come here would not find their way.

The lighthouse is said to have been built by the same man as built the pyramids of Al-Fustat, to the west of the Nile. Others though claim that this building was one of several erected by Alexander when the city was founded. Only God knows the truth of it.

1225 ZHAO RUGUA

Zhao Rugua (1170–1228) was a Chinese government official whose book Zhu Fan Zhi *was a compilation of Chinese knowledge of the world before their borders, including South East Asia, the Silk Route and the eastern Mediterranean. Inevitably, some of the information was gathered from hearsay, and was unreliable.*

The country of O-kön-t'o [Alexandria] belongs to Wu-ssï-li [Egypt]. According to tradition, in olden times a stranger, Tsu-ko-ni [Alexander the Great] by name, built on the shore of the sea a great tower under which the earth was dug out and two rooms were made, well connected and very well secreted. In one vault was grain, in the other were arms. The tower was two hundred *chang* high. Four horses abreast could ascend to two-thirds of its height. In the centre of the building was a great well connecting with the big river. To protect it from surprise by troops of other lands, the whole country guarded this tower that warded off the foes. In the upper and lower parts of it 20,000 men could readily be stationed to guard, and to sally forth to fight. On the summit there was a wondrous great mirror; if war-ships of other countries made a sudden attack, the mirror detected them beforehand, and the troops were ready in time for duty.

In recent years there came a foreigner who asked to be given work in the guardhouse of the tower; he was employed to sprinkle and sweep. For years no one entertained any suspicion of him, when suddenly one day he found an opportunity to steal the mirror and throw it into the sea, after which he made off.

1798 VIVANT DENON

In 1798 Napoleon invaded Egypt in order to cut off the British route to India, but his respect for the ancient civilization led him to take scholars and archaeologists with him. Prominent among them was French diplomat and artist Vivant Denon (1747–1825), who, the evening before disembarking at Alexandria, mused on what he would find, as he recorded in his Travels in Upper and Lower Egypt *(1803).*

By the help of our glasses we saw the tricolour flag displayed over our consul's house. I figured to myself the surprise he was about to feel, and that which we were preparing against the following day for the sheik of Alexandria.

When the long shadows of evening had marked the outlines of the city, I distinguished the two ports, the lofty walls flanked by numerous towers, no longer enclosing anything but heaps of sand, and a few gardens, the pale green of whose palm trees scarcely tempered the ardent whiteness of the soil; the Turkish castle, the mosques, their minarets; the celebrated pillar of Pompey; and my imagination went back to the past. I saw art triumph over nature; the genius of Alexandria employ the active hands of commerce, to lay, on a barren coast, the foundations of a magnificent city and select that city as the depository of the trophies of the conquest of a world; I saw the Ptolemies invite the arts and sciences, and collect that library which it took barbarism so many years to consume; it was there, said I, thinking of Cleopatra, Caesar and Anthony, that the empire of glory was sacrificed to the empire of voluptuousness! After this, I saw stern ignorance establish itself on the ruins of the masterpieces of the arts, labouring to destroy them, but unable, notwithstanding, even yet to have disfigured utterly those beautiful fragments which display the noble principles of their first design.

From this preoccupation, from this happiness of meditating in view of great objects, I was roused by a gun fired from our frigate, to bring too a vessel which had set all her sails to get into the port of Alexandria in spite of us, and without doubt to carry thither the tidings of the arrival of our fleet.

1849 JAMES LAIRD PATTERSON

James Laird Patterson (1822–1902) was a British Catholic clergyman who later served as Auxiliary Bishop of Westminster. As a young man, and before his ordination in 1855, he visited the Holy Land and the eastern Mediterranean, a journey he described in the well-known account Journal of a Tour in Egypt, Palestine, Syria, and Greece *(1849). For him, as for many Western travellers in the 19th century, Alexandria represented his first encounter with the 'Orient' and Islam, both of which he observed through his strongly British and Christian lens.*

4 December Hotel d'Orient We were pleasantly awoke this morning by an announcement that our pilot was come on board, and shortly after found ourselves gliding in between Ottoman, Austrian, French and English men of war and merchantmen in this fine harbour. A letter to the agent of the transit administration procured us a speedy and easy landing, and we were driven rapidly through the narrow and crowded half-oriental streets to this hotel in the great Frank Piazza. The tall camels, the thousandfold orientals on foot and donkeys, the veiled women, the cross-legged shopkeepers, the latticed houses and occasional minarets, quite gave one the 'Arabian Night' feeling I had anticipated. But this came in fuller force at the baths, whither of course we went as soon as we were established in our rooms. I will not rewrite the thousand-times-written ceremonies of the oriental bath; suffice it to say that we were duly conducted from one room to another, scrubbed and shampooed, rubbed, patted, parboiled with hot water, cooled with cold water, attired in a variety of linen robes and turbans, and finally found ourselves, exhausted with the fatigues of bathing, and above all of laughing at each other, reclining on divans in an outer apartment, with long pipes in our hands, and silent attendants presenting small cups of coffee every other minute.... After a short rest at home, we again went out on donkeys, attended by our little Nubian, Hassan, to make purchases in the bazaars. The European quarter of Alexandria is much like other seaports in the West; but our shopping led us into the Turkish quarter, where we were duly edified by the sight of long narrow streets, the houses with overhanging windows of latticed woodwork painted and gilt, small shops, in which the wrangling of oriental bargains was vociferously carried on by merchant and purchaser, etc. The great wonder seemed, how on earth our donkeys, careering along at a fearful pace, managed to elude the long strings of camels and other obstacles which blocked the way.... We bought some red fezzes and sashes, which are *de rigeur* for eastern travellers, and then threaded our way out of the city towards the old harbour, to see Pompey's Pillar (or, 'Bombey's Billar', as the natives call it) and Cleopatra's Needles. The former is a truly noble monument – a single granite shaft, with a lofty base and Corinthian capital; the whole being about ninety-five feet in height, and appearing even higher, from its elevated position.... The entourage of this column is wretched; the ground is squalid and broken; and by way of giving a lesson in civilization to its semi-barbarous possessors, sundry European worthies have scrawled their names all over the base. The great Mr Thompson, and the equally famous Mr Button, have respectively inscribed their ample names on it, at an evident sacrifice of several bottles of Day and Martin – a proceeding which leaves it next to an impossibility for posterity further to blacken those illustrious names. This pillar was, in fact, erected by the Alexandrians...as a propitiatory offering to their conqueror, Diocletian (as an inscription, now nearly effaced by the noble enthusiasm of successive Thompsons and Buttons, testifies); and the sockets to receive his statue, on the summit, still remain.

Cleopatra's Needles are on the shore, at the east point of the old harbour. To arrive at them we passed close to a very handsome mosque, in which I saw many Mussulmans at their devotions, one of whom insulted us elaborately (as Christians); and we remarked that several people, especially women, either spat or muttered some words of contempt or malediction, as we went by.

It is very striking to see persons in the midst of occupations, at their shops, or on the house-tops, spread out their praying carpets, perform their ablutions (of face, arms and legs), and then prostrate themselves towards Mecca, at the stated times of prayer. I understand, too, that they observe the fast of the Ramadan very strictly here; and I confess these public and ordinary recognitions of religion, however false it be, go far with me to excuse the exhibition by individuals of fanaticism and hatred towards Christians. But what a frightful and diabolical parody of Christian practices are these! The immorality and uncharitableness of these poor people are a striking sight, when coupled to, and the result of, their very religion.

The sadness of seeing so many thousands held in the bonds of the devil, with many lawful things forbidden them, and many most unlawful permitted and enjoined, would be intolerable, were one not to call to mind the Christian verity of the death of our Blessed Lord for all mankind, even for those who know Him not.

AMSTERDAM

Amsterdam developed as a fishing village in the early Middle Ages, and had become a significant city by the late 15th century. In 1578 it joined the 'revolt of the Netherlands' against Spanish rule (1568–1648) and grew to supersede Antwerp as the main city of the Low Countries.

The 17th century represented Holland's golden age, with Amsterdam at the heart of a worldwide trading empire, as well as a cultural hub.

Artists such as Rembrandt were in high demand to provide paintings to hang on the walls of the homes of the city's many wealthy burghers. By the 18th century, however, Amsterdam had lost much of its commercial pre-eminence, and in 1787 it was occupied by the Prussians, then liberated by the Revolutionary French in 1795 and incorporated in the Napoleonic empire (until 1813).

Amsterdam has been the capital of the Kingdom of the Netherlands since 1814, even though its trade had suffered badly during the Napoleonic Wars, not recovering fully until the 1850s. It was, however, increasingly recognized as a destination for tourists. Occupied by Germany in the Second World War (1940–45), in post-war years it has become a commercial and financial centre as well as a much-loved place to live and visit.

1592 FYNES MORYSON

Fynes Moryson (1566–1630) was an English gentleman who travelled widely in Europe and the Middle East with the intention of recording local conditions, customs and institutions. He published three volumes of An Itinerary Containing his Ten Yeeres Travell through the Twelve Dominions of Germany, Bohmerland, Sweitzerland, Netherland, Denmarke, Poland, Italy, Turky, France, England, Scotland & Ireland *(1617), writing a fourth in the 1620s. Moryson visited Amsterdam during the long war with Spain; an English army led by the Earl of Leicester to support the revolt had arrived in 1584 but achieved little.*

Five streets of this city are divided with water. The River Tay [IJ] flows like a large and calm sea on the north side, where is a safe port.... Upon the haven lies a field or marketplace, where the citizens use to behold their friends going to sea and returning home. From this place towards the south lies Warmoesstraat, a long and large street between two rivers, which part of the city is called, the new ditch. The merchants in summer meet upon the bridge, and in winter they meet in the New Church [Nieuwe Kerk], in very great number, where they walk in two ranks by couples, one rank going up, and another going down, and there is no way to get out of the church except they slip out of the doors, when in one of those ranks they pass by them. On the east side of the city there is a wall of stone, higher than the city, having a pleasant walk upon it....

The city hath five gates, which are shut at dinners and suppers, though the danger of the war be far from them. There be two churches in which they have two sermons each second day, and four on Sunday.... They have two almshouses (called *Gasthausen*, that is, houses for strangers) which were of old monasteries. One of these houses built round, was a cloister for nuns, wherein 60 beds were made for poor women diseased, and in another chamber thereof were 52 beds made for the auxiliary soldiers of England, being hurt or sick, and in the third room were 81 beds made for the hurt and sick soldiers of other nations: to which soldiers and sick women they gave clean sheets, a good diet and necessary clothes, with great cleanliness, and allow them physicians and surgeons to cure them.

1640 PETER MUNDY

Peter Mundy (c. 1596–1667) was a Cornish-born British trader who travelled in Europe, Russia and India, and as far afield as China. He visited Amsterdam during its commercial and cultural golden age. He wrote and illustrated an account of his travels, but it was not published until the 20th century.

14 April In the morning we came to Amsterdam, and there I took a lodging in the Nieuw Markt....

For the building of a house, they must drive in certain timbers or masts 42 or 43 foot deep before they meet with any fast ground, which is a sand at last, on which is laid the foundation. These timbers are said to continue hundreds of years sound, as long as they lie in the moist earth. They are forced in by a certain engine, being a great weight, whereunto is fastened a main rope, and unto that again about 40 other smaller, there being so many several men which pull at them in the same manner and with the same action, as sometimes many men do at the ringing of some great bell. The weight, by the help of a large pulley, is forced up, and with his fall drives the piles till they meet with the sand.

I have seen a whole house of brick, etc., sundry storeys high, standing altogether upon screws, as on stilts, the foundation being clean taken away.

With these, by report, they will remove large buildings from one place to another. Also sundry other ingenious devices with which they abound, as wind sawing-mills, windmills for draining of water, etc....

As for the art of painting and the affection of the people to pictures, I think none other go beyond them, there having been in this country many excellent men in that faculty, some at present, as Rembrandt, etc. All in general striving to adorn their houses, especially the outer or street room, with costly pieces; butchers and bakers not much inferior in their shops, which are fairly set forth, yea many times blacksmiths, cobblers, etc. will have some picture or other by their forge and in their stall. Such is the general notion, inclination and delight that these country natives have to paintings. Also their other furniture and ornaments of their dwellings very costly and curious, full of pleasure and home contentment, as rich cupboards, cabinets, etc., imagery, porcelain, costly fine cages with birds, etc.; all these commonly in any house of indifferent quality; wonderful neat and clean, as well in their houses and furniture, service, etc. within doors, as in their streets....

For their shipping, traffic and commerce by sea, I conceive no place in the world comes near it. There being at once come into the Texel at my being there 26 ships: from East India 8, from West India 9, and 9 from Guinea, etc.... The number of other ships which perpetually ebb and flow to this city, etc., is incredible, by which means, as by their industry and labour, they have made of this land, which naturally...is unprofitable and unuseful for man or beast.... Notwithstanding these inconveniences, they have by their ingenious labours and cleanliness so corrected them, that they have made a place where they live in health and wealth, ease and pleasure. For although the land, and that with much labour, is brought only to pasture, and that but in summer neither, yet by means of their shipping, they are plentifully supplied with... corn, pitch, tar, flax, hemp, etc.; from Danzig, Konigsberg, etc. in the Baltic Sea; masts, timber, fish, etc., from Norway; from Denmark, cattle; and from any part of the world besides, either in Europe, Asia, Africa or America, where any trade is, with the most precious and rich commodities of those parts, with which supplying other countries they more and more enrich their own....

The want of walking fields and meadows which others enjoy in other places, have made these to seek to countervail it in home delights, as in their streets, houses, rooms, ornament, furniture, little gardens, flower pots, in which later very curious or rare roots, plants, flowers, etc.; incredible prices for tulip roots. Also manufactures and rarities of foreign countries, of which this place doth abound and wherein they take delight.

1789 SAMUEL IRELAND

The British artist and engraver Samuel Ireland (1744–1800) produced many topographical views of Britain and northern Europe, assembled in books with accounts of his journeys. He was an enthusiastic proponent of the theatre, particularly of Shakespeare's plays.

At night we were entertained with a Dutch play, which for aught I know was well enough: the house is very plain, and but ill-lighted. I felt myself unfortunate in not arriving here one night sooner, to have enjoyed the sight of the Dutch Hamlet, a character which was performed last Saturday; and, according to the country report, is better filled and much superior to ours....

In our return we visited one of the musico's or licensed brothels. Our stay was but short, the ugliness and impudence of the women soon causing us to make a precipitate retreat. The number of those houses is incredible. A chandelier is lighted up in the middle of the room, at the farther end of which are placed a sleepy fiddler and harper, who play, if necessary, till morning; you pay a florin at entrance, and see all that is necessary through immense clouds of tobacco smoke. No indecency is permitted and I am told it is not uncommon to meet a sober citizen and his wife (particularly at the time of the annual fair) introducing a virtuous young woman, their daughter, merely to view the horrid tendency of immorality imagining with the poet, that: 'Vice is a monster of so frightful mien / As to be hated, needs but to be seen.'

This may be Dutch policy, but the experiment is surely dangerous; as the following couplet of the same elegant author more fully illustrates: 'Yet seen too oft, familiar with her face, / We first endure, then pity, then embrace.'

It is true that the Spartans publicly exhibited their slaves when drunk, to expose the deformity of drunkenness and deter their youth from the practice of it. With a loathsome object before their eyes, the dignity of our nature humiliated and nothing to invite, no passion could be inflamed: but the case of intoxication and the species of licentiousness before alluded to is widely different.

The situation of these wretched females is lamentable beyond description; immured within the walls for life, and only permitted to breathe a purer air one day in the year, they are then attended by their tyrant keeper, who never suffers them out of his sight. But somewhat too much of this. We retired to our hotel.

The Rasp-house or Bridewell is worthy notice: here the wretched culprit is chained to a block, and employed in cutting and rasping Brazil wood. In passing we saw a miserable creature, who asked charity through a barricadoed [sic] cellar window; he had before been imprisoned in the house and was now sentenced to six weeks additional confinement in this cellar for stealing some of the wood, piled in the yard to make his fire, where he was incessantly to pump or drown, as the water was generally up to his shoulders....

The workhouse contains near twelve thousand persons, who are admitted of all nations; the neatness and good management of this place is beyond description. In one of the apartments is a large picture, very finely painted, by Rembrandt, containing portraits of the first promoters of this charity; and another equally fine, of the same size and subject, intended as a companion, by Van Dyck. Part of this building is devoted to the reception of poor females; not those who have only deviated from the nicer rules of virtue and whose stars, perhaps, 'were more in fault than they;' but those who lost to all sense of shame, had abandoned themselves to an open state of prostitution.

In the Surgeons Hall is a fine picture by Rembrandt; the subject, a dissection. It contains portraits of the professors and principal members of the college, large as life, in half-length; and is executed in his best manner. The effect of it is astonishing; and yet, judicious and indeed indispensable as it was to make such a subject the ornament of such a place, we cannot but regret that so noble a specimen of art cannot be dwelt upon without disgust by any other than a medical eye....

1836 JOHN MURRAY III

The British writer and publisher John Murray III (1808–1892) published a series of popular handbooks from the 1830s, packed with practical information on travel and accommodation, as well as details of the major sights of Europe. He himself wrote volumes on Holland, Belgium, Germany, Switzerland and France.

The principal city of Holland is situated at the confluence of the river Amstel with the arm of the Zuider Zee called the IJ.... It has 225,000 inhabitants. Its ground-plan has somewhat the shape of a crescent, or half-bent bow; the straight line, representing the string, rests on the IJ and the curved line forms its boundary on the land side. Its walls are surrounded by a semicircular canal or wide fosse, and within the city are four other great canals, all running in curves, parallel with the outer one.... They are lined with handsome houses; each of the first three is at least two miles long, and in their buildings as well as dimensions may bear comparison with the finest streets in Europe. The various small canals which intersect the town in all directions are said to divide it into 95 islands, and to be traversed by no less than 290 bridges. It has been calculated that the repair of bridges, cleansing and clearing canals, and repairing dykes, in Amsterdam alone, amounts to several thousand guilders daily. This will be better understood when it is known that, were it not for the most skilful management of sluices and dykes, the city of Amsterdam might be submerged at any moment. All things considered, it is one of the most wonderful capitals in Europe; in the bustle of its crowded streets, and in the extent of its commercial transactions, it is surpassed by very few.... In the strange intermixture of land and water it may be compared to Venice; and the splendour of some of its buildings, though not equalling that of the Sea Cybele [Venice], may be said to approximate to it, but the houses are almost all of brick, and the canals differ from those of Venice in being lined with quays.

The whole city, its houses, canals and sluices, are founded upon piles; which gave occasion to Erasmus to say that he had reached a city whose inhabitants, like crows, lived on the tops of trees. The upper stratum is literally nothing more than bog and loose sand; and until the piles are driven through this into the firm soil below, no structure can be raised with a chance of stability. In 1822 the enormous corn warehouses, originally built for the Dutch East India Company, actually sank down into the mud, from the piles having given way. They contained at the time more than 70,000cwt of corn: a weight which the foundation beneath was incapable of supporting.... It has been often said that a police regulation restricts the use of wheels, from fear lest the rattling of heavy carriages over the stones should shake and injure the foundation of the buildings: this, however, is not true. Heavy burdens are almost entirely transported along the canals, and from thence to the warehouses on similar sledges. Omnibuses ply through the town and to the railway station.

The havens and canals are shallow, being about 8ft deep at ordinary water. They are, therefore, fit for the Rhine vessels and Dutch coasters, but do not admit vessels for foreign trade. These lie along the booms and in front of the town, and the goods are transferred by means of the numerous canals of the city. There is a good deal of mud deposited at the bottom of the canals, which when disturbed by the barges produces a most noisome effluvia in hot weather, when the water is said to 'grow'. Dredging machines are constantly at work to clear out the mud, which is sent to distant parts as manure. Mills have also been employed to give an artificial motion to the waters and prevent their becoming stagnant; but the same object is now attained by more simple means. To effect a circulation in the canals is most essential to the health of the inhabitants.

The vast dams thrown up within a few years in front of the town, for a great distance along the side towards the IJ, resist the influx of the sea into the mouths of the canals, and are provided with floodgates of the strongest construction, to withstand the pressure of high tides.

The Palace, formerly the Stadhuis, is a vast and imposing edifice of stone, standing upon 13,659 piles driven 70ft deep into the ground. The architect was Van Campen; the first stone was laid 1648, and the building finished 1655. It was originally occupied by the magistracy, for town councils, judicial tribunals and the like. During the reign of Louis Buonaparte it became his palace, and the late king resided in it whenever he visited Amsterdam. The main entrance is behind. The treasures of the once-celebrated bank of Amsterdam, which used to regulate the exchanges of Europe, were kept in the vaults below the building. It is chiefly remarkable for one grand Hall, occupying the centre of the building, lined with white Italian marble.... Many [sculpted bas-reliefs] in the interior are appropriate and well executed: over the door of the room which was the Secretary's is a dog watching his dead master, and a figure of Silence with her finger on her lips, as emblems of fidelity and secrecy. The Bankrupt Court contains a group representing Daedalus and Icarus – in allusion to rash speculations and their ruinous consequences.... It is worthwhile to see the view from the tower on the summit of the building. This is the best place to obtain a tolerably correct idea of this wonderful city, with its broad canals, avenues of green trees running through the heart of the town, houses with forked chimneys and projecting gables, many of them bowing forward or leaning backwards, from subsidence in their foundations.

1945 JOZEF HILEL BORENSZTAJN

Jozef Hilel Borensztajn (1898–1985) was a Polish Jew who emigrated to Amsterdam in early life and was sent to the death camps by the Nazis in the Second World War. He described his eventual return to Amsterdam in his diary (published 1998).

Tuesday, 12 June We finally arrive in Amsterdam at ten in the evening. There are cheering people and flags everywhere, but the platform is dark. Following the sole light, we reach the waiting room where there is soup for us. We can have as much as we want. Then the usual registration; finally, food stamps. At last we can leave.

It is late – at least half past twelve – and I do not know where to go. There are no trams, and Amsterdam is shrouded in darkness. I think of my friend Meier, but I can hardly turn up unannounced in the middle of the night. I hear that a car is coming to take us [to the] PIZ (the Portuguese Israelite Hospital). I decide to wait. Eventually the bus arrives and we get in. It is so dark I can barely see my hand in front of my eyes.

The bus drives through the quiet, dark night. To my astonishment I see the lights are on in the hospital – I learn later it is the only building for miles around with electricity. I am given a bed with sheets that are cleaner, whiter than any I have seen for a long time. The next day I am given a food card (number 73542) and an address, Weteringschans 104, where I can learn what to do next, and the address of an aid organization.

Wednesday, 13 June Next morning I check whether my old friend Lewinsohn is still in Amsterdam. I go to his apartment...and he is indeed there, as if nothing had happened. What joy!

After leaving him I go to the Kerkstraat where I meet another friend, Fuks, and then my cousin Frits Mindlin....

I walk everywhere, because there are no trams. And there is no light. Amsterdam is not yet back to life. It seems full of broken houses. The winter was tough, and the people took over the buildings that once housed Jews, demolished them and burned the wood. The food supply is not perfect, but I am told it's better than it was a few weeks ago. In the hospital we get quite decent food to eat. The time of celebration is over, and life somehow has to go on. Things are getting better every day. There are strange newspapers with amateurish content as if they are published by children. They have just two pages. People are mainly interested in articles about the distribution of ration cards. But today there is some really important news: the trams should work again next week, even if just for a few hours a day.

There is white bread...but I cannot eat it. But people mainly eat canned food from America and England. These cans – empty ones – lie around all over the streets. There are ration cards for chocolate, and people can't wait to swap them for a real chocolate bar. A few vegetables and a little fruit are available here and there – strawberries for example. Soon there will be fish in the market again. If you are lucky, you might find beer, on sale at 35 cents for a glass of pils.

People look exhausted. They talk constantly about last winter, which was terrible. It is called the 'hunger winter'. Thousands died of starvation. But now we have to look optimistically to the future.

ATHENS

The golden age of Athens in the 5th century BC was, from the point of view of writers about the city, always in the past. Ever since the Roman era, writers on Athens have evoked the echoes of the greats in literature, theatre, philosophy, science, politics, painting, sculpture and many other fields, and the unparalleled architecture legacy on the Acropolis. Though loved and beautified by the Roman emperor Hadrian in the early 2nd century AD, the city was otherwise denuded of much of its talent and interest by the Romans and Byzantine empires, and though conquered by the Ottoman Turks in 1456, still failed to thrive.

The 19th century saw a revival of interest in Athens and its unique heritage, in no small part thanks to Lord Byron, who almost singlehandedly inspired a Romantic interest in the cause of Greek independence, which was eventually won in 1832. From that time, it has become a major stop on the tourist circuit.

c.100 BC HERACLEIDES OF CRETE

Little is known of this author; his text was originally attributed to Dicaearchus of Messana.

The road to Athens is a pleasant one, running between cultivated fields the whole way. The city itself is dry and ill supplied with water. The streets are nothing but miserable old lanes, the houses mean, with a few better ones among them. On his arrival a stranger could hardly believe that this is the Athens of which he has heard so much. Yet he will soon come to believe that it is Athens indeed. A Music Hall, the most beautiful in the world, a large and stately theatre, a costly, remarkable and far-seen temple of Athena called the Parthenon rising above the theatre, strike the beholder with admiration. A temple of Olympian Zeus, unfinished but planned on an astonishing scale: three gymnasiums, the Academy, Lyceum and Cynosarges, shaded with trees that spring from greensward; verdant gardens of philosophers; amusements and recreations; many holidays and a constant succession of spectacles – all these the visitor will find in Athens.

The products of the country are priceless in quality but not too plentiful. However, the frequency of the spectacles and holidays makes up for the scarcity to the poorer sort, who forget the pangs of hunger in gazing at the shows and pageants. Every artist is sure of being welcomed with applause and of making a name: hence the city is crowded with statues.

Of the inhabitants some are Attic and some are Athenian. The former are gossiping, slanderous, given to prying the business of strangers, fair and false. The Athenians are high-minded, straight-forward and staunch in friendship.... The true-born Athenians are keen and critical auditors, constant in their attendance at plays and spectacles. In short, Athens as far surpasses all other cities in the pleasures and conveniences of life as they surpass the country. But a man must beware of courtesans lest they lure him to ruin.

c.AD 150 PAUSANIAS

Pausanias (AD 110–180) was a geographer and antiquarian from Asia Minor who wrote a detailed Description of Greece, *much of it from his own observations. The Athens he saw was some half a millennium past its Periclean prime, but shortly after the Roman emperor Hadrian had spent time in the city and re-beautified it.*

On entering the city there is a building for the preparation of the processions. Next is a temple of Demeter, with images of the goddess and of her daughter, and of Iacchus holding a torch. On the wall, in Attic characters, is written that they are works of Praxiteles. Not far from the temple is Poseidon on horseback, hurling a spear against the giant Polybotes. But the inscription of our time assigns the statue to another, and not to Poseidon. From the gate to the Ceramicus there are porticoes with brazen statues of such men and women as had some title to fame....

The district of the Ceramicus has its name from the hero Ceramus, reputed son of Dionysus and Ariadne. On the right is the Royal Portico, where sits the king when holding his yearly office. On the tiling of this portico are images of baked earthenware, of Theseus throwing Sciron into the sea and Day carrying away the beautiful Cephalus, who was ravished by Day, who was in love with him. This tale was told by Hesiod in his poem on women....

A portico behind carries pictures of the gods; on the wall opposite are painted Theseus, Democracy and Demos. It shows Theseus as the man who gave the Athenians political equality. Theseus is also remembered for bestowing sovereignty upon the people, and from his time they continued under a democratic government, until Peisistratus rose up and became despot....

Here is built also a sanctuary of the Mother of the gods; the image is by Pheidias. Hard by is the council chamber of the Five Hundred, the Athenian councillors for a year.... Near this is the Tholos (Round House) where the presidents sacrifice, and a few small statues made of silver.

Farther up stand statues of *eponymoi*, or heroes from whom the Athenian tribes received their names.... Before the entrance of the theatre called the Odeum or Music Hall are statues of Egyptian kings.... After the Egyptians come statues of Philip and his son Alexander. The events of their lives were too important to form a mere digression in another story. Whereas the Egyptians were honoured out of genuine respect and because they were benefactors, but it was rather through sycophancy that the people gave statues to Philip and Alexander.

395 SYNESIUS OF CYRENE

Synesius (c. 373–c. 414) visited Alexandria and Athens as a young man, then spent three years as an ambassador in Constantinople in 399. He was appointed bishop of Ptolemais in Cyrenaica, now part of Libya, in 410.

Letter 136 to his brother

May the sailor who brought me here die miserably: Athens contains nothing magnificent except its place names. When a sacrificial victim is burnt, only the skin remains as an indication of what animal that once was: just so, now that philosophy has deserted Athens, all that remains is to wander and wonder at the Academy and the Lyceum; and that colourful portico from which the sect of Chrysippus took its name (not that there is much colour in it now; the proconsul has removed the panels on which Polygnotus of Thasos had expended all his art). In our day, Egypt nourished the seeds of wisdom taken from Hypatia; Athens was indeed once a city, the home of the wise; now it is inhabited by beekeepers. The Plutarchean philosophers are very conscious of this, and they attract the young to the theatres, not by the reputation of their rhetoric but by amphoras of Hymettian honey.

1806 VICOMTE DE CHATEAUBRIAND

François-René, vicomte de Chateaubriand (1768–1848) was a French aristo-crat whose novels and travel writing marked him out as a leader of the French Romantic movement. Despite years in exile in London in the early years of the French Revolution, he became a diplomat under Napoleon. In 1806, he travelled to the Holy Land, via Greece.

It is not in the first moment of a strong emotion that you derive most enjoyment from your feelings. I proceeded towards Athens with a kind of pleasure which derived me of the power of reflexion; not that I experienced anything like what I had felt at the sight of Lacedaemon. Sparta and Athens have, even in their ruins, retained their different characteristics; those of the former are gloomy, grave and solitary; those of the latter pleasing, light and social. At the sight of the land of Lycurgus, every idea becomes serious, manly and profound; the soul, fraught with new energies, seems to be elevated and expanded; before the city of Solon, you are enchanted, as it were, by the magic of genius; you are filled with the idea of the perfection of man, considered as an intelligent and immortal being. The lofty sentiments of human nature assumed at Athens a degree of elegance which they had not had at Sparta. Among the Athenians, patriotism and the love of independence were not a blind instinct but an enlightened sentiment springing from that love of the beautiful in general with which Heaven had so liberally endowed them. In a word, as I passed from the ruins of Lacedaemon to the ruins of Athens, I felt that I should have liked to die with Leonidas, and to live with Pericles.

We advanced towards that little town whose territory extended 15 or 20 leagues, whose population was not equal to that of a suburb of Paris and which, nevertheless rivals the Roman Empire in renown....

I perceived, at some distance on my left, the ruins of the bridge over the Cephisus built by Xenocles of Lindus. I mounted my horse without looking for the sacred fig tree, the altar of Zephyrus or the pillar of Anthemocritus, for the modern way deviates in this part from the ancient Sacred Way. On leaving the olive-wood we came to a garden surrounded by walls which occupies nearly the site of the outer Ceramicus. We proceeded for about half an hour through wheat stubble before we reached Athens. A modern wall, recently repaired and resembling a garden wall, encompasses the city. We passed through the gate and entered little rural streets, cool and very clean; each house has its garden planted with orange and fig trees. The inhabitants appeared to me to be lively and inquisitive and had not the dejected look of the people of the Morea [the Peloponnese]. We were shown the house of the consul.

I could not have had a better recommendation than to M. Fauvel for seeing Athens. He has resided for many years in the city of Minerva and is much better acquainted with its minutest details than a Parisian is with Paris.... Invested with the appointment of consul at Athens, which merely serves him as a protection, he has been and still is engaged as draughtsman upon the *Voyage pittoresque de la Grece.*

1812 LORD BYRON

The poet George Gordon Byron, 6th Baron Byron (1788–1824), travelled widely in Europe after scandalizing British society, but the long narrative poem based on his travels, Childe Harold's Pilgrimage, *established his reputation as a genius. A British philhellene who devoted much effort, and finally his life, to the cause of Greek independence from Ottoman rule, he also despised the way in which his countrymen were despoiling Greece, removing Classical treasures such as the Elgin Marbles from the Parthenon. These feelings were vividly expressed in this extract from* Childe Harold's Pilgrimage.

Canto the Second

I.

Come, blue-eyed maid of heaven!—but thou, alas,
Didst never yet one mortal song inspire—
Goddess of Wisdom! here thy temple was,
And is, despite of war and wasting fire,
And years, that bade thy worship to expire:
But worse than steel, and flame, and ages slow,
Is the drear sceptre and dominion dire
Of men who never felt the sacred glow
That thoughts of thee and thine on polished breasts bestow.

II.

Ancient of days! august Athena! where,
Where are thy men of might, thy grand in soul?
Gone—glimmering through the dream of things that were:
First in the race that led to Glory's goal,
They won, and passed away—is this the whole?
A schoolboy's tale, the wonder of an hour!
The warrior's weapon and the sophist's stole

Are sought in vain, and o'er each mouldering tower,
Dim with the mist of years, grey flits the shade of power.

III.
Son of the morning, rise! approach you here!
Come—but molest not yon defenceless urn!
Look on this spot—a nation's sepulchre!
Abode of gods, whose shrines no longer burn.
E'en gods must yield—religions take their turn:
'Twas Jove's—'tis Mahomet's; and other creeds
Will rise with other years, till man shall learn
Vainly his incense soars, his victim bleeds;
Poor child of Doubt and Death, whose hope is built on reeds.

X.
Here let me sit upon this mossy stone,
The marble column's yet unshaken base!
Here, son of Saturn, was thy favourite throne!
Mightiest of many such! Hence let me trace
The latent grandeur of thy dwelling-place.
It may not be: nor even can Fancy's eye
Restore what time hath laboured to deface.
Yet these proud pillars claim no passing sigh;
Unmoved the Moslem sits, the light Greek carols by.

XI.
But who, of all the plunderers of yon fane
On high, where Pallas lingered, loth to flee
The latest relic of her ancient reign—
The last, the worst, dull spoiler, who was he?
Blush, Caledonia! such thy son could be!
England! I joy no child he was of thine:
Thy free-born men should spare what once was free;
Yet they could violate each saddening shrine,
And bear these altars o'er the long reluctant brine.

XIII.

What! shall it e'er be said by British tongue
Albion was happy in Athena's tears?
Though in thy name the slaves her bosom wrung,
Tell not the deed to blushing Europe's ears;
The ocean queen, the free Britannia, bears
The last poor plunder from a bleeding land:
Yes, she, whose generous aid her name endears,
Tore down those remnants with a harpy's hand.
Which envious eld forbore, and tyrants left to stand.

XV.

Cold is the heart, fair Greece, that looks on thee,
Nor feels as lovers o'er the dust they loved;
Dull is the eye that will not weep to see
Thy walls defaced, thy mouldering shrines removed
By British hands, which it had best behoved
To guard those relics ne'er to be restored.
Curst be the hour when from their isle they roved,
And once again thy hapless bosom gored,
And snatched thy shrinking gods to northern climes abhorred!

1849 JAMES LAIRD PATTERSON

Athens left Patterson (see page 17) torn between his admiration for the city's glorious but pagan past, and his commitment to Christian values.

Thursday, 12 September. At five o'clock this morning we were in the harbour of Piraeus, after a rough ten hours' passage from Syra [Syros, island in the Cyclades]. The harbour is (for its size) the most perfect, I should think, in the world. Certainly its adoption instead of, or rather in addition to, the adjacent Phalerum and Munichium, was not the least benefit for which Athens had to thank Themistocles, and did not. How wide seems the application of that law which, by denying their reward to good and useful works in this life, points to some future condition, where this shall be rectified. Great robberies, bloodshed and injustice seldom fail to challenge the regard and obtain the rewards of the world, or, more properly, of its prince.

We stood on deck watching the grey dawn, as it revealed the outline of the coast and that of Salamis; and the charm of Greece dawned with it, indefinable and inexpressible, that most subtle and refined *genius loci* – that mastery of our souls, which sways them with a rod so strong, and yet so gentle, that to escape it is at once beyond our power and beside our will.

In a letter of L's, which I got in Egypt, he talks of the *Nilosity* of the Nile: it is a good expression. Athens has also its *Atticity*. Its sway increased upon me as we drove up from Piraeus, while W pointed out the headland where Themistocles lay buried; the strong substructures of the long walls; the sweet groves of the Academy; the long range of Fames, with the dip through which winds the sacred way to Eleusis, on the left – Cithaeron, gold-fringed to the rising sun; the round thyme-clad Hymettus, and the lofty marble peaks of Pentelicon, on the right. As we near the city, and open the Museum hill, the Pnyx and Areopagus appear; while the temple of Theseus (the most perfect specimen of its style in the world), and the Propylea and Parthenon, on the Acropolis above, claim alternately our regard. The sun meanwhile kept seconding my desires, and revealing more and more of these glorious scenes, till it emerged to view, and darted its bright slanting rays over the whole plain. These rays disclosed at a glance all that scene of the struggles and development of the human mind, in the beauty and majesty of its blighted perfection, to which the civilized world looked for ages, as to the source of all wisdom and knowledge, the model of martial prowess, and the type of every form of poetry. Here Plato walked; here Socrates lived and suffered; here sang Aeschylus and Sophocles; hence went forth Miltiades and Themistocles, to fight and conquer by sea and land. Here lived a race who conquered their conquerors, and captive at last in body, brought under captivity the proud spirits of their victors, and through them of all mankind. This is the sacred place of humanity, the temple of man's intelligence and the centre of its history. Rome, once the mistress of the world, lives again by the force of that divine system to which her fall was as a temporary scaffold; but Athens, ruined, trodden down, oppressed by the yoke of a foreign invader, and now made ludicrous by the feigned friendship of foreign allies, by the force of her past history, and the might of her ancient intelligence, yet rules in the minds of men, and sways the destiny of nations who despise her present weakness.

How I wish I could wish her greatness restored; but this is as impossible, as it is to a Christian undesirable. Whatever attempts have been made in that direction, have been so plainly 'philosophic' – that is, in the French sense of anti-Christian – that it seems manifest that we must look back on the times of pagan Greek intellectual sway as passed (and happily so) forever.

We drove nearly through the town, which is wonderfully formed, considering that twenty years ago it was a mere Turkish village, to the Hotel d'Orient, which is opposite the English Embassy, and is a very good one.

BAGHDAD

Baghdad, 'the city of the Arabian nights', unlike so many other cities of Mesopotamia does not date back to earliest antiquity, but was founded in AD 764 by the Abbasid caliph al-Mansur. It was in its economic, cultural and intellectual prime about 800, during the reign of Caliph Harun al-Rashid. The world's largest city through the early Middle Ages, it was destroyed by the Mongol emperor Hulagu in 1258, and did not properly recover until the 20th century, when it became the capital of the Kingdom of Iraq, both under the British Mandate from 1920 and as an independent state from 1932. The Kingdom was ended by a Ba'athist coup in 1958. Baghdad suffered from heavy bombing during the wars of 1990–91 and 2003, and in the subsequent civil unrest.

1160 BENJAMIN OF TUDELA

Benjamin of Tudela (1130–1173) was a Jew from Navarre in northern Spain who travelled widely in Europe, Africa and the Middle East, and whose writings were influential in the Middle Ages and Renaissance. He was never explicit about the purpose of his travels, but frequently described the Jewish communities he encountered in his book The Itinerary of Benjamin of Tudela. *He visited Baghdad towards the end of the long caliphate of al-Muqtafi, at a time when the authority of the Abbasids was under challenge from the Seljuk Turks.*

It is two days to Baghdad, the great city and the royal residence of the caliph emir...of the family of Muhammad. He is at the head of the Muslim religion, and all the kings of Islam obey him; he occupies a similar position to that held by the Pope over the Christians. He has a palace three miles in extent, with a great park with all varieties of trees, fruit-bearing and otherwise, and all manner of animals. The whole is surrounded by a wall, and in the park is a lake whose waters are fed by the river Tigris.... He is kind unto Israel, and many belonging to the people of Israel are his attendants; he knows all language and is well versed in the Law of Israel.... He is truthful and trusty, speaking peace to all men.

The men of Islam see him but once in the year...at the feast which the Muslims call El-eid-bed Ramadan.... He rides on a mule, and dressed in royal robes of gold and silver and fine linen; on his head is a turban adorned with precious stones and over the turban is a black shawl as a sign of his modesty, implying that all this glory will be covered by darkness on the day of death. He is accompanied by all the nobles of Islam dressed in fine garments and riding on horses, the princes of Arabia, the princes of Torgarma and Daylam and the princes of Persia, Media and Ghuzz [in northern Iran], and the princes of the land of Tibet which is three months' journey distant, and westward of which lies the land of Samarkand. He proceeds from his palace to the great mosque by the Basra Gate. Along the road the walls are adorned with silk and purple, and the inhabitants receive him with all kinds of song and exultation, and they dance before him.... Then he proceeds to the court of the mosque, mounts a wooden pulpit and expounds to them their Law.... He does not return the way he came; and the road which he takes along the riverside is watched all year through so that no man shall tread in his footsteps. He does not leave the palace again for a whole year. He is a benevolent man....

In Baghdad there are 40,000 Jews, and they dwell in security, prosperity and honour under the great caliph, and among them are great sages.... At the head of them all is Daniel the son of Hisdai, who is styled 'Our Lord the Head of the Captivity of all Israel'....

There are 28 synagogues, either in the city itself or in Karkh on the other side of the Tigris; for the river divides this metropolis into two parts. The great Synagogue of the Captivity has columns of marble of various colours overlaid with silver and gold, and on these columns are sentences of the psalms in golden letters. And in front of the ark are about ten steps of marble, and on the topmost are the seats of the Head of the Captivity and of the princes of the House of David. The city is 20 miles in circumference, situated in a land of palms, gardens and plantations, the like of which is not to be found in the whole land of Shinar [Mesopotamia]. People come thither with merchandise from all lands. Wise men live there, philosophers who know all manner of wisdom, and magicians expert in all manner of witchcraft.

1224 YAQUT AL-HAMAWI

Yaqut al-Hamawi (1179–1229) was an Arab geographer born in Constantinople who travelled widely in the Middle East and Central Asia as the slave of a Baghdad trader. His Mu'jam ul-Buldān *(Geographical Encyclopaedia) also covers the history and ethnography of the regions he visited. He was one of the last to describe Baghdad before its destruction by the Mongols in 1258.*

The city of Baghdad forms two vast semicircles on the right and left banks of the Tigris, twelve miles in diameter. The numerous suburbs, covered with parks, gardens, villas and beautiful promenades, and plentifully supplied with rich bazaars and finely built mosques and baths, stretch for a considerable distance on both sides of the river. In the days of its prosperity the population of Baghdad and its suburbs amounted to over two million. The palace of the caliph stands in the midst of a vast park several hours in circumference which beside a menagerie and aviary comprises an enclosure for wild animals reserved for the chase. The palace grounds are laid out with gardens, and adorned with exquisite taste with plants, flowers and trees, reservoirs and fountains, surrounded by sculptured figures. On this side of the river stands the palaces of the great nobles. Immense streets, none less than forty cubits wide, traverse the city from one end to the other, dividing it into blocks or quarters, each under the control of an overseer, who looks after the cleanliness, sanitation and the comfort of the inhabitants.

The water exits both on the north and the south are like the city gates, guarded night and day by relays of soldiers stationed on the watch towers on both sides of the river. Every household is plentifully supplied with water at all seasons by the many aqueducts which intersect the town; and the streets, gardens and parks are regularly swept and watered, and no refuse is allowed to remain within the walls. An immense square in front of the imperial palace is used for reviews, military inspections, tournaments and races; at night the square and the streets are lighted by lamps.

There is also a vast open space where the troops whose barracks lie on the left bank of the river parade daily. The great platforms at the different gates of the city are used by the citizens for gossip and recreation or for watching the flow of travellers and country folk into the capital. The different nationalities in the capital have each an officer to represent their interests with the government, and to whom the stranger can appeal for counsel or help.

Baghdad is a veritable city of palaces, not made of stucco and mortar, but of marble. The buildings are usually of several storeys. The palaces and mansions are lavishly gilded and decorated, and hung with beautiful tapestry and hangings of brocade or silk. The rooms are lightly and tastefully furnished with luxurious divans, costly tables, unique Chinese vases and gold and silver ornaments.

Both sides of the river are for miles fronted by the palaces, kiosks, gardens and parks of the grandees and nobles, marble steps lead down to the water's edge, and the scene on the river is animated by thousands of gondolas, decked with little flags, dancing like sunbeams on the water and carrying the pleasure-seeking Baghdad citizens from one part of the city to the other. Along the wide-stretching quays lie whole fleets at anchor, sea and river craft of all kinds, from the Chinese junk to the old Assyrian raft resting on inflated skins.

The city's mosques are at once vast and remarkably beautiful. There are also in Baghdad numerous colleges of learning, hospitals, infirmaries for both sexes and lunatic asylums.

1928 FREYA STARK

The British writer and photographer Freya Stark (1893–1993) travelled widely in Turkey, Arabia and the Middle East after the First World War and wherever possible sought to encounter directly the life and people of the regions she visited, and to maintain her independence from officialdom. The early 20th-century Baghdad she visited was renowned for its cultural diversity.

To awaken quite alone in a strange town is one of the pleasantest sensations in the world. You are surrounded by adventure. You have no idea of what is in store for you, but you will, if you are wise and know the art of travel, let yourself go on the stream of the unknown and accept whatever comes in the spirit in which the gods may offer it. For this reason your customary thoughts, all except the rarest of your friends, even most of your luggage – everything, in fact, which belongs to your everyday life, is merely a hindrance. The tourist travels in his own atmosphere like a snail and stands, as it were, on his own perambulating doorstep to look at the continents of the world. But if you discard all this, and sally forth with a leisurely and blank mind, there is no knowing what may not happen to you.

For this reason I sent off only one of my letters of introduction – and that was to the friend of the Damascus tanner – and wandered out the morning after my arrival in Baghdad to find a house.

What you first see of the caliphs' city is a most sordid aspect: the long low straight street, a dingy hybrid between East and West, with the unattractiveness of both. The crowd looks unhealthy and sallow, the children are pitiful, the shops are ineffective and compromises with Europe; and the dust is wicked, for it turns to blood-poisoning at the slightest opportunity and bears out the old Babylonian idea of an atmosphere inhabited by demons.

But you can soon leave the main street and walk into the long bazaars and their twilight; or you can turn to the right among the narrow ways and lattice-work balconies of the Jewish and Moslem quarters; or better still, you can cross the old bridge of boats to Karkh, which was the southern suburb of the Round City built by Mansur, where the produce of the land, once coming in great boats down the 'Isa canal, had to unload into barges at the port near the ruin of Aqqar Kuf where now is desert, since the masts of the ships could not pass under the many stone bridges of the town.

The glory has departed, but the life is unchanged.

White-turbaned Indians, Jewish and Armenian merchants, are still here, though their silks and spices, their indigo and pepper, the sugar and velvets of Khuzistan no longer take the Aleppo road. Persian pilgrims or their descendants still walk with silent bare feet and long fanatic faces through the shadows of the dark and airless ways; and the sons of the Prophet in green turbans, with flowing gowns and brown rosary, still pass in grave abstraction, able no doubt to split hairs in Tradition or Grammar, though the Mustanseriya, the great college, is filled with the bales of the custom houses, and the old disputes which rent the lives of men, the Creation of the Quran or its Eternal Existence, have now given place to the cheerful badinage of Kurdish porters under those carved arcades.

I did not, of course, find all this out that very morning.

In fact I soon got lost in a labyrinth of ways so narrow that donkeys with panniers filled them from side to side. I was just thinking of enquiring the road home when I saw an empty house.

It was a tumbledown-looking place, with brick walls and grated windows evidently looking on to a small yard, and there was an Arabic notice to say that it was empty and for sale. But what attracted me was the house next door.

There, in a little garden court sitting under a shed on rows of matting, were twenty or thirty children learning their lessons from an old Mulla who sat cross-legged among them. They had only about ten books between them, so they sat in groups, three or four round each volume, and chanted the words in their childish voices. Now and then a newcomer would pass me at the gate, slip off his shoes and find an empty place and a corner of a book to read from. Now and then some of them got bored, strolled away among the plants and flowers, and returned after a while with renewed energy. The Mulla had a white turban and red hennaed beard, and a kind old face;

his scholars evidently had no fear of him. It was such a pleasant sight, and I thought it would be delightful to live next door to it, that I accepted the unnecessary assistance of five passers-by to decipher the address of the owner of the house and made my way back to the depressing atmosphere of my hotel with a feeling of wonderful elation....

True happiness, we consider, is incompatible with an inefficient drainage system. It is one of those points on which we differ most fundamentally from the East, where happiness and sanitation are not held to have any particular connection.

In spite of many efforts, Baghdad still remains triumphantly Eastern in this respect. It lies so low and in so flat a land that there is no possibility of draining anything anywhere. This is what makes it so depressing for Officers of Health and so amusing for people who like to study microbes.

Every house is built around a paved yard, large or small: in the middle of the yard is a trap-door, which does not usually fit extremely well: under that is a cistern where all the refuse waters go. The Sumerians used to bury their relatives under the dining-room floor close by, a thing which is no longer done.

My little court as time wore on seemed to smell more and more like a Sumerian ancestor. I used to lie awake and wonder about it at night and admire the malignity of a smell which could lie dormant all day when one might escape it by going out, and leapt upon one as soon as one was safely imprisoned in one's bedroom. There was something of the Babylonian fiend about it. Indeed I believe it was an affliction called up by the Mulla next door, who did not like infidels in his quarter. What could be more easy to one who knows the ropes than to call up a smell from the Baghdad underworld? The only difficulty would be to choose which, for there is a great variety. This was a particularly wily one. It never appeared by day so I was unable to prove its existence to my friends and neighbours; it never troubled Marie, who slept with her head in the very midst of it over our diminutive cistern-court; but it curled through or under my closed door, crept to the corner where I lay trying to breathe the comparatively innocent air of the street, and had me at its mercy for the rest of the night. It left me with a sore throat every morning.

1933 ROBERT BYRON

British writer Robert Byron (1905–1941) created a classic of travel writing in
The Road to Oxiana *(1937), in which he related a trip to Persia and Afghanistan,
combining an acute sensitivity to Islamic architecture with a strong sense of absurd-
ity and the daily practical challenges of travelling in remote regions. The Iraq he
visited was a recent creation as an independent state; Gertrude Bell (1868–1926)
had been instrumental in having Faisal (r. 1921–33) placed on the throne.*

It is little solace to recall that Mesopotamia was once so rich, so fertile of
art and invention, so hospitable to the Sumerians, the Seleucids and the
Sasanids. The prime fact of Mesopotamian history is that in the 13th century
Hulagu destroyed the irrigation system; and that from that day to this
Mesopotamia has remained a land of mud deprived of mud's only possible
advantage, vegetable fertility. It is a mud plain, so flat that a single heron,
reposing on one leg beside some rare trickle of water in a ditch, looks as
tall as a wireless aerial. From this plain rise villages of mud and cities of
mud. The rivers flow with liquid mud. The air is composed of mud refined
into a gas. The people are mud-coloured; they wear mud-coloured clothes,
and their national hat is nothing more than a formalized mud-pie. Baghdad
is the capital one would expect of this divinely favoured land. It lurks in a
mud fog; when the temperature drops below 110, the residents complain of
the chill and get out their furs. For only one thing is it now justly famous:
a kind of boil which takes nine months to heal, and leaves a scar....

The hotel is run by Assyrians, pathetic, pugnacious little people with
affectionate ways, who are still half in terror of their lives. There is only one
I would consign to the Baghdadis, a snappy youth called Daood (David),
who has put up the prices of all cars to Teheran and referred to the arch
of Ctesiphon as 'Fine show, sir, high show.'

This arch rises 121½ feet from the ground and has a span of 82. It also
is of mud; but has nevertheless lasted fourteen centuries. Photographs
exist which show two sides instead of one, and the front of the arch as well.
In mass, the ill-fired bricks are a beautiful colour, whitish buff against a sky
which is blue again, now that we are out of Baghdad. The base has lately
been repaired; probably for the first time since it was built.

The museum here is guarded, not so that the treasures of Ur may be
safe, but lest visitors should defile the brass of the showcases by leaning

on them. Since none of the exhibits is bigger than a thimble, it was thus impossible to see the treasures of Ur. On the wall outside, King Feisal has erected a memorial tablet to Gertrude Bell. Presuming the inscription was meant by King Feisal to be read, I stepped up to read it. At which four policemen set up a shout and dragged me away. I asked the director of the museum why this was. 'If you have short sight, you can get special leave,' he snapped. So much, again, for Arab charm.

BEIJING
(PEKING)

The site of modern Beijing has been an important political centre at least since the 5th century BC, when the kingdom of Yan had its capital, named Ji, on the site. Though Ji was destroyed by the first emperor in the 3rd century BC, the city, now called Yan, was rebuilt during the Han era (206 BC–AD 220), becoming a key military centre for defending the northern frontier of the now-unified China. During the Tang dynasty (618–907) it was rebuilt again as Youzhou;

in the 12th century it was rebuilt as Zhongdu. The Mongol invaders who conquered northern China in 1215 made their own capital on the same site; in 1271 Kublai Khan (r. 1260–94) rebuilt it as Dadu, making it capital of his Yuan dynasty.

After the Mongol Yuan dynasty was replaced by the native Ming in 1368, Dadu was renamed Beiping, and rebuilt again as Beijing ('Northern Capital'; formerly transliterated as Peking) in 1403 at a time of dispute with a branch of the dynasty based in Nanjing ('Southern Capital'). In 1644, Beijing fell to the Manchu invaders, became the capital of their new Qing dynasty and expanded, with the addition of many palaces and temples.

Beijing remained China's capital after both the fall of the Qing in 1911 and the Communist revolution of 1949. The subsequent forced modernization and homogenization of all aspects of life caused a total rupture with the traditions of the imperial past, most dramatically seen in the Cultural Revolution of the late 1960s. Following the death of Chairman Mao Zedong in 1976, a cautious liberalization was seen, until the 21st century when much of the old city was swept away.

1280s MARCO POLO

Marco Polo (1254–1324) was a Venetian trader who set off in 1271 to travel the Silk Road and spent years in Dadu, or Tatu ('great capital' in Mongolian, Khanbaliq or 'City of the Khan' in Chinese, sometimes Westernized as Cambaluc) with Kublai Khan. He returned to Venice in 1295, where he was imprisoned until 1299, during which time he wrote Il Milione, *the account of his travels, which quickly became a sensation across Europe.*

Now there was in old times a great and noble city called Cambaluc, which is to say 'The city of the Emperor'. But the Great Khan was informed by his astrologers that this city would prove rebellious and raise great disorders against his imperial authority. So he caused the present city to be built close beside the old one, with only a river between them. And he caused the people of the old city to be removed to the new town that he had founded;

50

and this is called Tatu. However, he allowed a portion of the people which he did not suspect to remain in the old city, because the new one could not hold the whole of them, big as it is.

This new city has a compass of 24 miles; each side has a length of 6 miles, and it is four-square. It is walled with walls of earth ten paces thick at bottom, and a height of more than ten paces; but at top they are about three paces thick. And they are provided throughout with loop-holed battlements, which are all whitewashed.

There are twelve gates, and over each is a great and handsome palace, so that there are on each side of the square three gates and five palaces; for there is at each angle also a great and handsome palace. In those palaces are vast halls in which are kept the arms of the city garrison.

The streets are so straight and wide that you can see along them from end to end and from one gate to the other. And up and down the city there are beautiful palaces, and many great and fine hostelries, and fine houses in great numbers.

Moreover, in the middle of the city there is a great clock – a bell – which is struck at night. And after it has struck three times no one must go out in the city, unless it be for the needs of a woman in labour, or of the sick. And those who go about on such errands have to carry lanterns. Moreover, the guard at each gate of the city is 1,000 armed men; not that for fear of any attack, but as a guard of honour for the sovereign and to prevent thieves from doing mischief in the town.

1541 FERNÃO MENDES PINTO

The Portuguese adventurer Fernão Mendes Pinto (c. 1509–1583) travelled through China, Japan and South East Asia between 1537 and 1558. He was shipwrecked off China and imprisoned, then taken prisoner by invading Tatars. Later shipwrecked again off Japan, Pinto claimed to be the first Westerner to visit those islands. His sometimes incredible account of his travels, published in Portugal in 1614, was translated into many languages.

The city is 30 leagues in circuit; and environed with two rows of strong walls, where there are a number of towers and bulwarks after our fashion; but without this circuit, which is of the city itself, there is another far greater...

that the Chinese affirm was anciently all inhabited, but at this present there are only some boroughs and villages, as also a many of fair houses, or castles, about it, among which are...the houses of the proctors of the 1,600 cities and most remarkable towns of the 32 kingdoms of this monarchy, who repair unto this city at the general assembly of the estates, which is held every three years for the public good. Without this great enclosure... are 80,000 tombs of the mandarins: little chapels all gilded within, and compassed about with balusters of iron and latten, the entries whereunto are through very rich and sumptuous arches.... It hath also 500 very great palaces, which are called the 'houses of the son of the sun', whither all those retire that have been hurt in the wars for the service of the king, as also many other soldiers, who in regard of age or sickness are no longer able to bear arms.... We saw also another long street of low houses, where there were 24,000 oarsmen; and another where 14,000 taverners that followed the court dwelt; as also a third street, where live a great number of light women, exempted from the tribute which they of the city pay, for that they are courtesans, whereof the most part had quitted their husbands for to follow that wretched trade.... In this enclosure do likewise remain all the laundresses...above 100,000. Within this same enclosure...there are 1,300 very sumptuous houses of religious men and women.... We saw also a great many...inns, whither come people of all ages and sexes, as to see comedies, plays, combats, bull-baiting, wrestling and magnificent feasts....

There were some feasts that lasted ten days, which in regard of the state, pomp and charge thereof, as well in the attendance of servants and waiters, as in the costly fare of all kind of flesh, fowl, fish and all delicacies in music, in sports of hunting and hawking, in plays, comedies, games, tourneys and in shows both of horse and foot, fighting and skirmishing together, do cost above twenty thousand *taels*. These inns are maintained by companies of very rich merchants, who...employ their money therein, whereby they gain far more than if they should venture it to sea.... Whensoever any one will be at a charge that way, he goes to the superintendent of the house, and declares what his design is; whereupon he shews him a book...which treats of the ordering and bumptiousness of feasts, the rates of them.... This book I have seen, and heard it read; in the three first chapters thereof, it speaks of the feasts whereunto God is to be invited, and of what price they are; and then it descends to the king of China.... After it hath done with the king in China, it speaks of the feasts of the tutons, which are the ten sovereign dignities that command over the 40 ghaems, who are as the viceroys of the state.

1655 PETER DE GOYER AND JAKOB DE KEYZER

De Goyer and de Keyzer, merchants from the Dutch trading post of Batavia (now Jakarta, Indonesia), travelled to China as representatives of the Dutch East India Company (VOC) to seek a trading agreement with the Ming. Their embassy included an artist, and the illustrated account of their journey was widely published and contributed significantly to European perceptions of China in the late 17th century.

The city is called Peking which signifies the northern chief city, to distinguish it from Nanking, which we interpret the southern city. But the other name Xuntien, wherewith it is so commonly called by the Chinese geographers, signifies Obedient to Heaven; it is called by the Tartars Cambalu, that is the City of the Lord....

All rarities in China are brought hither so that this city abounds in everything either for pleasure or humane sustenance. Several thousand royal vessels (beside those of private persons) are continually employed to fetch all manner of wares and curiosities for the emperor and his council at Peking.... The Chinese use great endeavours to make all rivers navigable that so they may come with ease by water to the emperor's court with the products of several provinces....

By this importation this place, though in an unfruitful and barren soil possesses everything in great abundance and may be called the granary of the whole empire; for they have a proverb among them that, 'there grows nothing in Peking, yet there is no want of anything'....

The streets are not paved, insomuch that in wet weather (which is seldom) they are hardly passable, but when the northern winds blow, and the weather dry, the soil which is of a light substance makes a dust far more noisome to passengers than the deep and miry streets; for such it is that it blinds a man as he goes along. The inhabitants therefore to prevent this inconvenience are fain to wear silk hoods over their faces; and the extraordinary foulness of the way makes very many to keep horses to carry them after a rainy day;

for the infinite number of common people that are continually up and down turns this dusty soil into mire and dirt after a little rain.

There are also horses and sedans to be hired at any time for the accommodation of passengers; but none make use of sedans or chairs but persons of quality. The sedan is made very artificially of bamboo or rushes in the middle whereof stands a chair which is covered with a tiger's skin upon which he that is carried seats himself, having behind him a boy with an umbrella in his hand to keep off the sun. His servants likewise attend him, some whereof go before and others follow with ensigns upon their shoulders whereby the quality of the person is known and is respected accordingly as he passes along.

1721 JOHN BELL

China has long been renowned for its acrobats, as recalled in this account by the Scottish doctor John Bell (1691–1780) who lived in St Petersburg, where he was appointed medical assistant to Russian embassies to Persia, China (1721–22) and Constantinople. The illustrated account of his travels was published in Britain and France in the 1760s.

We dined at the French or western convent, where again we found all the missionaries.... The emperor's band of music played all the time of dinner; after which we had jugglers and tumblers of great activity. Among the many feats and tricks performed by these people I shall mention only two or three which seemed most uncommon. The roof of the room where we sat was supported by wooden pillars. The juggler took a gimlet with which he bored one of the pillars and asked whether we chose red or white wine? The question being answered, he pulled out the gimlet and put a quill in the hole, through which ran, as from a cask, the wine demanded. After the same manner he extracted several sorts of liquors, all of which I had the curiosity to taste and found them good of their kinds.

Another of these expert youths took three long sharp-pointed knives and, throwing them up by turns, kept one always in each hand and the third in the air. This he continued to perform for a considerable time, catching constantly the falling knife by the handle without ever allowing it to touch the floor. The knives were exceeding sharp so that, had he missed laying hold of the handles, he must infallibly have lost some of his fingers....

I shall only mention one instance more. There were placed erect upon the pavement of the room two bamboos, which are a kind of cane. The length of them was about twenty-five feet; at the lower end I reckon them to be near five inches diameter and at the top, about the breadth of a crown piece. They were straight, light and smooth, and each supported by two men. Two boys then climbed up the poles without the least assistance and having reached the top stood upright, sometimes on one foot and sometimes on the other, and then upon their heads. This being done, they laid one hand on the top of the pole and stretched out their bodies almost at right angles to it. In this posture they continued for a considerable time and even shifted hands. I observed that much depended on the men who held the poles; one of the two having it fixed to his girdle; and they kept a steady eye on the motions of the boys. There were about twenty or thirty of these performers who all belong to the emperor and never display their art without his permission. I am fully persuaded that in tricks and feats of dexterity, few nations can equal and none excel the Chinese.

1887 HARRY DE WINDT

In the later 19th century China was forcibly opened to Western travellers and traders, who commonly both admired the rich and ancient culture they encountered and despised the people for their supposed servility and 'inscrutability'. Harry de Windt (1856–1933) was a British soldier and explorer who wrote accounts of several long journeys across Asia, including overland from Paris to New York via Siberia, and Russia to India via Persia. His description of arriving in Beijing in 1887 shows a typical disdain for the people among whom he was travelling.

A few hundred yards brought us to the gate of the Tartar city, and, ye gods! what a city! Upon first entering, it seemed as if a dense fog had suddenly descended upon one, but a look back at the bright sunshine outside the gate soon dispelled the illusion and explained the mystery: it was nothing but dust, the black, fine and searching dust, for which Pekin is famous. Everything was coated with it. One breathed it in with every inhalation, till eyes, mouth and nose were choked up, and breathing became almost an impossibility. No one seemed to mind it much, though our donkeys laboured through it nearly knee-deep.

We rode for some distance along the filthy, dusty streets. There is no rule of the road in Pekin, and it took one all one's time to steer safely through the carts, sedans, mule litters and camel caravans which thronged the streets. At length we turned into the principal thoroughfare, a broad unpaved street, raised in the centre, on either side of which one saw a long vista of low-roofed houses, scrubby trees and gaudy shop signs, lost in the distance in a cloud of dust. We were in Pekin at last.

In Pekin but apparently a long way yet from our destination, the Hotel de Pekin; and judging from our small guide's very erratic movements, we were not likely for some time to reach that friendly hostelry.... The disagreeable suspicion that our guide had lost his way became a certainty, when turning down a narrow by-lane, he brought us up at the door of a filthy tea-house. It was not a pleasant predicament. Imagine a Central African suddenly turned loose in the streets of London, and you have our position – with this difference, that the African would have had the advantage over us in the shape of a policeman to befriend him. Here, in this city of nearly two million inhabitants, it seemed unlikely enough that we should come across any of the English-speaking inhabitants, who number fifty to sixty at the most.

Threats of punishment and vengeance on the small boy were useless. He simply seated himself, and calling for a cup of tea, informed us we must find our way ourselves, he did not know it – at least that is what we inferred from his gestures, which were disrespectful in the extreme. With a lively recollection of our escape of the afternoon, we did not care to risk another disturbance, so, resigning ourselves to circumstances, dismounted and called for tea.

It was not a pleasant half-hour, for we were surrounded in less than five minutes by a crowd of dirty, villainous-looking ruffians. We had evidently been brought to one of the very lowest quarters of the town, and were not sorry to have left our watches in the carts. With the exception of the revolvers and a few cash [sic] they would not have been much the richer for robbing us. I should be sorry to have much to do with the inhabitants of the Chinese capital. There is no more obliging and hospitable being than the Chinese peasant, no more insolent, arrogant thief than the lower order of Pekinese. The victory of the imperial troops over the French in Tonkin [northern Vietnam; in 1884–85, Chinese forces caused setbacks for France in the Sino-French War] is, in a great measure, responsible for the insolence displayed by the inhabitants of Pekin towards Europeans. Insults are perpetrated almost daily, and in the open streets, for which there is no redress, and it is only necessary to go for a very short walk in the streets of the capital to see that the lesson taught the Celestials by the allied troops in 1860 has long since been forgotten.

We should probably have had to pass the night in this unsavoury den, had not a European passed and by the greatest luck caught sight of us through the narrow gateway. Our deliverer, Mr P., an American missionary, himself escorted us through a labyrinth of crowded streets and squares to Legation Street. We should certainly never have found our way otherwise, for there were no outward and visible signs even here of European inhabitants, till, just before reaching the hotel, we passed the French Embassy, and saw, through an open gateway, a spacious shady garden with smooth-shaven lawns, cedars and fountains, while over the doorway, in large gold letters on a vermilion ground, were the words 'Legation de France'. A couple of hundred yards further on we pulled up at the door of our caravanserai. Thanking and taking leave of our friend, we entered the building and were not sorry to find ourselves in the cool, grey-tiled, flower-bordered courtyard of the hotel, where a whisky and soda with plenty of ice washed the dust out of our throats and refreshed us not a little after our long and somewhat eventful ride.

The baggage arrived an hour after, and after a bath and change we felt well-disposed to do justice to the excellent dinner provided for us.... Sitting out after dinner in the little moonlit courtyard redolent of heliotrope and mignonette, one might have fancied oneself hundreds of miles from the dusty, ill-smelling city, and its barbaric population. The smells did not, thank goodness, penetrate here; and for the first time since leaving Tientsin [Tianjin], we thoroughly enjoyed an after-dinner cigar, not a little relieved that the starting-point, at any rate, of our long land journey had been safely reached.

1987 COLIN THUBRON

British travel writer Colin Thubron (b. 1939) travelled thousands of miles across China in the 1980s, often alone and on foot or by public transport, observing the country in the aftermath of Mao's radical upheavals, and at a time when cautious liberalization was under way.

Something impersonal and unfinished pervaded the whole metropolis of Beijing. Often I felt as if I was not in a city at all, but on a building site where a city might one day be created. I tramped the streets in disorientation, looking for a core which was not there. Across the tarmac desert of its roads the flat-blocks and Soviet-style institutions rose as featureless as cardboard, and the sycamores and silver poplars planted along them paled beneath too vast an expanse of sky. I was feeling displaced from some other capital, perhaps an imagined city – imperial Peking whose walls and temples had been hacked away.

Along the quiet streets commuters moved in unisexual flocks, jacketed in olive green and boilersuit blue. The boyish hair and tobacco-stained teeth of a million factory workers bobbed and grimaced from jam-packed trams and buses, while sallow girls, their plaits and pony-tails bound in elastic bands, bicycled solemnly all together down special lanes in regimental shoals. Staring at passing faces I wondered if I would ever come to know them. They conspired to fulfil Western clichés of themselves: inscrutable and all alike. The pavements fell noiseless under the uniform tread of their canvas shoes and black cloth slippers. I smiled at the gentler faces. They looked bemused, smiled slowly back. Nobody approached me.

Even the city's plan was vaguely estranging. The medieval Chinese who invented the magnetic compass, laid out their capital according to an intricate geomancy, so that its dead-straight streets and gates inscribed a sacred force-field out from the emperor's inner palaces to the farthest reaches of the empire....

The walls and gates had almost gone now, pulled down in the Revolutionary ferment, but they had left behind them this mystic gridiron fattened to six or eight lanes with scarcely a motor on them. Its roads sliced through the mesh of alleys and courtyards like the imposition of some unrepealable law, a giant idea driven through the throbbing softness of private life....

A few trams and Russian-style taxis clatter by, with an occasional Chinese-made 'Shanghai' or Japanese saloon (but never privately owned), while here and there a black Mercedes or lumpish 'Red Flag' conveys its officials between residence and ministry, concealed by curtains. For the rest, the roads are given up to a drifting river of five million bicyclists.

But as I approached the city's centre, I noticed differences. They came in apparent trivia – girls wearing skirts and tentative lipstick, markets spilling over the pavements with sacks of bananas, improvised stalls piled with cheap clothes. Arguments flared, and reticent tenderness: women walking arm in arm, a man's hand drifting to his workmate's shoulder. Compared to the Beijing of ten years ago – a city still frozen in the puritanism of Mao's Revolution – all this was unimaginable. But the changes now were everywhere. Window-dressing had appeared, with hairstyles, fashion, advertisements – all the messengers of a gentler, more self-centred, more humanely varied life....

I abandoned the avenues and slipped down side streets into a maze-world of alleys and courtyards. These *hutongs* are still the living flesh of Beijing, and once you are inside them it shrinks to a sprawling hamlet. The lanes are a motley of blank walls and doorways, interspersed by miniature factories and restaurants. Each street is a decrepit improvisation on the last. Tiled roofs curve under rotting eaves. The centuries shore each other up. Modern brick walls, already crumbling, enclose ancient porches whose doors of beaten tin or lacerated pinewood swing in carved stone frames. Underfoot the tarmac peels away from the huge, worn paving-slabs of another age, and the traffic thins to a tinkling slipstream of pedicabs and bicycles....

In these lanes, too, the inhabitants drifted into solitude and became individual. As they gossiped or bartered at little stalls of private enterprise, they looked mysteriously cleaner and trimmer than the houses from which they came. And they no longer seemed alike. Already I was mentally separating the dark southern immigrant from the taller Beijingnese, and identifying the deep chestnut hair of northern girls. People detached themselves into portraits – a bright-cheeked tomboy skipping with a frayed strand of rope; a man pulling his wife on a handcart, to work; while beside me an old woman hobbled on feet crippled by binding – they were less than six inches long, and their broken bones rose in a pained hillock close to the ankle. She smiled weakly at nothing.

BERLIN

Berlin was founded in the 1230s and came to dominate first Brandenburg and then Prussia, becoming the residence of the king of Prussia in 1701; the palace of Charlottenburg was built around this time.

The city was embellished throughout the 18th century, the most commonly noted feature being the Brandenburg Gate, built in 1788–91 by Frederick William II to symbolize peace. As capital of the most powerful state of early 19th-century Germany, and from 1871, capital of the German Empire, Berlin exerted an increasing cultural sway, while the reactionary Prussian monarchy dominated the political life of the city.

The early 20th century brought dramatic change to Berlin, which suffered a failed Communist revolution after the First World War, and remained economically highly divided between rich and poor. As the capital of the Weimar Republic in the 1920s, it was notorious for its liberal modernist culture, but this succumbed to the National Socialists, who won power in 1933. Adolf Hitler, chancellor from 1933, used the Berlin Olympic Games in 1936 as a showpiece to present his Nazi regime to the world.

At the end of the Second World War, when the Red Army liberated Berlin in April 1945 the city was devastated and the population starving. The post-war settlement left Berlin, now deep in Soviet-controlled East Germany, divided between zones administered by each of the four Allied powers: the Soviet Union, the United States, Britain and France. Whereas the Western sectors gradually regained economic and cultural vitality, the Soviet sector of East Berlin did not. In 1961, the Soviets erected a wall to prevent a constant stream of defections from East to West; the wall remained until 1989. Since its fall, the eastern sector has been revitalized and Berlin has become a centre for radical youth.

1803 CATHERINE WILMOT

Irish-born Catherine Wilmot (1773–1824) travelled across Europe in 1801–3 in the party of the Irish Lord and Lady Mount Cashell, meeting Napoleon and the Pope; an account of her journeys was published in 1920, based on her diaries. She lived in Russia until 1808, and later moved to France, where she died.

The drive from Potsdam to Berlin is highly cultivated and fine and the entrance into Berlin is perfectly magnificent. The new gate is like a grand triumphal arch, ornamented on the top by four bronze colossal horses, held in from bounding into the place beneath. The streets are extremely wide and delightfully planted with acacia trees, and a variety of others. We lodge in the most cheerful situation I ever saw; the public walk is immediately under our window, where we see all the ladies walking about with a little basket on their arms, instead of a reticule as in France....

Sunday we sallied forth in pursuit of churches and mounted up to the top of the highest to take a view of the town; to an amazing extent the country is perfectly flat. I think Berlin much prettier in detail, than looked at, at a *coup d'oeil*. I sat out most of the service at a Lutheran Church; the forms appeared pretty much like that of the Church of England.... In the evening we drove to Charlottenburg through beautifully planted avenues and woods which reach the extent of the way. The palace is handsome and in the midst of a paradise of a garden; this is the favourite royal residence, and the king, queen and their six little children with the brothers, and all the court, walked about during a great part of the evening....

The house in which the royal family lives is quite like a private gentleman's, furnished comfortably enough. All the present House of Prussia are esteemed stingy and shabby to the greatest degree.... The king walks about and rides without attendants. The people hardly make way for him in the streets, but as he is not noble in his character, this freedom does not flatter, as it is assumed from convenience, and no proof of confidence in his subjects. He is reckoned selfish, and fond of money, and his ministers manage his kingdom for him entirely.

1842 MARY SHELLEY

Mary Wollstonecraft Godwin, later Shelley (1797–1851) was the English author of Frankenstein *and wife of the poet Percy Bysshe Shelley, who died in 1822. In the 1840s she undertook several journeys with her son Percy Florence, which were written into a book in which she freely expressed her political views as well as describing more conventional sightseeing.*

27 July We are here in the best street, which has a double avenue of lime trees in the middle, running its whole length. One way it leads to the Brandenburg gate, the other to a spot that forms the beauty of Berlin as a capital – a wide open space, graced by a beautiful fountain, and an immense basin of

polished granite, made from one of those remarkable boulders found on the sandy plain, fifty miles from Berlin; adorned also by the colonnade of the New Museum, opposite to which stands the Guardhouse, the Italian Opera and the University. The building of the Arsenal is near and the whole forms a splendid assemblage of buildings. After dinner we have walked under the lime trees to the Brandenburg gate – a most beautiful portal built on the model of the Propylaeum at Athens, on a larger scale. Napoleon carried off the car of Victory which decorates the top; it was brought back after the battle of Waterloo. Before its capture it was placed as if leaving the city behind, to rush forward on the world; on its return, it was placed returning to and facing the city....

28 July Our first visit in the morning was to the museum. It is at some little distance from the hotel, and the walk led us through the best part of Berlin. The building itself is beautiful; the grand circular hall by which you reach the statue gallery, and which again you look down upon from the open gallery that leads to the pictures, surpasses in elegance and space anything I have ever seen, except in the Vatican. At once we rushed among the pictures – our only inducement, except curiosity to see a renowned capital city, to visit Berlin. The gallery is admirably arranged in schools, and the pictures have an excellent light on them; and in each room is hung up a list of pictures and their painters contained in it....

The gallery is open from ten till three. Unfortunately, the fatigue of the journey made me very ill able to endure much toil; and you know – who knows not? – that visiting galleries produces extreme weariness. I went back to the hotel several times to repose, and then returned to the gallery. I desired to learn by heart – to imbibe – to make all I saw a part of myself, so that never more I may forget it. In some sort I shall succeed. Some of the forms of beauty on which I gazed, must last in my memory as long as it endures; but this will be at the expense of others, which even now are fading and about to disappear from my mind.... The gallery of Berlin will, I fear, become a vague, though glorious dream, for the most part, leaving distinct only a few images that can never be effaced.

29 July Today, we have been doing our duty in sightseeing; though I grudged every minute spent away from the gallery.... I desired to visit some of the manufactures of Berlin steel, and expected to see beautiful specimens. It is a curious fact, how difficult it is to find out where you ought to go, and how to see any sight, unless it be a regular lion, or you have an exact address. We took a *drosky* [open carriage] and drove to a shop; it was closed: to another; there was no such thing. We returned to our hotel and learnt that we had been spending many useless *groschen* by not taking the *drosky* by the hour instead of the course. Having reformed this oversight, we set off again in search of the manufactory....

At length...we reached the Eisengieserei, or iron foundry, just outside the Oranienburg gate.... The men were at work making moulds in sand. At length a vast cauldron of molten metal was brought from the furnace and poured into a mould. There is something singular in boiling metal, the sight of which gives a new idea to the mind, a new sensation to the soul. Boiling water or other liquid presents only an inanimate element changed to the touch, not to the eye; but molten metal, red and fiery, takes a new appearance and seems to have life – the heat appears to give it voluntary action, and the sense of its power of injury adds to the emotion with which it is regarded; as well as the fact that it takes and preserves the form into which it flows.... Certainly, seeing the diminutive Cyclops pour the glowing living liquid from their cauldron, viewing it run fiercely into the various portions of the mould, and then grow tranquil and dark as its task was fulfilled, imparted, I know not why or how, a thrill to the frame.

After this we were taken to an outhouse in which there were articles for sale – no bracelets, nor chains nor necklaces; chiefly small statuettes of Napoleon and Frederick the Great.

1936 THOMAS WOLFE

In his posthumously published novel You Can't Go Home Again *(1940), American novelist Thomas Wolfe (1900–1938) described the city he had loved during Hitler's 1936 Olympics.*

The organizing genius of the German people, which has been used so often to such noble purpose, was now more thrillingly displayed than he had ever seen it before. The sheer pageantry of the occasion was overwhelming, so much so that he began to feel oppressed by it. There seemed to be something ominous in it. One sensed a stupendous concentration of effort, a tremendous drawing together and ordering in the vast collective power of the whole land. And the thing that made it seem ominous was that it so evidently went beyond what the games themselves demanded. The games were overshadowed, and were no longer merely sporting competitions to which other nations had sent their chosen teams. They became, day after day, an orderly and overwhelming demonstration in which the whole of Germany had been schooled and disciplined. It was as if the games had been chosen as a symbol of the new collective might, a means of showing to the world in concrete terms what this new power had come to be.

With no past experience in such affairs, the Germans had constructed a mighty stadium which was the most beautiful and most perfect in its design that had ever been built. And all the accessories of this monstrous plant – the swimming pools, the enormous halls, the lesser stadia – had been laid out and designed with this same cohesion of beauty and of use. The organization was superb. Not only were the events themselves, down to the minutest detail of each competition, staged and run off like clockwork, but the crowds – such crowds as no other great city has ever had to cope with, and the like of which would certainly have snarled and maddened the traffic of New York beyond hope of untangling – were handled with a quietness, order and speed that was astounding.

The daily spectacle was breathtaking in its beauty and magnificence. The stadium was a tournament of colour that caught the throat; the massed splendour of the banners made the gaudy decorations of America's great parades, presidential inaugurations and World's Fairs seem like shoddy carnivals in comparison. And for the duration of the Olympics, Berlin itself was transformed into a kind of annex to the stadium. From one end of the city to the other, from the Lustgarten to the Brandenburger Tor, along the whole broad sweep of Unter den Linden, through the vast avenues of the faery Tiergarten, and out through the western part of Berlin to the very portals of the stadium, the whole town was a thrilling pageantry of royal banners – not merely endless miles of looped-up bunting, but banners fifty feet in height, such as might have graced the battle tent of some great emperor.

And all through the day, from morning on, Berlin became a mighty Ear, attuned, attentive, focused on the stadium. Everywhere the air was filled with a single voice. The green trees along the Kurfürstendamm began to talk: from loud-speakers concealed in their branches an announcer in the stadium spoke to the whole city – and for George Webber it was a strange experience to hear the familiar terms of track and field translated into the tongue that Goethe used. He would be informed now that the *Vorlauf* was about to be run – and then the *Zwischenlauf* – and at length the *Endlauf* – and the winner: 'Owens – Oo Ess Ah!'

Meanwhile, through those tremendous banner-laden ways, the crowds thronged ceaselessly all day long. The wide promenade of Unter den Linden was solid with patient, tramping German feet. Fathers, mothers, children, young folks, old – the whole material of the nation was there, from every corner of the land. From morn to night they trudged, wide-eyed, full of wonder, past the marvel of those banner-laden ways. And among them one saw the bright stabs of colour of Olympic jackets and the glint of foreign faces: the dark features of Frenchmen and Italians, the ivory grimace of the Japanese, the straw hair and blue eyes of the Swedes, and the big Americans, natty in straw hats, white flannels and blue coats crested with the Olympic seal.

And there were great displays of marching men, sometimes ungunned but rhythmic as regiments of brown shirts went swinging through the streets. By noon each day all the main approaches to the games, the embannered streets and avenues of the route which the Leader would take to the stadium, miles away, were walled in by the troops. They stood at ease, young men, laughing and talking with each other – the Leader's bodyguards, the Schutz Staffel units, the Storm Troopers, all the ranks and divisions in their different uniforms – and they stretched in two unbroken lines from the Wilhelmstrasse up to the arches of the Brandenburger Tor. Then, suddenly, the sharp command, and instantly there would be the solid smack of ten thousand leather boots as they came together with the sound of war.

It seemed as if everything had been planned for this moment, shaped to this triumphant purpose. But the people – they had not been planned. Day after day, behind the unbroken wall of soldiers, they stood and waited in a dense and patient throng. These were the masses of the nation, the poor ones of the earth, the humble ones of life, the workers and the wives, the mothers and the children – and day after day they came and stood and waited. They were there because they did not have money enough to buy the little cardboard squares that would have given them places within the magic ring. From noon till night they waited for just two brief and golden moments of the day: the moment when the Leader went out to the stadium, and the moment when he returned.

At last he came – and something like a wind across a field of grass was shaken through that crowd, and from afar the tide rolled up with him, and in it was the voice, the hope, the prayer of the land. The Leader came by slowly in a shining car, a little dark man with a comic-opera moustache, erect and standing, moveless and unsmiling, with his hand upraised, palm outward, not in Nazi-wise salute, but straight up, in a gesture of blessing such as the Buddha or Messiahs use.

1960 GEORGE KENNAN

George Kennan (1904–2005) was an American diplomat who did much to define the way the West thought about the Cold War. He had studied in Berlin in the late 1920s, and visited again in 1960. His impressions of the 'new Berlin' are recorded in his memoir Sketches from a Life *(1989).*

16–22 June Berlin was bright, open, sprawling – with its characteristic energetic air, in which one burns one's self out (at least I do) with the sheer output of energy, on first arrival.... For the first time, one had the impression of a wholly new Berlin, with a quite different arrangement of functions arising – or, better, superimposed – on the skeleton of the old one, the street pattern being largely unchanged. It was a shock to reflect how much of the old city, particularly the parts of it that had once been so central and so imposing, so seemingly timeless and indestructible – the great, teeming business center between Potsdamer Platz and the Friedrichstrasse and the old residential Tiergartenviertel – had passed utterly into history, so that coming generations, in fact even today's young people, would not even know that those quarters had ever been there, and would be unable to picture them even if told. Five years ago the old Berlin, if only in the form of its ruins and rubble, had still prevailed: the new life had only camped, tentatively and almost apologetically, on what was left of it. Today the new Berlin has taken over. The old one, the scene of such vitality, such pretensions, such horrors and such hopes, is being thrust down into the oblivion of history, before the eyes of those of us who knew it....

On Monday evening I went to the theater, over in the Communist eastern sector of the city with M. It was the former Theater am Schiffbauerdamm – the theater where, until his recent death, Brecht had directed. The area around the theater, once the very teeming center of this entire city, was now empty, silent, almost deserted....

The play was a dramatization of Sholokhov's *And Quiet Flows the Don* – translated, obviously, from the Russian. The acting was good. The house was not full. In the corridors people whispered and glanced furtively at one another. One had suddenly the feeling that we – the actors and the little band of spectators – were the only living people in the great, ruined and deserted area that stretched for miles around, that we were going through a ceremony of sorts in the midst of this great void, as in a dream, as though some menacing spirit were mocking us, putting us through our paces....

M and I sat, in stony silence, in the second row, behind two silent figures in some sort of Communist officer's uniform. Even when the curtain was drawn, there was not a sound among the audience. A whisper would have been heard all over the hall. It was clear: I was back in Russia – not the Russia of today, but Stalin's Russia. The dreadful, furtive spirit which Khrushchev had largely exorcized among his own people had found refuge here in this distant Russian protectorate and it now presided, like a posthumous curse of the dead Stalin on the 'faithless' Germans, over the ruins of the 'eastern sector'.... We left during the intermission....

We drove across the bridge and turned left along the river, behind the university, heading toward one of the great squares that fronted on the one-time (now-destroyed) Imperial Palace. Suddenly, we emerged onto this vast open area from the little park in front of the ruins of the old Zeughaus. We got out of the car, walked out onto the deserted square, and were suddenly overwhelmed – but utterly, profoundly, as I have not been in many years – by what we saw and felt around us.

It was now late twilight – the long-drawn twilight of the northern night. Under the trees it was dark, but the sky was still partly bright. There was a touch of gold in the air. Before us there was only the great square confronting the ruins of the enormous Wilhelminian Romanesque cathedral. The entire area was unbelievably silent and empty. Only one pair of lovers, standing under the trees by the Zeughaus, moved uneasily away at our approach. All about us were the ruins of the great old buildings, semi-silhouetted against the bright sky. And what ruins! In their original state, they had seemed slightly imitative and pretentious. Now they suddenly had a grandeur I had never seen even in Rome. We both became aware that this was, somehow, a moment like no other. There was a stillness, a beauty, a sense of infinite, elegiac sadness and timelessness such as I have never experienced. Death, obviously, was near, and in the air: hushed, august, brooding Death – nothing else. Here all the measureless tragedy of the Second World War – the millions of dead, the endless seas of bereavement and sorrow, the extinction of a whole great complex of life and belief and hope – had its perpetuation. So overpowering was the impression that we spoke only in whispers, as though we were in a cathedral, instead of standing in the open before the ruins of one. Not a soul was now in sight. But no – far up, at the top of an enormous flight of steps leading up to what was left of the cathedral, on the pedestal of one of the huge marble columns, we saw half-hidden in the shadows three adolescent boys – motionless, themselves like statues, themselves silent, endlessly alone and abandoned; and their lost, defiant figures burned themselves into my vision to the point where I see them still today – elbows on the knees, chins resting on the palms of their hands – the embodiment of man's lost and purposeless state, his loneliness, his helplessness, his wistfulness and his inability to understand.

CAIRO

Built just a few miles from the ancient pyramids of Giza, Cairo was founded by the Arabs as a fortified camp named Al-Fustat in AD 641, and it soon became a mercantile and manufacturing centre. In 969 the conquering Fatimid dynasty created a new capital, Al-Qahira, for a caliphate that endured until 1171.

In the 12th century Cairo became the capital of Saladin's Ayyubid empire, and from 1260 the capital of the Mamluk empire. By the mid-14th century, it was the largest city in Europe and the Middle East, a centre of learning and faith as well as political power. In 1517 it was taken over by the Ottoman Turks.

By the 19th century ancient Egypt was a place of fascination to many Westerners following Napoleon's invasion of 1798, when he had taken with him a team of scholars and antiquarians to document the ancient culture (see pages 16–17). Most visitors stayed in Cairo en route to Giza.

From 1882 to 1952, Egypt was under British rule, although formal independence was granted in 1922. In the First World War, Cairo was the headquarters for the British campaign against the Ottoman Turks; in the Second, it was the British headquarters for the Middle East Command and the North Africa campaign against Germany and Italy. Following the Egyptian nationalist revolution of 1952, it remains a capital very much in touch with its history.

1050 NASIR KHUSRAW

Persian poet Nasir Khusraw (1004–1088) is acknowledged as a great writer who travelled very widely across the Muslim world in the years 1046–52, recording what he saw in his Safarnama.

Coming south from Syria, the first city encountered is New Cairo, Old Cairo being situated farther south. New Cairo is called al-Qahira al-Muizziyya, and the garrison town is called Fustat....

The sultan's palace is in the middle of Cairo, encompassed by an open space so that no building abuts it.... As the ground is open all around it, every night there are a thousand watchmen, five hundred mounted and five hundred on foot, who blow trumpets and beat drums at the time of evening prayer and then patrol until daybreak.

Viewed from outside the city, the sultan's palace looks like a mountain because of all the different buildings and the great height. From inside the city, however, one can see nothing at all because the walls are so high. They say that twelve thousand servants work in the palace, in addition to the women and slave-girls, whose number no one knows. It is said, nonetheless, that in the palace which consists of twelve buildings, there are thirty thousand individuals.

The harem has ten gates on the ground level.... And a subterranean entrance through which the sultan may pass on horseback. Outside the city, he has built another palace connected to the harem palace by a passageway with a reinforced ceiling. The walls of his palace are of rocks hewn to look like one piece of stone and there are belvederes and tall porticoes....

The city of Cairo has five gates; there is no wall, but the buildings are even stronger and higher than the ramparts and every house and building is itself a fortress. Most of the buildings are five storeys tall, although some are six. Drinking water is from the Nile, and water carriers transport water by camel. The closer the wall is to the river, the sweeter the water; it becomes more brackish the farther you get from the Nile. Old and New Cairo are said to have a thousand camels belonging to water carriers. The water carriers who port water on their backs are separate: they have brass cups and jugs and go into the narrow lanes where a camel cannot pass....

Old Cairo is situated on a promontory. It was built on a hill for fear of the Nile waters. Looking at Old Cairo from a distance, you would think it was a mountain. There are places where the houses are fourteen storeys tall and others seven. I heard from a reliable source that one person has on top of a seven-storey house a garden where he raised a calf. He also has a waterwheel up there turned by this ox to lift water from a well down below. He has orange trees and also bananas and other fruit-bearing trees, flowers and herbs planted on the roof.

1326 IBN BATTUTA

Ibn Battuta (1304–1368/69 or 1377) was the greatest traveller of the medieval world. Born in Morocco, he travelled through much of North Africa, the Middle East and South and East Asia, and dictated his book, The Travels, *towards the end of his life. He visited Cairo on his first pilgrimage to Mecca (see page 182).*

I arrived at length at Cairo, mother of cities and seat of Pharaoh the tyrant, mistress of broad regions and fruitful lands, boundless in multitude of buildings, peerless in beauty and splendour, the meeting place of comer and goer, the halting place of feeble and mighty, whose throngs surge as the waves of the sea, and can scarce be contained in her for all her size and capacity....

On the bank of the Nile opposite Old Cairo is the place known as The Garden, which is a pleasure park and promenade, containing many beautiful gardens, for the people of Cairo are given to pleasure and amusements. I witnessed a fete once in Cairo for the sultan's recovery from a fractured hand; all the merchants decorated their bazaars and had rich stuffs, ornaments and silken fabrics hanging in their shops for several days.

The mosque of 'Amr is highly venerated and widely celebrated. The Friday service is held in it and the road runs through it from east to west. The madrasas of Cairo are so numerous they cannot be counted. As for the hospital 'between the two castles' near the mausoleum of Sultan Qala'un, no description is adequate: it contains an innumerable quantity of appliances and medicaments, and its daily revenue is as high as a thousand dinars.

There are a large number of religious establishments called *khanqahs*, and the nobles vie with one another in building them. Each of these is set apart for a separate school of *darwishes*, mostly Persians, who are men of good education and adepts in the mystical doctrines. Each has a superior and a doorkeeper and their affairs are admirably organized. They have many special customs, one of which has to do with their food. The steward of the house comes in the morning to the *darwishes*, and each indicates what food he desires, and when they assemble for meals, each person is given his bread and soup in a separate dish, none sharing with another. They eat twice a day. They are each given winter clothes and summer clothes, and a monthly allowance of from twenty to thirty dirhams. Every Thursday night they receive sugar cakes, soap to wash their clothes, the price of a bath and oil for their lamps. These men are celibate; the married men have separate convents.

At Cairo too is the great cemetery of al-Qarafa, a place of peculiar sanctity which contains the graves of innumerable scholars and believers. In the Qarafa the people build beautiful pavilions surrounded by walls, so that they look like houses. They also build chambers and hire Koran-readers who recite night and day in agreeable voices. Some of them build religious houses and madrasas beside the mausoleums and on Thursday nights they go out to spend the night there with their children and women-folk, and make a circuit of the famous tombs. They go out to spend the night there also on the 'Night of mid Sha'ban', and the market-people take out all kinds of food to eat. Among the many sanctuaries is the holy shrine where there reposes the head of al-Husayn. Beside it is a vast monastery, on the doors of which are silver rings and plates.

1850 GUSTAVE FLAUBERT

The 27-year-old novelist Gustave Flaubert (1821–1880) saw Egypt – and Cairo in particular, where he spent seven weeks – as the polar opposite of his native Normandy, which he despised for its dullness and small-mindedness. For him, as for many others in the 19th century, Cairo provided the allure of the exotic Orient, the supposed sensuality of which was highly prized by the 19th-century Western imagination. The following is from a letter Flaubert wrote to his mother from Cairo in 1850.

3 February I have caught a bad cold by staying five hours upright on a wall to see the ceremony of the Danseh. This is what it is: the word 'danseh' means 'trampling', and never was a name better given. It has to do with a man, who passes on horseback over several others crouched on the ground like dogs. At certain epochs of the year this festival is repeated only at Cairo in memory of, and to renew the miracle of, a certain holy Mussulman, who once entered Cairo marching thus on horseback over earthen vessels without breaking them. The sheik, who repeats this ceremony, should wound the men no more than the saint broke the earthen vessels. If the men die of it, their sins are the cause. I saw dervishes there, who had iron spits passed through their mouths and their chests. Oranges were spitted at the two ends of the iron rods. The crowd of the faithful howled with enthusiasm; to that you must join music savage enough to drive one mad. When the sheik appeared on horseback, my gentlemen laid themselves on the ground with their heads down; they were put in rows like herrings, and heaped close to one another, so that there should be no interval between the bodies. A man walked over them to see if the platform of humanity was firm and close, and then to clear the course, a hail, a tempest, a hurricane of whacks administered by eunuchs began to rain right and left at random, on whatever happened to be there. We were perched on a wall, Sassetti and Joseph at our feet. We stayed there from eleven till nearly four. It was very cold, and we had hardly room to stir, so great was the crowd, and so small the place we had taken; but it was a very good one and nothing escaped us. We heard the palm sticks sound dully on the tarbouches [fezzes] like the drumsticks on drums full of tow, or rather on balls of wool. This is exact. The sheik advanced, his horse held by two attendants, and himself supported by two others; and the good gentleman needed it. His hands began to tremble, a nervous attack seized him, and at the end of his parade, he was almost unconscious. His horse passed at a slow walk over the bodies of more than two hundred men lying flat on their stomachs. As for how many died of it, it is impossible to know anything about them; the crowd pours in behind the sheik in such a way, when once he has passed, that it is no easier to know what has become of these unfortunates, than to make out the fate of a pin thrown into a torrent.

1863 GEORGE HOSKINS

British Egyptologist G. A. Hoskins (1802–1864) visited Egypt in the 1830s and again thirty years later, a visit described in his book A Winter in Upper and Lower Egypt *(1864).*

Cairo has changed little within the last quarter of a century. The mosques are more dilapidated, and the colours in them much less bright. One great improvement has been effected. The Uzbekeeh, a large square containing 450,000 square feet, which, during the inundation, was formerly covered with water, and at other times a cornfield, is now beautifully planted, affording the greatest of all luxuries in a hot climate – delicious shade.

Under the trees are some indifferent cafés, where excellent coffee, sherbet and punch may be had, and where a very poor band plays in the evenings. On Sundays the promenade is very crowded – Franks and Turks in their Nizam dresses. European tradesmen, who have not adopted the latter, generally wear the red *tarboosh*, while their wives and daughters appear in European dresses, though not in the best taste.

The groups that will interest the stranger most are the citizens playing at dominoes, chess and backgammon, and the peasants collected round the jugglers. If the cafés were good, and the gardens better taken care of, few promenades in the world would be more delightful. Some of the houses which surround it are handsome, especially the palace of the late pasha's sister, and Shepheard's large hotel – with all its defects, the best in Cairo – as well as the Hotel d'Orient, the next best, on the opposite side of the square; but the artist will admire more the old houses, with their picturesque latticed wood windows, or Mushrebeehs. The minaret of a mosque, surrounded by trees, adds to the effect....

These are a few of the architectural attractions of the streets of Cairo, but the crowds which animate them are not less interesting. Rich and poor, high and low, are conglomerated together. Every variety of costume, and every shade of complexion, from the swarthy Nubian to the fair Circassian. Sometimes the attention is drawn to the harem of a rich Turk, enveloped in silks of black and gay colours, of a breadth that would satisfy even a Parisienne's taste (though they wear no crinoline), as if, like fair Fatima, of Tripoli, 'they had been bought by the hundred-weight, and trundled home in a wheelbarrow'. They are often mounted on donkeys, richly caparisoned, of a merit and value unknown in Europe.

Besides the harems, the most extraordinary groups of women are often seen on foot in the bazaars; nothing human distinguishable except a pair of fine black eyes, not sparing in their glances, peeping over the linen masks that cover their faces from the eyes downwards, the rest of the body having the appearance of an immense lump of merchandise covered with folds of linen or silk, scarcely showing their yellow boots. They are mostly attended by slaves, or some elderly female relation....

The mosques are the pride of Cairo. Unwashed, unpainted, unrepaired and even crumbling into dust, as many of them are, their beautiful minarets rival the palms in gracefulness; and, combined with the glorious street architecture, the elegant fountains and picturesque costumes, are enough to drive an artist crazy, that the noise and confusion of the ever-moving crowds prevent their drawing them. While the sun shines, nothing but the plague thins the bazaars of Cairo....

At all the mosques which are now used for prayer, it is necessary to submit to put on slippers at the entrance, or have the feet covered with cloths. The Moslems always take off their shoes when there are people praying, and every right-minded visitor, whatever may be his creed, will be careful not to offend their feelings.

The visit to the mosques is rather expensive; a carriage costs ten shillings, and a fee of about two shillings is expected at each mosque; the janissary also looks for, at least, four shillings.

The citadel, which forms so grand a feature in the views of Cairo, is well worth seeing, and may be visited on donkeys or in a carriage.... The whole of the city is seen, with its innumerable minarets; that of Sultan Hassan, immediately beneath, being particularly distinguishable. In the distance, the desert, the Nile and the Pyramids of Geezeh [sic] and Sakkara. The inundation, like a lake, adds now to the interest of the view, though it nearly doubles the distance of the pyramids for those who wish to visit them in October.

1940S G. S. FRASER

Scottish poet G. S. Fraser (1915–1980) was one of many Allied soldiers who visited Cairo during the Second World War. In his memoir A Stranger and Afraid *(1983) he recalled his sojourn in olfactory fashion.*

When I think of Cairo now, I think of something sick and dying; an old beggar, propped up against a wall, too palsied to raise a hand or supplicate alms; but in a passive way he can still enjoy the sun.... But who can possess a city? Who can possess it, as he possess his own body, so that a vague consciousness of its proportions is always in his mind?...

Cairo probably seemed to me a more confusing city than it really is because I saw it through a haze of heat and odours – the smells of spice, of cooking fat, of overripe fruit, of sun-dried sweat, of hot baked earth, of urine, of garlic, and, again and again, too sweet, of jasmine; a complex that, in the beginning of the hot weather, seemed to melt down to the general consistency of smouldering rubber...a smell of the outskirts of hell. Ceasing, soon, consciously to notice all this, I would sometimes, in the Garden City near the Embassy, pass a lawn of thin, patchy grass that had just been watered through a sprinkler; and I would realize, for a moment, how parched and acrid my nostrils were. The smell of the Nile itself, of course, was different; by its banks, at night, there was a damp, vegetative coolness, that seemed to have, in a vague, evocative way, something almost sexual about it. And it was voluptuousness, in a cool large room, to bend over and sniff, in a glass bowl on a table, at a crisp red rose. But in such a room there would be European women; and their skins would have dried a little, in that cruel climate, and one would be aware of their powder, and their scent. Beauty, whether of body or character, lay, in that city, under a constant siege. In my memory, that hot baked smell prevails; that, and the grittiness – the dust gathering thickly on the glossy leaves of the evergreens, and the warm winds stinging eyes and nostrils with fine sand – and the breathlessness, the inner exhaustion. Under the glaring day, one seemed to see the human image sagging and wilting a little, and expected sallow fingers and faces to run and stretch, as if they were made of wax.

CHICAGO

Chicago, originally a French trading post, did not grow significantly until the opening of canal and rail links in 1848, which made it an important transport hub for the American Midwest, particularly important for its grain siloes, its huge stockyards and meat-packing industry. Much of the early city was destroyed in a devastating fire in 1871.

Following the fire the city was speedily rebuilt, with major public health improvements and grand office building and department stores, giving rise to the so-called Gilded Age; the population passed one million in 1890. In the early 20th century it saw considerable immigration of a range of ethnic groups, including Irish, Italians and blacks from the Southern states.

1866 JOHN WALTER

British newspaperman and Liberal MP John Walter (1818–1894) was managing editor of The Times. *He travelled to the United States in 1866, and published his letters privately on his return.*

We left Detroit at 10 the next morning, and arrived here at 9 p.m.... Next morning we went up to the top of the courthouse, to get a bird's-eye view of the town, which covers a vast area, bounded by the lake on one side, and by the prairie on the other. The streets, as in all other American towns, are laid out at right angles. Some of them are extremely handsome. Michigan Avenue, which runs along the shore of the lake, and Wabash Avenue, which runs parallel to it, are particularly striking. The latter is paved with wood and contains the principal churches. In a few years, when the wooden houses are replaced by stone ones, it will be one of the finest streets in the States.

No town in America appears to have gone ahead like this. Forty years ago it was a poor village, inhabited chiefly by Indians, and the whole place might have been bought for a few thousand dollars; now it contains 200,000 inhabitants, and is one of the richest and most flourishing towns in the Union. Among other curious feats of engineering, the art of houselifting has been practised here to an extraordinary extent. After the town had been regularly laid out, and most of the houses built, it was discovered that the streets were on too low a level; so they had to be raised several feet, and, as a necessary consequence, the houses were raised too. The Tremont House, where we are staying, and which makes up 150 beds, was raised bodily four or five feet, without sustaining any damage. I am told that a printing office was treated in a similar manner, without having to suspend its business for a single day.

The chief trade of Chicago is in corn and cattle; and in every direction along the quays you see huge, unsightly structures, called elevators, in which the grain which arrives from the country is received and transferred to the ships. They are mere loading machines – that is all – and are only used to economize time and labour. The grain is brought in on one side in the railway trucks, from which it is shovelled out into pits under the floor of the building, and thence is lifted by an endless web into a trough, down which it pours, in a continual stream, into the hold of the ship, which lies along the other side of the quay....

The next morning, Mr Bross, the Deputy Governor of the State, called upon us, and took us to see the principal establishments in the town. We first visited the Exchange Rooms, where all the corn jobbers carry on their operations. This is a grand field for gambling, and fortunes are made and lost here in no time. We next visited the Illinois Central Railway Depot, where we were shown specimens of the various productions of the State and samples of its soil, taken from different places. The company has still several hundred thousand acres of its original grant of land to dispose of; and a purchaser has no difficulty here in suiting himself, both as to quantity and quality. Some of the farms are on an enormous scale. Mr Sullivant, of Douglas County, farms 40,000 acres, and has farmed half as many more.... We next visited several private establishments, which almost rival those of New York in size and splendour. One of the most remarkable is that of Mr Bowen, a dry goods merchant, who told me that he began business twelve years ago without a dollar, and is now turning over $8,000,000 a year. He owns a good deal of real property in the town, and lives in one of the best houses in Michigan Avenue. Mr Griggs, the principal publisher and bookseller in this place, also possesses a first-rate establishment. One of the wealthiest inhabitants of the place is a man who began business as a waggon builder twenty-five years ago, when the town was in its infancy, and sold last year 5,000 waggons, and could have sold as many more if he could have supplied the demand. Such are the rewards of industry and perseverance in this extraordinary place....

On Sunday we attended morning service at Trinity Church – a large, handsome building, capable of accommodating 1,800 people. Dr Cummins, the bishop elect of Kentucky, preached his farewell sermon – a very effective one. At the conclusion he made a special appeal for a supply of cast-off clothing, to enable the poorer children of his flock to go to school. So that, in spite of social equality, &c., there are ragged children, it seems, even in Chicago.

1884–85 MRS HOWARD VINCENT

While still a hub for the meat industry, in the 1880s the city was already a centre for political conventions, as observed by Mrs Howard (Ethel) Vincent (1861–1952), wife of a British Conservative MP, who was struck by the different approaches to politics across the Atlantic. Her book Forty Thousand Miles Over Land and Water *(1886) recounts a journey she undertook in the USA, New Zealand and East Asia in 1884–85.*

After the great fire of October, 1871, Chicago rose like a phoenix from its ashes. A curious calculation resulted in the discovery that in the period of six months one building, from four to six storeys high, was completed each hour in a day of eight working hours. It certainly presents an unprecedentedly rapid growth, and the population entirely keeps pace with it.

Chicago is just settling down after the intense excitement of the Convention, held here only the other day, when Blaine was chosen as the Republican candidate, and Cleveland by the Democrats. Every four years the whole country is convulsed with these Presidential elections, a tenure of office far too short to allow of any settled policy to attain to maturity. The country is blazoned with portraits of the rival candidates; debased often to the use of advertisements, as when Mr Blaine (who is dyspeptic) is seen standing by a bottle as big as himself of 'Tippecande'. The newspapers resound throughout the country with their mutual vituperations. 'Blaine is corrupt!' cry the Democrats; 'Cleveland is immoral!' retort the Republicans.

Party warfare descends even to the shape of the hat. In New York we had several times noticed the predominating number of tall white hats. It was explained they were Blaine's followers; whereas Cleveland's wore a wider brim in a brown felt. In America, where every adult male, be he householder or not, has a vote, politics have a wider range, and are discussed eagerly among all classes. We got at last to have quite a 'national' interest, and should like to have been in America during the final struggle coming in November....

It was five miles to the stockyards, which really constitute the great sight of Chicago. The cable cars, running so swiftly and silently as if by magic, by means of invisible underground machinery, down State Street, conveyed us thither and back for the modest sum of 5d. The yards, with their well-filled pens on either side, presented a wild appearance. Droves of cattle were being driven by men on horseback, galloping and cracking their long whips, with the curious wooden stirrups and peaked saddle of old Spanish Mexican make.

We threaded our way through them to Armour & Co.'s, one of the largest establishments, where daily many thousands of pigs, sheep and oxen are purchased, killed, cut up, cooked, salted and packed in the shortest possible space of time. We were allowed to wander about the reeking, blood-stained floors, and thoroughly sickened, and fearful that every turn would reveal more bloody horrors, I stopped opposite a gory pile of horns being carted away, while C. went to see the oxen killed. He described how they are driven in single file through a narrow passage into separate pens, over the top of which runs a broad plank, on which the 'gentleman who does the shooting' stands with a small rifle. The poor beast looks up a second after his admission to the pen, and the rifle bullet fells him instantly stone dead. The further door is opened, and the carcase dragged away by cords to the cutting-up room. There could be no more merciful mode of killing without any unnecessary brutality.

1889 RUDYARD KIPLING

The brash commercialism of Chicago in the late 19th century struck many visitors from Britain; journalist and novelist Rudyard Kipling (1865–1936) – who toured America in 1889 after living several years in India – was outspoken in his criticisms, though he later settled in New England.

I have struck a city – a real city – and they call it Chicago.

The other places do not count. San Francisco was a pleasure resort as well as a city, and Salt Lake was a phenomenon.

This place is the first American city I have encountered. It holds rather more than a million people with bodies, and stands on the same sort of soil as Calcutta. Having seen it, I urgently desire never to see it again. It is inhabited by savages. Its water is the water of the Hooghly, and its air is dirt. Also it says that it is the 'boss' town of America.

I do not believe that it has anything to do with this country. They told me to go to the Palmer House, which is overmuch gilded and mirrored, and there I found a huge hall of tessellated marble crammed with people talking about money and spitting about everywhere. Other barbarians charged in and out of this inferno with letters and telegrams in their hands, and yet others shouted at each other. A man who had drunk quite as much as was good for him told me that this was 'the finest hotel in the finest city on God Almighty's earth'. By the way, when an American wishes to indicate the next country or state, he says, 'God Almighty's earth'. This prevents discussion and flatters his vanity.

Then I went out into the streets, which are long and flat and without end. And verily it is not a good thing to live in the East for any length of time. Your ideas grow to clash with those held by every right-thinking man. I looked down interminable vistas banked with nine, ten and fifteen-storeyed houses, and crowded with men and women, and the show impressed me with a great horror.

Except in London – and I have forgotten what London was like – I had never seen so many white people together, and never such a collection of miserables. There was no colour in the street and no beauty – only a maze of wire ropes overhead and dirty stone flagging under foot.

A cab-driver volunteered to show me the glory of the town for so much an hour, and with him I wandered far. He conceived that all this turmoil and squash was a thing to be reverently admired, that it was good to huddle men together in fifteen layers, one atop of the other, and to dig holes in the ground for offices.

He said that Chicago was a live town, and that all the creatures hurrying by me were engaged in business. That is to say they were trying to make some money that they might not die through lack of food to put into their bellies. He took me to canals as black as ink, and filled with untold abominations, and bade me watch the stream of traffic across the bridges....

Then my cab-driver showed me business blocks, gay with signs and studded with fantastic and absurd advertisements of goods, and looking down the long street so adorned, it was as though each vender stood at his door howling: 'For the sake of money, employ or buy of me, and me only!'

Have you ever seen a crowd at a famine-relief distribution? You know then how the men leap into the air, stretching out their arms above the crowd in the hope of being seen, while the women dolorously slap the stomachs of their children and whimper. I had sooner watch famine relief than the white man engaged in what he calls legitimate competition. The one I understand. The other makes me ill....

Sunday brought me the queerest experiences of all – a revelation of barbarism complete. I found a place that was officially described as a church. It was a circus really, but that the worshippers did not know. There were flowers all about the building, which was fitted up with plush and stained oak and much luxury, including twisted brass candlesticks of severest Gothic design.

To these things and a congregation of savages entered suddenly a wonderful man, completely in the confidence of their God, whom he treated colloquially and exploited very much as a newspaper reporter would exploit a foreign potentate. But, unlike the newspaper reporter, he never allowed his listeners to forget that he, and not He, was the centre of attraction. With a voice of silver and with imagery borrowed from the auction room he built up for his hearers a heaven on the lines of the Palmer House (but with all the gilding real gold, and all the plate-glass diamond) and set in the centre of it a loud-voiced, argumentative, very shrewd creation that he called God. One sentence at this point caught my delighted ear. It was apropos of some question of the Judgment, and ran: 'No! I tell you God doesn't do business that way.' He was giving them a deity whom they could comprehend, and a gold and jewelled heaven in which they could take a natural interest. He interlarded his performance with the slang of the streets, the counter and the exchange, and he said that religion ought to enter into daily life. Consequently, I presume he introduced it as daily life – his own and the life of his friends.

1939 HENRY MILLER

Interwar Chicago was infamous both for its gang warfare and for the poverty of its segregated districts and ghettos, despite major public works instituted under the New Deal and other schemes during the Depression. American novelist Henry Miller (1891–1980) described the wretchedness in his memoir (published 1945) of a long road-trip around the United States undertaken in 1939, after nine years living in Paris.

Meanwhile I have good news for you – I'm going to take you to Chicago, to the Mecca Apartments on the South Side. It's a Sunday morning and my cicerone has borrowed a car to take me around. We stop at a flea market on the way. My friend explains to me that he was raised here in the ghetto;

he tries to find the spot where his home used to be. It's a vacant lot now. There are acres and acres of vacant lots here on the South Side. It looks like Belgium did after the World War. Worse, if anything. Reminds me of a diseased jawbone, some of it smashed and pulverized, some of it charred and ulcerated. The flea market is more reminiscent of Cracow than of Clignancourt, but the effect is the same. We are at the back door of civilization, amid the dregs and debris of the disinherited. Thousands, hundreds of thousands, maybe millions of Americans, are still poor enough to rummage through this offal in search of some sorely needed object. Nothing is too dilapidated or rust-bitten or disease-laden to discourage the hungry buyer. You would think the five-and-ten cent store could satisfy the humblest wants, but the five-and-ten cent store is really expensive in the long run, as one soon learns. The congestion is terrific – we have to elbow our way through the throng. It's like the banks of the Ganges except that there is no odor of sanctity about. As we push our way through the crowd my feet are arrested by a strange sight. There in the middle of the street, dressed in full regalia, is an American Indian. He's selling a snake oil. Instantly the thought of the other miserable derelicts stewing around in this filth and vermin is gone. *A World I Never Made*, wrote James Farrell. Well, there stands the real author of the book – an outcast, a freak, a hawker of snake oil. On that same spot the buffaloes once roamed; now it is covered with broken pots and pans, with worn-out watches, with dismantled chandeliers, with busted shoes which even an Igorote would spurn. Of course if you walk on a few blocks you can see the other side of the picture – the grand facade of Michigan Avenue where it seems as if the whole world were composed of millionaires. At night you can see the great monument to chewing gum lit up by floodlights and marvel that such a monstrosity of architecture should be singled out for special attention....

We dig further into the South Side, getting out now and then to stretch our legs. Interesting evolution going on here. Rows of old mansions flanked by vacant lots. A dingy hotel sticking up like a Mayan ruin in the midst of yellow fangs and chalk teeth. Once respectable dwelling places given up now to the dark-skinned people we 'liberated'. No heat, no gas, no plumbing, no water, no nothing – sometimes not even a windowpane. Who owns these houses? Better not inquire too closely. What do they do with them when the darkies move out? Tear them down, of course. Federal housing projects.

Model tenement houses.... I think of old Genoa, one of the last ports I stopped at on my way back to America. Very old, this section. Nothing much to brag about in the way of conveniences. But what a difference between the slums of Genoa and the slums of Chicago! Even the Armenian section of Athens is preferable to this. For twenty years the Armenian refugees of Athens have lived like goats in the little quarter which they made their own. There were no old mansions to take over – not even an abandoned factory. There was just a plot of land on which they erected their homes out of whatever came to hand. Men like Henry Ford and Rockefeller contributed unwittingly to the creation of this paradise which was entirely built of remnants and discarded objects. I think of this Armenian quarter because as we were walking through the slums of Chicago my friend called my attention to a flowerpot on the windowsill of a wretched hovel. 'You see,' he said, 'even the poorest among them have their flowers.' But in Athens I saw dovecotes, solariums, verandahs floating without support, rabbits sunning themselves on the roofs, goats kneeling before ikons, turkeys tied to the door-knobs. Everybody had flowers – not just flowerpots. A door might be made of Ford fenders and look inviting. A chair might be made of gasoline tins and be pleasant to sit on. There were bookshops where you could read about Buffalo Bill or Jules Verne or Hermes Trismegistus. There was a spirit here which a thousand years of misery had not squelched. Chicago's South Side, on the other hand, is like a vast, unorganized lunatic asylum. Nothing can flourish here but vice and disease. I wonder what the great Emancipator would say if he could see the glorious freedom in which the black man moves now. We made them free, yes – free as rats in a dark cellar.

DAMASCUS

Perhaps the oldest continuously inhabited city in the world, occupied since about 9000 BC, Damascus has been a major cultural, religious and trading centre since ancient times. Part of the Hellenistic and then the Roman Empire (when it was the site of the crucial conversion of Paul to Christianity in the 30s AD), the city was fully Christianized in the 4th century; in AD 635 it was conquered by the Arabs, and the Great Mosque was built by Caliph al-Walid in the 8th century.

From 1516 it was held by the Ottomans until 1918 when it became the capital of Syria. The city grew quickly in the 20th century, and survived the Syrian Civil War of the 2010s relatively unscathed.

1326 AND 1348 IBN BATTUTA

The great Muslim traveller Ibn Battuta (see page 72) visited Damascus in the 1320s when it was a provincial capital of the Mamluk dynasty of Egypt; during a second visit in 1348, the Black Death killed up to half the population.

Damascus surpasses all other cities in beauty, and no description, however full, can do justice to its charms. The Umayyad Mosque is the most magnificent in the world, the finest in construction and noblest in beauty, grace and perfection; it is matchless. Its construction was undertaken by Caliph Walid I, who sought the Roman emperor at Constantinople to send craftsmen to him, and the emperor sent him twelve thousand. The mosque is on the site of a church, and when the Muslims captured Damascus, one of their commanders entered from one side by the sword and reached the middle of the church, while another entered peaceably from the eastern side and reached the middle also. So the Muslims made the half of the church which they had entered by force into a mosque while the half which they had entered peacefully remained as a church. When Walid decided to extend the mosque over the entire church he asked the Greeks to sell him their church, but they refused, so he seized it....

One of the principal doctors at Damascus was Taqi ad-Din Ibn Taymiya, a man of great ability and wide learning, but with some kink in his brain. The people idolized him. One day he said something from the pulpit that the other theologians disapproved, and he was imprisoned.... His mother interceded for him, so the sultan set him at liberty until he did the same thing again. I was in Damascus at the time. In his discourse he said 'Truly God descends from Heaven in the same bodily fashion that I make this descent,' and stepped down one step of the pulpit. A Malikite doctor objected, but the people beat him with their hands and their shoes so severely that his turban fell off and disclosed a silken skullcap on his head. Inveighing against the doctor for wearing this skullcap, they hauled him before the authorities who had him imprisoned and beaten.... But the other doctors accused Ibn Taymiya of heresy; and the sultan had him imprisoned in the citadel, where he remained until his death.

One of the celebrated sanctuaries at Damascus is the Mosque of the Footprints (al-Aqdam), which lies two miles south of the city, alongside the main highway which leads to the Hijaz, Jerusalem and Egypt. It is a large mosque, richly endowed and highly venerated. The footprints from which it derives its name are impressed upon a rock and are said to be the mark of Moses' foot....

I saw a remarkable instance of the veneration in which the Damascenes hold this mosque during the great pestilence on my return journey through Damascus in July 1348. The viceroy ordered all the people to fast for three days and that no one should cook anything in the market during the daytime (for most of the people there only eat food prepared in the market). So the people fasted for three days, then they assembled in the Great Mosque... until the place was filled to overflowing, and they spent the Thursday night in prayers and litanies. After the dawn prayer next morning they all went out holding Korans in their hands, and the emirs barefooted. The procession was joined by the entire population of the town; the Jews came with their Book of the Law and the Christians with their Gospel, all of them with their women and children. The whole concourse, weeping and supplicating and seeking the favour of God through His Books and His Prophets, made their way to the Mosque of the Footprints, and there they remained until near midday. They then returned to the city and held the Friday service, and God lightened their affliction; for the number of deaths in a single day at Damascus did not attain 2,000, while in Cairo it reached the figure of 24,000 a day....

The people of Damascus have a high opinion of North Africans, and freely entrust them with the care of their moneys, wives and children. Strangers are handsomely treated and never forced to any action that might injure their self-respect.

1849 JAMES LAIRD PATTERSON

The future Catholic Auxiliary Bishop of Westminster, Patterson (see page 17) was a recent convert when he undertook his journey to Egypt, Palestine, Syria and Greece in 1849. His perceptions of Damascus were strongly influenced by his religious interests.

We left about seven o'clock, and had the hottest ride across the plain I have ever undergone; and that in spite of a very fresh breeze. We halted near a stream for lunch, and let the poor mules (who trudge away bravely under their burthens) precede us to Damascus. On the right, the plain in which S. Paul's miraculous conversion took place was shewn us.... I pictured to myself 'the persecutor Saul' riding in his glittering armour, on a steed proud apparently of its noble burthen, as he himself was, in his mistaken zeal and purpose, of his own charge from the chief priests of his nation. Thus he pricked forward across the hot plain, in all the excitement of speedy arrival, heedless of the noonday glare and fierce heat which fanned his cheek, flushed with yet fiercer passion from within; when suddenly, 'above the brightness of the midday sun', a light from heaven smites him to the earth, and rolls horse and rider, in their brilliant trappings, in the dust which they seemed just now to spurn beneath their feet. Trembling and blind, and yet for the first time truly brave and truly seeing, he is raised from the earth by his astonished followers and led slowly by the hand into Damascus. The outward change was great; yet how much greater that of the inner man....

We stopped at the Hotel de Palmyre. I was so much tired with the journey that I could not sleep and went therefore to a late mass at nine.... After mass and Holy Communion, we accompanied the two Nazarist fathers who are here to their house and church. They are both French, and the national taste and neatness comes out in the arrangement and decorations of the house. As usual, they have very large schools, and have taught the children French, so that that language begins to be much spoken here. The Protestants have also a mission, and disseminate their Bibles and other books, but without much effect: the people take them for the sake of the covers, and burn the insides! These missionaries are always called 'Ingliz', though many are Americans and Germans and the name is used as one of opprobrium (among both Turks and Christians), tantamount to 'infidel' or misbeliever.... We also looked into the great square of the mosque, once the cathedral of S. John Damascene, which has been a cruciform church. The court appears to have been surrounded by a magnificent cloister, of pointed arches on Roman marble columns....

We spent a great part of the morning in buying some Damascus silks. The khan in which our silk merchant lived was a fine one, but not so much so as that of the banker, which consists of a large quadrangle, roofed in and divided into six arcades, supporting as many domes. Round this space, in which is a range of shops or chambers, there runs a gallery, corresponding with one on the ground floor, in front of which, on wooden divans, the shopkeepers squat and transact their business. We also visited the jewel bazaars; but I saw nothing worth having. The bazaars here are very extensive, and almost all roofed in. Some are handsome, but on the whole they are decidedly inferior to those of Cairo. We went to a café to eat ice, or rather milk and snow from Hermon, which is its substitute here, and found a large shed built over running water, opposite the castle (a fine Saracen building, with great towers), in which various groups were reposing on the divans. In the evening we went to the convent...and visited the place where S. Paul was let down from the wall.... We also went, about as far again westward, to the Catholic burial ground, which it seems is now generally regarded as the true place of the conversion of S. Paul. Certainly the account seems to imply a much nearer vicinity to Damascus than that shewn us on Saturday.

1870–71 ISABEL BURTON

Isabel, Lady Burton (1831–1896) was a renowned English traveller and the wife of explorer Richard Burton, whose biography she wrote. Her Inner Life of Syria, Palestine, and the Holy Land *(1876) described her stay there in 1870–71.*

After a long residence in Damascus, I always say to my friends, 'If you have two or three days to spare, follow the guidebooks; but if you are pressed for time come with me, and you shall see what you will best like to remember, and you shall buy the things that are the most curious.' We will make our purchases first, visiting on the way everything of interest....

Before we enter the bazars, look at that Afghan sitting under yonder tree. If you like to invest in a little brass or silver seal, he will, for a few piastres, engrave your name upon it in Arabic. We will then enter the sadlery bazar, where you can buy magnificent trappings for a pony or donkey for the children at home. This is a pretty *Suk*. There are saddle-cloths of every colour in cloth, embossed with gold, holsters, bridles of scarlet silk, with a silken cord – a single rein, which makes you look as if you were managing a fiery horse by a thread, and the bridle is effectively covered with dangling silver and ivory ornaments. There are mule and donkey trappings of every colour in the rainbow, mounted with little shells....

We should do wisely to go into the shoemakers' bazar. You see how gaudy the stalls look. I want you to buy a pair of lemon-coloured slippers, pointed at the toe, and as soft as a kid glove. The stiff red slippers and shoes are not so nice, and the red boots with tops and tassals and hangings, are part of the Bedawi dress, and that of the Shaykhs generally. Why must you buy a pair of slippers? Because you must never forget at Damascus that you are only a 'dog of a Christian', that your unclean boots must not tread upon sacred ground, and that if you wish to see anything you must be prepared at any moment to take off the impure Giaour things, put on these slippers and enter reverently; all around you will do the same for that matter. Here we cover our heads and bare our feet to show respect; you Franks cover your feet and uncover your heads. Do not forget always to have your slippers in your pocket, as naturally as your handkerchief and your purse, until you return to the other side of Lebanon, or you will often be hindered by the want of them.

We will now inspect the marqueterie bazar, where we shall find several pretty things inlaid with choice woods, mother-of-pearl or steel; the former are the best, if finely worked. These are the large chests which form part of the bride's trousseau. Those ready-made are generally coarse, but you can order a beautifully fine and very large one for about five napoleons. There are tables, and the clogs used by the hanam in marble courts.... Now we will go to the smithy-like gold and silver bazar, where they sit round in little pens, hammering at their anvils. Each seems to have a strongbox for his treasures. All this is the greatest possible rubbish for a European to wear, but you will pick up many barbarous and antique ornaments, real gold and real stones, though unattractive. You may buy all sorts of spangling things as ornaments for your horse; you will find very beautiful *Zarfs*, or filigree coffee-cup-holders; you may order, on seeing the pattern, some very pretty *raki* cups of silver, inlaid with gold, very minute, with a gold or silver fish trembling on a spring, as if swimming in the liqueur.

While we are here, I will take you up a ladder on to the roof, not to lose time. The men will give me the key of the door for a little *bakshish*. By this way we shall reach the southern side of the Great Mosque, and after scrambling over several roofs, and venturing a few awkward jumps, we shall arrive at the top of a richly ornamented triple gateway; it is outside the Mosque, and hardly

93

peers above the mud and debris and bazar roofs, which cover up what is not already buried. Over the central arch is a cross, and Greek inscription: 'Thy kingdom, O Christ! is an everlasting kingdom, and thy dominion endureth throughout all generations.' It is a serious reflection that this bit of truth should have remained upon a mosque, perhaps for 1,762 years. It doubtless belonged to the stupendous Temple of the Sun, befitting the capital. After the birth of our Saviour it became a Christian Cathedral, dedicated to St John the Baptist, whose head is said to lie under a little railed-off cupola'd tomb, and is still venerated by the Moslems. The Christian Cathedral was divided at the conquest between Christians and Moslems, but it has long since become wholly and exclusively Moslem. Yet this inscription testifying to the truth has lived down every change of masters.

We will now pass down a narrow lane joining two bazars. A wretched wooden stall with shelves, filled with dirty bottles, and odds and ends of old china, here attracts your eye, and squatting on the counter a shrivelled little old man sits under his turban, with his palsied chin shaking like the aspen leaves. You see how smilingly he salutes me: out of those unwashed bottles he is looking for his finest *atr* (ottar) and his best sandalwood oil. Being fond of ladies' society, he will saturate our handkerchiefs and clothes with his perfumes, and we shall be traceable for a week to come – it is not easy to divest yourself of ottar when it has once touched clothes. He has long ago given me all his confidence. He is not so poor as he looks. He has sold ottar and sandalwood oil all his life, some 95 years; he has 15 wives and 102 children, and he would still like, he says, to marry again. I reprove him for having married eleven more than allowed by the Koran....

You can also buy an *izar*, to walk about the bazars *incognita* like a native. It covers all, except your face, from head to foot, like a shroud. It is pure silk, and you can choose your own colours; they are mostly brilliant, but I care only for black. Some are worked beautifully in gold. If you wish to pass for a Christian, you may expose your face, or wear an apology for a covering; but as Moslemahs we must buy *mandils*, white handkerchiefs, or coloured, with flowers and figures so thickly laid on that no one can recognize our features. If you have one of the black and gold or coloured *izars*, you will be a great personage. If you want to pass unobtrusively, you must wear a plain white linen sheet, with a thick *mandil*, and in that costume you might walk all day with your own father and not be known except by the voice.

1928 FREYA STARK

Writer and photographer Freya Stark (see page 44) was always concerned to get as close as possible to the people she met on her travels. She recounted some hair-raising adventures in Syria in her letters to her mother.

2 April

Darling B

I am much better again today, and hope to be quite well by the end of the week. I was able to be out this morning and enjoy my walk through Damascus slums, trying to find the 'four great gates'. I had an adventure which might really make the mission hair stand up and gave me a nasty qualm. I fell into it because it was so like the Arabian nights. An old man with a venerable beard came up as I was strolling along with my camera and said, just as anyone would expect, 'Follow me, oh lady, and I will show you a beautiful place.' So I followed. He told me it was an ancient bath, unused I supposed; and turned down a very narrow dark passage which went below the level of the street. I did hesitate but he said, 'Have no fear', and it is not so easy as it seems to change one's course when once started. We came to a heavy studded door on which he knocked; ten centuries dropped from me by magic: I should not have been at all surprised to see the caliph and his two companions on the other side! The door opened from the inside and there was a great vaulted hall, lighted from a window in the roof, and with a cistern of flowing water in the centre. There were alcoves with carpets on a raised platform round three sides, and various men lying about on them with their heads wrapped in turbans and nothing much except their big bath wraps on. I did feel I was not at all in a suitable place! They gathered round me in an instant. Then I heard the door clank to behind me with a horrid sound as if a chain were dropped.

I had an unpleasant sensation as if my heart were falling – literally a sinking of the heart in fact – but I did remain outwardly calm; only I put my back against the wall so as to face them. I said to the old man: 'Oh my father, wilt thou hold my gloves while I take the picture?', and got my camera ready with complete disregard to the rules of photography. They had all come up so close to me and I thought them a villainous-looking crowd. Someone murmured to the old man, 'French?' 'English,' said I hastily: 'We are your people's friends.' This had an extraordinarily soothing effect on the atmosphere. I asked if they would mind moving away from me for the picture, which they did in silence. When I had taken it I thanked the man who seemed master of the bath and turned to my old man to have the door unfastened: this was also done in complete silence but just as I was stepping out two or three asked me to turn back and look over the baths. This you may imagine I did not do. I was very glad to have that door open, though I suppose it was really quite all right. I wish now I had taken the picture with more care, for I don't imagine any European had been in that particular place before. I am not mentioning this episode here, for as it is I am being almost shadowed by the family who are evidently fearfully anxious. Think of it! My landlady has never in all her life been even to the Great Mosque.

DUBLIN

Dublin was founded by Vikings in the 10th century, and the town rose to prominence in the Middle Ages when it became the centre for the precarious English hold over Ireland. In the mid-17th century, it saw a Catholic uprising against Protestant English rule that left much of the city derelict, but following the Restoration of Charles II in 1660 its fortune revived, based in large part on the wool trade.

In the 18th century, Dublin flourished economically, becoming the second largest city in the British Isles: culturally, with many well-known writers and musicians based there; and architecturally, with elegant classical squares and terraces. The late 18th century saw the emergence of a nationalist movement in Ireland, fuelled in large part by grievances at the treatment of the majority Catholic population, which contributed to social and political unrest in 1798 and political union with England in 1800.

In the 19th century, Dublin was marked by the general poverty that caused widespread emigration from Ireland. Independence in 1922 saw Dublin the capital of essentially Catholic and introverted Eire, but in the 21st century the city has become more cosmopolitan in outlook and has attracted large businesses from across the world.

1666 FRANÇOIS DE LA BOULLAYE LE GOUZ

French aristocrat François de La Boullaye Le Gouz (1623–1668) wrote of his travels in India, Persia, Greece, the Middle East, Denmark, Germany, Netherlands, England, Ireland and Italy. Published in English in 1837, The Tour of the French traveller M. de La Boullaye Le Gouz in Ireland, A.D. 1644 *was one of the first books to give practical information for travellers.*

The city of Dublin is the capital of Ireland. It is on the east of the island: its size equal to that of Angers. The quay of the harbour is very fine, but receives only small craft: large vessels remain in the roads, two miles from the city. There is no curiosity except a well which is two or three miles from the city, on the northern coast, which works miracles for the lame and the blind. So say the natives.

There are fine buildings in Dublin: a college and many churches, among which is that of St Patrick, the apostle of the country. In the choir are displayed the arms of the old English knights, with their devices. I went there on Sunday to witness the ceremonial attending on the Viceroy. I saw much that was really magnificent. On leaving the church there marched before him a company of footmen, beating the drum, and with matchlocks ready for action. Then followed a company of halberdiers, his bodyguards

98

and sixty gentlemen on foot, with four noblemen well mounted, and the Viceroy in the midst upon a white Barbary horse. I followed the train in order to enter more freely into the castle; but at the door they ordered me to lay down my sword, which I would not do, saying, that being born of a condition to carry it before the king, I would rather not see the castle than part with my arms. A gentleman in the suite of the Viceroy seeing from my gallant bearing that I was a Frenchman, took me by the hand, saying, 'Strangers shall on this occasion be more favoured than residents.' And he brought me in. I replied to him that his civility equalled that of the French towards his nation, when they met them in France. Being within, I found this castle indifferently strong, without any outworks, and pretty well furnished with guns of cast metal.

1776 ARTHUR YOUNG

The English economist and agriculturalist Arthur Young (1741–1820) visited Dublin in 1776 as part of an extended journey that he described in Tour in Ireland *(1780). He liked what he saw.*

19 June Arrived at Holyhead, after an instructive journey through a part of England and Wales I had not seen before. Found the packet, the Claremont, captain Taylor, would sail very soon. After a tedious passage of twenty-two hours, landed on the 20th, in the morning, at Dunlary, four miles from Dublin, a city which much exceeded my expectation; the public buildings are magnificent, very many of the streets regularly laid out, and exceedingly well built. The front of the Parliament House is grand; though not so light as a more open finishing of the roof would have made it. The apartments are spacious, elegant and convenient, much beyond that heap of confusion at Westminster, so inferior to the magnificence to be looked for in the seat of empire. I was so fortunate as to arrive just in time to see Lord Harcourt, with the usual ceremonies, prorogue the Parliament.

Trinity College is a beautiful building and a numerous society; the library is a very fine room, and well filled. The new Exchange will be another edifice to do honour to Ireland; it is elegant, cost £40,000, but deserves a better situation. From everything I saw, I was struck with all those appearances of wealth which the capital of a thriving community may be supposed to exhibit.

Happy if I find through the country in diffused prosperity the right source of this splendor! The common computation of inhabitants 200,000, but, I should suppose, exaggerated. Others guessed the number 140, or 150,000.

23 June Lord Charlemont's house in Dublin is equally elegant and convenient, the apartments large, handsome and well disposed, containing some good pictures, particularly one by Rembrandt, of Judas throwing the money on the floor, with a strong expression of guilt and remorse; the whole group fine. In the same room is a portrait of Caesar Borgia by Titian. The library is a most elegant apartment, of about 40 by 30, and of such a height as to form a pleasing proportion, the light is well managed, coming in from the cove of the ceiling, and has an exceeding good effect.

Before I quit the city, I observe, on the houses in general, that what they call their two-roomed ones, are good and convenient. Mr Latouche's, in Stephen's Green, I was shown as a model of this sort, and I found it well contrived, and finished elegantly. Drove to Lord Charlemont's villa at Marino, near the city, where his lordship has formed a pleasing lawn, margined in the higher part by a well-planted thriving shrubbery, and on a rising ground a banqueting room, which ranks very high among the most beautiful edifices I have anywhere seen; it has much elegance, lightness and effect, and commands a fine prospect; the rising ground on which it stands slopes off to an agreeable accompaniment of wood, beyond which, on one side, is Dublin harbour, which here has the appearance of a noble river crowded with ships moving to and from the capital. On the other side is a shore spotted with white buildings, and beyond it the hills of Wicklow, presenting an outline extremely various....

Having the year following lived more than two months in Dublin, I am able to speak to a few points, which, as a mere traveller I could not have done.... Fish and poultry are plentiful and very cheap. Good lodgings almost as dear as they are in London; though we were well accommodated (dirt excepted) for two guineas and an half a week. All the lower ranks in this city have no idea of English cleanliness, either in apartments, persons or cookery. There is a very good society in Dublin in a Parliament winter – a great round of dinners, and parties; and balls and suppers every night in the week, some of which are very elegant, but you almost everywhere meet a company much too numerous for the size of the apartments.

They have two assemblies on the plan of those of London, in Fishamble street, and at the Rotunda; and two gentlemen's clubs, Anthry's and Daly's, very well regulated; I heard some anecdotes of deep play at the latter, though never to the excess common at London. An ill-judged and unsuccessful attempt was made to establish the Italian Opera, which existed but with scarcely any life for this one winter; of course they could rise no higher than a comic one.... The house was generally empty and miserably cold.

1796 JACQUES-LOUIS DE BOUGRENET DE LA TOCNAYE

The Chevalier de La Tocnaye (1767–1823) was a French royalist aristocrat exiled to London from 1792, who toured Ireland on foot in 1795–96 (saying he had 'nothing better to do'), enjoying the countryside and its people. He described his adventures in A Frenchman's Walk through Ireland *(1797).*

Dublin is a very considerable city, about one-fourth the size of London, of which it is the image in little – even the streets bear the same names; the beauty of the buildings may dispute for precedence with those of the capital; one is astonished at their magnificence and number. The Parliament House does honour to the nation's representatives; it is an immense circular building surrounded by a magnificent colonnade....

I occupied my leisure in the early days of my sojourn as I do ordinarily in such times elsewhere, by moving from one place to another, and mixing as much as possible with the crowd. I joined one which seemed, on a certain day, to be expecting something with impatience, and found myself among them in front of a large building which had something of the look of an old castle. There was a little platform at the level of a window in the second storey; two men of somewhat disagreeable look made their appearance on it, and I thought I was about to witness some peculiar ceremony. But I was promptly disabused of this idea, for one of them passed a loop of rope round the neck of the other and fastened the cord to a bar of iron above him. I turned to get away, but the crowd was too dense for movement; the poor wretch stood for a moment, alone, in view of the people, then a bolt slipped, and the little platform on which he stood fell against the wall. The Irish have, perhaps, got the better of their neighbours in the matter of hanging people with grace, but to me it appears a great cruelty to make a sort of parade of the death of a man, and in diminishing the horror of the punishment crime is increased and executions multiplied.

I think I am not far wrong in assigning this as the reason why there are more people hung in Great Britain and Ireland than in all the rest of Europe.

The crowd seemed to move steadily in one direction, and I followed again – this time to be led to Phoenix Park, where there was a horse race. I really could not say which of the two – execution or race – gave the greater pleasure to the hundred-headed monster.

Although the part of the city where the well-to-do people live is perhaps as beautiful as anything similar in Europe, nothing anywhere can compare with the dirt and misery of the quarters where the lower classes vegetate. They call these quarters 'The Liberties' of Dublin, and this made me think often of 'liberties' of France under Robespierre, than which there was nothing more disgusting in the universe....

From seeing Irishmen abroad one would imagine them to be most gallant and incapable of living without society. The very same men who appear to find so much pleasure in dancing attendance on our ladies allow cavaliers to flirt with their own. When an Irishman presents himself at the door of a Jacques Roastbeef in England, the latter fears immediately an attack on his purse, his wife, his daughter, or his wine. In revenge Dublin is shy in receiving the foreigner. One would say that the Dubliners remember their own faults of youth.

There are few social functions except those that are called routs. Where a house might comfortably entertain twenty persons, sixty are invited, and so in proportion. I have seen routs where, from vestibule to garret, the rooms were filled with fine ladies beautifully dressed, but so crushed against each other that it was hardly possible to move. A foreigner has cause for embarrassment in these too brilliant assemblies, for he may here see really charming women in greater number than in most cities, and he thinks it a pity to see them lose on a stairway the time which might be passed much more agreeably with a small number of appreciative friends.

1828 HERMANN VON PÜCKLER-MUSKAU

Hermann von Pückler-Muskau (1785–1871) was a German prince who fought against Napoleon and studied landscape gardening, a subject on which he wrote to much acclaim. He visited Britain several times in the 1820s, and later travelled in North Africa and the eastern Mediterranean. Von Pückler-Muskau drew on these tropes for his description of the capital in 1828. His Tour in England, Ireland, and France, *based on his letters, was published in 1833.*

11 August This country has more resemblance to Germany than to England. That universal and almost over-refined industry and culture disappears here, and with it, alas!, English neatness. The houses and streets have a dirty air, although Dublin is adorned with many magnificent palaces and broad straight streets.... The environs of the city have no longer the accustomed freshness; its soil is more neglected, the grass and trees scantier. The grand features of the landscape, however, the bay, the distant mountains of Wicklow, the Hill of Howth, the amphitheatrical mass of houses, the quays, the harbour, are beautiful. Such, at least, is the first impression....

As soon as I had a little refreshed myself I took a walk through the city; in the course of which I passed two rather tasteless monuments. The one represents William of Orange on horseback, in Roman costume. Both man and horse are deformed: the horse has a bit in his mouth, and head-gear on, but no appearance of reins, though the king's hand is stretched out exactly as if he were holding them. Does this mean that William wanted no rein to rid John Bull?

The other monument is a colossal statue of Nelson, standing on a high pillar, and dressed in modern attire. Behind him hangs a cable, and the figure is too high to be distinctly seen.

I afterwards came to a large round building, towards which the people crowded, keeping watch on the outside. On inquiry I learned that the yearly exhibition of fruits and flowers was held there. They were just taking away the former as I entered; notwithstanding which, I saw many fine specimens. In the midst of the flowers, which formed a sort of temple, there was an enclosed space railed round for the fruits which the judges ate with great gravity and apparent satisfaction. They must have been a long time in coming to a decision; for rinds of melons, pears and apples, fragments of pines, stones of plums, apricots and peaches, lay in mountains on the table beneath; and although the flowers were all gradually removed by the proprietors, I did not see that any of the fruits found their way out of this temple of Pomona.

13 August Having seen enough of the city, I have begun my rides in the neighbourhood, which is much more beautiful than its appearance at my first approach, on the least favourable side, led me to expect. A road commanding charming views...brought me to Phoenix Park, the Prater of Dublin, which in no respect yields to that of Vienna, whether we regard its expanse of beautiful turf for riding, long avenues for driving or shady walks. A large but ill-proportioned obelisk is erected here to the Duke of Wellington. I found the park rather empty, but the streets through which I returned full of movement and bustle. The dirt, the poverty and the ragged clothing of the common people often exceed all belief. Nevertheless they seemed always good-natured and sometimes have fits of merriment in the open streets which border on madness; whiskey is generally at the bottom of this. I saw a half-naked lad dance the national dance in the marketplace so long, and with such violent exertion, that at last he fell down senseless amid the cheers of the spectators, totally exhausted like a Mohammedan *dervise*.

The streets are crowded with beggar-boys, who buzz around one like flies, incessantly offering their services. Notwithstanding their extreme poverty, you may trust implicitly to their honesty, and wretched, lean and famished as they appear, you see no traces of melancholy on their open, good-natured countenances. They are the best-bred and most contented beggar-boys in the world. Such a little fellow will run by your horse's side for hours, hold it when you alight, go on any errand you like. And is not only contented with the few pence you give him, but full of gratitude which he expresses with Irish hyperbole. The Irishman appears generally more patient than his neighbours, but somewhat degraded by long slavery.

14 August Another friend...paid me a visit this morning. Scarcely had he quitted me, when I was told that Lady B––, an Irish peeress and one of the most beautiful women in the country, whose acquaintance I had cultivated during the last season in the metropolis, was in her carriage below and wished to speak to me. As I was still in the most absolute '*negligé*', I told the waiter...that I was not dressed, as he saw, but that I would be ready immediately. He announced the state of my toilet, but added, '*de son chef*', that 'my Lady had better come up'. Imagine my astonishment when he came back and told me that Lady B–– had laughed very much, and had bid him say that she would willingly wait but that to pay gentlemen morning visits in their chambers was not the custom of Ireland.

In this answer appeared the cordial, frank and good-natured character of the true Irish woman, which I had already learned to love and admire. A prudish Englishwoman would have driven away in high displeasure, and perhaps have ruined the reputation of a young man for such a 'quid pro quo' as this.

1889 MARIE ANNE DE BOVET

The most famous export of Dublin since the 18th century has been the stout, or dark beer, Guinness. The French traveller de Bovet (fl. 1893–1930) wrote several books about Ireland in the 1880s and 1890s, and was particularly struck by the grand scale of operations surrounding the brewery.

One should not leave the Liberties without visiting the immense industrial establishment which, on the confines of this miserable quarter, represents the fortune of Dublin. I mean the Guinness Brewery, where is manufactured the black beer called stout, or porter, which looks like bottled blacking, and in every part of the world where the English language is spoken is the rival of Bass and Co.'s pale ale. Founded in 1750, the Guinness Brewery has grown to such proportions that in 1885 its business transactions were five times greater than in 1837. Three years ago the business was sold for six millions sterling to a company, Sir Edward Cecil Guinness, Bart., remaining Chairman of the Board.

By way of a joke, people say that Dublin beer is black because it is made with the water of the Liffey. The truth is, that its colour as well as its peculiar taste is due to the malt having been first roasted.... To reduce it to malt it is soaked for two or three days in vats, then it is left in the air to sprout, after which it is dried and baked in an oven. The malt is then warehoused in airtight rooms till the moment it is wanted. The brick building used for this purpose is the largest in Dublin, and can hold a million bushels. After being carefully winnowed, the malt is crushed by metal rollers, and then macerated with warm water. From this process comes an insipid and colourless mush, removed by suction pumps into copper boilers that hold nearly twenty-two thousand gallons, where it is boiled with hops which give a bitter taste to the malt liquor. The peaty soil of the country not being fit for the cultivation of hops, they are sent over here in bales, from England, Germany and America. The mixture then passes through pipes into refrigerators, whence, once reduced to a proper temperature, it is again poured into vats, where it comes into contact with yeast. It is then that fermentation is produced, the result being the decomposition of the saccharine matter into alcohol. This operation, which lasts from three to four days, is overlooked by excise-men, and the sum received by the Treasury in this way comes to a daily amount of £1,200. The vats are twenty-seven in number, and together hold over a million gallons.

The visitor who has the curiosity to poke his nose through one of the openings made in the side may have a very good idea of the feelings the Duke of Clarence experienced when he was drowning in the butt of Malmsey, with this difference, that if he fell headlong into this seething frothy mixture, he would be asphyxiated by the carbonic acid gas it gives off, before he could arrive at the surface. It would be a very pleasant way of committing suicide. Before one has experienced it one can form no idea of the strength of the fermenting fumes of stout, nor of the delicious perfume that emanates from it – absolutely different from that of any other spirituous liquor. After a vat is emptied the washers are obliged to wait four and twenty hours before they can enter it. One second of it is enough to turn you dizzy, and two to make you insensible, and unless you are anxious to get rid of life, it is as well that someone should hold on to your coat tails. When the fermentation is nearly complete the liquid is poured into troughs where it is cleared from the scum which rises to the surface. When it is perfectly clear the manufacture is finished. There is nothing left but to pump the beer into tuns where the clearing process is completed.... The underground vaults are one of the curiosities of the brewery. There are endless galleries where by the blue light of electricity one has an indefinitely multiplied vision of the tun of Heidelberg. One hundred and fifty strongly iron-bound oak tuns standing on pedestals of masonry, hold from 200 to 1,700 hogsheads each; there are something like eleven or twelve millions of gallons warehoused at one time in these immense cellars. It makes one's head turn to think of it. A network of subterranean lines connects these tuns with the dock at the Victoria quay, where the casks are filled by an ingenious process which prevents all waste and leakage.

FLORENCE

The Tuscan city of Florence rose to eminence through its domination of long-distance trade and banking in the Middle Ages, and in the 14th and 15th centuries saw a remarkable artistic and intellectual Golden Age. Although it was in relative decline in the 16th century, it remained irresistibly attractive to cultural visitors, as it has been ever since. From the mid-17th century, Florence became an essential stop on the 'Grand Tour', undertaken by many young British aristocrats to visit Italy, acquire some education and enjoy themselves in equal measure.

In the 20th century, Florence became almost overwhelmed by mass tourism in search of its wealth of art and architecture, yet it still managed to retain the atmosphere of a provincial Italian town.

1580 MICHEL DE MONTAIGNE

The French philosopher Michel de Montaigne (1533–1592) is renowned for his thoughtful, self-examining and highly personal essays written in 1580. Later that year he visited Italy, including Florence, seeking a cure for his kidney stones. His dyspeptic impressions were recorded in a journal by his valet.

This is a smaller town than Ferrara, placed in a plain and surrounded by a vast number of well-cultivated hills. The Arno, which is crossed by divers bridges, runs through it and the walls of the town have no ditches. This day M. de Montaigne passed two stones and a large amount of gravel without perceiving anything more than a slight pain in the lower part of the stomach. On the same day we visited the stables of the Grand Duke, which are large and arched in the roofs, but no valuable horses were therein. The Grand Duke is not at present in residence. We saw there a strange kind of sheep, a camel, some lions and bears, and an animal as big as a large mastiff, the shape of a cat, and spotted black and white, which they called a tiger.

We went to the church of San Lorenzo where those banners of ours which Marshal Strozzi lost in his Tuscan defeat are still hanging. In this same church are several specimens of painting on the flat, and some beautiful statues of excellent workmanship, the work of Michael Angelo. We next saw the Dome, a very large church, and the bell tower, covered with black and white marble and one of the fairest and richest works in the world.

M. de Montaigne affirmed that he never saw a nation so lacking in fair women as the Italian, and the lodgment he found far less well arranged than in France or Germany; the food, indeed, was not half so abundant or well served as in Germany. In neither country is the meat larded, but in Germany it is far better seasoned, and there is greater variety in sauces and soups. The rooms themselves in Italy are vastly inferior, no saloons, the windows large, and all uncovered save by a huge wooden shutter, which would exclude all daylight if it should be necessary to keep off the sun or the wind, an inconvenience which M. de Montaigne found still more intolerable than the lack of curtains in Germany....

I cannot tell why this city should be termed 'beautiful', as it were by privilege. Beautiful it is, but no more so than Bologna, and little more than Ferrara, while it falls far short of Venice.... The city is paved with flat stones without pattern or regularity. After the dinner the four gentlemen and a guide took the post to go to visit a place belonging to the duke which is called Castello. There is nothing of merit in the house, but around it are divers gardens, the entire place being set on the slope of a hill, so that the main walks are on the slope, and the cross alleys straight and level; also many arbours, thickly covered with interwoven twigs of sweet-smelling shrubs, such as cedar, cypress, orange, citron and olive, the branches being enlaced so closely that the sun at his fiercest could not pierce thereinside....

In a part of the garden they encountered a very humorous experience, for, as they were walking about therein and marking its curiosities, the gardener for a certain purpose withdrew, and while they stood gazing at some marble statues, there sprang up under their feet and between their legs an infinite number of tiny jets of water, so minute that they resembled exactly drops of rain, and with this they were sprinkled all over. It was produced by the working of subterranean machinery which the gardener, being two hundred paces distant, set in motion. So delicately was it constructed that he was able from where he was stationed to raise and depress the outflow as he willed. The same device is to be found in divers other places. They saw also the great fountain which finds a channel through two vast bronze figures, one of which, clasped by the other in a violent embrace, seems half-fainting, and, with head thrown back, belches forth the stream from his mouth. So great is the force that the column of water rises some thirty-seven fathoms above the top of these figures, which are themselves twenty feet high.

c.1660 RICHARD LASSELS

Richard Lassels (1603–1668) was an English Catholic priest who lived much of his life in Paris, but travelled in Italy in the 1650s and 1660s accompanying young Catholic aristocrats. He described the important cultural sights in his posthumous book The Voyage of Italy, *which remained popular into the 18th century and introduced the term 'Grand Tour'. Not all his information was correct, such as his misattribution of the Baptistery doors, actually done by Ghiberti and Pisano.*

The Domo, I believe, was the finest church in Italy when it was built.... The foundations and architecture of it were contrived by Arnolfo di Lapo, a Dutchman, and *a la maniera rustica*, saith Vasari of it, in his *Lives of the Painters*. It's one of the neatest churches without that I have ever beheld, being clad in white, red and black marble, but it's only white plastered within, with pillars of a dark coloured freestone. What if the architect of this church were somewhat of Diogenes' mind? And as Diogenes thought the world would be turned upside down one day, so this architect thought that the world would be turned inside out one day, and that then his church would be the fairest in the world and all lined with marble. As it is, it looks a little hypocritically; though the structure within be of noble contrivance. On the top of it stands mounted a fair cupola made by Brunelleschi, a Florentine. This was the first cupola in Europe, and therefore the more admirable for having no idea after which it was framed; and for being the idea of that of St Peter's in Rome, after which so many young cupolas in Rome and elsewhere have been made since. Hence it is said that Michael Angelo, coming now and then to Florence (his native country) while he was make the cupola in Rome of St Peter's church, and viewing attentively this cupola of Florence, used to say to it *'Come te non voglio; meglio di te non posso'* [I have no wish to do it as you do; yet I cannot do it better than you do]. It's said also that Brunelleschi, making this cupola, caused taverns, cookshops and lodgings to be set in it, that the workmen which find all things necessary there and not spend time going up and down; and he had reason for this cupola from the ground below to the top of the lantern, is two hundred and two *braccie*, or yards high....

Near to the Domo stands the Campanile or high steeple of Florence made by Giotto. It's a hundred and fifty *braccie*, or little yards, high, and half as deep in the ground. It's flat at top and crusted all over with curious little polished marble stones, marble pillars and statues, so that (as Charles V said of it) if it had a case to cover it withal and hinder it from being seen too frequently, men would flock thither at the taking off of this cover, as to see a wonder. Indeed it's a kind of wonder to see that in three hundred years space, not the least part of that steeple (all crusted over with marble) is perished....

Near to the Domo also stands the Baptistery or round church of St John where all the children of the town are baptized. The brazen doors of it (three in all) are admirable, especially that which looks towards the great church, of which Michael Angelo, being asked his opinion, answered that it was so well made it might stand at the entrance of Paradise. These doors are all of brass historied into figures, containing the remarkable history of both the Testaments. They were the work of Laurentius Cion who spent fifty years making them: a long time I confess but this is it which Apelles called *aeternitati pingere*, to work things which will outlast brass and be famous for ever.

1770 ANNA MILLER

Poet Anna Miller (1741–1781), from Bath, England, toured Italy in 1770 with her husband; her collected letters were published anonymously.

28 December I hope you have had no alarm from any newspaper article relating to the shock of an earthquake felt here yesterday morning at five o'clock. I happened to be awake and heard a confused noise which at first seemed to be at a considerable distance but came rolling on and was immediately followed by a shock which seeming to proceed from the foundation of the house, ascended to the very top.

I do not know anything it resembled so much (but in a far greater degree) as that of a horse shaking himself when you are on his back, with this difference that this being the shuddering of a house instead of a horse, the various moveables in the room balanced to one side and the other, and some light furniture fell down. The bedstead was lifted up a little way from the ground and came down again with a great shock. M–– awaked and persuading me there was no danger, added to there not being any uncommon noise in the hotel, and Mrs Vanini's keeping quiet, I was not alarmed though an almost insupportable closeness of air continued for more than a minute, as well as I could judge.

All the bells in the churches were rung out to warn the people to quit their houses. Many of the poorer sort fled from their habitations and repaired to the churches. After sitting up about a quarter of an hour and perceiving all to be still, I went to sleep and did not wake till nine o'clock. The earthquake had done no mischief to any of the houses of the town. This morning a violent clap of thunder fell on the Duomo and split some of the pinnacles and other ornaments on the top, without further damage. Several risible stories have circulated in regard to the disturbances and discoveries the earthquake occasioned, among some polite societies here.

1853 T.Q. (SAMUEL YOUNG)

Samuel Young (1812–1855) was an American banker whose letters from a trip to Europe in 1853 were published in a Saratoga newspaper and collected under the title A Wall-street bear in Europe, with his familiar foreign journal of a tour through portions of England, Scotland, France and Italy *(1855). He was less than impressed with Florence.*

Florence is the favorite city in Italy of the Americans and English. If I can content myself here, I shall remain some months, making an excursion to Rome, &c. If not, I shall first visit Rome, and then return to England, where I will endeavour to be satisfied for the winter. If I fail in that, I shall go back to the United States 'per first steamer', thoroughly, entirely and conclusively satisfied and disgusted with all traveling; and firmly resolved never again to take my feet away from the shores of my native land; one town of which – with all its faults – containing more honesty and sincerity than the whole continent of Europe. Right or wrong, there is my opinion.

26 **November** Several of us who came up together from Leghorn, have com- pared notes, and all are disappointed in the external appearance of Florence.

The town is old and yellow. The streets are narrow and nearly all without sidewalks. The carriages, however, keep to the middle, and do not drive over fast. Where there are sidewalks, they are only about two feet wide, and consequently almost useless. Florence is not as cheerful a city outwardly, as Leghorn; but it is the residence of a great many Americans and English, because it is cheaper, and they can here husband their resources. At night Florence is badly lighted; and pedestrians, who are not keen-sighted, had better keep to the house....

Yellow is the prevailing colour of the buildings in Florence. The lower windows are protected by a framework of iron bars, set about four inches apart. Many of the houses along the Arno are let for lodgings. These lodgings are now pretty full. A single man can live cheaper here than at many other European towns, but not so cheaply as I had been told; that is, if he live comfortably. He can get his meals at the Cafe Doney at a very fair price. The cafes here are few and not equal to the French. I am staying at the Grand Hotel de New York kept by a man who cannot speak English. The 'master of the hotel', as he is called, is, like some of the keepers of the public houses in New York, perfectly competent in his own estimation. He is of a good figure, portly, requires much space to revolve in, and of course wears hair under his nose. All the men here, except a very few Americans and English, look as if some giant had taken them by the legs and forced their heads into coal-scuttle....

27 **November** In America we hear exaggerated accounts of the licentiousness of the French and Italians. I speak of the visible sinfulness. What takes place within doors, I profess to know nothing of. All I do know, is this; that in Paris and in the Italian cities I have seen, licentiousness does not meet the eye. No inducements are held out to you in the streets at night, to stray from the straight and narrow path. The presence of a watchful police has doubtless some influence. Yet, in London there is a good police, but you are often annoyed by abandoned females. London is worse that way than New York. I am told, also, by those that ought to know, that French and Italian women in general, are quite as virtuous as the women of England and America. Their manners are more free and easy; hence, their reputations suffer.

1956 MARY MCCARTHY

An American writer and campaigner for radical causes, Mary McCarthy (1912–1989) summed up the characteristic pleasures of the city in her 1956 book The Stones of Florence.

A 'characteristic' Florentine street – that is, a street which contains points of touristic interest (old palaces, a Michelozzo portal, the room where Dostoievski finished *The Idiot*, etc.) – is not only extremely narrow, poor and heavily populated, lined with florists and greengrocers who display their wares on the strip of sidewalk, but is also likely to be one of the principal traffic arteries. The main route today from Siena and Rome, for example, is still the old Roman 'way', the Via Romana, which starts at an old arched gate, the Porta Romana (1326; Franciabigio fresco in the archway), bends north-east, passing the gardens of the Annalena (suppressed convent) on the left and the second gate of the Boboli on the right, the church of San Felice (Michelozzo facade) on the left again, to the Pitti Palace, after which it changes its name to the Via Guicciardini, passes Palazzo Guicciardini (birthplace of the historian), the ancient church of Santa Felicita ('Deposition' by Pontormo inside, in a Brunelleschi chapel), and one continues to Ponte Vecchio, which it crosses, changing its name again to Por Santa Maria and again to Calimala before reaching the city centre. The traffic on the Via Romana is highly 'characteristic'. Along the narrow sidewalk, single file, walks a party of Swiss or German tourists, barelegged, with cameras and other equipment hanging bandoleer-style from various leather straps on their persons; clinging to the buildings, in their cleated shoes, they give the effect of a scaling party in the Alps. They are the only walkers, however, who are not in danger of death. Past them, in both directions (Via Romana is a two-way street), flows a confused stream of human beings and vehicles: baby carriages wheeling in and out of the Boboli Garden, old women hobbling in and out of church, grocery carts, bicycles, Vespas, Lambrettas, motorcycles, *topolinos*, Fiat *seicentos,* a trailer, a donkey cart from the country delivering sacks of laundry that has been washed with ashes, in the old-fashioned way, Cadillacs, Alfa-Romeos, *millecentos*, Chevrolets, a Jaguar, a Rolls-Royce with a chauffeur and a Florence licence plate, bands of brawny workmen carrying bureaus, mirrors and credenzas (for this is the neighbourhood of the artisans), plumbers tearing up the sidewalk, pairs of American tourists with guidebooks and maps, children, artists from the Pensione Annalena, clerks, priests, housemaids with shopping baskets stopping to finger the furred rabbits hanging upside down outside the poultry shops, the sanitation brigade (a line of blue-uniformed men riding bicycles that propel wheeled platforms holding two or three garbage cans and a broom made of twigs each), a pair of boys transporting a funeral wreath in the shape of a giant horseshoe, big tourist buses from abroad with guides talking into microphones, trucks full of wine flasks from the Chianti, trucks of crated lettuces, trucks of live chickens, trucks of olive oil, the mail truck, the telegraph boy on a bicycle, which he parks in the street, a tripe-vendor with a glassed-in cart full of smoking-hot entrails, outsize Volkswagen station wagons marked 'US Forces in Germany', a man on a motorcycle with an overstuffed armchair strapped to the front of it, an organ-grinder, horse-drawn fiacres from the Pitti Palace. It is as though the whole history of human locomotion were being recapitulated on a single street; an airplane hums above; missing only is the Roman litter.

But it is a pageant no one can stop to watch, except the gatekeeper at the Boboli who sits calmly in his chair at the portal, passing the time of day. In his safe harbour, he appears indifferent to the din, which is truly infernal, demonic. Horns howl, blare, shriek; gears rasp, brakes squeal, Vespas sputter and fart, tyres sing. No human voice, not even the voice of a radio, can be distinguished in this mechanical babel, which is magnified as it rings against the rough stone of the palaces. If the Arno valley is a natural oven, the palaces are natural amplifiers. The noise is ubiquitous and goes on all day and night. Far out in the suburbs, the explosive chatter of a Vespa mingles with the cock's crow at four in the morning; in the city an early worker, warming up his scooter, awakens the whole street.

GUANGZHOU
(CANTON)

The Chinese coastal city of Guangzhou (formerly romanized as Canton) was an important port under the Song (960–1279) and Ming (1368–1644) dynasties, and was one of the main points of contact for European traders in China from the 17th century.

In the 19th century the British used Canton for importing opium to China, and a Chinese protest against this led to the First Opium War

(1839–42), after which the port was forcibly 'opened' as a British (later American and French) treaty port. In the later 19th century Canton's prosperity declined somewhat following decades of internecine bloodshed (the leader of the Taiping rebellion against the Qing dynasty of 1850–64 came from the Canton region) and in the face of competition from Shanghai and Hong Kong as Western entry points to China's interior.

Guangzhou was deeply involved in the modernizing, nationalist and Communist conflicts of the first half of the 20th century, but it did not become an industrial centre until the late 1950s.

1655 PETER DE GOYER AND JAKOB DE KEYZER

The Dutch East India Company (VOC) was active in the city in the 17th century; its representatives de Goyer and de Keyzer (see page 53) visited in 1655.

Canton, the first chief city of this kingdom, lies upon the height of twenty-three degrees northern latitude, and is surrounded toward the east, west and north with very fruitful and delightful hills, and borders toward the south so very much upon the sea that on that side there is no part of all China so commodious to harbour shipping, where they likewise arrive daily from all quarters of their world, with all manner of goods, wherewith they make a considerable gain. It lies likewise upon the right side of the river Ta, where it grows somewhat narrow; but lower toward the sea it spreads such a breadth that it seems more like an ocean than a stream. For three miles upon this river is this city of Canton walled in, and some places adorned with rich and populous suburbs which are not much inferior to the ordinary cities both in bigness and number of inhabitants.

On the water side, the city is defended with two rows of high and thick walls which are strengthened with several bulwarks, watchtowers and other forts; though besides these works there are two other strong water castles which are built in the middle of the river which render this city invincible....

The city is likewise defended and surrounded on the land side with a strong wall, and five strong castles, whereof some are within the walls and others without upon the tops of steep hills so that this city is sufficiently both by land and sea defended against all the invasions of any enemy what-soever, and in the opinion of some seems invincible.

1853 BAYARD TAYLOR

The American poet and man of letters Bayard Taylor (1825–1878) undertook a journey from Britain to South and East Asia in 1853; like many Westerners, he was fascinated with the lore surrounding opium usage. In the 1860s he served as a US diplomat in St Petersburg.

In spite of the penalties attached to it by Chinese law, the smoking of opium is scarcely a concealed practice at present. I have seen it carried on in open shops in Shanghai, where there are some streets which are never free from the sickening smell. It had always been my intention to make a trial of the practice, in order to learn its effects by personal experience, and being now on the eve of leaving China, I applied to a gentleman residing in Canton, to put me in the way of enjoying a pipe or two. He was well acquainted with a Chinaman who was addicted to the practice, and by an agreement with him, took me to his house one evening. We were ushered into a long room, with a divan, or platform about three feet high, at the further end. Several Chinamen were in the room, and one, stretched out on the platform, was preparing his pipe at a lamp. The host invited me to stretch myself opposite to him, and place my head upon one of those cane head-stools which serve the Chinese in lieu of pillows.

The opium pipe is a bamboo stick, about two feet long, having a small drum inserted near the end, with an aperture in its center. A piece of opium, about twice the size of a pin's head, is taken up on a slender wire and held in the flame of the lamp until it boils or bubbles up, when it is rolled into a cylindrical shape on the drum, by the aid of the wire. It loses its dark color by the heating and becomes pale and soft. Having been sufficiently rolled, it is placed over the aperture, and the wire, after being thrust through its center, to allow the air to pass into the pipe, is withdrawn. The pipe is then held to the flame, and as the opium burns, its fumes are drawn into the lungs by a strong and long-continued inspiration. In about half a minute the portion is exhausted, and the smoker is ready for a second pipe.

To my surprise I found the taste of the drug as delicious as its smell is disagreeable. It leaves a sweet, rich flavor, like the finest liquorice, upon the palate, and the gentle stimulus it communicates to the blood in the lungs, fills the whole body with a sensation of warmth and strength. The fumes of the opium are no more irritating to the windpipe or bronchial tubes than common air, while they seem imbued with a richness of vitality far beyond our diluted oxygen. I had supposed that opium was smoked entirely for the purpose of mental exhilaration, and that to the smokers, as to many who intoxicate themselves with ardent spirits, there was no sensual gratification in the mere taste of the article. The reverse is undoubtedly the truth, and the practice, therefore, is doubly dangerous. Its victim becomes hopelessly involved in its fascinating illusions, and an awful death, such as I had witnessed not long before, is sure, sooner or later, to overtake him who indulges to excess. I have a pretty strong confidence in my own powers of resistance, but do not desire to make the experiment a second time.

Beyond the feeling of warmth, vigor and increased vitality, softened by a happy consciousness of repose, there was no effect until after finishing the sixth pipe. My spirits then became joyously excited, with a constant disposition to laugh; brilliant colors floated before my eyes, but in a confused and cloudy way, sometimes converging into spots like the eyes in a peacock's tail, but oftenest melting into and through each other, like the hues of changeable silk.... I went home feeling rather giddy and became so drowsy, with slight qualms at the stomach, that I went to bed at an early hour.

I had made an arrangement to walk around the walls of Canton the next morning, with Mr Bonney, and felt some doubt as to whether I should be able to undertake it; but, after a deep and refreshing sleep, I arose at sunrise, feeling stronger and brighter than I had done for weeks.

1879 ISABELLA BIRD

The British explorer and photographer Isabella Bird (1831–1904) was one of the most distinguished female travel writers of the 19th century. Her extensive journeys, including those in North America, Oceania and South, East and Central Asia, did not begin until she was in her forties, when she was advised to travel for her health, but continued up to her death.

4 January Viewing Canton from the 'five-storeyed pagoda', or from the dignified elevation of a pawn tower, it is apparent that it is surrounded by a high wall, beyond which here and there are suburban villages, some wealthy and wood-embosomed, others mean and mangy. The river divides it from a very populous and important suburb. Within the city lies the kernel of the whole, the Tartar city, occupied by the garrison and a military colony numbering about twenty thousand persons. This interesting area is walled round, and contains the residence of the Tartar General, and the consulates of the great European powers. It is well wooded and less closely built than the rest of Canton. Descending from any elevation one finds oneself at once involved at any and every point in a maze of narrow, crowded streets of high brick and stone houses, mostly from five to eight feet wide. These streets are covered in at the height of the house roofs by screens of canvas matting, or thin boards, which afford a pleasant shade, and at the same time let the sunbeams glance and trickle among the long, pendant signboards and banners which swing aloft, and upon the busy, many-coloured, jostling throng below....

There are heavy and ancient gates or barricades which enclose each street, and which are locked at night, only to be opened by favour of the watchmen who guard them. Their closing brings to an end the busy street life, and at 10 p.m. Canton, cut up into small sections, barred out from each other, is like a city of the dead. Each gate watchman is appointed and paid by the 'vestry' of the street in which he keeps guard. They wear uniform, but are miserable dilapidated-looking creatures, and I have twice seen one fast asleep.... These men are on the look-out for armed bands of robbers, but specially for fire. They are provided with tom-toms and small gongs on which to proclaim the hours of the night, but, should fire arise, a loud, rapid, and incessant beating of the gong gives the alarm to all the elevated brotherhood in turn, who at the same time, by concerted signals, inform the citizens below of the ward and street in which the fire has originated. In each principal street there is a very large well, covered with granite slabs, with its exact position denoted on a granite slab on the adjoining wall. These wells, which are abundant reservoirs, are never opened except in case of fire....

In the streets the roofs of the houses and shops are rarely, if ever, regular, nor are the houses themselves arranged in a direct line. This queer effect results from queer causes. Every Chinese house is built on the principles of geomancy, which do not admit of straight lines, and were these to be disregarded the astrologers and soothsayers under whose auspices all houses are erected, predict fearful evils to the impious builders....

The public buildings and temples, though they bear magnificent names, are extremely ugly, and are the subjects of slow but manifest decay, while the streets of shops exceed in picturesqueness everything I have ever seen. Much of this is given by the perpendicular signboards, fixed or hanging, upon which are painted on an appropriate background immense Chinese characters in gold, vermilion or black. Two or three of these belong to each shop, and set forth its name and the nature of the goods which are to be purchased at it. The effect of these boards as the sun's rays fall upon them here and there is fascinating. The interiors of the shops are lofty, glass lamps hang from the ceilings and large lanterns above every door, and both are painted in bright colours, with the characters signifying happiness, or with birds, butterflies, flowers or landscapes. The shop wall which faces the door invariably has upon it a gigantic fresco or portrait of the tutelary god of the building, or a sheet of red paper on which the characters forming his name are placed, or the character Shan, which implies all gods, and these and the altars below are seen from the street. There is a recess outside each shop, and at dusk the joss sticks burning in these fill the city with the fragrance of incense....

This is a meagre outline of what may be called the anatomy of this ancient city.... At this date it has probably greater importance than it ever had, and no city but London impresses me so much with the idea of solid wealth and increasing prosperity.

My admiration and amazement never cease. I grudge the hours that I am obliged to spend in sleep; a week has gone like half a day, each hour heightening my impressions of the fascination and interest of Canton, and of the singular force and importance of the Chinese. Canton is intoxicating from its picturesqueness, colour, novelty and movement. Today I have been carried eighteen miles through and round it, revelling the whole time in its enchantments, and drinking for the first time of that water of which it may truly be said that who so drinks 'shall thirst again' – true Orientalism.

1955 SIMONE DE BEAUVOIR

When the French writer and philosopher Simone de Beauvoir (1908–1986) visited in 1955, Canton appeared more traditional than modern; most of the traditional city was destroyed during the Cultural Revolution of the 1960s.

Between 1911 and 1927 Canton spearheaded the revolutionary movement. Today however the 'march towards socialism' is much less apparent than in the rest of China. Late to be liberated, possessing almost no industry, virtually no proletariat, twelve hundred miles by air from Peking, this city of small shopkeepers and small artisans had yet to feel the transforming impact of the regime.... For me, coming from Peking and Shanghai, it is like sliding back into the old semifeudal world.

My hotel is fourteen storeys high, the main skyscraper in the city. It is greyish, squat, quite awful, but it dominates the 'Long Quay' and from my window I look out upon a considerable strip of river.... The river is literally surfaced by boats beating upstream, and coasting down with the current; enormous rafts freighted with logs edge softly in the direction of the sea while junks sail for inland destinations. There are sampans whose deckhouses seem roofed with some sort of raffia – woven bamboo perhaps, greyish at any rate, and sloping downwards towards the prow. I love the great paddle-wheel boats, some of which transport passengers and goods seaward, still more of which head for the hinterlands. They are wooden, painted in fine green and gold tints; they have two decks astern, one deck amidships; the stern, boxlike, perpendicular and with windows, resembles a house front, a kind of ledge painted yellow is sandwiched between the two decks and above it runs an inscription in Chinese; the overall effect recalls Columbus' caravels. On the wharf crates and bales are being loaded and unloaded. An entire system of streams and canals connects the river with the inland country. Traffic slackens little if at all at night. The river then becomes alive with little red lamps: candles, lanterns are lit on the small craft where as many as 60,000 Cantonese have their permanent dwellings....

I especially remark the number of teahouses and their lavishness; plenty of tea is drunk in the South, not only because the heat breeds thirst but because people like to get together in public places. The salons are so big that one will often take up what would be an entire block of houses. The tables are of dark wood, in the middle a stairway leads up to a second floor, and on the farther side a window gives out upon another street. There are also ice-cream parlours where seated at a marble-top table you are served all sorts of flavours: vanilla, pineapple, banana, red pea. I lunch in one Canton restaurant.... I am brought fried shrimp, duck pates, breast of chicken, vol-au-vents, puffs, little stuffed rolls, rissoles, little thumb-sized bits of bread accompanying morsels of pickled pork, a dessert made of cookies and ample whipped cream.

HAVANA

Havana (originally San Cristóbal de la Habana) was founded by the
Spaniards in the early 16th century on an excellent natural harbour
in Cuba, and it became the base for further conquests; later in the
century it became the collecting point for treasure fleets returning
to Spain. After being held by the British briefly in the 1760s, it was
heavily fortified by Spain. From 1800 increasing numbers of visitors
came to Havana, and after Cuba won its independence from Spain

in 1898, it became the capital of the new republic. Treated as a playground — and centre of gangsterism — by many Americans in the first
half of the century, Havana and Cuba underwent a Marxist revolution
led by Fidel Castro in 1959 and were subjected to an embargo by the
United States until the 2000s.

1800 ALEXANDER VON HUMBOLDT

*The Prussian naturalist and explorer Humboldt (1769–1859) became the first
person to popularize Havana following a three-month-long visit in 1800–1, writing
about the island's human society and natural history (and even measuring its
latitude and longitude more accurately than ever before). For this he is often
described as the 'second discoverer' of Cuba (after Columbus).*

The view of Havana from the entrance to the port is one of the most picturesque and pleasing on the northern equinoctial shores of America. This
view, so justly celebrated by travellers of all nations, does not possess the
luxury of vegetation that adorned the banks of the Guayaquil, nor the wild
majesty of the rocky coasts of Rio de Janeiro...but the beauty that in our
climate adorns the scenes of cultivated nature, unites here with the majesty
of the vegetable creation, and with the organic vigour that characterizes the
torrid zone. The European who experiences this union of pleasing impressions, forgets the danger that menaces him in the midst of the populous
cities of the Antilles, and strives to comprehend the different elements of
so vast a country, gazing upon the fortresses crowning the rocks east of
the port, the opening arm of the sea surrounded with villages and farm-
houses, the tall palms, and the city itself half hidden by a forest of spars
and sails of shipping.

The principal edifices of Havana, the cathedral, the Government House,
the residence of the Comandante of Marine, the navy yard, the post office
and the Royal Tobacco factory, are less notable for their beauty than for the
solidity of their construction. The streets are generally narrow, and many
of them not paved. As the paving stone is brought from Vera Cruz, and its
transportation is costly, the singular idea had been entertained, shortly
before my arrival, of supplying its place with great trunks of trees, as is
done in Germany and Russia, in the construction of dykes across swampy

places. This project was speedily abandoned; but travellers who arrived sub-
sequently to the making of the experiment, were surprised to see beautiful
trunks of mahogany buried in the ruts of Havana.

During my residence in Spanish America few of the cities presented
a more disgusting appearance than did Havana, from the want of a good
police. One walked through the mud to the knees, and the many carriages,
or *volantes*, which are the characteristic carriages of this city, and the drays
laden with boxes of sugar, their drivers rudely elbowing the passer-by,
made walking in the streets both vexatious and humiliating. The offensive odour of the salted meat, or *tasajo*, infected many of the houses, and
even some of the ill-ventilated streets. It is said the police have remedied
these evils, and that lately there has been a marked improvement in the
cleanliness of the streets. The houses are well ventilated, and the street de
los Mercaderes presents a beautiful view. There, as in many of our older
cities in Europe, the adoption of a bad plan when laying out the city can
only be slowly remedied.

1839 FRANCES CALDERÓN DE LA BARCA

*Frances Calderón de la Barca (1804–1882), also known as Frances 'Fanny'
Erskine Inglis, was a Scottish writer who married Calderón de la Barca, the
Spanish minister to the United States in 1838. The following year he was posted
to Mexico, where she wrote a highly acclaimed account of her stay (see page
192) based on the letters she wrote to her family. She stopped briefly in Havana
on the way.*

Last evening, as we entered the beautiful bay, everything struck us as
strange and picturesque. The soldiers of the garrison, the prison built by
General Tacon, the irregular houses with their fronts painted red or pale
blue, and with the cool but uninhabited look produced by the absence of
glass windows; the merchant ships and large men-of-war; vessels from every
port in the commercial world, the little boats gliding among them with their
snow-white sails, the negroes on the wharf – nothing European. The heat
was great, that of a July day, without any freshness in the air....

Finally, we were hoisted over the ship's side in a chair, into the government boat, and rowed to the shore. As it was rather dark when we arrived,

and we were driven to our destination in a *volante*, we did not see much of the city. We could but observe that the streets were narrow, the houses irregular, most people black, and the *volante*, an amusing-looking vehicle, looking behind like a black insect with high shoulders, and with a little black postilion on a horse or mule, with an enormous pair of boots and a fancy uniform.

The house in which, by the hospitality of the H—a family we are installed, has from its windows, which front the bay, the most varied and interesting view imaginable. As it is the first house, Spanish fashion, which I have entered, I must describe it to you before I sleep. The house forms a great square, and you enter the court, round which are the offices, the rooms for the negroes, coalhouse, bathroom, etc., and in the middle of which stand the *volantes*. Proceed upstairs and enter a large gallery which runs all round the house. Pass into the *Sala*, a large cool apartment, with marble floor and tables, and chaise-longues with elastic cushions, chairs and armchairs of cane. A drapery of white muslin and blue silk divides this from a second and smaller drawing room, now serving as my dressing room, and beautifully fitted up, with Gothic toilet table, inlaid mahogany bureau, marble centre and side tables, fine mirrors, cane sofas and chairs, green and gold paper. A drapery of white muslin and rose-coloured silk divides this from a bedroom, also fitted up with all manner of elegances. French beds with blue silk coverlids and clear mosquito curtains, and fine lace. A drapery divides this on one side from the gallery; and this room opens into others which run all round the house. The floors are marble or stucco – the roofs beams of pale blue wood placed transversely, and the whole has an air of agreeable coolness. Everything is handsome without being gaudy, and admirably adapted for the climate. The sleeping apartments have no windows, and are dark and cool while the drawing rooms have large windows down to the door, with green shutters kept closed till the evening.

The mosquitoes have now commenced their evening song, a signal that it is time to put out the lights. The moon is shining on the bay, and a faint sound of military music is heard in the distance, while the sea moans with a sad but not unpleasing monotony. To all these sounds I retire to rest.

1957 GRAHAM GREENE

British novelist Graham Greene (1904–1991) described the fleshpots of pre-revolutionary Havana in his autobiography Ways of Escape *(1980).*

I had visited Havana several times in the early fifties. I enjoyed the louche atmosphere of Batista's city and I never stayed long enough to be aware of the sad political background of arbitrary imprisonment and torture, I came there...for the sake of the Floridita restaurant (famous of daiquiris and Morro crabs), for the brothel life, the roulette in every hotel, the fruit-machines spilling out jackpots of silver dollars, the Shanghai Theatre where for one dollar twenty-five cents one could see a nude cabaret of extreme obscenity with the bluest of blue films in the intervals. (There was a pornographic bookshop in the foyer for young Cubans who were bored by the cabaret.)...

Destiny had produced [a] driver in a typically Cuban manner. I had employed him some two or three years before for a few days in Havana. I was with a friend and on our last afternoon we thought of trying a novelty – we had been to the Shanghai. We had watched without much interest Superman's performance with a mulatto girl (as uninspiring as a dutiful husband's). We had lost a little at roulette, we had fed at the Floridita, smoked marijuana, and seen a lesbian performance at the Blue Moon. So now we asked our driver if he could provide a little cocaine. Nothing apparently was easier. He stopped at a newsagent's and came back with a screw of paper containing some white powder – the price was the equivalent of five shillings which struck me as suspiciously cheap.

We lay on our bed and sniffed. Once or twice we sneezed.

'Do you feel anything?'

'Nothing at all.'...

I was soon convinced that we had been sold – at what now appeared an exorbitant price – a little boracic powder. Next morning I told the driver so. He denied it. The years passed.

When I came back to Havana in 1957 I looked for him in all the quarters where drivers congregated.... The man I remembered might be a swindler, but he was a good guide to the shadier parts of Havana, and I had no desire for a dull and honest man to be my daily companion on this long trip. One night, I went to the Shanghai Theatre. When I came out into the dingy street I saw a number of taxis drawn up. A driver advanced towards me. 'I have to apologize humbly, senor. You had reason. It *was* boracic powder. Three years ago I was deceived too. The accursed newspaper seller. A swindler, senor. I trusted him. I give you back the five shillings.' In the course of the tour which followed he made a better profit than he lost. Every hotel, every restaurant, every cantina paid him his commission. I never saw him again on my next two visits to the island. Perhaps he was able to retire on his gains.

HONG KONG

The fishing port of Hong Kong, built on an island off the southern coast of China, was ceded to Britain in 1842 (the lease was eventually extended until 1997) and swiftly turned into a major British outpost in the Far East. By the later 19th century it was a leading commercial and industrial centre, as it remained throughout the 20th century and after its return to China.

1853 BAYARD TAYLOR

American Bayard Taylor (see page 118) visited eleven years after Hong Kong was leased to the British, and found colonial life already in full swing.

Seen from the water, the town, stretching for a mile along the shore, at the foot of Victoria Peak, whose granite cliff towers eighteen hundred feet above, bears considerable resemblance to Gibraltar. The Governor's mansion, the Bishop's Palace, the church and barracks occupy conspicuous positions, and the houses of merchants and government officials, scattered along the steep sides of the hill, give the place an opulent and flourishing air. So far from being disappointed in this respect, one is surprised to find that ten years of English occupation have sufficed to civilize so completely a barren Chinese island....

For amusements, besides riding, boating, yacht regattas, &c., there is a club, with a library, reading and billiard rooms, and a bowling alley, much frequented by Americans. The society is not extensive, but intelligent and agreeable, and the same lordly hospitality, with which I first became acquainted in India, prevails not only here but throughout all the foreign communes in China. This custom originated long ago, in the isolation to which the foreign merchant was condemned, and the infrequency of visitors from the distant world, which he had temporarily renounced. Then all houses were open to the guest, and the luxury which had been created to soften the gilded exile, was placed at his command....

I doubt if there be another class of men, who live in more luxurious state than the foreign residents in China. Their households are conducted on a princely scale, and whatever can be laid in the way of furniture, upholstery or domestic appliances of any sort, to promote ease and comfort, is sure to be found in their dwellings. Their tables are supplied with the choicest which the country can afford, and a retinue of well-drilled servants, whose only business it is to study their habits, anticipate all their wants....

These little communities, nevertheless, are subject to iron laws of etiquette, any infraction whereof, either purposely or through ignorance, makes society tremble to its foundations.... The newly arrived, unless he wishes to avoid all society, must go the rounds of the resident families and make his calls. The calls are returned, an invitation to dinner follows in due course of time and everything is in train for a footing of familiar intercourse.

This custom seems to me to reverse the natural course of social ethics. It obliges the stranger to seek his welcome, instead of having it spontaneously tendered to him. The residents defend the practice, on the ground that it allows a man to choose his own society – an obvious bull, since he cannot know who are congenial to him until he has met them....

There are private balls occasionally – public, rarely, if ever – where quadrilles, and waltzes, and polkas, are danced with as much spirit as at any outside the Tropics; but there is a considerate departure from the etiquette of the North, in allowing the gentlemen to appear, on such occasions, in a white linen jacket, and with a simple ribbon in place of a cravat. Nay, if so minded, he may even throw wide his collar, and enjoy a cool throat.

1878 ISABELLA BIRD

By the time the much-travelled Isabella Bird (see page 119) arrived in 1878, the city was growing fast and attracting immigrants from across the region. Her visit unluckily coincided with a major fire, which began on Boxing Day and destroyed 10 acres of housing, causing a million dollars' worth of damage.

Turning through another channel, we abruptly entered the inner harbour, and sailed into the summer, blue sky, blue water, a summer sun and a cool breeze, while a tender veil of blue haze softened the outlines of the flushed mountains. Victoria, which is the capital of the British colony of the island of Hong Kong, and which colloquially is called Hong Kong, looked magnificent, suggesting Gibraltar, but far, far finer, its peak eighteen hundred feet in height – a giant among lesser peaks, rising abruptly from the sea above the great granite city which clusters upon its lower declivities, looking out from dense greenery and tropical gardens, and the deep shade of palms and bananas, the lines of many of its streets traced in foliage, all contrasting with the scorched red soil and barren crags which were its universal aspect before we acquired it in 1843.

A forest of masts above the town betoken its commercial importance, and 'P. and O.' and Messageries Maritimes steamers, ships of war of all nations, low-hulled, big-masted clippers, store and hospital ships, and a great fishing fleet lay at anchor in the harbour. The English and Romish cathedrals, the Episcopal Palace, with St Paul's College, great high blocks of commercial buildings, huge sugar factories, great barracks in terraces, battery above battery, Government House and massive stone wharves came rapidly into view, and over all, its rich folds spreading out fully on the breeze, floated the English flag.

But dense volumes of smoke rolling and eddying, and covering with their black folds the lower slopes and the town itself made a surprising spectacle, and even as we anchored came off the rapid tolling of bells, the roll of drums and the murmur of a 'city at unrest'. No one met me.

A few Chinese boats came off, and then a steam launch with the M. M. agent in an obvious flurry. I asked him how to get ashore, and he replied, 'It's no use going ashore, the town's half burned, and burning still; there's not a bed at any hotel for love or money, and we are going to make up beds here.' However, through the politeness of the mail agent, I did go ashore in the launch, but we had to climb through and over at least eight tiers of boats, crammed with refugees, mainly women and children, and piled up with all sorts of household goods, whole and broken, which had been thrown into them promiscuously to save them. 'The palace of the English bishop,' they said, was still untouched; so, escaping from an indescribable hubbub, I got into a bamboo chair, with two long poles which rested on the shoulders of two lean coolies, who carried me to my destination at a swinging pace through streets as steep as those of Varenna [north Italy]. Streets choked up with household goods and the costly contents of shops, treasured books and nick-nacks lying on the dusty pavements, with beds, pictures, clothing, mirrors, goods of all sorts; Chinamen dragging their possessions to the hills; Chinawomen, some of them with hoofs rather than feet, carrying their children on their backs and under their arms; officers, black with smoke, working at the hose like firemen; parties of troops marching as steadily as on parade, or keeping guard in perilous places; Mr Pope Hennessy, the governor, ubiquitous in a chair with four scarlet bearers; men belonging to the insurance companies running about with drawn swords; the miscellaneous population running hither and thither; loud and frequent explosions; heavy crashes as of tottering walls, and, above all, the loud bell of the Romish cathedral tolling rapidly, calling to work or prayer, made a scene of intense excitement; while utterly unmoved, in grand Oriental calm (or apathy), with the waves of tumult breaking round their feet, stood Sikh sentries, majestic men, with swarthy faces and great, crimson turbans.

Through the encumbered streets and up grand flights of stairs my bearers brought me to these picturesque grounds, which were covered over with furniture and goods of all descriptions brought hither for safety, and Chinese families camping out among them. Indeed, the Bishop and Mrs Burdon had not only thrown open their beautiful grounds to these poor people, but had accommodated some Chinese families in rooms in the palace under their own. The apathy or calm of the Chinese women as they sat houseless amid their possessions was very striking.... The Bishop and I at once went down to the fire, which was got under, and saw the wreck of the city and the houseless people camping out among the things they had saved. Fire was still burning or smouldering everywhere, high walls were falling, hose were playing on mountains of smouldering timber, whole streets were blocked with masses of fallen brick and stone, charred telegraph poles and fused wires were lying about, with half-burned ledgers and half-burned everything. The coloured population exceeds one hundred and fifty-two thousand souls, and only those who know the Babel which an eastern crowd is capable of making under ordinary circumstances can imagine what the deafening din of human tongues was under these very extraordinary ones. In the prison, which was threatened by the flames, were over eight hundred ruffians of all nations, and it was held by one hundred soldiers with ten rounds of ammunition each, prepared to convey the criminals to a place of safety and to shoot any who attempted to escape....

On returning, I was just beginning to unpack when the flames burst out again. It was luridly grand in the twilight, the tongues of flame lapping up house after house, the jets of flame loaded with blazing fragments, the explosions, each one succeeded by a burst of flame, carrying high into the air all sorts of projectiles, beams and rafters paraffin soaked, strewing them over the doomed city, the leaping flames coming nearer and nearer, the great volumes of smoke, spark-laden, rolling toward us, all mingling with a din indescribable.

Burning fragments shortly fell on the windowsills, and as the wind was very strong and setting this way, there seemed so little prospect of the palace being saved that important papers were sent to the cathedral and several of the refugees fled with their things to the hills. At that moment the wind changed, and the great drift of flame and smoke was carried in a comparatively harmless direction, the fire was got well in hand the second time, the official quarter was saved, and before 10 p.m. we were able for the first time since my arrival at midday to sit down to food.

1959 IAN FLEMING

British novelist Ian Fleming (1908–1964) published his first 007 title, Casino Royale, *in 1953. In 1959 the* Sunday Times *newspaper commissioned him to tour the world and write about the cities he visited. One was Hong Kong, now a burgeoning capitalist city off the coast of Communist China. The city was returned to Chinese rule in 1997.*

Apart from being the last stronghold of feudal luxury in the world, Hong Kong is the most vivid and exciting city I have ever seen, and I recommend it without reserve to anyone who possesses the fate. It seems to have everything – modern comfort in a theatrically Oriental setting; an equable climate except during the monsoons; beautiful country for walking or riding; all sports, including the finest golf course – the Royal Hong Kong – in the East, the most expensively equipped racecourse and wonderful skin-diving; exciting flora and fauna, including the celebrated butterflies of Hong Kong; and a cost of living that compares favourably with any other tourist city. Minor attractions include really good Western and Chinese restaurants, exotic night life, cigarettes at 1s. 3d. for twenty and heavy Shantung silk suits, shirts, etc., expertly tailored in forty-eight hours....

The streets of Hong Kong are the most enchanting night streets I have trod.... Avoiding harsh primary colours, the streets of Hong Kong are evidence that neon lighting need not be hideous, and the crowded Chinese ideograms in pale violet and pink and green with a plentiful use of white are entrancing not only for their colours but also because one does not know what drab messages and exhortations they spell out. The smell of the streets is seaclean with an occasional exciting dash of sandalwood from a joss-stick factory, frying onions and the scent of sweet perspiration that underlies Chinese cooking. The girls, thanks to the *cheong sams* they wear, have a deft and coltish prettiness which sends Western women into paroxysms of envy. The high, rather stiff collar of the *cheong sam* gives authority and poise to the head and shoulders, and the flirtatious slits from the hem of the dress upwards, as high as the beauty of the leg will allow, demonstrate that the sex appeal of the inside of a woman's knee has apparently never occurred to Dior or Balmain. No doubt there are fat or dumpy Chinese women in Hong Kong, but I never saw one. Even the men, in their spotless white shirts and dark trousers, seem to have better, fitter figures than we in the West, and the children are a constant enchantment....

The Peking Restaurant was bright and clean.... Dick insisted that then, and on all future occasions when we were together, I should eat with chopsticks, and I pecked around with these graceful but ridiculous instruments with clumsy enthusiasm. To my surprise the meal, most elegantly presented and served, was in every respect delicious. All the tastes were new and elusive, but I was particularly struck with another aspect of Oriental cuisine – each dish had a quality of gaiety about it, assisted by discreet ornamentation, so that the basically unattractive process of shovelling food into one's mouth achieved, whether one liked it or not, a kind of elegance. And the background to this, and to all my subsequent meals in the East, always had this quality of gaiety – people chattering happily and smiling with pleasure and encouragement.

But by now it was late and the after-effects of jet travel – a dull headache and a bronchial breathlessness – had caught up with me, and we ended our evening with a walk along the thronged quays in search of a taxi and home. On the way I commented on the fact that there is not a single seagull in the whole vast expanse of Hong Kong harbour. Dick waved towards the dense flood of junks and sampans on which families of up to half a dozen spend the whole of their lives, mostly tied up in harbour. There hadn't used to be any seagulls in Shanghai either, he said. Since the communists took over they have come back. The communists have put it about that they had come back because they no longer have to fight with the humans for the harbour refuse. It was probably the same thing in Hong Kong. It would [have] taken an awful lot of seagulls to compete for a living with three million Chinese. On this downbeat note I closed my first enchanted day.

ISTANBUL
(CONSTANTINOPLE)

Istanbul, on the north coast of the Bosphorus strait linking the Mediterranean and Black seas, has always been one of the world's great cities from its foundation in AD 330 as the capital of the Eastern Roman (or Byzantine) Empire.

A vast entrepôt for trade between the Mediterranean world and the East, Constantinople had a diverse population and was renowned for its wealth until the final centuries of the Byzantine Empire, when it had been diminished by assaults from Arabs, Turks and even Christian Crusaders, who took and looted the city in 1204.

The expansion of the Ottoman Turks from the 11th century left Byzantium with little more than a small area around Constantinople by the mid-15th century. Nevertheless, the city remained iconic, and its fall to Ottoman sultan Mehmed II in 1453 was devastating.

The Ottomans made Constantinople, which they often called Istanbul (the Great City), their capital although the old name continued to be used widely. The city's great church, Hagia Sophia, built by Emperor Justinian in the 6th century, was converted into a mosque. Istanbul remained a trading hub as well as a key strategic location in the politics of Eastern Europe and the Levant.

In the early 20th century the Ottoman Empire was swept away by the nationalist revolution of Young Turks, losing its position as capital of Turkey to Ankara in 1923. It remains Turkey's largest city.

AD 950 CHIU T'ANG SHU

The Chiu T'ang shu, *the official history of China's Tang dynasty (AD 618–907), was compiled in the mid-10th century, and included much of what was known of the world across Asia and the Middle East. The Chinese had long had trading contacts with the Roman Empire, which was known to the Chinese as Ta-ts'in.*

The country of Fu-lin also called Ta-ts'in, lies above the western sea. In the south-east it borders on Po-si [Persia].

The walls of the capital are built of granite, and are of enormous height. The city contains in all over 100,000 households. In the south it faces the great sea. In the east of the city there is a large gate; it is covered with yellow gold and shines at a distance of several miles. Coming from outside to the royal residence there are three large gates beset with all kinds of precious stones.

On the upper floor of the second gate they have placed a large golden scale, with twelve golden balls suspended from the scale-stick by which the twelve hours of the day are shown. A human figure has been made of gold, on whose side, one of the golden balls will drop whenever an hour has come; the sound makes known the divisions of the day without the slightest mistake.

It is customary for men to have their hair cut and wear robes leaving the right arm bare. Women have no lapels on their dresses, and wear turbans of embroidered cloth. The possession of a great fortune confers superior rank on its owner. They drive in small carriages with white canopies; when going in or out they beat drums and hoist flags, banners and pennants. The country contains much gold, silver and rare gems, corals and amber; and all the valuable curiosities of the West are exported from this country.

1170 BENJAMIN OF TUDELA

Benjamin of Tudela's (see page 41) book, The Itinerary of Benjamin of Tudela, *described the conditions for trade, though whether this or some other purpose inspired his travels is never fully clear from his text. The traders he encounters in the great entrepôt of Constantinople come from as diverse locations as central Europe to the Middle East and central Asia.*

All sorts of merchants come here, from Babylon, Shinar, Persia, Media, Egypt, Canaan and the empire of Russia, from Hungaria, Patzinakia, Khazaria, Lombardy and Sepharad. It is a busy city and there is none like it in the world except Baghdad....

Close to the palace is the Hippodrome, where every year on the anniversary of the birth of Jesus the king gives a great entertainment. Men from all over the world come before the king and queen with jugglery and without jugglery, and they introduce lions, leopards, bears and wild asses and engage them in combat with one another; and the same thing is done with birds....

They hire barbarian warriors to fight with the sultan Masud, king of the Seljuk Turks; for the natives of Constantinople themselves are not warlike but are as women who have no strength to fight.

1332 IBN BATTUTA

Ibn Battuta (see page 72) travelled from Astrakhan (now in southern Russia) to Constantinople with the wife of Uzbeg, khan of the Golden Horde (she was

daughter of the Byzantine emperor) and a caravan of five thousand horsemen.
He stayed five weeks, before returning to Astrakhan and resuming his journey
to India and China.

The city is vast, in two parts separated by a great tidal river. On the eastern bank of the river is the Great City; it contains the residence of the emperor, the nobles and the rest of the population. Its bazaars and streets are spacious and paved with flagstones; most of the artisans and sellers in them are women. The city lies at the foot of a hill which carries a small citadel and the emperor's palace. The principal church is here.

The second part, called Galata, is reserved to the Frankish Christians who dwell there. They are bound to pay taxes to the king of Constantinople, but often they revolt and he makes war on them until the Pope makes peace between them. They are all men of commerce and their harbour is one of the largest in the world; I saw a hundred galleys and other large ships, and the small ships were too many to be counted. The bazaars here are good but filthy.

The great church called Hagia Sophia was reputedly built by Asaph, the son of Berechiah, the cousin of King Solomon. It is one of the greatest churches of the Greeks, and is encircled by a wall so that it looks like a town. It is the custom of the king, the nobles and the rest of the people to come every morning to this church.

The number of monks and priests in this church runs into thousands, some the descendants of the apostles, and inside is another church exclusively for women, containing more than a thousand virgins and a greater number of aged women who devote themselves to religious practices. Most of the population of the city are monks, ascetics and priests, and its churches are numberless. The soldiers and civilians all carry over their heads huge parasols, both in winter and summer, and the women wear large turbans.

I was out one day with my Greek guide, when we met the former king Andronicos II who had become a monk. He was on foot, wearing haircloth garments and a bonnet of felt, and had a long white beard. His fine face bore signs of his austerities. When the Greek saw him he said to me, 'Dismount, for this is the king's father.' When my guide saluted him the king asked about me. Then he took my hand and said to the Greek to translate his words, 'I clasp this hand which has entered Jerusalem and this foot which has walked within the Dome of the Rock and the churches of the Holy

Sepulchre and Bethlehem.' He then laid his hand upon my feet and passed it over his face. I was astonished at their good opinion of one who, though not of their religion, had entered these places. As I walked with him he asked me about Jerusalem and the Christians there.

1437 PERO TAFUR

Pero Tafur (c. 1410–1487), a Castilian aristocrat from Córdoba in southern Spain, travelled widely in Europe, Asia and North Africa in the 1430s, in part acting as ambassador for the king of Castile. He described his journeys in his Travels and Adventures *(1454). His visit to Constantinople came in the final years of Byzantine rule.*

There is a great place where the people used to watch the games when they celebrated their holidays, and in the centre are two snakes entwined, made of gilded brass, and they say that wine once poured from the mouth of one and milk from the other. It seems to me that too much credit must not be attached to the story.

In the centre of this square is a brass statue of a man. When merchants could not agree as to price they would go to this statue, which they called the Just, and whatever it signified as correct by shutting the hand, that was the true price of the goods, and both parties had to accept it. There was once a nobleman who valued his horse at 300 ducats, and a gentleman desired to buy it but they could not agree on the price. They went to the statue, and the purchaser took out some ducats and laid one in the hand of the statue, which thereupon shut its hand, meaning that the horse was not worth more. The purchaser took the horse and the seller the ducat, but the seller was so incensed that he took out his scimitar and cut off the statue's hand, and after that it never judged again. When the buyer reached home the horse fell dead, and the hide and shoes fetched just one ducat....

The emperor's palace must once have been magnificent, but now it is in such state that it, like the entire city, shows the evils which the people have suffered.... The emperor's state is as splendid as ever, for nothing is omitted from the ancient ceremonies, but really he is like a bishop without a see. When he rides abroad all the imperial rites are strictly observed. The empress rides astride, with two stirrups, and when she desires to mount, two lords hold up a rich cloth while turning their backs upon her, so that when she throws her leg across the saddle no part of her person can be seen....

The city is sparsely populated. The inhabitants are sad and poor, showing the hardship of their lot which is, however, not so bad as they deserve, for they are a vicious people, steeped in sin....

During my stay the Grand Turk [Murad II] marched to a place on the Black Sea, and his road took him close to the walls of Constantinople. I had the good fortune to see him in the field, and I observed the manner in which he went to war, and his arms, horses and accoutrements. I am of opinion that if the Turks were to meet the armies of the West they could not overcome them, not because they are lacking in strength, but because they want many of the essentials of war.

1547 JEAN CHESNEAU

The Frenchman Jean Chesneau (fl. 1545–52) visited in 1547 as secretary to the French ambassador to the court of Sultan Suleiman the Magnificent (r. 1520–66), and accompanied him on an expedition in Persia. He describes the Ottoman city at its peak.

We arrived in Constantinople on 14th May, 1547, and found lodgings not far from the port.

The most distinguished building is the palace of the Great Lord, which is called the Seraglio. It is around three miles in circumference, surrounded with high walls and has 11 iron gates. The Seraglio is very fine, and decorated with marble of many colours, porphyry, columns and other marvellous items brought from all of Greece and Asia.

It is permitted only to enter the great court and a few galleries and low rooms where audiences are held four times a week. But even the exterior view makes it plain that this is a magnificent edifice.

There is also the seraglio of the Great Lord's harem; the seraglio of the Janissaries, the palace of the patriarch, the partially ruined palace of the emperor Constantine, also the church of Santa Sophia, a marvellous construction built by Emperor Justinian with ancient columns and marbles of magnificent quality and size. Nearby the Great Lord has created his stables, as it is close to the Seraglio, while the church has been made into a mosque.

Near it is a mosque built by Sultan Mehmet, which has a hospital for people of all states of life, law, faith or country, and where for three days they are given honey, rice, meat, bread and a room in which to sleep. This is why there are so few poor people or beggars.

There are also other mosques, of Sultan Selim, Sultan Bajazet and other lords, and these are wonderfully beautiful and sumptuous. These show that they know well enough how to build in stone, yet they only use that material for their places of worship and palaces. All their other houses are low and made of earth or wood, and this is the case throughout Turkey.

1834 ALEXANDER KINGLAKE

Alexander Kinglake (1809–1891), a British travel writer and politician, published Eothen, or, Traces of Travel Brought Back from the East *anonymously in 1844, describing a journey made in the Middle East ten years previously. His picturesque account of an 'Oriental' city suffering from the plague also prefigures the widely held image of late 19th-century Ottoman Turkey as the 'sick man of Europe'.*

All the while that I stayed at Constantinople the plague was prevailing, but not with any degree of violence. Its presence, however, lent a mysterious and exciting, though not very pleasant, interest to my first knowledge of a great Oriental city; it gave tone and colour to all I saw, and all I felt – a tone and a colour sombre enough, but true, and well befitting the dreary monuments of past power and splendour....

The Europeans during the prevalence of the plague, if they are forced to venture into the streets, will carefully avoid the touch of every human being whom they pass. Their conduct in this respect shows them strongly in contrast with the 'true believers': the Moslem stalks on serenely, as though he were under the eye of his God, and were 'equal to either fate'; the Franks go crouching and slinking from death, and some (those chiefly of French extraction) will fondly strive to fence out destiny with shining capes of oilskin!...

As for me, I soon got 'compromised'.... Faithfully promising to shun the touch of all imaginable substances, however enticing, I set off very cautiously, and held my way uncompromised till I reached the water's edge; but before my *caïque* was quite ready some rueful-looking fellows came rapidly shambling down the steps with a plague-stricken corpse, which they were going to bury among the faithful on the other side of the water. I contrived to be so much in the way of this brisk funeral, that I was not only touched by the men bearing the body, but also, I believe, by the foot of the dead man, as it hung lolling out of the bier. This accident gave me such a strong interest in denying the soundness of the contagion theory, that I did in fact deny and repudiate it altogether; and from that time, acting upon my own convenient view of the matter, I went wherever I chose, without taking any serious pains to avoid a touch....

Perhaps as you make your difficult way through a steep and narrow alley, shut in between blank walls, and little frequented by passers, you meet one of those coffin-shaped bundles of white linen that implies an Ottoman lady.... Of her very self you see nothing except the dark, luminous eyes that stare against your face, and the tips of the painted fingers depending like rosebuds from out of the blank bastions of the fortress. She turns, and turns again, and carefully glances around her on all sides, to see that she is safe from the eyes of Mussulmans, and then suddenly withdrawing the *yashmak*, she shines upon your heart and soul with all the pomp and might of her beauty.

The Osmanlees speak well.... Even the treaties continually going on at the bazaar for the buying and selling of the merest trifles are carried on by speechifying rather than by mere colloquies, and the eternal uncertainty as to the market value of things in constant sale gives room enough for discussion. The seller is for ever demanding a price immensely beyond that for which he sells at last, and so occasions unspeakable disgust in many Englishmen, who cannot see why an honest dealer should ask more for his goods than he will really take!...

The vendor, perceiving that the unfolded merchandise has caught the eye of a possible purchaser, commences his opening speech. He covers his bristling broadcloths and his meagre silks with the golden broidery of Oriental praises, and as he talks, along with the slow and graceful waving of his arms, he lifts his undulating periods, upholds and poises them well, till they have gathered their weight and their strength, and then hurls them bodily forward with grave, momentous swing. The possible purchaser listens to the whole speech with deep and serious attention; but when it is over *his* turn arrives. He elaborately endeavours to show why he ought not to buy the things at a price twenty times larger than their value. Bystanders attracted to the debate take a part in it as independent members; the vendor is heard in reply, and coming down with his price, furnishes the materials for a new debate. Sometimes, however, the dealer, if he is a very pious Mussulman, and sufficiently rich to hold back his ware, will take a more dignified part, maintaining a kind of judicial gravity, and receiving the applicants who come to his stall as if they were rather suitors than customers. He will quietly hear to the end some long speech that concludes with an offer, and will answer it all with the one monosyllable '*Yok*', which means distinctly 'No'.

1942 STEVEN RUNCIMAN

The British historian Sir Steven Runciman (1903–2000) was professor of Byzantine Art and History at Istanbul University 1942–45, and his three-volume work A History of the Crusades *was published in 1951–54.*

No city is more splendidly situated than Istanbul; but its setting has one cruel disadvantage. I have often thought that the inherent melancholy and pessimism of the Byzantines was due to the climate of their imperial city, to the cold wind that blows in winter down the funnel of the Bosphorus from the Black Sea and the steppes of Russia beyond it, to the hot, enervating wind, the *melteme*, blowing from the south in summer, and to the all-pervading damp.

JERUSALEM

The ancient home of the Jews and capital of Israel's kings including David and Solomon, Jerusalem became part of the Roman province of Judaea in AD 6 and saw the climax of the life and death of Jesus, so that it was a uniquely holy place for both Jews and Christians thereafter. Following the Great Jewish Revolt against the Romans, the Jewish Temple was destroyed by Emperor Titus in AD 70. Emperor Hadrian rebuilt it as a Roman city, and Emperor Constantine embellished it with fine churches. Following capture by the Arab caliph Umar in 638, it was celebrated by the Muslims as the place from which Muhammad ascended to heaven, and the mosque known as the Dome of the Rock was built on the reputed spot.

The most important destination for Christian pilgrimage since Roman times, Jerusalem became the objective of the Crusaders from the later 11th century; the city was in Christian hands to 1187, when it was captured by Saladin. It remained in Arab, Egyptian or Ottoman hands until 1917, and was then taken by British and Arab forces. It remained under British mandate to 1948, when it became the capital of the new state of Israel, though divided so that East Jerusalem (including the old city) remained in Jordanian hands. In 1967, Israel captured and occupied the whole city.

AD 333 BORDEAUX PILGRIM

An anonymous pilgrim from Bordeaux to Jerusalem gave an account of the religious sights of Jerusalem just a few decades after Constantine had built several churches, including the Church of the Holy Sepulchre, and his mother Helen had collected important relics of Christ's life and death.

From Caesarea Palaestina to Jerusalem 116 miles, 4 halts, 4 changes.

There are in Jerusalem two large pools at the side of the temple, which were made by Solomon; and further in the city are twin pools with five porticoes, which are called Bethsaida. There persons who have been sick for many years are cured; the pools contain water which is red when it is disturbed. There is also here a crypt, in which Solomon used to torture devils.

Here is also the corner of an high tower, where our Lord ascended and the tempter said to Him, 'If thou be the Son of God, cast thyself down from hence.'... Under the pinnacle of the tower are many rooms, and here was Solomon's palace. There also is the chamber in which he wrote the Book of Wisdom; this chamber is covered with a single stone. There are also large subterranean reservoirs and pools constructed with great labour. And in the building itself, where stood the temple that Solomon built, they say that the blood of Zacharias which was shed upon the stone pavement before the altar remains to this day. There are also the marks of the nails in the shoes of the soldiers who slew him, throughout the whole enclosure, so plain that you would think they were impressed upon wax. There are two statues of Hadrian, and not far from the statues is a perforated stone, to which the Jews come every year and anoint it, bewail themselves with groans, rend their garments, and so depart. There also is the house of Hezekiah King of Judah....

As you go out of the wall of Sion and you walk towards the gate of Neapolis, towards the right, below in the valley, are walls, where was the house of Pontius Pilate. Here our Lord was tried before His passion. On the left hand is the little hill of Golgotha where the Lord was crucified. About a stone's throw from thence is a vault wherein His body was laid and rose again on the third day. There, at present, by the command of the emperor Constantine has been built a basilica, that is to say, a church of wondrous beauty having at the side reservoirs from which water is raised, and a bath behind in which infants are baptized.

Also as one goes from Jerusalem to the gate which is to the eastward, in order to ascend the Mount of Olives, is the valley called that of Josaphat. Towards the left, where are vineyards, is a stone at the place where Judas Iscariot betrayed Christ; on the right is a palm tree, branches of which the children carried off and strewed in the way when Christ came. Not far from thence are two notable tombs of wondrous beauty; in the one, which is a true monolith, lies Isaiah the prophet, and in the other Hezekiah, King of the Jews. From there you ascend to the Mount of Olives, where before the Passion, the Lord taught His disciples. There by the orders of Constantine a basilica of wondrous beauty has been built. Not far from thence is the little hill which the Lord ascended to pray, when he took Peter and John with Him, and Moses and Elias were beheld.

1050 NASIR KHUSRAW

Persian poet Nasir Khusraw (see page 71) visited Jerusalem in the course of a pilgrimage to Mecca and provided the most detailed pen-portrait of medieval Jerusalem in his Safarnama.

Jerusalem, situated on top of a hill, has no source of water but rain. The villages have springs, but there are none inside the city. Around the city is a rampart of stone and mortar with iron gates. Near the city there are no trees, since it is built on rock. It is a large city, with some twenty thousand men there when I saw it. The markets are fine, the buildings tall and the ground paved with stone.... There are many artisans, each group having its own streets. The eastern wall is attached to the congregational mosque. Passing out of the mosque you come out onto a large, flat plain called Sahira. They say that this is where the Resurrection will take place, where all people will be gathered together. For this reason people have come there from all over the world and taken up residence in order to die in that city. When God's appointed time comes, they will already be in the stipulated place. O God! On that day wilt Thou be Thine own servants' protector and Thy mercy. Amen. O Lord of the Universe!

On the edge of the plain is a large cemetery, where there are many spots in which men pray and make special requests, which are granted by God. God, receive our supplications and forgive our sins and evil deeds. Have mercy upon us, O Most Merciful!

Between the sanctuary and the plain of Sahira is a large, deep valley shaped like a trench. Therein are large edifices laid out by the ancients. I saw over the door of one house a carved stone dome, and anything more amazing could scarcely exist: I could not figure out how it had been raised. Everybody said it was Pharaoh's House and that this was the valley of Gehenna. I asked how it came to be called thus and was told that, in the days of the caliphate of Umar, the Plain of Sahira had been the site of an army camp. When Umar looked at the valley he said, 'This is the valley of Gehenna.' The common people say that anyone who goes to the edge of the valley can hear the voices of the people in hell. I went there but heard nothing.

1494 PIETRO CASOLA

From a wealthy Milanese family, Pietro Casola (1427–1507) was a canon who undertook a pilgrimage to Jerusalem, writing about his journey from Italy in his Pilgrimage to Jerusalem in the Year 1494. *His wide-ranging interests went far beyond the purely devotional. Despite his evident interest in the prosperity and way of life of the Muslim inhabitants, he betrayed the intolerance and lack of understanding of their faith that had been common for Europeans since the days of the Crusades.*

On Tuesday, 5th August, at sunrise...we set out towards Jerusalem by a very stony, mountainous and disagreeable road.... The country seemed very bare and wild; there was no fruit to be seen, nor did we come across any beautiful fountains. These are not like the countries of Italy. God willing, at an early hour we reached the Holy City of Jerusalem, almost dead of heat and thirst....

When we were all gathered together and counted again we were conducted into the city by friars of Mount Sion and quartered in the Hospital of St John. After asking for water, we began to lie down; each pilgrim was given a carpet to spread on the ground. The magnificent captain was in the habit of lodging with two persons in Mount Sion, a good way outside the city; but this prior had taken a house within the city near to the Sepulchre. The captain went there to rest, and then he sent to fetch me from the hospital, and made me lodge with him.

We lived like lords in the house of the captain, but the poorer pilgrims fared badly, as the prior had little charity for them; not a single person was satisfied with him. The friars shrugged and excused themselves because they could not treat the pilgrims as they used to do in the time of the former priors....

We visited the sacred places on the Mount of Olives where the mysteries which preceded the passion of Our Lord Jesus Christ were shown to us.... Then we mounted to a small church, and over the altar was a stone still bearing the mark of the foot of Our Lord Jesus Christ when he ascended into heaven, and this was touched with the rosaries and other objects of devotion. Afterwards we went into the valley of Jehoshaphat, which will be the place of the Last Judgment of Our Lord Jesus Christ. In this valley there is a beautiful church containing the Sepulchre in which the body of Our Lady was placed by the eleven Apostles. The place of the Sepulchre proper is governed by the Latin friars of Mount Sion. In the same church there are several other altars served by Greek priests. The church is also held in great veneration by the Moorish women. At the entrance the Moors made a charge for each person. I do not know how much it was because the captain paid....

We went to see the Probatic pool [Pool of Bethesda]. This has running water, and there are vestiges of the five porches which the Holy Scripture says were there at the time of Christ. This was a pool which had the virtue that an angel descended from heaven into the said pool and moved the water, and the first sick person who entered the pool after the moving of the water was cured of all his infirmities.... Now the Moors use it to wash hides which have been in lime. Many of the pilgrims drank the water. When I saw that filth I left it alone, it was enough for me to wash my hands there.

We afterwards saw the Mosque which they say stands on the site of the temple of Solomon. It is a beautiful building from the outside, and strong compared with the greater part of the habitations in Jerusalem. It is wonderful to see the courts – so well paved with the whitest marble – which are built around at the base of the Mosque.

When we had seen what the friars wanted us to see, we returned at the hospital all hot and covered with dust, and took a little repose. The prior of Mount Sion now sent to tell the pilgrims that we must be ready to enter the Holy Sepulchre that evening. But when he tried to arrange for the entrance with the person in authority, he demanded a thousand ducats. An altercation followed, and the project of entering the Sepulchre was given up.

As the captain's house was frequented by a very agreeable Moor who had formerly been forced into slavery at Rhodes, and who knew a little Latin, I got him to take me to see the city.... What pleased me most was the sight of the bazaars – long, vaulted streets extending as far as the eye can reach. In one of them all the provisions are sold – including cooked provisions, as they sell the chestnuts at home. I was told that not a single person in Jerusalem does the cooking in the house; and whoever wishes to eat goes to buy in the bazaar. However, they make bread at home, flat unleavened cakes; these are good when there is no other bread to be got.... Cooked fowls, cooked meat, eggs and all other eatables are very cheap. I saw another long bazaar, with both sides full of merchandise, and of the things the people know how to make, and this was a great sight....

Among the inhabitants of Jerusalem there are many of good condition and handsome men. They all go about dressed in the same way, with those clothes that look like quilts. Many are white, others are made of goat's hair, and of other silks of the Moorish kind. According to their means they display great care and magnificence in the cloths they wear on their heads....

They eat on the ground on carpets. They do not drink wine in public – but if they get the chance they take a good long drink of it. They like cheese very much. They would not eat a fowl which had had its neck drawn, as is the custom with us. They always cut the fowls' throats; otherwise they are clean in their cooking. For sleeping they have no place but the ground. They lie upon carpets, of which they have a great many. In their manner of eating they are very dirty; even persons of importance thrust their hands into the dishes. They do not use knives or forks or spoons, but they thrust their hands into everything.

With regard to their prayers, when they rose they went through so many genuflexions – throwing themselves all their length stretched out on the ground – that it was a marvel to see them. When they go to pray in the mosque they go barefooted, and first they wash themselves in certain places set apart for that purpose, but only from the waist downwards, and then they uncover their heads, which they never uncover even in the presence of the greatest lord in the world. It is great madness to talk to them about our faith, because they have no rational sentiment in them. They are very impetuous and easily excited to anger, and they have no gracious or courteous impulses or actions. And I declare that they may be as great and as learned as you like, but in their ways they are like dogs.

I was never able to see a beautiful woman, for they go about with their faces covered by a black veil. They wear on their heads a thing which resembles a box, a braccio long, and from that a long cloth, like the white towels in Italy, hangs down.

1811 VICOMTE DE CHATEAUBRIAND

An associate of Napoleon, Chateaubriand (see page 33) undertook a pilgrimage to Jerusalem in 1811. Following the fall of Napoleon's empire, he supported the restored Bourbon dynasty.

We pursued our course through a desert where wild fig trees, thinly scattered, waved their embrowned leaves in the southern breeze.... Presently, all vegetation ceased; even the very mosses disappeared. The confused amphitheatre of the mountains was tinged with a red and vivid colour. In this dreary region we kept ascending for an hour to gain an elevated hill that we saw before us; after which we proceeded for another hour across a naked plain bestrewed with loose stones. All at once, at the extremity of this plain, I perceived a line of Gothic walls, flanked with square towers, and the tops of a few buildings peeping above them. At the foot of this wall appeared a camp of Turkish horse, with all the accompaniments of oriental pomp. *El Cods* 'the Holy City' exclaimed the guide, and away he went at full gallop.

I can now account for the surprise expressed by the Crusaders and pilgrims at the first sight of Jerusalem, according to the reports of historians and travellers. I can affirm that whoever has, like me, had the patience to read near two hundred modern accounts of the Holy Land, the rabbinical compilations and the passages in the ancients relative to Judea, still knows nothing at all about it. I paused with my eyes fixed on Jerusalem, measuring the height of its walls, reviewing at once all the recollections of history from Abraham to Godfrey of Bouillon, reflecting on the total change accomplished in the world by the mission of the Son of man, and in vain seeking that Temple, not one stone of which is left upon another. Were I to live a thousand years, never should I forget that desert which yet seems to be pervaded by the greatness of Jehovah and the terrors of death.

The cries of the interpreter to keep close together as we were at the entrance of the camp, roused me from the reverie. We passed among the tents covered with black lambskins; a few, among others that of the pasha, were formed of striped cloth. The horses, saddled and bridled, were fastened to stakes. I was surprised to see four pieces of horse artillery; they were well mounted and the carriages appeared to be of English construction. Our mean equipage and pilgrims' dress excited the laughter of the troops. The pasha was coming out of Jerusalem as we drew up to the gate of the city. I was obliged to take off the hand-kerchief which I had tied over my head to keep off the sun, lest I should draw upon myself a similar affront to that which poor Joseph incurred at Tripolizza [Tripoli, Greece].

We entered Jerusalem by the Pilgrims' Gate near which stands the Tower of David, better known by the appellation of the Pisans' Tower. We paid the tribute and followed the street that opened before us; then, turning to the left between a kind of prison of plaster, denominated houses, we arrived at 22 minutes past 12, at the convent of the Latin Fathers. I found it in the possession of Abdallah's soldiers, who appropriated to themselves whatever they thought fit.

Those only who have been in the same situation as the Fathers of the Holy Land can form a conception of the pleasure which they received from my arrival. They thought themselves saved by the presence of one single Frenchman. I delivered a letter from General Sebastiani to Father Bonaventura di Nola, the superior of the convent. 'Sir,' said he, 'it is Providence that has brought you hither. You have travelling *firmans* [permits]. Permit us to send them to the pasha. He will thence find that a Frenchman has arrived at the convent; he will believe we are under the special protection of the Emperor.'

1949 AND 1967 ELIE WIESEL

Elie Wiesel (1928–2016) was a Romanian-born American activist and writer, Holocaust survivor and winner of the Nobel Prize for Peace for his work on human rights. He visited Jerusalem in 1949, shortly after the establishment of the Israeli state, and again following its capture by Israel in the 1967 Six Days' War.

When did I see Jerusalem for the first time? I don't even know. When I visited the city for the first time, it seemed to me that it was not for the first time. At the same time, each visit since then I have had the feeling it is my first visit....

Before I even began to speak I dreamed of the widow, the daughter of Zion, who sits alone in the Temple of Jerusalem. I would wait for the little goat that was to give me raisins and almonds and then carry me, and all of us, far away to the city where everything breathes Yiddishkeit, where even the stones tell tales of wonder in Yiddish about Jewish kings and princes....

While studying, we seemed to find ourselves in Jerusalem. All the hills, all the little streets, all the buildings looked familiar. Priests and Levites met us with smiles. Talmudic scholars stopped us in the street and asked us to recite our lesson. Students of Talmud pulled us away to hear Hillel the Elder or Rabbi Akiba lecture.

Though far from Jerusalem we lived between its walls.

It took a whole year, until the summer of 1949, before I had the opportunity to go to Eretz Yisrael. A Paris newspaper agreed to send me there as a correspondent. My assignment: to portray the life of the new immigrants to the new – yet old – land, theirs and ours. Naturally, I immediately ran to Jerusalem. The city was still divided. The Old City belonged to Jordan. I spent long hours in the tower of the YMCA building facing the King David Hotel, unable to satisfy myself with the picture of the true Jewish Jerusalem, so near and yet so far.

It was peculiar: the average Israeli citizen hardly missed the Old City. I seldom heard anyone speak of the deep longing that must dominate every Jew who reminds himself of the Kotel Hamaarivi, the Western Wall. How could one go on with his daily activities in the new Jerusalem when the old Jerusalem was in captivity? No one could answer this question for me. The truth is, one gets used to everything....

June 1967 Exactly like many other Jews, I also feared the outcome of the war between Israel and her neighbors. Too many elements reminded me of historic betrayals committed by the world with respect to our people. The enemy openly threatened annihilation, and in the UN no one responded....

The war still raged in the Sinai, but it was only the fate of Jerusalem that caught the imagination of the Jewish people. The Arabs were still shooting from the rooftops, but Jews, in the thousands, ran to the Old City, and no one could stop them.

A bizarre, elemental force had suddenly taken possession of all Jews, rabbis and merchants, *yeshiva* boys and *kibbutznikes*, officers and schoolchildren, cynics and artists – all had forgotten everything. Each wanted to be at the Kotel Hamaaravi, to kiss the stones, to cry out prayers or memories. Each knew that on that historic day, in that week, the place of the Jew was at the Temple Mount. I had the privilege to run with them. I have never run with such an impetus. I have seldom said 'amen' with such devotion as when the paratroops, in their exaltation, prayed Minhah. I have never understood the profound meaning of Ahavat Yisrael, love of Israel, as I did on that day when I stood, as in a dream, under the burning sun and thought with pride of Jewish existence.

At that time an elderly Jew – I thought he was one of the main characters who had stepped out of one of my novels – remarked to me, 'Do you know why and how we defeated the enemy and liberated Jerusalem? Because six million souls took part in our battle.' Then I actually saw what the naked eye seldom sees: souls on fire floated high above us, praying to the Creator to protect them and all of us.

And this prayer itself was also transformed into a soul.

LHASA

Lhasa became the political and religious capital of Tibet in the 17th century, when the Potala Palace, winter home of the Dalai Lama, spiritual and religious leader of Tibet, was built, as well as many large monasteries. It was taken over by the Chinese Qing dynasty in 1750. A British expedition in 1904 took the city and the Chinese left shortly thereafter. A closed city that was rarely visited by Westerners, Lhasa was retaken by the Chinese Red Army in 1950, and following a rising in 1959 the Dalai Lama went into exile in India. In recent decades, new transport links and large-scale immigration by Han Chinese has changed the character of the city, with traditional Tibetan culture sidelined as a tourist attraction.

1811 THOMAS MANNING

Thomas Manning (1772–1840) was a scholar of China and the first Briton to visit Lhasa, where he met the seven-year-old ninth Dalai Lama, as he recorded in his journal.

We passed under a large gateway whose gilded ornaments at top were so ill fixed that some leaned one way and some another, and reduced the whole to the rock appearance of castles and turrets in pastry work. The road here, as it winds past the palace, is royally broad; it is level and free from stones, and combined with the view of the lofty towering palace, which forms a majestic mountain of building, has a magnificent effect. The road about the palace swarmed with monks; its nooks and angles with beggars lounging and basking in the sun. This again reminded me of what I have heard of Rome. My eye was almost perpetually fixed on the palace, and roving over its parts, the disposition of which being irregular, eluded my attempts at analysis. As a whole, it seemed perfect enough; but I could not comprehend its plan in detail. Fifteen or twenty minutes now brought us to the entrance of the town of Lhasa.

If the palace had exceeded my expectations, the town as far fell short of them. There is nothing striking, nothing pleasing in its appearance. The habitations are begrimed with smut and dirt. The avenues are full of dogs, some growling and gnawing bits of hide which lie about in profusion, and emit a charnel-house smell; others limping and looking livid; others ulcerated; others starved and dying, and pecked at by the ravens; some dead and preyed upon. In short, everything seems mean and gloomy, and excites the idea of something unreal. Even the mirth and laughter of the inhabitants I thought dreamy and ghostly. The dreaminess no doubt was in my mind, but I never could get rid of the idea; it strengthened upon me afterwards. A few turns through the town brought us into a narrow by-lane, and to the gate of a courtyard, where we dismounted, and, passing through that yard, entered another smaller one surrounded by apartments. We mounted a ladder, and were shown into the room provided for us.

1901 EKAI KAWAGUCHI

The Japanese Buddhist monk Ekai Kawaguchi (1866–1945) made four visits to Tibet between 1900 and 1915, where he posed as a Tibetan doctor; he was not impressed with conditions in Tibet. His account of them was seen by the British and influenced Francis Younghusband, leader of the 1904 expedition that brought Tibet into the British sphere of influence.

There are many cheap inns in Lhasa, but as I had been informed that they were not respectable, I desired to stay with a friend, a son of the premier of Tibet. While at Darjeeling I had become acquainted with this young noble, and he had offered me a lodging during my stay in Lhasa.... So I called at his house...and asked if he was in, but heard that my friend had become a lunatic. They told me that he had gone out of his mind two years before, and that he went mad at regular periods.... I waited there for over two hours, as I was told he might come, and then I reflected that it would be of no use for me to see a madman, on whom I could not depend, so I made up my mind to direct my steps to the Sera monastery, for I thought it would be better for me to be temporarily admitted in the college, and then to pass the regular entrance examinations. So I at once hired a coolie to carry my baggage, and started for the monastery....

I arrived at the monastery at four o'clock and at once called at the dormitory of Pituk Khamtsan, giving myself out as a Tibetan. Hitherto I had passed for a Chinaman, but...I had not trimmed my hair nor shaved my face, nor bathed for a long time, and I cannot have been much cleaner than a Tibetan, so I made up my mind to pass for one and to live among them. The examinations for a Tibetan might be too difficult for me; still I could command the Tibetan language almost as well as a native, and I was often treated as one. I thought, therefore, that I could pass without detection, and so for my own safety I entered the monastery in this guise....

I had trimmed and shaved neither hair nor beard in my journey of over ten months, so that they had grown very long. On the day after my arrival, therefore, when I got a priest to shave my head, I asked him to shave off my beard also. He wondered why I wanted to have it shaved off, and told me that it would be very unwise of me to do so when it had grown so beautiful. He seemed to think that I was joking, and I was obliged to let it grow. A beard is much valued by the Tibetans, because they generally have none, though the inhabitants of Kham and other remote provinces grow beards. They are so eager to have a beard, that after I was known to be a doctor I was often asked to give medicine to make the beard grow. They would say that I must have used some medicine to make my beard grow so long....

I bought a hat, a pair of shoes and a rosary, according to the regulations of the monastery.... I went to the chief professor of the department which I was to enter...but found that no examinations were to be given. I called on the professor with a present of the best tea to be procured in Tibet. His first question was: 'Where are you from? You look like a Mongolian; are you not one?' Being answered in the negative, he asked me several geographical questions, for he was well acquainted with the geography of the country. But I answered well, as I had travelled through the provinces on my own feet. It was thus settled that I might be admitted on probation. So I saluted the Lama with my tongue out, and he put his right hand on my head, as usual, and put a red cloth about two feet long round my neck as the sign of my admission.

1904 FRANCIS YOUNGHUSBAND

Francis Younghusband (1863–1942) was a British army officer who led a British expedition to Tibet in 1904 that defeated the Tibetans at Gyantse and, against orders, advanced to Lhasa and signed a treaty that secured British influence in Tibet, which was at that time under Qing Chinese sovereignty.

Practically, then, the religion of the Tibetans is but of a degraded form. Yet one does see gleams of real good radiating through. The Tashi Lama whom Bogle met was a man of real worth. His successor of the present day produced a most favourable impression in India, and excited the enthusiasm of Sven Hedin. Deep down under the dirty crust there must be some hidden source of strength in these Lamas, or they would not exert the influence they do. Millions of men over hundreds of years are not influenced entirely by chicanery or fraud. And I think I caught a glimpse of that inner power during a visit that I paid to the Jo Khang Temple....

I visited this temple with full ceremony after the Treaty was signed, and was received with every mark of cordiality by the Chief Priest. I was even showed round what might be called the high-altar, in spite of my protestations that I might be intruding where I should not go. The actual building is not imposing. The original temple, built about AD 650, according to Waddell, has been added to, and the result is a confused pile without symmetry, and devoid of any single complete architectural idea. One sees a forest of wooden pillars grotesquely painted, but no beautiful design or plain simple effect. Moreover, dirt is excessively prevalent, there is an offensive smell of the putrid butter used in the services, and the candlesticks, vases and ceremonial utensils, some of solid gold and of beautiful design, are not orderly arranged.

Still, this temple, from its antiquity, from its worn pavements marking the passage of innumerable pilgrims, from the thought that for a thousand years those wanderers from distant lands had faced the terrors of the desert and the mountains to prostrate themselves before the benign and peaceful Buddha, possessed a halo and an interest which the beauty of the Taj itself could never give it.

Here it was that I found the true inner spirit of the people. The Mongols from their distant deserts, the Tibetans from their mountain homes, seemed here to draw on some hidden source of power. And when from the far recesses of the temple came the profound booming of great drums, the chanting of monks in deep reverential rhythm, the blare of trumpets, the clash of cymbals, and the long rolling of lighter drums, I seemed to catch a glimpse of the source from which they drew. Music is a proverbially fitter means than speech for expressing the eternal realities; and in the deep rhythmic droning of the chants, the muffled rumbling of the drums, the loud clang and blaring of cymbals and trumpets, I realized this sombre people touching their inherent spirit, and, in the way most fitted to them, giving vent to its mighty surgings panting for expression.

1946 HEINRICH HARRER

Heinrich Harrer (1912–2006) was an Austrian mountaineer who was interned in India during the Second World War. He escaped to Tibet, where he entered Lhasa and befriended the young Dalai Lama, staying from 1946 to 1952.

It was 15 January 1946, when we set out for our last march.... We turned a corner and saw, gleaming in the distance, the golden roofs of the Potala, the winter residence of the Dalai Lama and the most famous landmark of Lhasa. The monument compensated us for much. We felt inclined to go down on our knees like the pilgrims and touch the ground with our foreheads....

Nobody stopped us or bothered about us. We...finally realized that no one, not even a European, was suspect, because no one had ever come to Lhasa without a pass.

As we approached, the Potala towered ever higher before us. As yet we could see nothing of the town itself, which lay behind the hills on which the palace and the school of medicine stood. Then we saw a great gate crowned with three Chorten [stupas], which spans the gap between the two hills and forms the entrance to the city. Our excitement was intense. Now we should know our fate for certain. Almost every book about Lhasa says that sentries are posted here to guard the Holy City. We approached with beating hearts. But there was nothing. No soldiers, no control post, only a few beggars holding out their hands for alms. We mingled with a group of people and walked unhindered through the gateway into the town.... We spoke no word, and to this day I can find no terms to express how overwhelming were our sensations. Our minds, exhausted by hardships, could not absorb the shock of so many and such powerful impressions.

We were soon in front of a turquoise-roofed bridge and saw for the first time the spires of the Cathedral of Lhasa. The sun set and bathed the scene in an unearthly light. Shivering with cold we had to find a lodging, but in Lhasa it is not so simple to walk into a house as into a tent in the Changthang [western Tibetan plateau]. We should probably be reported to the authorities. But we had to try. In the first house we found a dumb servant, who would not listen to us. Next door there was only a maid who screamed for help till her mistress came and begged us to go somewhere else. She said she would be driven out of the quarter if she received us. We did not believe that the government could be as strict as all that, but we did not want to cause her unpleasantness and so went out again. We walked through some narrow streets and found ourselves already at the other side of town. There we came to a house much larger and finer-looking than any we had yet seen, with stables in the courtyard. We hurried in to find ourselves confronted by servants, who abused us and told us to go away. We were not to be moved and unloaded our donkey....

We too felt far from comfortable at the idea of exacting hospitality by force, but we did not move. More and more people were attracted by the din.... We remained deaf to all protestations. Dead-tired and half-starved we sat on the ground by our bundles, indifferent to what might befall us. We only wanted to sit, to rest, to sleep.

The angry cries of the crowd suddenly ceased. They had seen our swollen and blistered feet, and, open-hearted simple folk as they were, they felt pity for us. A woman began it. She was the one who had implored us to leave her house. Now she brought us butter-tea. And now they brought us all sorts of things – *tsampa*, provisions and even fuel. The people wanted to atone for their inhospitable reception. We fell hungrily on the food and for the moment forgot everything else.

Suddenly we heard ourselves addressed in perfect English. We looked up, and though there was not much light to see by, we recognized that the richly clad Tibetan who had spoken to us must be a person of the highest standing. Astonished and happy, we asked him if he was not, perchance, one of the four young Tibetan nobles who had been sent to school at Rugby. He said he was not but that he had passed many years in India. We told him shortly what had happened to us, saying we were Germans, and begging to be taken in. He thought for a moment and then said he could not admit us to his house without the approval of the town magistrate, but he would go to that official and ask for permission.

LONDON

Roman London was founded *c.* AD 43, and built at the northern end of the bridge over the Thames; following the Norman Conquest the city was dominated by the Tower, built by William I from 1066 to subdue the native people. London, and its closely associated city of Westminster — which became the seat of government with the royal palace at Whitehall and home of Parliament — was one of the great cities of medieval and early modern Europe, its cultural importance emphasized by the emergence of Shakespeare's theatre. Following the Great Fire of 1666, the late 17th and 18th centuries saw a building boom both within the City of London itself and expanding its close suburbs in the 'West End', culminating in the major building projects of the Prince Regent (later George IV) including Regent Street and Regent's Park.

Victorian London, a city of 5-6 million people and capital of the global British Empire, became notorious for its extremes of wealth and poverty and for its dank weather, both vividly described by many visitors. In the 20th century, London continued to expand, despite the bombing (Blitz) of 1940; a wave of immigration that began in 1948 with people from the West Indies on the HMT *Empire Windrush* has made London one of the most multicultural cities in the world.

1599 THOMAS PLATTER

Thomas Platter the Younger (1574–1628) was born in Berne, Switzerland, the son of a humanist scholar of the same name. His journals, which cover both his life at home and his travels in England, Spain and France, provide much vivid detail of everyday life. His descriptions of the entertainments of late Elizabethan London, including visits to the Globe Theatre where he saw a play (probably) by Shakespeare, offer important insights into the popular entertainment of the day.

On 21st September after lunch, about two o'clock, I and my party crossed the water, and there in the house with the thatched roof witnessed an excellent performance of the tragedy of the first Emperor Julius Caesar with a cast of some fifteen people; when the play was over, they danced very marvellously and gracefully together as is their wont, two dressed as men and two as women.... Daily at two in the afternoon, London has two, sometimes three plays running in different places, competing with each other, and those which play best obtain most spectators.

The playhouses are so constructed that they play on a raised platform, so that everyone has a good view. There are different galleries and places, however, where the seating is better and more comfortable and therefore more expensive. For whoever cares to stand below only pays one English penny, but if he wishes to sit he enters by another door, and pays another penny, while if he desires to sit in the most comfortable seats which are cushioned, where he not only sees everything well, but can also be seen, then he pays yet another English penny at another door. And during the performance food and drink are carried round the audience, so that for what one cares to pay one may also have refreshment....

There are a great many inns, taverns and beer-gardens scattered about the city, where much amusement may be had with eating, drinking, fiddling and the rest, as for instance in our hostelry, which was visited by players almost daily. And what is particularly curious is that the women as well as the men, in fact more often than they, will frequent the taverns or alehouses for enjoyment. They count it a great honour to be taken there and given wine with sugar to drink; and if one woman only is invited, then she will bring three or four other women along and they gaily toast each other; the husband afterwards thanks him who has given his wife such pleasure, for they deem it a real kindness.

1725 CÉSAR DE SAUSSURE

De Saussure (1703–1783) was from a noble Protestant family in Lausanne, Switzerland. From 1724 he travelled across Europe for fifteen years, including a four-year stay in London from 1725, and a second visit at the end of the 1730s. He published an account of his travels in 1742. An Anglophile, he saw St Paul's Cathedral as, with Hagia Sophia in Constantinople, the most beautiful building in the world, and believed England was marred only by its religious divisions.

A few days after my arrival in London I had an unpleasant experience. Wishing one evening to walk in the park, and having already visited it twice, I thought I could easily find my way there and back alone. The evening was very fine, and I stayed in the park till ten o'clock, enjoying my stroll and the amusing sights around me, the park being very crowded that evening. When I wished to go home again and cross the Mews, a large square occupied by the King's stables, by which way I had come, I found the gates already closed. I immediately set about trying to find out my whereabouts and a new way home.

Unfortunately I could not speak a word of English, and wandered aimlessly about, trying to find my way, unable to ask anyone's help or to hire a hackney coach, as I could not make a driver understand me or give him my address. The only thing I could do was to walk from street to street, in the hopes of recognizing some landmark or other; but after hoping this for about an hour I found myself in an entirely unknown part. It was now past midnight; the streets were empty, and I did not know what to do. I sat down on a seat in front of a shop and longed for day.

After I had been seated there for half an hour or so, to my intense relief two gentlemen happened to go by, and you can imagine my delight when I heard them conversing in French. I almost thought they were angels sent to my help! I hastened to stop them, to explain to them my unpleasant situation. They inquired where I lived, which I could not tell them, the name of the street having completely escaped my memory. After questioning me for some minutes as to what country I came from, how long I had been in London, whether I had any acquaintances, it turned out most fortunately for me that these gentlemen were acquainted with a friend of mine, and that they lived at no great distance from him. They were kind enough to show me the way themselves, and we walked two miles together before I got back to my rooms. Since then I have taken good care not to lose myself again. I am too much afraid of spending such another weary night.

1790 XIA QINGGAO (HSIEH CH'ING KAO)
Xia Qinggao (1765–1822) travelled through western Europe between 1783 and 1797. He worked as a seaman on a Chinese merchant ship. He was illiterate and went blind during the course of his travels; towards the end of his life, he dictated his memoirs.

England is a sparsely settled island, separated from the mainland, with a large number of rich families. The dwelling houses have more than one storey. Maritime commerce is one of the chief occupations of the English, and wherever there is a region in which profits could be reaped by trading, these people strive for them, with the result that their commercial vessels are to be seen on the seven seas. Traders are to be found all over the country. Male inhabitants from 15 to 60 are conscripted into the service of the king as soldiers; a large foreign mercenary army is also maintained. Consequently, although the country is small, it has such a large military force that foreign nations are afraid of it.

Near the sea is London which is one of the largest cities in the country. In this city is a fine system of waterworks. From the river, which flows through the city, water is raised by means of revolving wheels, installed at three different places, and poured into pipes which carry it to all parts of the city. Anyone desirous of securing water would just have to lay a pipe between his house and the water mains, and water would be available. The water tax for each family is calculated on the number of persons in that family.

Men and women all wear white ordinarily; for mourning, however, black is used. The army wears a red uniform. Women wear long dresses that sweep the floor, with the upper part tight and the lower part loose. At the waist is a tight belt with a buckle. Whenever there is a celebration of a festive occasion, then some young and beautiful girls are asked to sing and dance to the accompaniment of music. Girls of rich and noble families learn these arts when they are very young.

1811 LOUIS SIMOND

The French-born writer Louis Simond (1767–1831) lived in America as a young man and, with his English wife, made a two-year journey across the British Isles while the Napoleonic Wars were still raging.

11 January A sort of uniform dinginess seemed to pervade everything, that is, the exterior; for through every door and window the interior of the house, the shops at least, which are most seen, presented, as we drove along, appearances and colours most opposite to this dinginess; everything there was clean, fresh and brilliant. The elevated pavement on each side of the streets full of walkers, out of the reach of carriages, passing swiftly in two lines without awkward interference, each taking to the left. At last a very indifferent street brought us in front of a magnificent temple, which I knew immediately to be St Paul's, and I left the vehicle to examine it. The effect was wonderfully beautiful; but it had less vastness than grace and magnificence. The colour struck me as strange – very black and very white, in patches which envelope sometimes half a column; the base of one; the capital of another; here, a whole row quite black, there, as white as chalk. It seemed as if there had been a fall of snow, and it adhered unequally. The cause of this is evidently the smoke which covers London; but it is difficult to account for its unequal operation. This singularity has not the bad effect which might be expected from it....

My friend conducted me very obligingly back again through the whole town. In our walk we passed several large squares, planted in the middle with large trees and shrubs, over a smooth lawn, intersected with gravel walks; the whole enclosed by an iron railing, which protects these gardens against the populace, but does not intercept the view.... I have heard no cries in the streets, seen few beggars, no obstructions or stoppages of carriages, each taking to the left....

24 January The people of London, I find, are quite as disposed to answer obligingly to the questions of strangers as those of Paris. Whenever I have made inquiries, either in shops, or even from porters, carters and market-women in the streets, I have uniformly received a civil answer, and every information in their power. People do not pull off their hats when thus addressing anybody, as would be indispensable at Paris; a slight inclination of the head, or motion of the hand, is thought sufficient. Foot-passengers walk on with ease and security along the smooth flagstones of the side-pavement. Their eyes, mine at least, are irresistibly attracted by the allurements of the shops....

17 February We have been a whole month in London, and for the last three weeks I have set down nothing in this journal. It is not, as might be supposed, from having been too much taken up, or too little. A French traveller once remarked sagaciously, that there is a malady peculiar to the climate of England, called the catch-cold; this malady, under the modern title of influenza, has recently afflicted all London, and we have been attacked by it. A friend of F. who had come to London on purpose to receive us, has been obliged to fly precipitately; others dare not come.

1826 HERMANN VON PÜCKLER-MUSKAU

On one of his visits to Britain in the 1820s, Hermann von Pückler-Muskau (see page 102) was much taken with the rebuilding of London recently done by the Prince Regent and John Nash.

5–6 October The huge city is...full of fog and dirt, and the macadamized streets are like well-worn roads; the old pavement has been torn up and replaced by small pieces of granite, the interstices between which are filled with gravel; this renders the riding more easy and diminishes the noise, but on the other hand changes the town into a sort of quagmire. Were it not for the admirable *'trottoirs'* people must go on stilts as they do in the Landes near Bordeaux. Englishwomen of the lower classes do indeed wear an iron machine of the kind on their large feet.

London is, however, extremely improved in the direction of Regent Street, Portland Place and the Regent's Park. Now for the first time it has the air of a seat of government and not of an immeasurable metropolis of 'shopkeepers', to use Napoleon's expression. Although poor Mr Nash (an architect who has great influence over the King and is the chief originator of these improvements) has fared so ill at the hands of connoisseurs – and it cannot be denied that his buildings are a jumble of every sort of style, the result of which is rather 'baroque' than original – yet the country is, in my opinion, much indebted to him for conceiving and executing such gigantic designs for the improvement of the metropolis.... It's true, one must not look too nicely into the details. The church, for instance, which serves as *'point de vue'* to Regent Street ends in a ridiculous spire which every part seems at variance with every other. It is a strange architectural monster....

Faultless, on the other hand, is the landscape-gardening part of the park, which also originates with Mr Nash, especially in the disposition of the water. Art has here completely solved the difficult problem of concealing her operations under an appearance of unrestrained nature. You imagine you see a broad river flowing on through luxuriant banks and going off in the distance in several arms, while in fact you are looking upon a small piece of standing, though clear, water created by art and labour. So beautiful a landscape as this, with hills in the distance and surrounded by an enclosure of magnificent houses a league in circuit, is certainly a design worthy of one of the capitals of the world, and when the young trees are grown into majestic giants, will scarcely find a rival.

1854 HARRIET BEECHER STOWE

*The American author and social campaigner Harriet Beecher Stowe (1811–1896)
is best known for her novel* Uncle Tom's Cabin *(1852) about the conditions
of life for slaves in the United States; she also wrote on a wide range of social
issues. In 1854 she visited England on a triumphant tour of lecturing and
campaigning.*

At about seven o'clock we took our carriage to go to the Earl of Carlisle's,
the dinner hour being here somewhere between eight and nine. As we
rode on through the usual steady drizzling rain, from street to street
and square to square, crossing Waterloo Bridge, with its avenue of lamps
faintly visible in the seethy mist, plunging through the heart of the city,
we began to realize something of the immense extent of London.

Altogether the most striking objects that you pass, as you ride in the
evening thus, are the gin shops, flaming and flaring from the most conspicuous positions, with plate-glass windows and dazzling lights, thronged
with men, and women, and children, drinking destruction. Mothers go
there with babies in their arms and take what turns the mother's milk
to poison. Husbands go there and spend the money that their children
want for bread, and multitudes of boys and girls of the age of my own.
In Paris and other European cities, at least the great fisher of souls baits
with something attractive, but in these gin shops men bite at the bare,
barbed hook. There are no garlands, no dancing, no music, no theatricals,
no pretence of social exhilaration, nothing but hogsheads of spirits, and
people going in to drink. The number of them that I passed seemed to
me absolutely appalling.

After long driving we found ourselves coming into the precincts of the
West End and began to feel an indefinite sense that we were approaching
something very grand, though I cannot say that we saw much but heavy,
smoky-walled buildings, washed by the rain. At length we stopped in
Grosvenor Place and alighted. We were shown into an anteroom adjoining
the entrance hall, and from that into an adjacent apartment, where we met
Lord Carlisle. The room had a pleasant, social air, warmed and enlivened
by the blaze of a coal fire and wax candles.

1885 HIPPOLYTE TAINE

The French literary and art critic Taine (1828–1893) was a champion of the naturalistic novelist Emile Zola. Following a visit to England, he published a series of essays on English life in a Paris newspaper.

Sunday in London in the rain: the shops are shut, the streets almost deserted; the aspect is that of an immense and a well-ordered cemetery. The few passers-by under their umbrellas, in the desert of squares and streets, have the look of uneasy spirits who have risen from their graves; it is appalling.

I had no conception of such a spectacle, which is said to be frequent in London. The rain is small, compact, pitiless; looking at it one can see no reason why it should not continue to the end of all things; one's feet churn water, there is water everywhere, filthy water impregnated with an odour of soot. A yellow, dense fog fills the air, sweeps down to the ground; at thirty paces a house, a steamboat appear as spots upon blotting paper. After an hour's walk in the Strand especially, and in the rest of the City, one has the spleen, one meditates suicide. The lofty lines of fronts are of sombre brick, the exudations being encrusted with fog and soot. Monotony and silence; yet the inscriptions on metal or marble speak and tell of the absent master, as in a large manufactory of bone-black closed on account of a death.

A frightful thing is the huge palace in the Strand, which is called Somerset House. Massive and heavy piece of architecture, of which the hollows are inked, the porticoes blackened with soot, where, in the cavity of the empty court, is a sham fountain without water; pools of water on the pavement, long rows of closed windows – what can they possibly do in these catacombs? It seems as if the livid and sooty fog had even befouled the verdure of the parks. But what most offends the eyes are the colonnades, peristyles, Grecian ornaments, mouldings and wreaths of the houses, all bathed in soot; poor antique architecture – what is it doing in such a climate? The flutings and columns in front of the British Museum are be-grimed as if liquid mud had been poured over them.

St Paul's, a kind of Pantheon, has two ranges of columns, the lower range is entirely black, the upper range, recently scraped, is still white, but the white is offensive, coal smoke has already plastered it with its leprosy.

1956 SAM SELVON

*The Trinidad-born writer Sam Selvon (1923–1994) migrated to Britain in 1950,
and his novel* The Lonely Londoners *(1956) described the lives of the West
Indian immigrants of the so-called Windrush generation. Written mainly in
Creole and patois, it includes experimental sections of stream-of-consciousness.*

Oh what a time it is when summer come to the city and all them girls
throw away heavy winter coat and wearing light summer frocks you could
see the legs and shapes that was hiding away from the cold blasts and
you could coast a lime in the park and negotiate ten shillings or a pound
with the sports as the case may be or else they have a particular bench
near the Hyde Park Corner that they call the Play Around Section where
would could go and sit with one of them what a time summer is because
you bound to meet the boys coasting lime in the park and you could go
walking through the gardens and see all them pretty pieces of skin taking
suntan and how the old geezers like the sun they would sit on the benches
and smile everywhere you turn the English people smiling isn't it a lovely
day as if the sun burn away all the tightness and strain that was in their
faces for the winter and on a nice day every manjack and his brother going
to the park with his girl and laying down on the grass and making love in
the winter you would never think that the grass would ever come green
again but if you don't keep your eyes open it look like one day they have
clothes on sometimes walking up to the Bayswater Road from Queensway
you could look on a winter day and see how grim the trees looking and a
sort of fog in the distance though right near to you you ain't have no fog
but that is only deceiving because if someone down the other side lookup
by where you are it would look to them as if it have fog by where you are
and this time so the sun in the sky like a force-ripe orange and it giving
no heat at all and the atmosphere like a sullen twilight hanging over the
big city but it is different too bad when is summer for then the sun shine
for true and the sky blue and a warm wind blowing it look like when is
winter a kind of grey nasty colour does come to the sky and it stay there
and you forget what it was like to see blue skies like back home where blue
sky so common people don't even look up in the air and you feel miserable
and cold but when summer come is fire in the big town big times fete like
stupidness and you have to keep the blood cool for after all them cold and

wet months you like you roaring to go though to tell truth winter don't make much difference to some of the boys they blazing left and right as usual all the year round to talk of all the episodes that Moses had with woman in London that would take bags of ballad....

MADRID

Although the origins of Madrid date to pre-Roman times, the town did not acquire major significance until 1561 when Philip II effectively made it his capital by building the nearby palace-monastery of El Escorial as the seat of his court and government. In the 17th century it became one of the largest cities in Europe and a major cultural centre, much of the finest art now being housed in the Prado. In the 1930s, Madrid suffered a long siege at the hands of the Nationalist forces of Francisco Franco;

its fall in March 1939 led to the end of the civil war. Since the return to democracy in 1975, Madrid has become an international business and cultural centre.

1623 RICHARD WYNN

Richard Wynn (1588–1649) was a politician and courtier to James I and Charles I of England. In 1623 he accompanied the then Prince Charles on a secret and ill-fated journey to the Spanish court to seek the hand of the Infanta. His account of the adventure was not published until a century later.

The place resembles Newmarket, both for the country and for the sharpness of the air. It is but a village, and lately grown to this greatness by this king and his father's residing there. It stands very round, thick with buildings, having neither back-premises nor gardens in all the town.

We were brought in at the far end of the town, which lay near the place we were to alight at. Coming through the streets, I observed most of the buildings to be of brick, and some few of stone, all set forth with balconies of iron, a number of which were gilt. I found likewise that some of their buildings were but of one storey, and the rest five or six storeys high. Enquiring the reason, I was told those low buildings were called in Spanish *Casa de Malitia* – in English, House of Malice. For there the king has the privilege that no man can build above one storey without his leave, and for every upper storey the king is to receive half the rent, to save which charge there be infinite numbers of houses but one storey high....

Towards evening I went to my Lord of Bristol's to wait upon my Lady, and in my return through one street I met at least five hundred coaches. Most of them had all women in, going into the fields (as they usually do at this time of day) to take the air. Of all the women, I dare take my oath, there was not one unpainted – so visibly, that you would thing they rather wore vizards than their own faces. Whether they be handsome or no I cannot tell, unless they did unmask; yet a great number of them have excellent eyes and teeth; the boldest women in the world, for as I passed along, numbers of them called and beckoned to me: whether their impudence or my habit was the cause of it I cannot tell....

175

1855 RICHARD FORD

Richard Ford (1796–1858) was a wealthy English art collector who lived in Spain for some thirty years, writing an anecdotal travel guide in 1843 that was so critical of the Spanish government and French behaviour during the Peninsular War that publication was withdrawn while it was at the printing press. An expurgated edition was published two years later.

It is quite refreshing on the Prado to see what good friends all Spaniards seem to be. There is no end to compliments and Judas kissings, but deep and deadly are the jealousies which lurk beneath. And double-edged are the ideal knives grasped by the murders of the wish, for *muchos besan a manos, que quieren ver cortadas* [many kiss the hand where they would seek to plunge the knife]: arsenic mixed with honey is not more sweet. All this is very Roman.

1857 WILLIAM CULLEN BRYANT

The American poet William Cullen Bryant (1794–1878) spent much of his career in New York, where he edited the Evening Post *and was a major influence on the creation of Central Park. In 1857 he visited Spain and North Africa, and published his letters home.*

15 November There are many native Spaniards who tell you that seeing Madrid is not seeing Spain. 'Madrid,' said a very intelligent person to me, 'is not a Spanish city; it is French – it is inhabited by *afrancesados* people who take pains to acquire French tastes, and who follow French fashions and modes of living.... If you want to see Spain, you must seek it in the provinces, where the national character is not yet lost; you will find Spain in Andalusia, in Estremadura, in the Asturias, in Galicia, in Biscay, in Aragon; but do not look for it in Madrid.'...

One of the first places we were taken to see on our arrival in Madrid was the Prado. Here, beyond the pavements and yet within the gates of the capital, is a spacious pleasure-ground, formed into long alleys, by rows of trees, extending north and south, almost out of sight. In the midst, between the colossal figures of white marble which form the fountain of Cybele on the north, to those of the fountain of Neptune in the other direction, is an area of ten or twelve acres, beaten as hard and smooth as a threshing floor, by the feet of those who daily frequent it. Into this, two noble streets, the finest in Madrid, widening as they approach it, the Calle de Alcalá and the Calle de Atocha, pour every afternoon in fine weather, at this season, a dense throng of the well-dressed people of the capital, to walk up and down, till the twilight warns them home. They move with a leisurely pace from the lions of Cybele to the sea-monsters of Neptune, and then turning, measure the ground over again and again, till the proper number of hours is consumed. The men are unexceptionably dressed, with nicely brushed hats, glittering boots and fresh gloves; the favorite color of their kids is yellow; the ladies are mostly in black, with the black veil of the country resting on their shoulders; they wear the broadest possible hoops, and skirts that trail in the dust, and they move with a certain easy dignity which is thought to be peculiar to the nation. On these occasions, dress of a light color is a singularity, and a bonnet attracts observation. Close to the walk is the promenade for carriages, which pass slowly over the ground, up one side and down the other, till those who sit in them are tired. Here are to be seen the showy liveries of the grandees and opulent *hidalgos* of Spain, and of the foreign ambassadors. It seemed to me that the place was thronged on the day that I first saw it, but this the Spanish gentleman who conducted us thither absolutely denied. 'There is nobody here,' said he, 'nobody at all. The weather is chilly and the sky threatening; you should come in fine weather.' The threat of the sky was fulfilled before we could get home, and we reached the door of our hotel in a torrent of rain....

Here at Madrid they live upon very unceremonious terms with each other, dropping in at each other's houses in the evening, and calling each other by their Christian names, without the prefix of Don or Doña. They get perhaps, if anything, a cup of tea or chocolate, and a *biscocho*. I was several times at the house of a literary lady of Madrid and saw there some of the most eminent men of Spain, statesmen, jurists, ecclesiastics, authors, leaders of the liberal party and chiefs of the absolutists, who came and went, with almost as little ceremony as if they met on the Prado. The *tertúlia* is something more than this; there is more dress, illumination, numbers; but the refreshments are almost as frugally dispensed. The stranger in Spain does not find himself excluded from native society, as he does in Italy, but is at once introduced to it, on the same footing with the natives.

I find one objection, however, to the social arrangements of Madrid: that they make the evenings frightfully long.

1862 HANS CHRISTIAN ANDERSEN

The Danish writer Andersen (1805–1875), best known for his fairy stories, also wrote travel books, notably about Scandinavia and the Iberian Peninsula, written in conversational tone with occasional philosophical diversions.

In the north, in the cloudy land, the wind sweeps across the open strand, and through the corner of every street. There are many corners, and a poet may dwell in each of them. Is there one well born and brought up, he delights in the beautiful, he is full of longing after romantic Spain. Let him come here, let them all come direct to Madrid, at any period of the year they choose! If that be in summer, they will be roasted alive by the sun; if it be in winter, they will receive the icicles' kiss, they will be favoured with frosted fingers, and thawing snow into their very galoshes. And if they remain here, what have they seen of Spain? Madrid has none of the characteristics of a Spanish town, not to mention the capital of Spain. That it became such, was a fancy of Philip II, and he would assuredly have frozen and perspired for this, his royal whim.

One very great advantage, however, this place possesses the first of its kind; it is the picture gallery – a pearl, a treasure worthy to be sought and deserving a journey to Madrid to see it. During our stay here, there was another very charming place of resort open – the Italian opera; but when you have mentioned this and the picture gallery, you have named what are the most remarkable and most interesting places for strangers. Outside all was raw and damp, but within the theatre you sat as if in a warm bath, amid smoke and steam; the thick mist from the numerous cigars the people smoked between the acts, and the smell of the gas, pervaded even the boxes. Yet, notwithstanding these disagreeables, we remained until after midnight, fascinated by the richness of the tones with which Signora La Grange astonished and delighted us....

Madrid reminds me of a camel that has fallen down in the desert: I felt as if I was sitting on its hump and though I could see far around, I was not sitting comfortably.

Besides the Puerto del Sol, the plaza in which we resided, there are in Madrid some other plazas which ought to be mentioned, and which has each its peculiarity. The prettiest is the large Plaza de Oriente, planted with trees and bushes; it is situated near the palace. Under the leafy trees stand here, in a circle, statues of the kings and queens of Leon and Castile. The palace itself is a large, heavy building; but from its terrace, and even from part of the plaza, there is an extensive and lovely view over the garden and the fields down to the river Manzanares, and of the hills behind the Escurial; they were now quite covered with snow, and looked very picturesque when the atmosphere was clear. The Plaza Major, which is at no great distance, has quite an opposite character; one feels one's self, as it were, in it, confined in a prison yard; but it is unquestionably the most peculiar of all the plazas in Madrid. It savours of the Middle Ages; is more long than broad; and has in its centre a bronze statue of Philip III on horseback. The lofty arcade around it contains but small, insignificant shops, where are sold bonnets, woollen goods and hardware. In former days, this plaza was the scene of the bloody bullfights and the terrible autos-da-fé. Even now stands here the old building, with its turrets and curiously formed window frames, from the balconies of which the Spanish kings and courts beheld the bullfight, or saw the unfortunate victims of the Inquisition roasted alive. The little clock which gave the death-signal hangs still upon the wall.

I always observed a number of soldiers in this plaza. They stood in groups, looking at different jugglers who, during the whole day, were performing here. In the evening poor boys kindled a large fire here to warm themselves. On the steps leading up to the arcade sat a couple of wretched-looking objects, an old woman in rags, and a grey-haired old man wrapped up in a dirty Spanish cloak. Each of them were playing on some little instrument, which was quite out of tune, to which they sang in husky voices equally out of tune. Not one of the people passing by gave them anything. Nevertheless, they continued to sit where they were, as if they had grown fast to the damp stone, in the bitterly cold weather, and perhaps they were singing about that hero, El Cid, or of happy love.

1916 LEON TROTSKY

The Russian revolutionary Leon Trotsky (1879–1940) went into exile during the First World War and spent a brief period in Spain. He recounted in his autobiography My Life *(1930) how he passed a week at liberty and alone in Madrid before being sent to prison and then expelled from the country.*

From San Sebastian, where I was delighted by the sea and appalled by the prices, I went to Madrid and found myself in a city in which I knew no one, not a single soul, and no one knew me. And since I did not speak Spanish, I could not have been lonelier even in the Sahara or in the Peter-Paul fortress. There remained only the language of art. The two years of war had made one forget that such a thing as art still existed. With the eagerness of a starved man, I viewed the priceless treasures of the Museum of Madrid and felt again the 'eternal' element in this art. The Rembrandts, the Riberas. The paintings of Bosch were works of genius in their naive joy of life. The old caretaker gave me a lens so that I might see the tiny figures of the peasants, little donkeys and dogs in the pictures of Miel. Here there was no feeling of war, everything securely in its place. The colours had their own life, uncontrolled.

This is what I wrote in my notebook in the museum: 'Between us and the old artists – without in the least obscuring them or lessening their importance – there grew up before the war a new art, more intimate, more individualistic, one with greater nuances, at once more subjective and more intense. The war, by its mass passions and suffering, will probably wash away this mood and this manner for a long time – but it can never mean a simple return to the old form, however beautiful – to the anatomic and botanic perfection, to the Rubens thigh (though thighs are likely to play a great role in the new post-war art, which will be so eager for life). It is difficult to prophesy, but out of the unprecedented experiences filling the lives of almost all civilized human beings, surely a new art must be born.'

MECCA

The ancient city in the western Arabian Peninsula was the birthplace of Muhammad and site of his revelations of the Quran, so that the city in present-day Saudi Arabia has always been the focus of Muslim daily prayers and — in particular, the black granite structure of the Kaaba (House of God) at the heart of its main mosque — of the Hajj, or pilgrimage, undertaken by every Muslim at least once in a lifetime. No non-believer is permitted to enter the city.

1326 IBN BATTUTA

The famous North African traveller Ibn Battuta (see page 72) visited Mecca on pilgrimage four times, the first in 1326.

We then set out from Medina towards Mecca, and halted near the mosque of Dhu'l-Hulayfa, five miles away. It was at this point that the Prophet assumed the pilgrim garb and obligations, and here too I divested myself of my tailored clothes, bathed, and putting on the pilgrim's garment I prayed and dedicated myself to the pilgrimage.... Thence we travelled through 'Usfan to the Bottom of Marr, a fertile valley with numerous palms and a spring supplying a stream from which the district is irrigated.

We set out at night from this blessed valley, with hearts full of joy at reaching the goal of our hopes, and in the morning arrived at the City of Surety, Mecca (may God ennoble her!), where we immediately entered the holy sanctuary and began the rites of pilgrimage.

The inhabitants of Mecca are distinguished by many excellent and noble activities and qualities, by their beneficence to the humble and weak, and by their kindness to strangers. When any of them makes a feast, he begins by giving food to the religious devotees who are poor and without resources, inviting them first with kindness and delicacy. The majority of these unfortunates are to be found by the public bakehouses, and when anyone has his bread baked and takes it away to his house, they follow him and he gives each one of them some share of it, sending away none disappointed. Even if he has but a single loaf, he gives away a third or a half of it, cheerfully and without any grudge.

Another good habit of theirs is this. The orphan children sit in the bazaar, each with two baskets, one large and one small. When one of the townspeople comes to the bazaar and buys cereals, meat and vegetables, he hands them to one of these boys, who puts the cereals in one basket and the meat and vegetables in the other and takes them to the man's house, so that his meal may be prepared. Meanwhile the man goes about his devotions and his business. There is no instance of any of the boys having ever abused their trust in this matter, and they are given a fixed fee of a few coppers.

The Meccans are very elegant and clean in their dress, and most of them wear white garments, which you always see fresh and snowy. They use a great deal of perfume and kohl and make free use of toothpicks of green arak-wood. The Meccan women are extraordinarily beautiful and very pious and modest. They too make great use of perfumes to such a degree that they will spend the night hungry in order to buy perfumes with the price of their food. They visit the mosque every Thursday night, wearing their finest apparel; and the whole sanctuary is saturated with the smell of their perfume. When one of these women goes away the odour of the perfume clings to the place after she has gone.

1503 LUDOVICO OF VARTHEMA

Ludovico of Varthema (c. 1470–1517), an adventurer from Bologna, Italy, became the first Westerner to visit Mecca on pilgrimage. It needed all his ingenuity to escape once he had been identified as an Italian.

On 18th May we entered into Mecca from the north, and afterwards we descended into the plain.... We found the caravan from Cairo, which had arrived eight days before us.... In the said caravan there were sixty-four thousand camels and one hundred Mamluks.... Truly I never saw so many people collected in one spot as during the twenty days I remained there. Of these people some had come for the purposes of trade, and some on pilgrimage for their pardon....

In the midst of the city there is a very beautiful temple, similar to the Colosseum of Rome, but not made of such large stones, but of burnt bricks, and it is round in the same manner; it has ninety or one hundred doors around it, and is arched, and has many of these doors. On entering the temple you descend ten or twelve steps of marble, and here and there...stand men who sell jewels, and nothing else. And when you have descended the said steps you find the said temple all around, and...the walls, covered with gold. And under the arches there stand about 4,000 or 5,000 persons, men and women, which persons sell all kinds of odoriferous things; the greater part are powders for preserving human bodies, because pagans come there from all parts of the world. Truly, it would not be possible to describe the sweetness and the odours which are smelt within this temple. It appears like a spicery full of musk, and of other most delicious odours....

Having gone to make some purchases for my captain, I was recognized by a Moor who looked me in the face and said to me: 'Where are you from?'

I answered: 'I am a Moor.' He replied: 'You are not telling the truth.' I said to him: 'By the head of Mahomet, I am a Moor.' He answered: 'Come to my house,' and I went with him. When I had arrived at his house, he spoke to me in Italian, and told me he knew that I was not a Moor, and that he had been in Genoa and in Venice, and gave me proofs of it. When I heard this, I told him that I was a Roman, and that I had become a Mameluke at Cairo. He was much pleased, and treated me with very great honour.... When he saw that I displayed hostility to the Christians, he showed me yet greater honour, and told me everything point by point.... I said to him: 'O, friend, I beg you to tell me some mode or way by which I may escape from the caravan, because my intention is to go to find those beings who are hostile to the Christians; for I assure you that, if they knew what I am capable of, they would send to find me even to Mecca.' He answered me: 'By the faith of our prophet what can you do?' I answered him that I was the most skilful maker of large mortars in the world. Hearing this he said: 'Mahomet be ever praised, who has sent us such a man to serve the Moors and God.' So he concealed me in his house with his wife. And he begged me that I would induce our captain to drive out from Mecca fifteen camels laden with spices, and this he did in order not to pay thirty seraphim to the sultan for the toll. I replied that if he would save me in this house, I would enable him to carry off a hundred camels if he had so many, for the Mamluks have this privilege. And when he heard this he was much pleased.

1767 CARSTEN NIEBUHR

The German mathematician and explorer Carsten Niebuhr (1733–1815) was the sole survivor of a scientific expedition in Arabia in 1762–67 sent by the Danish king. Though unable to visit Mecca itself, he described what he gleaned about it from others who had.

This city is situated in a dry and barren tract of country, a full day's journey from Jidda.... In the summer months, the heat is excessive; and, to avoid and moderate it as much as possible the inhabitants carefully shut their windows and water the streets. There have been instances of persons suffocated in the middle of the streets by the burning wind called Samoum or Samieli.

As a great part of the first nobility in Hedjas live at Mecca, the buildings are better here than in any other city in Arabia. Among its elegant edifices, the most remarkable is the famous Kaba or house of God, which was held in high veneration by the Arabians even before the days of Mahomet.

My curiosity would have led me to see this sacred and singular structure; but no Christian dares enter Mecca. Not that there is any such express prohibition in the laws of Mahomet, or that liberal-minded Mahometans could be offended; but the prejudices of the people in general...make them think that it would be profaned by the feet of infidel Christians. They even persuade themselves that Christians are restrained from approaching it by a supernatural power. They tell of an infidel who audaciously advanced within sight of Mecca but was there attacked by all the dogs of the city, and was so struck with the miracle, and with the august aspect of the Kaba, that he immediately became Mussulman....

Although the Mahometans permit not Europeans to visit Mecca, they make no difficulty of describing the Kaba to them. I even obtained a drawing of that holy place, which I had afterwards an opportunity of correcting, from another draught by a Turkish painter. This painter gained his livelihood by making such draughts of the Kaba and selling them to pilgrims.

To judge from those designs...the Kaba must be an awkward shapeless building; a fort of square tower it is, covered on the top with a piece of black gold-embroidered silk stuff. This stuff is wrought at Kahira, and changed every year at the expense of the Turkish sultan. The gutters upon this building are of pure gold.

What seems to be most magnificent about this sacred edifice, is the arcades around the square in which the Kaba stands. They speak, in terms of high admiration, of a vast number of lamps and candlesticks of gold and silver with which those arcades are illuminated. However, even by these accounts...the riches of the Kaba are far from equal in value to what is displayed in some Catholic churches in Europe.

In the Kaba is particularly one singular relic, which is regarded with extreme veneration. This is the famous black stone, said to have been brought by the angel Gabriel.... The stone, according to the account of the clergy, was, at first, of a bright white colour, so as to dazzle the eyes at the distance of four days journey; but it wept so long and so abundantly for the sins of mankind, that it became at length opaque, and at last absolutely black....

The Arabs venerate the Kaba, as having been built by Abraham, and having been his house of prayer. Within the same enclosure is the well of Zemzem, valued for the excellence of its water, and no less for its miraculous origin: Hagar, when banished by her master, set little Ismael down here while she should find some water to quench his thirst. Returning after an unsuccessful search, she was surprised to see a spring bursting up from the ground between the child's legs. That spring is the present well of Zemzem.

Another ornament of the Kaba, is a row of metal pillars surrounding it. These pillars are joined by chains, on which hang a vast number of silver lamps. The porticoes or arcades above mentioned are designed to protect the pilgrims from the torrid heat of the day.... The merchants, of whom great numbers accompany the caravans, expose their wares for sale under those arcades.

1853 RICHARD BURTON

The British explorer and translator Richard Burton (1821–1890) sensationally visited Mecca in 1853, disguised as an Afghan Muslim, and was able to measure and sketch the Kaaba, at great risk to his life.

After a journey of twenty hours across the desert, we passed the barriers which mark the outermost limit of the sacred city, and ascending some giant steps, pitched our tents on a plain, or rather plateau, surrounded by barren rock, some of which, distant, but a few yards, mask from view the birthplace of the Prophet. It was midnight; a few drops of rain were falling, and lightning played around us. Day after day we had watched its brightness from the sea, and many a faithful haji had pointed *out* to his companions those fires which were Heaven's witness to the sanctity of the spot. 'Alhamdu Lillah!' Thanks be to God! we were now at length to gaze upon the Kiblah, to which *every* Mussulman has turned in prayer since before the days of Muhammed, and which, for long ages before the birth of Christianity was reverenced by the Patriarchs of the East. Soon after dawn arose from our midst the shout of 'Labbaik! Labbaik!' and passing between the rocks, we found ourselves in the main street of Mecca, and approached the 'Gateway of Salvation', one of the thirty-nine portals of the 'Temple of Salvation'.

On crossing the threshold we entered a vast unroofed quadrangle, a mighty amplification of the Palais Royal, having on each side of its four sides a broad colonnade, divided into three aisles by a multitude of slender columns, and rising to the height of about thirty feet. Surmounting each arch of the colonnade is a small dome: in all there are a hundred and twenty, and at different points arise seven minarets, dating from various epochs, and of somewhat varying altitudes and architecture. The numerous pigeons which have their home within the temple have been believed never to alight upon any portion of its roof, thus miraculously testifying to the holiness of the building. This marvel, however, of late years having been suspended, many discern another omen of the approach of the long-predicted period when unbelievers shall desecrate the hallowed soil.

In the centre of the square area rises the far-famed Kabah, the funereal shade of which contrasts vividly with the sunlit walls and precipices of the town. It is a cubical structure of massive stone, the upper two-thirds of which are mantled by a black cloth embroidered with silver, and the lower portion hung with white linen. At a distance of several yards it is surrounded by a balustrade provided with lamps, which are lighted in the evening, and the space thus enclosed is the circuit ground along which, day and night, crowds of pilgrims, performing the circular ceremony of Tawaf, realize the idea of perpetual motion. We at once advanced to the black stone embedded in the angle of the Kabah, kissed it, and exclaimed 'Bismillah wa Allahu Akbar' – 'In God's name, and God is Greatest.' Then we commenced the usual seven rounds, three at a walking pace, and four at a brisk trot. Next followed two prayer-flections at the tomb of Abraham, after which we drank of the water of Zamzam, said to be the same which quenched the thirst of Hagar's exhausted son.

Besides the Kabah, eight minor structures adorn the quadrangle, the well of Zamzam, the library, the clockroom, the triangular staircase and four ornamental resting-places for the orthodox sects of Hanafi, Shafi, Maliki and Hanbali.

We terminated our morning duties by walking and running seven times along the streets of Safa and Marwa, so named from the flight of seven steps at each of its extremities. After a few days spent in visiting various places of interest, such as the slave-market and forts, and the houses of the Prophet and the caliphs Ali and Abu Bakr, we started on our six hours' journey to the mountain of Arifat, an hour's sojourn at which, even in a state of insensibility, confers the rank of *haji*. It is a mountain spur of about a hundred and fifty feet in height, presenting an artificial appearance from the wall encircling it and the terrace on its slope, from which the *iman* delivers a sermon before the departure of his congregation for Mecca. His auditors were, indeed, numerous, their tents being scattered over two or three miles of the country....

On 5th June, at sunset, commencing our return, we slept at the village of Muzdalifah, and there gathered and washed seven pebbles of the size of peas, to be flung at three piles of whitewashed masonry known as the Satans of Muna. We acquitted ourselves satisfactorily of this duty on the festival of 6th June, the 10th day of the Arabian month Zu'lhijah. Each of us then sacrificed a sheep, had his hair and nails cut, exchanged the *ikram* for his best apparel, and embracing his friends, paid them the compliments of the season. The two following days the Great, the Middle and the Little Satan were again pelted, and, bequeathing to the unfortunate inhabitants of Muna the unburied and odorous remains of nearly a hundred thousand animals, we returned, eighty thousand strong, to Mecca. A week later, having helped to insult the tumulus of stones which marks, according to popular belief, the burial place of Abulahab, the unbeliever, who we learn from the Koran, has descended into hell with his wife, gatherer of sticks, I was not sorry to relinquish a shade temperature of 120 degrees and wend my way to Jeddah en route for England, after delegating to my brethren the recital of a prayer in my behalf at the Tomb of the Prophet in Medina.

MEXICO CITY

Mexico City was established in the early 16th century when the Spanish conquistadors captured the old Aztec capital of Tenochtitlán, whose size and prosperity amazed them. Nevertheless, they razed the city, drained the site and built their own colonial city on top.

In the 19th century, Mexico City, capital of an independent nation from 1821, displayed the relics of its colonial past, with Baroque public buildings, many monasteries and little industry.

The capital was the scene of intense fighting during the Mexican Revolution (1910-20), but the population expanded with many immigrants from the countryside. Like Havana, it became a playground for wealthy Americans.

1520 HERNÁN CORTÉS

Hernán Cortés (1485–1547), leader of the Spanish conquistadors in Mexico, described the impressive Aztec capital Tenochtitlán in vivid terms in a letter to his king, Charles I of Spain (better known as Holy Roman Emperor Charles V).

The great city is situated in a salt lake, two leagues from the mainland. There are four entrances, formed by artificial causeways, each as wide as two spears' length. The city is as large as Seville or Cordoba; its principal streets are very wide and straight; some of these, and all the inferior ones, are half land and half water, and are navigated by canoes. All the streets at intervals have openings through which the water flows, crossing from one street to another; and at these openings there are wide bridges, well built of timber of great strength; on many of these bridges ten horses can go abreast....

This city has many public squares where markets are held continuously. There is one square twice as large as that of the city of Salamanca, surrounded by porticoes where more than 60,000 souls come each day to buy and sell; and where are found all kinds of merchandise: food, jewels of gold and silver, lead, brass, copper, tin, precious stones, bones, shells, snails and feathers. There are also wrought and unwrought stone, bricks burnt and unburnt, timber hewn and unhewn, of different sorts. There is a street for game birds; they also sell the skins of some birds of prey, with their feathers, head, beak and claws. There are also sold rabbits, hares, deer and little dogs raised for eating. There is an herb street, where may be obtained all sorts of roots and medicinal herbs. There are apothecaries' shops, where prepared medicines, liquids, ointments and plasters are sold; barbers' shops, where they wash and shave the head; and restaurateurs.... Wood and coal are seen in abundance, and earthenware braziers for burning coals; mats for beds, seats, halls and bedrooms.

There are all kinds of green vegetable, fruits, honey and wax from bees, and from the stalks of maize which are as sweet as the sugar-cane; honey is also extracted from the plant called maguey, which is superior to sweet or new wine; from the same plant they extract sugar and wine. Skeins of cotton thread of all colours are sold in one quarter of the market, which resembles the silk market at Granada, although the former is supplied more abundantly. Painters' colours, as numerous as can be found in Spain, and as fine shades; deerskins dressed and undressed, dyed different colours; earthenware of a large size and excellent quality; large and small jars, jugs, pots, bricks and endless variety of vessels, all made of fine clay, and all or most of them glazed and painted; maize or Indian corn, in the grain and in the form of bread; patés of birds and fish; great quantities of fish – fresh, salt, cooked and uncooked; the eggs of hens, geese and other birds in great abundance, and cakes made of eggs; finally, everything that can be found throughout the whole country is sold in the markets....

This city contains many temples, or houses, for their idols, very handsome edifices; in the principal ones reside religious persons of each sect. They dress in black, and never cut or comb their hair from the time they enter the priesthood until they leave it; and all the sons of the principal inhabitants are placed in the temples and wear the same dress from the age of seven or eight years until they are married....

Among these temples there is one which far surpasses all the rest, whose grandeur no human tongue can describe, for within its lofty wall there is room for a town of 500 families. The enclosure contains handsome edifices, with large halls and corridors, in which the priests reside. There are forty towers, lofty and well built, the largest of which has fifty steps leading to its main body, and is higher than the tower of the principal tower of the church at Seville....

Along one of the causeways that lead into the city are laid two pipes, constructed of masonry, each of which is two paces in width, and about five feet in height. An abundant supply of excellent water is conveyed by one of these pipes and distributed about the city, where it is used by the inhabitants for drink and other purposes. The other pipe is kept empty until the former requires to be cleansed, when the water is let into it and continues to be used till the cleaning is finished. As the water has to be carried over bridges on account of the salt water crossing its route, reservoirs resembling canals are constructed on the bridges, through which the fresh water is conveyed.... People carry fresh water in canoes through all the streets for sale, taking it from the aqueduct in the following manner: the canoes pass under the bridges on which the reservoirs are placed, when men stationed above fill them with water, for which service they are paid.

1839 FRANCES CALDERÓN DE LA BARCA

The Scottish writer Frances Calderón de la Barca (see page 126) moved to Mexico City in 1839 and stayed for two years. Her book Life in Mexico *was based on letters she wrote; it was not popular in Mexico itself but provides a vivid picture of the young nation.*

At length we arrived at the heights looking down upon the great valley, celebrated in all parts of the world, with its framework of everlasting mountains, its snow-crowned volcanoes, great lakes and fertile plains, all surrounding the favoured city of Montezuma, the proudest boast of his conqueror, once of Spain's many diadems the brightest. But the day had overcast, nor is this the most favourable road for entering Mexico. The innumerable spires of the distant city were faintly seen. The volcanoes were enveloped in clouds, all but their snowy summits, which seemed like marble domes towering into the sky. But as we strained our eyes to look into the valley, it all appeared to me rather like a vision of the Past than the actual breathing Present. The curtain of Time seemed to roll back, and to discover to us the great panorama that burst upon the eye of Cortes when he first looked down upon the tableland; the king-loving, God-fearing conqueror, his loyalty and religion so blended after the fashion of ancient Spain, that it were hard to say which sentiment exercised over him the greater sway. The city of Tenochtitlan, standing in the midst of the five great lakes, upon verdant and flower-covered islands, a western Venice, with thousands of boats gliding swiftly along its streets, long lines of low houses, diversified by the multitudes of pyramidal temples, the Teocalli, or houses of God – canoes covering the mirrored lakes – the lofty trees, the flowers and the profusion of water now wanting to the landscape – the whole fertile valley enclosed by its eternal hills and snow-crowned volcanoes – what scenes of wonder and of beauty to burst upon the eyes of these wayfaring men!...

But my thoughts...were soon recalled to the present by the arrival of an officer in full uniform at the head of his troop, who came out by order of the government to welcome the bearer of the olive-branch from ancient Spain, and had been on horseback since the day before, expecting our arrival. As it had begun to rain, the officer, Colonel Miguel Andrade, accepted our offer of taking shelter in the diligence [stagecoach]. We had now a great troop galloping along with us, and had not gone far before we perceived that in spite of the rain, and that it already began to grow dusk, there were innumerable carriages and horsemen forming an immense crowd, all coming out to welcome us. Shortly after, the diligence was stopped, and we were requested to get into a very splendid carriage, all crimson and gold, with the arms of the republic, the eagle and nopal [cactus], embroidered in gold on the roof inside, and drawn by four handsome white horses. In the midst of this immense procession of troops, carriages and horsemen, we made our entry into the city of Montezuma....

What most attracts our attention are the curious and picturesque groups of figures which we see from the windows – men bronze-colour, with nothing but a piece of blanket thrown round them, carrying lightly on their heads earthen basins, precisely the colour of their own skin, so that they look altogether like figures of terra cotta: these basins filled with sweetmeats or white pyramids of grease (*mantequilla*); women with *rebosos*, short petticoats of two colours, generally all in rags, yet with a lace border appearing on their under garment: no stockings, and dirty white satin shoes, rather shorter than their small brown feet; gentlemen on horseback with their Mexican saddles and sarapes, lounging *léperos*, moving bundles of rags, coming to the windows and begging with a most piteous but false-sounding whine, or lying under the arches and lazily inhaling the air and the sunshine, or sitting at the door for hours basking in the sun or under the shadow of the wall; Indian women, with their tight petticoat of dark stuff and tangled hair, plaited with red ribbon, laying down their baskets to rest, and meanwhile deliberately examining the hair of their copper-coloured offspring. We have enough to engage our attention for the present....

I made my debut in Mexico by going to mass in the cathedral. We drove through the Alameda, near which we live, and admired its noble trees, flowers and fountains, all sparkling in the sun....

The carriage drew up in front of the cathedral, built upon the site of part of the ruins of the great temple of the Aztecs; of that pyramidal temple, constructed by *Ahuitzotli*, the sanctuary so celebrated by the Spaniards, and which comprehended with all its different edifices and sanctuaries, the ground on which the cathedral now stands, together with part of the plaza and streets adjoining....

We entered the Christian edifice, which covers an immense space of ground, is of the Gothic form, with two lofty ornamented towers, and is still immensely rich in gold, silver and jewels. A balustrade running through it, which was brought from China, is said to be very valuable, but seems to me more curious than beautiful. It is a composition of brass and silver. Not a soul was in the sacred precincts this morning but miserable *léperos*, in rags and blankets, mingled with women in ragged *rebosos*.... The floor is so dirty that one kneels with a feeling of horror, and an inward determination to effect as speedy a change of garments afterwards as possible. Besides, many of my Indian neighbours were engaged in an occupation which I must leave to your imagination; in fact, relieving their heads from the pressure of the colonial system, or rather, eradicating and slaughtering the colonists, who swarm there like the emigrant Irish in the United States. I was not sorry to find myself once more in the pure air after mass; and have since been told that except on peculiar occasions, and at certain hours, few ladies perform their devotions in the cathedral. I shall learn all these particulars in time.

1938 GRAHAM GREENE

In 1938, Greene (see page 128), a well-known Catholic, visited Mexico to report on the effects of a recent anticlerical purge. His account was published as The Lawless Roads *(1939).*

The shape of most cities can be simplified as a cross; not so Mexico City, elongated and lopsided on its mountain plateau. It emerged like a railway track from a tunnel – the obscure narrow streets lying to the west of the Zócalo, the great square in which the cathedral sails like an old rambling Spanish galleon close to the National Palace. Behind, in the tunnel, the university quarter – high dark stony streets like those of the Left Bank in Paris – fades among the tramways and dingy shops into red-light districts and street markets. In the tunnel you become aware that Mexico City is older and less Central European than it appears at first – a baby alligator tied to a pail of water; a whole family of Indians eating their lunch on the sidewalk edge; railed off among the drug-stores and the tram-lines, near the cathedral, a portion of the Aztec temple Cortés destroyed....

Out of the Zócalo our imaginary train emerges into sunlight. The Cinco de Mayo and the Francisco Madero, fashionable shopping streets, run like twin tracks, containing smart Mayfair stations – the best antique shops, American teashops, Sanborn's, towards the Palace of Arts and the Alameda. Tucked behind them is the goods track – Tacuba – where you can buy your clothes cheap if you don't care much for appearances. After the Palace of Arts the parallel tracks are given different names as they run along beside the trees and fountains of Moctezuma's park – the Avenida Juárez full of tourist shops and milk bars and little stalls of confectionery, and the Avenida Hidalgo, where hideous funeral wreaths are made, ten feet high and six across, of mauve and white flowers. Then Hidalgo wanders off where no one troubles to go and Juárez is closed by the great Arch of the Republic, which frames a sky-sign of Moctezuma Beer, and the Hotel Regis, where the American Rotarians go and the place where they draw the lottery. We turn south-west into the Paseo de la Reforma, the great avenue Maximilian made, running right out of the city to the gates of Chapultepec, past Columbus and Guatemoc and the glassy Colon Café, like the Crystal Palace, where President Huerta, the man who shot Madero and fled from Carranza, used to get drunk (when he became helpless, they turned out the lights and people passing said, 'The President's going to bed'; it wouldn't have been a good thing to see the President of Mexico carried to his car), on past the Hotel Reforma and the Statue of Independence, all vague aspiration and expensive golden wings, to the lions at the gates. And on either side branch off the new smart streets, pink and blue wash and trailing flowers, where the diplomats live, and the smell of sweets blows heavily along from Juárez....

I changed my hotel – it was too brand-new – for a dustier, noisier, more native brand, though it called itself by an Anglo-Saxon name. Here I got a room with a shower and three meals a day for 5.50 pesos, say, seven shillings. Lunch consisted of six courses with a cocktail and coffee. Music was supplied through the street door; a succession of marimba players took up a collection – the marimba, gentle, sentimental, with the pleasing tinkle of a music-box. Beggars came in all through the meal (why not? It is a good strategic time) and people selling sheet music, and even rosaries, and of course lottery tickets. You couldn't get away from lottery tickets, even in the courtyard of the cathedral. I shall always associate Mexico City with the sick smell of sweets and the lottery sellers. The lottery is the next best thing to hope of heaven – there is a draw every week, with first prizes of twenty-five thousand, fifty thousand, and sometimes one hundred thousand pesos....

El Retiro is the swagger cabaret of Socialist Mexico, all red and gold and little balloons filled with gas, and chicken *à la* king. A film star at one table and a famous singer, and rich men everywhere. American couples moved sedately across the tiny dance floor while the music wailed, the women with exquisite hair and gentle indifference, and the middle-aged American businessmen like overgrown schoolboys a hundred years younger than their young women. Then the cabaret began – a Mexican dancer with great bold thighs, and the American women lost a little of their remote superiority. They were being beaten at the sexual game – somebody who wasn't beautiful and remote was drawing the attention of their men. They got vivacious and talked a little shrilly and powdered their faces, and suddenly appeared very young and inexperienced and unconfident, as the great thighs moved. But their turn came when the famous tenor sang. The American men lit their pipes and talked all through the song and then clapped heartily to show that they didn't care, and the women closed their compacts and listened – avidly. It wasn't poetry they were listening to or music (the honeyed words about roses and love, the sweet dim nostalgic melody), but the great emotional orgasm in the throat. They called out for a favourite song, and the rich plump potent voice wailed on – interminably, a whole night of love. This was not popular art, or intellectual art – it was, I suppose, capitalist art. And this, too, was Socialist Mexico.

MOSCOW

Moscow grew up around the fortress of the Kremlin on the banks of the Moskva River in the 14th century, becoming the capital of the Grand Duchy of Muscovy. It bore the brunt of attacks from the Mongols through the later medieval period. The capital of Russia was moved to St Petersburg in 1713, but Moscow remained culturally and politically key to Russia; it was occupied in 1812 by Napoleon but burned down by the Russian defenders to drive him from Russia. It was swiftly rebuilt and its status as capital was restored after the Bolshevik revolution of 1917, with the seat of government again in the Kremlin.

1636 ADAM OLEARIUS

Adam Olearius (or Oehlschlaeger) (1599–1671) was a German scholar who became secretary to the ambassador sent by Frederick III, Duke of Holstein, to the Shah of Safavid Persia. They travelled via Moscow, where they agreed a treaty with Tsar Mikhail I in 1634, and visited again in 1636.

The city is almost at an equal distance from all the frontiers, which is above 120 German leagues. It is about three leagues about and, no doubt, hath been hitherfore bigger than it is now. Matthieu de Michou, a canon of Cracow, who flourished at the beginning of the last age, says that in his time it was twice as big as the city of Prague. The Tartars of Crim and Precop burnt it in the year 1571, and the Poles set it afire in the year 1611 so as that there was nothing left of it but the castle; and yet now there are numbered in it above 40,000 houses and it is out of all controversy one of the greatest cities in Europe.

It is true that, the palaces of the great lords and the houses of some rich merchants excepted, which are of brick and stone, all the rest are of wood and made up of beams and cross-pieces of fir laid one upon another. They cover them with barks of trees upon which they sometimes put another covering of turfs. The carelessness of the Muscovites and the disorders of their housekeeping are such that there hardly passes a month, nay not a week, but some place or other takes fire, which, meeting with what is very combustible, does in a moment reduce many houses; nay, if the wind be any thing high, whole streets into ashes. Some days before our arrival the fire had consumed the third part of the city; and about 5 or 6 years since, the like accident had near destroyed it all. To prevent this the Strelitz of the guard and the watch are enjoined in the night-time to carry poleaxes wherewith to break down the houses adjoining to those which are afire, by which means they hinder the progress of it with much better success than if they attempted the quenching of it. And that it may not fasten on other more solid structures, the doors and windows are very narrow, having shutters of latten [tin plate], to prevent the sparks and flashes from getting in.

Those who have their houses burnt have this comfort withal that they may buy houses ready-built at a market for that purpose without the white-wall, at a very easy rate, and have them taken down, transported and in a short time set up in the same place where the former stood.

The streets of Moscow are handsome and very broad, but so dirty after rain hath ever so little moistened the ground that it were impossible to get out of the dirt were it not for the great posts which set together make a kind of bridge which like that of the Rhine near Strasbourg, which bridges in foul weather serve for a kind of pavement.

The city is divided into four quarters or circuits, whereof the first is called Cataygorod, that is the mid-city, as being in the midst of the others. This quarter is divided from the rest by a brick wall which the Muscovites called the *crasne stenna*, that is, red stone. The Moskva passes on the south side of it and the river Neglina, which joins the other behind the castle, on the north side. The Great Duke's palace, called Kremlin and of greater extent than many other ordinary cities, takes up almost one half of it and is fortified with strong walls and a good ditch and very well mounted with cannon. In the midst are two steeples, one very high and covered with copper gilt as all the other steeples of the castle are. This steeple is called Juan Welike, that is the Great John. The other is considerable only for the bell within it, made by the Great Duke Boris Godunov, weighing 33,600 pounds. It is not tolled but upon great festivals to honour the entrance and audience of ambassadors, but to stir it there must be 24 men who pull it by a rope that comes down into the court while some others are above to help it on by thrusting. The Great Duke's palace stands towards the farther side of the castle with that of the patriarch and apartments for several *boyars* [noblemen] who have places at court. There is also a very fair palace of stone according to the Italian architecture for the young prince but the Great Duke continues still in his wooden palace as being more healthy than stone structures. The exchequer and the magazine of powder and provisions are also within the castle....

In the spacious space before the castle is the chief market of the city kept; all day it is full of people but especially slaves and idle persons. All the marketplace is full of shops as also all the streets abutting upon it; but every trade has a station by itself, so as the mercers intermingle not with the linen or woollen drapers, nor goldsmiths with saddlers, shoemakers, tailors, furriers and the like, but every profession and trade hath its proper street, which is so much the greater convenience, in that a man does, of a sudden, cast his eye on all he can desire. Seamstresses have their shops in the midst of the market, where there is also another sort of women traders, who have rings in their mouths, and, with their rubies and turquoises, put off another commodity which is not seen in the market. There is a particular street where are sold the images of their saints. 'Tis true these go not under the name of merchandise among the Muscovites, who would make some difficulty to say they had *bought* a saint – but they say they receive them by way of exchange or trucking for money; and so when they buy they make no bargain, but lay down what the painter demands.

1812 EUGÈNE LABAUME

Captain Eugène Labaume (1783–1849) was a staff officer with Napoleon on the Russia campaign of 1812; he was of the few to survive the Grande Armée's disastrous retreat in October–December of that year. His account of the campaign was one of the first to be published after the return to France.

Being anxious to arrive at Moscow, we commenced our march at an early hour in the morning and passed through several deserted villages. On the banks of the Moskva towards our right were some magnificent chateaux, which the Tartars had pillaged to deprive us of every comfort which these places could afford; and the corn, ready for harvest, had either been trodden down or eaten by the horses. The haystacks, which covered the country were given to the flames and spread all around an impenetrable smoke.... About two o'clock we perceived, from the summit of a lofty hill, a thousand elegant and gilded spires which, glittering in the rays of the sun, seemed at a distance like so many globes of fire.

Transported with delight at this beautiful spectacle, which was the more gratifying from the memory of the melancholy objects we had hitherto seen, we could not suppress our joy, but, with a simultaneous movement, exclaimed, 'Moscow, Moscow!' At the sound of this long-wished-for name, the soldiers rushed up the hill in crowds, discovering new wonders at every step. One admired a noble château on our left, the elegant architecture of which displayed more eastern magnificence; another directed his attention towards a palace or temple; but all were struck with the superb picture which this immense town afforded. The Moskva flows through smiling meadows and having fertilized the country, passes through the capital, separating an immense group of houses built of wood, of stone and of brick, and constructed in a style in which were united the different sorts of architecture peculiar to every nation. The walls painted of different colours, the cupolas gilded or covered with lead or slates, the terraces of the palaces, the obelisks, and above all the spires, presented to our eyes the reality of one of those famous cities of Asia which hitherto we had believed only to exist in the rich imagination of the Arabian poets....

On 15th September we approached the city, which had no walls, a simple parapet of earth being the only work which constituted the outer enclosure. Nothing indicated that the town was inhabited and the road by which we arrived was so deserted that we saw neither Russian nor even French soldier. No cry, no noise was heard. In the midst of this awful solitude we pursued our march, a prey to the most utmost anxiety, and that anxiety was redoubled when we perceived a thick smoke, which arose in the form of a column from the centre of the town. Eager to know the cause of this conflagration we in vain endeavoured to find someone who might satisfy our irrepressible curiosity, and the impossibility of satisfying it increased our impatience and augmented our alarm.

1839 MARQUIS DE CUSTINE

The French nobleman and Romantic novelist Astolphe-Louis-Léonor, Marquis de Custine (1790–1857), is best known for his account of a visit to Russia in 1839. Though himself a reactionary, he was appalled at Russian autocracy and described its pernicious effects; nevertheless, he was impressed by the physical beauty of Moscow.

A multitude of spires gleamed alone above the dust of the road, the undulations of the soil and the misty line that nearly always clothes the distance, under the summer sun of these parts.... Before the eye spreads a landscape, wild and gloomy, but grand as the ocean; and to animate the dreary void, there rises a poetical city, whose architecture is without either a designating name or a known model.

To understand the peculiarity of the picture, it is necessary to remind the reader of the orthodox plan of every Greek church. The summit of these sacred edifices is always composed of several towers, which vary in form and height, but the number of which is five at the least.... The middle steeple is the most lofty; the four others respectfully surround this principal tower. Their form varies; the summits of some resemble pointed caps placed upon a head; the great towers of certain churches, painted and gilded externally, may be severally compared to a bishop's mitre, a tiara adorned with gems, a Chinese pavilion, a minaret and a clergyman's hat. They often consist of a simple cupola, in the shape of a bowl, and terminating in a point....

Bright chains of gilded or plated metal unite the crosses of the inferior steeples to the principal tower; and this metallic net, spread over an entire city, produces an effect that it would be impossible to convey, even in a picture. The holy legion of steeples, without having any precise resemblance to the human form, represent a grotesque assemblage of personages gathered together on the summits of the churches and chapels, a phalanx of phantoms hovering over the city.

The exteriors of the mystic domes...remind the stranger of a cuirass of Damascus steel; and the sight of so many scaly, enamelled, spangled, striped and chequered roofs, shining in the sun with various but always brilliant colours, strikes him with the most lively astonishment. The desert, with its dull sea-green tint, is, as it were, illuminated by this magical network of carbuncles. The play of light, in the aerial city, produces a species of phantasmagoria, in broad day, which reminds one of the reflected brilliance of lamps in the shop of a lapidary. These changing hues impart to Moscow an aspect altogether different from that of the other great European cities. The sky, when viewed from the middle of such a city, is a golden glory, similar to those seen in old paintings....

After passing Petrovski, the enchantment gradually disperses, so that by the time of entering Moscow, we feel as if waking from a brilliant dream to a very dull and prosaic reality – a vast city without any real monuments of art, that is to say, without a single object worthy of a discriminative and thoughtful approbation. Before so heavy and awkward a copy of Europe, we ask, with wonder, what has become of the Asia, whose apparition had struck us with admiration so short a time before? Moscow, viewed from without as a whole, is a creation of sylphs, a world of chimeras; when inspected close at hand and in detail, it is a vast trading city, without regularity, dusty, ill paved, ill built, thinly peopled; in short, though it unquestionably exhibits the work of a powerful hand, it betrays also the conceptions of a head whose idea of the beautiful has failed to produce one single *chef-d'oeuvre*....

Nevertheless, amid the chaos of plaster, brick and boards that is called Moscow, two points never cease to attract the eye – the church of St Basil, and the Kremlin – the Kremlin, of which Napoleon himself was only able to disturb a few stones! This prodigious fabric, with its white irregular walls, and its battlements rising above battlements, is in itself large as a city. At the close of day when I first entered Moscow, the grotesque piles of churches and palaces embraced within the citadel rose in light against a dimly portrayed background, poor in design and cold in colouring, though we are still burning with heat, suffocating with dust and devoured by mosquitoes. It is the long continuance of the hot season which gives the colour to southern scenery; in the north, we feel the effects of the summer, but we do not see them; in vain does the air become heated for a moment, the earth remains always discoloured....

On first entering the city of Moscow, I forgot poetry, and even history; I thought only of what I saw, which was not very striking, for I found myself in streets similar to those in the outskirts of all great cities: I crossed a boulevard which resembled other boulevards, and then, after driving down a gentle descent, found myself among straight and handsome lines of houses built of stone. At last I reached the Dmitriskoi-street, where a handsome and comfortable chamber had been engaged for me in an excellent English hotel. I had, at Petersburg, been commended to Madame Howard, who without this introduction would not have received me into her house. I took care not to reproach her for being so scrupulous, for it is owing to this precaution that one can sleep comfortably in her establishment. The means by which she has succeeded in maintaining there a cleanliness rarely seen anywhere, and which is an absolute miracle in Russia, is her having had erected, in her courtyard, a separate building, in which the Russian servants are obliged to sleep....

The first thing that struck me in the streets of Moscow was the more lively, free and careless bearing of the population as compared with that of Petersburg. An air of liberty is here breathed that is unknown to the rest of the empire. It is this which explains to me the secret aversion of the sovereigns to the old city, which they flatter, fear and fly. The emperor Nicholas, who is a good Russian, says he is very fond of it: but I cannot see that he resides in it more than did his predecessors, who detested it.

1931 BERNARD PARES

Distinguished British historian of Russia Bernard Pares (1867–1949) was a liberal critic of the Soviet Union, but romantically hoped that the industrialization of the 1930s represented an empowerment of the Russian people, as he described in his book Moscow Admits a Critic (1936).

Within an hour of my arrival at the hotel I was wandering freely about the streets and mixing with the crowds of holiday makers. Some of my friends have refused to believe that I was not followed throughout. I have a nose for that kind of thing from earlier times, so I was rather on the watch for anything of the kind; but there was nothing whatever to notice, and almost from the first the whole idea disappeared from my mind. I went out by myself, whenever I felt inclined to, and strayed casually in any direction that suggested itself....

My first feeling...was one of surprise at the simplicity of it all. Petersburg, Petrograd or Leningrad – whichever you like to call it – was a place that I always hated: in fact, I should not have been sorry for the plough to go over it. Moscow was, and still is, a home – someone else's home it may be, but anyhow a home – and here one knows that one is at the heart of the Russian people, which, whatever it is called, is still the Russian people. When I was a student in Moscow in 1898, I used, for the sheer sake of the sense of home in it, to walk through the Kremlin every day; and now, though the Kremlin has returned to its early role as a fortress – this time the fortress of Communism – I was constantly walking past it and all round it, and from my hotel I had a full view into it. There it stood, just as before, though now turned to different uses. The only notable difference was that a large gilt star was fixed to the top of each of the main gates or pinnacles, but this one soon gets used to....

I was constantly roaming the streets in this way, going through the big shops, watching the streams of buyers and noting the great accumulation of stores of every kind. My general impression was almost the same as that of the busy Christmas purchasing season in London, from which I had just come. The Moscow 'Selfridge' or 'Army and Navy Stores' might here belong to the State – and why should that be regretted? – but there was the same plenty of all the most useful things and the same busy buying. I nowhere noticed a superfluity of luxuries. There were signs of attention to smartness, but the general impression was one of well-being. I was quite aware, both from what I knew before and from what I heard in Moscow, that it was totally different two years ago, and, indeed, there was a general sense of satisfaction, novelty and even surprise in the general mood.

Familiar snatches of Russian conversation floated past me as I walked along the streets. It was the ordinary sort of talk which I might have heard in London – frank, open and familiar, and on subjects of everyday interest. One knew of the earlier theoretical attack on the family and its various appearances in legislation, but here were the families as they used to be before, father and mother perhaps holding their children by the hand and taking their pleasure together.... The people were neatly dressed, especially the children, and the general impression was that they were also well fed (I notice this particularly at a workers' club)....

I have always felt at home in great crowds of the common folk...for it is the great underground Russia that always fascinated me in the past. Personal worries, and even personal distinctiveness, disappear when you are thus 'in the lap of the people'. You share equally in its geniality, and every chance neighbour is a friend. Once you have the language, all the sights and sounds are common to you as to anyone else, including the posters on the streets, which were, here most numerous. They are short, easily readable sentences in white letters on a red ground, and they are all over the place. I noted down several of them in the great Park of Rest and Culture, the new playground of the city on the west side, where, in spite of a miserable thaw and drizzle, which had upset all the plans for skating competitions, everyone seemed good tempered and all were enjoying themselves.... 'Greetings to a New Year and new triumphs'; 'Hurrah for the best friend of physical culture – our native, beloved Stalin'; 'What October has done for me'; 'We must have soap'; 'Russia is growing and getting strong'; one of the commonest of all is 'The cadres settle everything.'...

Certainly there was, in all I saw, no suggestion whatever of a sullen and disgruntled people wondering when it could be relieved of a hated government. We must remember, of course, the wholesale deportations from Moscow on the introduction of the internal passport system in December 1932. Everyone who lives in Moscow now, and that means three million people or more, has to earn the right to do so by taking a hand in the vast work of construction which is everywhere in progress. That is, they are all playing a part in the big movement; and it is also quite clear that if one speaks only of Moscow, and I spent the whole of my month there, they are already profiting by doing so.

I kept on asking myself the question: how much of all this is the people, or, in other words, to what extent the circle of public support around the government has widened – both as compared with what I learned from other visitors of two years ago and, perhaps far more, as compared with my own instinct so well remembered out of pre-revolution times. To what extent was the government a foreigner to the people? In the times of Tsardom I had never failed to feel its almost complete isolation. The ministers of those times, and more especially in the last days of Tsardom, were for the most part obviously haphazard choices from a very narrow and by no means distinguished circle. I was, of course, one of those who longed to see the Russian public, as a whole, make its way into the precincts of government, and in 1917 for a very short time I had that satisfaction.

But even then there was the much less definable barrier though a very real one, which separated the Russian intelligentsia from the great mass of the Russian public.... Educated Russians of all sorts, and this applied to officials, officers, schoolmasters and revolutionary propagandists, seemed to me to regard the working folk far too much as recipients of any of the various lessons which they wished to teach them. I have to say that in Moscow today this frontier seems to have disappeared altogether, and in my many visits to public offices and great institutions government and people were of the same stock.

MUMBAI
(BOMBAY)

The ancient west Indian coastal city of Mumbai, built on a group of islands, was known by Europeans as Bombay from the 16th century. Held by Portugal from 1503 to 1661, when it was passed to the English crown, it became a headquarters of the British East India Company.

With the British holding increasing sway over India, in the mid-19th century Bombay began to thrive (and the islands united), and the 1860s

207

saw a huge growth in its cotton industry. It was already an important port for those travelling between Europe and India, a role which grew rapidly after the opening of the Suez Canal in 1869.

In 1896 a serious outbreak of plague and consequent population decline led to a degree of economic stagnation, although it also became the most Westernized city in India, which contributed to its emerging role as a focus for Indian nationalism. Since independence in 1947, it grew to become the largest city in India and was renamed Mumbai in 1995.

1786 WILLIAM FRANCKLIN

The junior East India Company soldier William Francklin (1763–1839) visited on his way from Bengal to Persia in 1786, assessing the city and its defences with a military eye, though the 'fish' he describes is more mysterious. He later became a distinguished scholar of Indian history and culture.

The island of Bombay is in the possession of the English East India Company; it is situated on the coast of Conkan, in lat. 19 north, and long. 72.38 east; it was granted, as part of the marriage portion with the Infanta of Portugal, to Charles II. The harbour is capable of containing three hundred sail of ships with the greatest safety: there is also a most excellent dock, in which ships of his Majesty's squadron, and others, are repaired, refitted and completely equipped for sea. They build also here all sorts of vessels; and the workmen in the yard are very ingenious and dexterous, not yielding to our best shipwrights in England. This island is very beautiful, and as populous for its size as any in the world; merchants and others coming to settle here from the different parts of the Deccan, Malabar and Coromandel, as well as the Gujarat country. Among those of the latter place are many Parsi families; these are descended from the remains of the ancient Gubres, or worshippers of fire; most of the country merchants, as well as the menial servants of the islands, are of this faith. They are very rich, and have in their hands the management of all mercantile affairs....

The island of Bombay is about eight miles in length, and twenty in circumference: the most remarkable natural curiosity the island produces

208

is a small fish; this fish, according to the description of a gentleman who has seen it, and from whom I received my information, is in form somewhat like a mussel, about four inches long, and has upon the top of its back, and near the head, a small valve, on the opening of which you discover a liquor of a strong purple colour, which, when dropped on a piece of cloth, retains the hue. It is found chiefly in the months of September and October, and it is observed the female fish has not this valve which distinguishes the sexes. It is not improbable to suppose that this fish is of the same nature as the ancient Murex, or shell-fish, by which the Romans attained the art of dyeing to such perfection, and is similar to that found formerly on the coasts of Tyre.

The Company's forces at this Presidency consist of eight battalions of sepoys, a regiment of European infantry, and a corps of European artillery and engineers. During the late long and very severe war, the Bombay troops have distinguished themselves in a peculiar manner, and the campaign of Bedanore and the sieges of Tellicherri and Mangalore will long remain testimonials of high military abilities, as well as of their bravery and patience under severe duty. The breed of sheep on this island is very indifferent, and all the necessaries of life are much dearer than in any other part of India.

1853 BAYARD TAYLOR

The American man of letters Bayard Taylor (see page 118) experienced colonial Bombay in the last years of British East India Company rule; the British crown assumed direct rule in 1858.

We came slowly up the splendid bay, until within half a mile of the town. The shores being low, nothing but an array of brown tiled roofs, and a small Gothic spire, was visible behind the crowd of vessels at anchor. On the other hand, however, the islands of Elephanta and Panwell, and the ranges of the Mahratta Ghauts, were gorgeously lighted up by the evening sun. But little time was allowed for admiring them; the anchor dropped, and a fleet of boats, conveying anxious friends and relatives, gathered about us. The deck was covered with pyramids of baggage, all was noise and confusion, here shouts of joy and there weeping, here meeting and there parting, many scenes of the drama of life enacted at the same moment. Finding myself left wholly to my own resources, I set about extricating myself from the bewilderment, and accepting the first native who addressed me, I embarked for the shore before the other passengers had thought of leaving.

'*Rupees*,' said the master of the boat, holding up three of his fingers. '*Ek*' (one) I answered. Up went two fingers. '*Ek*' again; and so I went ashore for one. We came to a stone pier, with a long flight of steps leading down to the water. The top of it was thronged with natives in white dresses and red turbans. Among them were the runners of the hotels, and I soon found the one I wanted.... A line of cabs, buggies and palanquins with their bearers was drawn up on the pier, and in order to be as Indian as possible, I took one of the latter.

It was not a pleasant sensation to lie at full length in a cushioned box, and impose one's whole weight (and I am by no means a feather) upon the shoulders of four men. It is a conveyance invented by Despotism, when men's necks were footstools, and men's heads playthings. I have never yet been able to get into it without a feeling of reluctance, as if I were inflicting an injury on my bearers. Why should they groan and stagger under my weight, when I have legs of my own? And yet, I warrant you, nothing would please them less than for me to use those legs. They wear pads on the shoulders, on which rests the pole to which the palanquin is suspended, and go forward at a slow, sliding trot, scarcely bending their knees or lifting their feet from the ground. The motion is agreeable, yet as you are obliged to lie on your back, you have a very imperfect view of the objects you pass. You can travel from one end of India to another in this style, but it is an expensive and unsatisfactory conveyance, and I made as little use of it as possible, in my subsequent journeys....

Bombay, as a city, presents few points of interest to a traveller. It is wholly of modern growth, and more than half European in its appearance. It is divided into two parts – the Fort, as it is called, being enclosed within the old Portuguese fortifications and surrounded by a moat. It is about a mile in length, extending along the shore of the bay. Outside of the moat is a broad esplanade, beyond which, on the northern side, a new city has grown up. The fortifications are useless as a means of defence, the water of the moat breeds mosquitoes and fevers, and I do not understand why the walls should not have been levelled, long since. The city within the fort is crowded to excess. Many of the streets are narrow, dark and dirty, and as the houses are frequently of wood, the place is exposed to danger from fire. The population and trade of Bombay have increased so much within the last few years, that this keeping up of old defences is a great inconvenience. So far are the old practices preserved, that at one particular gate, where there was a powder magazine twenty years ago, no person is permitted to smoke. Southward of the Fort is a tongue of land – formerly the island of Colaba, but now connected by a causeway – on which stands the lighthouse. To the north-west, beyond the city, rises Malabar Hill, a long, low height, looking upon the open ocean, and completely covered with the gardens and country houses of the native and European merchants....

My friend Cursetjee Merwanjee accompanied me one afternoon in a drive around the environs of Bombay. After passing the esplanade, which is thickly dotted with the tents of the military and the bamboo cottages of the officers, we entered the outer town, inhabited entirely by the natives. The houses are two or three stories in height, with open wooden verandahs in front, many of which have a dark, mellow old look, from the curiously carved posts and railings of black wood which adorn them. Mixed with the houses are groups of the beautiful cocoa palm, which rise above the roofs and hang their feathery crowns over the crowded highway. Outside of the town hall is shade and the splendor of tropical bloom. The roads are admirable, and we rolled smoothly along in the cool twilight of embowered cocoa, brab and date palms, between whose pillared trunks the afternoon sun poured streams of broad golden light. The crimson sagittaria flaunted its flame-like leaves on the terraces; a variety of the acacia hung thick with milky, pendulous blossoms, and every gateway disclosed an avenue of urns leading up to the verandah of some suburban palace, all overladen with gorgeous southern flowers. We rode thus for miles around and over Malabar Hill, and along the shores of the Indian Ocean, until the hills of Salsette, empurpled by the sunset, shone in the distance like the mountains of fairy land.

1939 JOHN MACCALLUM SCOTT

John MacCallum Scott (b. 1911) was a British Liberal politician whose volume Eastern Journey *(1939) described a journey around Malaya and India shortly before the Second World War, when Bombay was both unusually Westernized for India and a stronghold of the Indian nationalist movement.*

Bombay is a law unto itself. It is more a European city than an Eastern city.... To the newcomer who makes it his first experience of India, it must have a tremendous fascination but at the end of the journey it comes rather as an anticlimax. Its broad boulevards and huge apartment houses are far too modern and clean, its sea promenades and its sophisticated dance halls too out of tune with all that one has already seen....

Yet Bombay is the sign of the times; it stands in the very vanguard of India's future. Here a new India is being forged, an India which will be welded into one in spite of itself, not by force of arms but by the power of the rupee. Bombay is known as the Millionaire's City. It has fathered great commercial and industrial enterprises; railway companies, great trading systems and banks have grown from tiny beginnings in its back streets. And there is still more to come. The city, more than any other in India, has acquired the business point of view. Its citizens are on the lookout for opportunities....

Two very different factors have combined to make Bombay what it is. The first is its geographical position. It is the first port of call for ships coming from the West.... Almost every official from the Viceroy down to the junior civil servant out for the first time must arrive there, and go on by train to Delhi or wherever he is to be stationed. And when going home on leave or saying goodbye for the last time, the hills behind the city will be the last thing he will see from the ship's rail.... Tourists too are frequently to be seen in Bombay. They come on world cruises, stay for a couple of nights maybe, making whoopee in the hotels and nightclubs and then pass on to do the same thing somewhere else....

In the evenings we would stroll along the waterfront. Make no mistake about it, Bombay is a very beautiful city, ringed by soft hills and by the sea. To walk there at sunset is to enjoy one of India's highest prizes. Frequently we would go to the Gateway of India, the grandiose building on the water-front where the Viceroy receives the homage of the Indian princes when he arrives for the first time. Thousands would collect there in the evening, promenading up and down, women mixing indiscriminately with the men.... Often young Indians, straight down from Oxford by all appearances, would come racing down to the waterfront in sports cars accompanied by girls, just as though all the disabilities under which Indian women suffered were things of the past.

Sometimes we would go to one of the hotels to dance, and there we would see parties of Indians seated at the tables, the men in faultless evening dress, the women looking very lovely in saris which sparkled with gold and silver brocade.

1962 V. S. NAIPAUL

Many writers have commented on the dramatic contrasts between rich and poor in Mumbai, and the intensity of the poverty encountered by every traveller. The novelist V. S. Naipaul (1932–2018), Trinidad-born and of Indian descent, visited in the early 1960s. The bleak picture of Indian life he painted in An Area of Darkness *(1964) caused the Indian government to ban the book.*

They tell the story of the Sikh who, returning to India after many years, sat down among his suitcases on the Bombay docks and wept. He had forgotten what Indian poverty was like. It is an Indian story, in its arrangement of figures and properties, its melodrama, its pathos. It is Indian above all in its attitude to poverty as something which, thought about from time to time in the midst of other preoccupations, releases the sweetest of emotions. This is poverty, our especial poverty, and how sad it is! Poverty not as an urge to anger or improving action, but poverty as an inexhaustible source of tears, an exercise of the purest sensibility....

India is the poorest country in the world. Therefore, to see its poverty is to make an observation of no value; a thousand newcomers to the country before you have seen and said as you. And not only newcomers. Our own sons and daughters, when they return from Europe and America, have spoken in your very words. Do not think that your anger and contempt are marks of your sensitivity. You might have seen more: the smiles on the faces of the begging children, that domestic group among the pavement sleepers waking in the cool Bombay morning, father, mother and baby in a trinity of love so self-contained that they are as private as if walls had separated them from you: it is your gaze that violates them, your sense of outrage that outrages them. You might have seen the boy sweeping down his area of pavement, spreading his mat, lying down: exhaustion and under-nourishment are in his tiny body and shrunken face, but lying flat on his back, oblivious to you and the thousands who walk past in the lane between the sleepers' mats and house walls bright with advertisements and election slogans, oblivious of the warm, overbreathed air, he plays with fatigued concentration with a tiny pistol in blue plastic. It is your surprise, your anger, that denies him humanity. But wait. Stay six months. The winter will bring fresh visitors. Their talk will also be of poverty; they too will show their anger. You will agree; but deep down there will be annoyance; it will seem to you then, too, that they are seeing only the obvious; and it will not please you to find your sensibility so accurately parodied.

Ten months later I was to revisit Bombay and to wonder at my hysteria. It was cooler, and in the crowded courtyards of Colaba there were Christmas decorations, illuminated stars hanging out of windows against the black sky. It was my eye that had changed. I had seen Indian villages: the narrow broken lanes with green slime in the gutters, the choked back-to-back mud houses, the jumble of filth and food and animals and people, the baby in the dust, the swollen-bellied, black with flies, but wearing its good-luck amulet. I had seen the starved child defecating at the roadside, while the mangy dog waited to eat the excrement. I had seen the physique of the people of Andhra, which had suggested the possibility of an evolution downwards, wasted body to wasted body. Nature mocking herself, incapable of remission. Compassion and pity did not answer; they were refinements of hope. Fear was what I felt. Contempt was what I had to fight against; to give way to that was to abandon the self I had known. Perhaps in the end it was fatigue that overcame me.... I had learned too that escape was always possible, that in every Indian town there was a corner of comparative order and cleanliness in which one could recover and cherish one's self-respect. In India the easiest and most necessary thing to ignore was the most obvious. Which no doubt was why, in spite of all I had read about the country, nothing had prepared me for it.

But in the beginning the obvious was overwhelming, and there was the knowledge that there was no ship to run back to, as there had been at Alexandria, Port Sudan, Djibouti, Karachi. It was new to me then that the obvious could be separated from the pleasant, from the areas of self-respect and self-love. Marine Drive, Malabar Hill, the lights of the city at night from Kamala Nehru Park, the Parsi Towers of Silence: these are what the tourist brochures put forward as Bombay, and these were the things we were taken to see on three successive days by three kind persons. They built up a dread of what was not shown, that other city where lived hundreds of thousands who poured in a white stream in and out of Churchgate Station as though hurrying to and from an endless football match. This was the city that presently revealed itself, in the broad, choked and endless main roads of suburbs, a chaos of shops, tall tenements, decaying balconies, electric wires and advertisements, the film posters that seemed to derive from a cooler and more luscious world, cooler and more luscious than the film posters of England and America, promising a greater gaiety, an ampler breast and hip, a more fruitful womb. And the courtyards behind the main streets: the heat heightened, at night the sense of outdoors destroyed, the air holding on its stillness the odours of mingled filth, the windows not showing as oblongs of light but revealing lines, clothes, furniture, boxes, and suggesting an occupation of more than floor space. On the roads northwards, the cool redbrick factories set in gardens: Middlesex it might have been, but not attached to these factories and semi-detached or terrace houses, but that shanty town, that rubbish dump. And, inevitably, the prostitutes, the 'gay girls' of the Indian newspapers. But where, in these warrens where three brothels might be in one building and not all the sandal-oil perfumes of Lucknow could hide the stench of gutters and latrines, was the gaiety?

NAPLES

The ancient city of Naples was the dominant city of southern Italy from the Middle Ages, but from the 12th century was under the control of, successively, Norman, German, Aragonese and then Spanish dukes or kings, as capital of the Kingdom of Sicily. It was a centre for the Catholic Counter-Reformation in the 16th and 17th centuries. In the 18th century, Naples — together with its nearby volcano Vesuvius and, after its discovery in 1748, the Roman town of Pompeii — became an essential stop on the Grand Tour for British aristocrats, and then American tourists in the 19th century.

In 1870, Naples became part of the new Kingdom of Italy. In the 20th century it was notorious for its organized gangsterism. In the Second World War, heavy Allied bombing (1940–43) and eventual liberation in 1943 did little to shake this reputation.

Unlike most of the other Grand Tour destinations, Naples is no longer a can't-miss tourist destination, despite the close proximity of Pompeii, Capri and the popular Amalfi coast.

1782 WILLIAM BECKFORD

William Beckford (1760–1844), a wealthy English art collector, architect and traveller, undertook his journey to Italy to avoid scandal at home. On his arrival in Naples he attended the reception of Ferdinand IV, Bourbon king of Naples, who was renowned for his love of hunting.

As soon as we arrived in sight of Capua, the sky darkened, clouds covered the horizon and presently poured down such deluges of rain as floated the whole country. The gloom was general; Vesuvius disappeared just after we had discovered it. At four o'clock darkness universally prevailed, except when a livid glare of lightning presented momentary glimpses of the bay and mountains....

For three hours the storm increased in violence, and instead of entering Naples on a calm evening, and viewing its delightful shores by moonlight – instead of finding the squares and terraces thronged with people and animated by music, we advanced with fear and terror through dark streets totally deserted, every creature being shut up in their houses, and we heard nothing but driving rain, rushing torrents and the fall of fragments beaten down by their violence. Our inn, like every other habitation, was in great disorder, and we waited a long while before we could settle in our apartments with any comfort. All night the waves roared round the rocky foundations of a fortress beneath my windows, and the lightning played clear in my eyes.

4 November The sky was cloudless when I awoke, and such was the transparence of the atmosphere that I could clearly discern the rocks, and even some white buildings on the island of Caprea, though at the distance of thirty miles.... I lay half an hour gazing on the smooth level waters and listening to the confused voices of the fishermen, passing and repassing in light skiffs, which came and disappeared in an instant.

Running to the balcony the moment my eyes were fairly open (for till then I saw objects, I know not how, as one does in dreams), I leaned over its rails and viewed Vesuvius, rising distinct into the blue aether, with all that world of gardens and casinos which are scattered about its base; then looked down into the street, deep below, thronged with people in holiday garments, and carriages, and soldiers in full parade. The shrubby, variegated shore of Posillipo drew my attention to the opposite side of the bay. It was on those very rocks, under those tall pines, San Nazaro was wont to sit by moonlight, or at peep of dawn, composing his marine eclogues. It is there he still sleeps; and I wished to have gone immediately and strewed coral over his tomb, but I was obliged to check my impatience and hurry to the palace in form and gala.

A courtly mob had got thither upon the same errand, daubed over with lace and most notably be-periwigged. Nothing but bows and salutations were going forward on the staircase, one of the largest I ever beheld, and which a multitude of prelates and friars were ascending with awkward pomposity. I jostled along to the presence-chamber, where His Majesty was dining alone in a circular enclosure of fine clothes and smirking faces. The moment he had finished, twenty long necks were poked forth, and it was a glorious struggle among some of the most decorated who first should kiss his hand, the great business of the day. Everybody pressed forward to the best of their abilities. His Majesty seemed to eye nothing but the end of his nose, which is doubtless a capital object.

1838 JAMES FENIMORE COOPER

American romantic novelist James Fenimore Cooper (1789–1851) spent several years in Europe in the 1820s to early 1830s, describing them in two volumes published in 1838. On his visit to Italy he toured the usual tourist and cultural highlights.

The place is inexhaustible in street amusements. I never tire of wandering about it, but find something to amuse me at every turn. In one quarter, the population appear literally to live in the open air, and we have driven through a street in which cooking, eating, wrangling, dancing, singing, praying, and all other occupations, were going on at the same moment. I believe I mentioned this in the first visit, but I had not then fallen on the real scene of out-door fun. The horses could not move off a walk, as we went through this street; and their heads, suddenly thrust into the centre of a *ménage*, appeared to produce no more derangement than a puff from a smoky chimney in one of our own kitchens.

But the Mole is the spot I most frequent. Besides the charm of the port, which to me is inexhaustible, small as the place is, we have all sorts of buffoons there. One recites poetry, another relates stories, a third gives us Punch and Judy, who, in this country, bear the more musical names of Polichinello and Giulietta, or some other female name equally sonorous. The shipping is not very numerous, though it has much of the quaintness and beauty of the Mediterranean rig....

You will smile at my old passion for fine skies and landscape scenery, but I have climbed to the castle of St Elmo a dozen times within the last month to see the effect of the sunset. Just as the day disappears, a soft rosy tint illumines the base of Vesuvius, and all the crowded objects of the coast, throwing a glow on the broad Campagna that enables one almost to fancy it another Eden. While these beautiful transitions are to be seen on the earth, the heavens reflect them, as the sun. Of the hues of the clouds at such moments, it is impossible to speak clearly, for they appear supernatural. At one time the whole concave is an arch of pearl; and this perhaps is succeeded by a blush as soft and as mottled as that of youth; and then a hundred hues become so blended, that it is scarcely possible to name or to enumerate them. There is no gorgeousness, no dazzling of the eye in all this, but a polished softness that wins as much as it delights the beholder. Certainly, I have never seen sunsets to compare with these, on shore, before this visit to Naples; though at sea, in low latitudes, they are more frequent, I allow.

1854 T.Q. (SAMUEL YOUNG)

American banker Young, who wrote under the name T.Q. (see page 112), was unimpressed with much of what he found in Naples, being disappointed by the Carnival and unable to find the licentiousness he had expected.

January Naples is beautifully situated, partly on a hill and principally on the level space at its foot, extending to the edge of the Bay. To the left is Vesuvius, with its two heads usually in the clouds, which seem to have great affection for the crater and linger there when the rest of the sky is blue. The extinct crater, or the mountain where it is, is pointed at the top; then there is a small valley, and the round head of the present burning mountain rises higher in the air. When the wind is favorable a thin white smoke is seen hanging around it, changing its form momently.... From the rear of Vesuvius, there stretches a chain of hills along the shore of the Bay, for about twenty miles out to the ocean, where they seem to terminate abruptly. Two or three villages are scattered along them, and at their extremity by the sea stands Sorento [*sic*]. From the farthest point visible you bring your eye along the horizon to your right hand, ten miles, and you see the island of Capri rising high out of the water.... Along the face of the hills to the right, runs a handsome road, the fashionable drive of the city. From it you look down upon white villas and gardens, and get a fine view of Vesuvius, the city and the Bay....

Naples is said to contain three hundred and sixty thousand inhabitants. It does not look thus large; but I presume the poor people lie six in a bed. These Italian cities must be much crowded, for you see hardly any country residences in passing through the land. The streets are well paved. The houses mostly of a pale yellow, or white, five stories high, with green blinds; and often with balconies before every window. In these balconies the ladies may sit with their novels or needle work, looking quite unconscious all the time; yet the Toleda (Toledo Street) is the Broadway of Naples. The crowds on the sidewalks here are so great, that it is often difficult to make your way. The shops look quite stylish, much after the French fashion. The tailors make great display, as do the jewellers, confectioners, &c. A handsome silk hat, to all appearance as good as the French hat, can be bought for one dollar twenty-five cents. And kid gloves for fifteen cents a pair. I have seen some well-looking boots displayed for sale but did not ask the price. How these articles will wear, I cannot say.

At the doors of the bread shops you see bread hanging on nails and in all kinds of shapes; like hearts, *krullers*, small loaves ornamented, or in rings. The flower stands exhibit fine roses, great clusters of them half blown and each as big as a hen's eggs. Fresh grown peas can now be had of the vegetable merchants. Good plums, a little shrivelled from the manner in which they are kept, are plentiful. Oranges are, of course, a drug. A small Sicily or Malta orange, with a thin skin is the best. Many travelling pedlars go about the streets, with their wares upon their heads; and their cries make the air resound. This, added to the jingling bells worn by the flocks of goats continually being driven into the city to be milked, or out to pasture, makes Naples full of sound. The street musicians also, with horn, violin, guitar, &c., dancing as they play; also Punch and Judy, who were created in this region, squeaking in the streets, with multitudes of carts, carriages, &c., make Naples a noisy town....

I had heard much of the *lazzarone* [beggars] of Naples, but I can find no class answering the description given of them in books. The fishermen with their red woolen caps, hanging in bags by the side of their heads, and the younger of them with bare feet, answer nearest to my notion of the *lazzaroni*.... Beggars are as plentiful here as at Pisa; and that is saying enough. Priests are not so frequently seen here as at Rome; but soldiers are more visible....

The Carnival began on the 17th January, but it has amounted to but little thus far. A few fellows, dressed grotesquely, stop before the hotels, singing, playing and dancing, until some coppers are thrown to them; but such performances are nearly always to be seen. The 'nobility' have given a series of balls; and the King one or two on Sunday evenings; but all this does not make such a Carnival as you read or hear of. Are all travellers liars, or are they not? is an open question for debating societies. All I can say with regard to this common propensity is, that if I fall into the habit, it must be while entirely unconscious of it.

The visible wickedness of Naples, I do not see much of, even with spectacles. We have received too many of our accounts of continental licentiousness from English books and newspapers. If I had stopped a moment for reflection, I should have decided, that as the English have published so many wilful falsehoods about America and the Americans, they must have treated in like manner other countries not under their control. Hereafter I shall receive all English accounts of foreign countries with much distrust.

1943 NORMAN LEWIS

British novelist Lewis (1908–2003) arrived in Naples, newly liberated from German control by the Allies, in October 1943, and his diary of his work as an Intelligence Officer over the next twelve months catalogued the devastation, starvation and suffering of a society affected by years of war.

25 October It is astonishing to witness the struggles of this city so shattered, so starved, so deprived of all those things that justify a city's existence, to adapt itself to a collapse into conditions which must resemble life in the Dark Ages. People camp out like Bedouins in deserts of bricks. There is little food, little water, no salt, no soap. A lot of Neapolitans have lost their possessions, including most of their clothing, in the bombings, and I have seen some strange combinations of garments in the streets, including a man in an old dinner jacket, knickerbockers and army boots, and several women in lacy confections that might have been made up from curtains. There are no cars but carts by the hundred, and a few antique coaches such as barouches and phaetons drawn by lean horses. Today in Posilippo [*sic*] I stopped to watch the methodical dismemberment of a stranded German half-track by a number of youths who were streaming away from it like leaf-cutter ants, carrying pieces of metal of all shapes and sizes. Fifty yards away a well-dressed lady with a feather in her hat squatted to milk a goat. At the water's edge below, two fishermen had roped together several doors salvaged from the ruins, piled their gear on these and were about to go fishing. Inexplicably no boats are allowed out, but nothing is said in the proclamation about rafts. Everyone improvises and adapts.

Tonight I dined for the first time in a civilian house at the invitation of a Signora Gentile recently released by a member of the section from the Filangieri gaol, where with a number of other women she had been imprisoned by the partisans on vague charges of collaboration. Here the mood was one of escapism, even of nostalgic frivolity. Our friends had made a huge effort to cast out of mind the unpleasantness of the imme-diate past. Several beautiful women were present – one in a blouse made from a Union Jack; all the old-style airs and graces banished by Mussolini were back again....

We ate wurst, sipped schnapps, drank wine from glasses of the right shape and colour, somebody strummed a mandolin, and we talked about

Naples and its traditions – the city that had ignored and finally overcome all its conquerors, dedicated entirely and everlastingly to the sweet things of life. Other wars were mentioned in passing, but this one was not. Neither were politics, Mussolini, food shortages or the rumoured outbreak of typhus.

NEW YORK CITY

Founded by the Dutch as New Amsterdam in 1626, the young colony was taken by the English in 1664 and renamed New York. During the American War of Independence, New York was a British stronghold, but the British evacuation in 1783 marked the end of the war. New York, on Manhattan Island, became the first capital of the United States (1785–90).

In the 19th and early 20th centuries New York became the prime focus for immigration from Europe, the arrival marked by the Statue of Liberty (a gift from the French government in 1889). Skyscrapers, first seen in the 1890s, came to mark the Manhattan skyline, an image instantly recognizable across the world from countless movies since the 1930s.

1679 JASPER DANCKAERTS AND PETER SLUYTER

Fifteen years after the English takeover of New York, Jasper Danckaerts (1639–1702/04) and Peter Sluyter (1645–1722), envoys of a Dutch religious sect seeking a new home, encountered a flourishing but rough colonial society. They succeeded in founding their colony, but it failed after forty years.

24 September In church we found truly a wild worldly world. I say wild, not only because the people are wild, as they call it in Europe, but because most of the people partake of the nature of the country, that is, peculiar to the land where they live. We heard a minister preach, who had come from Fort Orange [Albany], an old man named Domine Schaats, of Amsterdam. We could only imagine that he had been drinking a little this morning. His text was, Come unto me all ye, etc., but he was so rough that even the roughest and most godless of our sailors were astonished.

The church being in the fort, we had an opportunity to look through the latter. It is not large; it has four points or batteries; it has no moat but is enclosed with a double row of palisades. It is built from the foundation with quarry stone; the parapet is of earth. It is well provided with cannon... all bearing the mark or arms of the Netherlanders. The garrison is small.... It has only one gate, on the land side, which opens upon a broad plain or street, called the Broadway or Beaverway.

27 September We started at two o'clock for Long Island. We went on, up the hill, along open roads and a little wood, through the first village, called Breukelen [Brooklyn], which has a small, ugly little church in the middle of the road.... We came upon several plantations where Gerrit was acquainted with the people, who made us very welcome, sharing bountifully whatever they had.

On our return, we went from the city, along the Broadway. On both sides lived negroes, mulattoes and whites. These negroes were formerly the slaves of the Dutch West India Company, but, the changes and conquests of the country have given them their freedom and they settled here, where they have enough land to live on. We left the Bouweri [Bowery] village and went through the woods to the village of New Harlem.

11 October We embarked early and rowed to Staten Island, where we arrived about eight o'clock.... There are about a hundred families on the island: mostly Dutch and French, and a few English....

When we arrived at Gouanes, we heard voices in the huts of the Indians living there. They were drunk, raving, striking, shouting, jumping, fighting each other and foaming at the mouth like raging wild beasts. Others had fled with their wives and children to Simon's house, where the drunken brutes followed, bawling in the house and outside. And this was caused by Christians selling liquor.... This subject is so painful and so abominable, that I will say no more for the present.

1819 ADLARD WELBY

Adlard Welby (1776–1861) was a wealthy British gentleman who visited America to improve relations between the two countries following the War of Independence and War of 1812. Although less than complimentary about New York, the city rose in his estimation when he compared it with Philadelphia, his next stop.

The heat of the weather in the city is so oppressive to English constitutions, that we have established ourselves across the river, on the Jersey shore, at a very pleasant place called Hoboken; here we pay $7 per week each, for board and lodging, and have a quick and pleasant communication with New York by steam ferry-boats every hour during the day to and from it.

On entering our present boarding house to inquire their terms, we encountered the first striking specimen of the effects of freedom without refinement; upon asking for the landlord, a young woman who was sweeping the floor slip-shod, desired us to walk into a room she pointed to; where, she said, we might wait for further orders!! We did as we were ordered, reflecting on this contrast to a good English inn where, upon the traveller's arrival, from the Landlord down to 'Boots', all are immediately upon the alert ready and willing to attend to your wishes....

The Americans at New York have not made a favourable impression upon me: almost every face expresses the game of desperate speculation.... Business here, with the exception of a few respectable houses, is conducted on an apparently slovenly plan; clerks at their banks look like our tavern waiters in *deshabillé*, and the bankers themselves not in appearance so respectable as our clerks.

The town is handsomely built, and several things constantly remind one that here the people rule, and their convenience and comfort are studied: the footways for example are in general twice as broad as ours, in some instances taking up at least as much of the street as that set apart for the carriages; and the hackney coaches are not only neat but elegant in our sense of the word, and both drivers and horses equally superior. In a late publication, it is observed that the goods in the stores are set out in a slovenly manner; my own observation is that their shops or stores are apparently as good, and the stock as well shewn as in many good houses in London: their coffee houses and dinner-rooms in the best lodging houses are even superbly fitted up, very much in the French style: the Tontine, the City and the Bank coffee houses are three of the first; and a person may now dine at any one of them for three dollars and a half per week, and fare sumptuously upon turtle, &c. every day; wine is but little drank, or any other liquor indeed, either at or immediately after dinner by Americans; the reason for this, as given to me by an American, seems good – 'We consider dinner as a sufficient stimulus,' says he 'without adding wine or spirits to it.'

1842 CHARLES DICKENS

British novelist Charles Dickens (1812–1870) visited America in 1842 on a highly publicized tour of a continent unrestrained by the restrictive conventions of the Old World. He stayed in New York for three weeks, where he was highly feted. Here as elsewhere, he made a point of visiting penitentiaries, orphanages and asylums, as well as the more conventional sights.

Was there ever such a sunny street as this Broadway! The pavement stones are polished with the tread of feet until they shine again; the red bricks of the houses might be yet in the dry, hot kilns; and the roofs of those omnibuses look as though, if water were poured on them, they would hiss and smoke, and smell like half-quenched fires. No stint of omnibuses here! Half-a-dozen have gone by within as many minutes. Plenty of hackney cabs and coaches too; gigs, phaetons, large-wheeled tilburies and private carriages – rather of a clumsy make, and not very different from the public vehicles, but built for the heavy roads beyond the city pavement. Negro coachmen and white; in straw hats, black hats, white hats, glazed caps, fur caps; in coats of drab, black, brown, green, blue, nankeen, striped jean and linen; and there in that one instance (look while it passes, or it will be too late), in suits of livery. Some Southern republican that, who puts his blacks in uniform, and swells with Sultan pomp and power....

Heaven save the ladies, how they dress! We have seen more colours in these ten minutes, than we should have seen elsewhere, in as many days. What various parasols! what rainbow silks and satins! what pinking of thin stocking, and pinching of thin shoes, and fluttering of ribbons and silk tassels, and display of rich cloaks with gaudy hoods and linings!...

This narrow thoroughfare, baking and blistering in the sun, is Wall Street: the Stock Exchange and Lombard Street of New York. Many a rapid fortune has been made in this street, and many a no less rapid ruin. Some of these very merchants whom you see hanging about here now, have locked up money in their strongboxes, like the man in the Arabian nights, and opening them again, have found but withered leaves. Below, here by the water side, where the bowsprits of ships stretch across the footway, and almost thrust themselves into the windows, lie the noble American vessels which have made their Packet Service the finest in the world. They have brought hither the foreigners who abound in all the streets: not, perhaps, that there are more here, than in other commercial cities; but elsewhere, they have particular haunts, and you must find them out; here, they pervade the town....

Again across Broadway, and...into another long main street, the Bowery.... The stores are poorer here; the passengers less gay. Clothes ready-made, and meat ready-cooked, are to be bought in these parts; and the lively whirl of carriages is exchanged for the deep rumble of carts and wagons. These signs which are so plentiful, in shape like river buoys, or small balloons, hoisted by cords to poles, and dangling there, announce, as you may see by looking up, 'Oysters in every Style'. They tempt the hungry most at night, for then dull candies glimmering inside, illuminate these dainty words, and make the mouths of idlers water, as they read and linger....

But how quiet the streets are! Are there no itinerant bands; no wind or stringed instruments? No, not one. By day, are there no Punches, Fantoccini, Dancing-dogs, Jugglers, Conjurors, Orchestrinas, or even Barrel-organs? No, not one. Yes, I remember one. One barrel organ and a dancing monkey – sportive by nature, but fast fading into a dull, lumpish monkey, of the Utilitarian school. Beyond that, nothing lively; no, not so much as a white mouse in a twirling cage.

Are there no amusements? Yes. There is a lecture room across the way, from which that glare of light proceeds, and there may be evening service for the ladies thrice a week, or oftener. For the young gentlemen, there is the counting house, the store, the bar-room; the latter, as you may see through these windows, pretty full. Hark! to the clinking-sound of hammers breaking lumps of ice, and to the cool gurgling of the pounded bits, as, in the process of mixing, they are poured from glass to glass. No amusements? What are these suckers of cigars and swallowers of strong drinks, whose hats and legs we see in every possible variety of twist, doing, but amusing themselves? What are the fifty newspapers, which those precocious urchins are bawling down the street, and which are kept filed within, what are they but amusements? Not vapid waterish amusements, but good strong stuff; dealing in round abuse and blackguard names; pulling off the roofs of private houses, as the Halting Devil did in Spain; pimping and pandering for all degrees of vicious taste, and gorging with coined lies the most voracious maw; imputing to every man in public life the coarsest and the vilest motives; scaring away from the stabbed and prostrate body-politic, every Samaritan of clear conscience and good deeds; and setting on, with yell and whistle and the clapping of foul hands, the vilest vermin and worst birds of prey. No amusements!

1866 JOHN WALTER

The New York John Walter (see page 80) saw and recorded included many features familiar today, but not the skyline.

We have been busy enough, as you may suppose, since we arrived here, and have seen most of the lions of the place. Our first visit was to the tower of Trinity Church, at the bottom of Broadway, in order to get a bird's-eye view of the city.... The view extends all over the bay and its surrounding shores on one side, and a long way up the Hudson and the Sound on the other; but chiefly reveals the fact that the roofs of the houses in New York are nearly flat.

The city is singularly destitute of fine public buildings, or other striking architectural features. It is the vast size of the 'stores' and hotels, and the beauty of the streets in the more fashionable quarters, that constitute its chief merits. The city is built on an island, called Manhattan, about seven or eight miles long, by two or three wide. It is laid out in 'avenues' and streets, which intersect each other at right angles, the avenues forming the longer, and the streets the shorter axis. Of these, Fifth Avenue is by far the finest; it extends from the centre of the city to the 'Central Park', and is the most aristocratic quarter in New York. It contains the principal clubs and the Fifth Avenue Hotel, the latest of those enormous caravansaries of which Astor House, in Broadway, was the first, and destined to be succeeded by others still vaster and more imposing. The private houses, as in all the best streets in New York, have a half-sunk basement, with a flight of ten or twelve steps up to the front door. This causes them, of course, to be well set back from the pavement, a great improvement upon our ordinary low-level system in London. They are built either of bright, red brick, relieved with green shutters, or of brown sandstone or white marble. The general appearance of the streets is remarkably bright and cheerful, and there is no smoke. To this agreeable picture, however, there are some drawbacks. The streets, as a general rule, are execrably paved, and there are no cabs. The bad paving is laid at the door of the Corporation, which enjoys the worst possible repu-tation, and is charged with every species of jobbery and rascality. The want of cabs is a great nuisance, though the inconvenience is less felt here than it would be in London, where the streets are too narrow and the traffic too great to admit of tramways and street cars. These latter monopolize the passenger traffic of most of the streets, but Fifth Avenue and Broadway are at present exempt from them. The 'Central Park', which may some day deserve that name, though at present quite at the extremity of the city, somewhat resembles the Bois de Boulogne, but is even more beautifully laid out. It is a wild, rocky district, of about 900 acres, and contains a beautiful lake and many miles of walks and carriage drives....

The Americans are early risers, and our breakfast table is pretty well filled by eight o'clock. The bill of fare is truly sumptuous, and receives ample justice at the hands of the guests. Oysters, fried or stewed; beefsteaks and mutton chops; kidneys and hashes of various kinds; omelettes; eggs, boiled, poached, or 'jobbled'; tomatoes, in various forms; hominy, boiled or fried; breadstuffs, and 'corn' cakes of all sorts form the staple of this important meal.

1947 SIMONE DE BEAUVOIR

French intellectual and feminist Simone de Beauvoir (see page 122) visited America in 1947, fascinated by the dissociation between her mental pictures of a city so well known from popular culture, and the actual city she encountered.

25 January I'm flying to New York.... Despite all the books I've read, the films, the photographs, the stories, New York is a legendary city in my past; there is no path from the reality to the legend. Across from old Europe, on the threshold of a continent populated by 160 million people, New York belongs to the future. How could I jump wholeheartedly over my own life? I try to reason with myself – New York is real and present – but this feeling persists.... I don't know if it will be through anger or hope, but something is going to be revealed – a world so full, so rich and so unexpected that I'll have the extraordinary adventure of becoming a different me....

D. P. has come to meet me; I don't know her. But off I go, borne away beside a young woman I've never seen, through a city my eyes don't yet know how to see. The car drives so fluidly, the road beneath the wheels is so smooth, that the earth seems as evanescent as air. We follow a river, we cross a metal bridge, and my neighbor says suddenly, 'That's Broadway.' Then, all at once, I see. I see broad, brightly lit streets where hundreds and hundreds of cars are driving, stopping, and starting again with such discipline you would think they were guided from above by some magnetic providence. The regular grid of the streets, the immovable stop signs at the perpendicular intersections, the mathematical sequence of red and green traffic lights all create such an impression of order and peace that the city seems silent. The fact is, you don't hear a single honk or exhaust backfiring, and now I understand why our American visitors are surprised by the awful screeching of brakes at our street corners. Here the cars glide by on a blanketed roadway punctuated by rising geysers of steam. It's like a silent film. The shiny cars look like they've just left the showroom, and the pavement seems as clean as the tiles of a Dutch kitchen. Light has washed away all the stains; it's a supernatural light that transfigures the asphalt, that wraps a halo around the flowers, silk dresses, candies, nylon stockings, gloves, bags, shoes, furs and ribbons offered in the shop windows. I look avidly.... Tomorrow New York will be a city. But this evening is magical....

26 January It's nine o'clock in the morning. It's Sunday. The streets are deserted. A few neon signs are still lit. Not a pedestrian, not a car; nothing disturbs the rectilinear grid of Eighth Avenue. Cubes, prisms, parallelograms; the houses are abstract solids and surfaces; the intersection, an abstract of two volumes – its materials have no density or structure; the space itself seems to have been set in molds. I do not move; I look. I'm here, and New York will be mine.... I go down Broadway; it's really me. I'm walking in streets not yet traveled by me, streets where my life has not yet been carved, streets without any scent of the past....

Slogans run through my head: 'City of contrasts'. These alleys smelling of spices and packing paper at the foot of facades with thousands of windows: that is one contrast. I encounter another contrast with each step, and they are all different. 'A vertical city', 'passionate geometries', 'thrilling geometries': such phrases are perfect descriptions of these skyscrapers, these facades, these avenues: I see that. And I've often read, 'New York with its cathedrals.' I could have invented the phrase – all these old clichés seem so hollow. Yet in the freshness of discovery, the words 'contrasts' and 'cathedrals' also come to my lips, and I'm surprised they seem so faded when the reality they capture is unchanged. People have told me something more precise: 'On the Bowery on Sundays, the drunks sleep on the sidewalks.' Here is the Bowery; the drunks are sleeping on the sidewalks. This is just what the words meant, and their precision disconcerts me. How could they have seemed so empty when they are so true? It isn't with words that I will grasp New York. I no longer think of grasping it: I will be transformed by it....

27 **January** If I want to decode New York, I must meet New Yorkers. There are names in my address book but no faces to match. I'll have to talk on the telephone, in English, to people whom I don't know and who don't know me. Going down into the hotel lobby, I'm more intimidated than if I were going to take an oral exam. This lobby stuns me with its exoticism, an unnatural exoticism. I'm the Zulu frightened by a bicycle, the peasant lost in the Paris Metro. There's a newspaper and a cigar stand, a Western Union office, a hairdresser, a writing room where stenographers and typists take dictation from clients – it's at once a club, an office, a waiting room and a large department store. I perceive around me all the conveniences of everyday life, but I don't know what to do.... I'm confused by the coins.... For ten minutes I try in vain to get a telephone line; all the machines reject the nickel I stubbornly keep sliding into the slot meant for quarters. I remain sitting in one of the booths, worn out. I want to give up: I hate this malicious instrument. But in the end I can't just stay wrapped in my solitude. I ask the Western Union employee for help. This time someone answers.... They weren't expecting me, and I have nothing to offer. I simply say, 'I'm here.' I have no face either; I'm just a name bandied about by mutual friends.... But the voices are almost friendly, natural. This naturalness already comforts me, as a kind of friendship. After three calls, though, I close my address book, flushed.

PARIS

Paris began as the Roman town of Lutetia. By the late 13th century it was the largest city in western Europe, a centre of learning based on the Sorbonne. Its architecture included the Gothic Basilica of St Denis, the mausoleum for the kings of France; Notre-Dame Cathedral; and the Sainte-Chapelle, built by Louis IX (r. 1226–70 — known as St Louis) as the home for expensive relics brought back from Crusade. The monarchs made the Louvre (originally a castle) and the Tuileries Palace their home.

In the early 16th century, Francis I introduced Renaissance art and architecture to Paris, but the city suffered in the religious wars later in the same century. In the 17th century the reign of Louis XIV saw a monumental building programme of churches, palaces and grand avenues (despite his moving the capital to Versailles); it became a high point on any Grand Tour. Louis XV (r. 1715–74) created the large Place Louis XV (now the Place de la Concorde) on the west side of the city, where his grandson Louis XVI would be guillotined in 1793.

The Revolution brought chaos to the city, but Napoleon I did much to reglorify Paris, building the Arc de Triomphe at the end of the Champs-Elysées; after further urban uprisings in 1830 and 1848, Paris was radically transformed in the 1850s and 1860s by Napoleon III and Baron Haussmann, who together built 40,000 houses in a unified style along wide, straight boulevards.

Early 20th-century Paris was acknowledged as the cultural heart of Europe, but was materially run down following the First World War. Artists, writers and thinkers were attracted from across the world to shiver in Rive Gauche garrets, drink in bars, make love and produce masterworks. Paris was occupied by Nazi Germany in June 1940 following the Blitzkrieg conquest of France. After liberation in 1944, it was gradually rebuilt and stylishly modernized.

1287 RABBAN BAR SAUMA

Rabban Bar Sauma (c. 1220–1294) was a Nestorian Christian monk, born near Beijing of a Mongol background. While on pilgrimage to Jerusalem, he was appointed ambassador of the Mongol Il-Khan Abaqa and his son Arghun, who sought an alliance with the Christian West to drive the Egyptian Mamluks from the Holy Land. Although he met the Cardinals in Rome, Philip IV (the Fair) of France in Paris and Edward I of England (in Gascony), nothing concrete came of his embassy. He died in Baghdad.

Afterwards they went to the country of Paris. And King Philip sent out a large company of men to meet them, who brought them into the city with great ceremony. The King assigned to Rabban Sauma a place to dwell, and three days later summoned him to his presence. And the King asked him, 'Why have you come? Who sent you?' Rabban Sauma replied, 'King Arghun and the Catholicus of the East have sent me concerning Jerusalem.' And he gave the King the letters and gifts he had brought. And the King answered, 'If it is true that the Mongols, though they are not Christians, will fight against the Arabs for the capture of Jerusalem, we should fight with them.'

Rabban Sauma said to him, 'Now we have seen the glory of your kingdom, we ask you to show us the churches and the shrines, and the relics of the saints, and everything else which is found here and not in any other country, so that when we return we may make known what we have seen.' Then the King commanded his Amirs, 'Show them all the wonderful things which we have here, and afterwards I myself will show them what I have.'

And Rabban Sauma and his companions remained for a month of days in this great city of Paris, and they saw everything. There were 30,000 scholars engaged in the study of ecclesiastical books of instruction, commentaries and exegesis of the Holy Scriptures, and also of profane learning; and they studied wisdom, philosophy and rhetoric, and the arts of healing, geometry, arithmetic, and the science of the planets and the stars; they engaged constantly in writing theses, and all of them received money for subsistence from the King.

They also saw a great church in which were the tombs of dead kings, with statues in gold and silver upon their tombs. 500 monks performed commemoration services here, and they too ate and drank at the expense of the king. And the crowns of those kings, as well as their armour and apparel, were laid upon their tombs. In short they saw everything that was splendid and renowned.

After this the King summoned them, and they went to him in the church. And he asked Rabban Sauma, 'Have you seen what we have?' Then they went into an upper chamber of gold, which the King opened, and he brought out a coffer of beryl in which was laid the Crown of Thorns that the Jews placed upon the head of our Lord when they crucified Him. The Crown was visible through the transparent beryl. And there was with it a piece of the wood of the Cross. The King said, 'When our fathers took Constantinople, and sacked Jerusalem, they brought these blessed objects from it.' And we blessed the King and besought him to permit us to return.

1612 THOMAS CORYAT

The English gentleman Thomas Coryat (c. 1577–1617) from Somerset travelled across northern Europe and Italy in 1608–11, much of the time on foot and mainly for reasons of curiosity. Coryat's Crudities, *the record of his journey, was highly popular, and introduced many Englishmen to Continental manners. The partially built bridge he describes is the Pont Neuf, built by Henry IV.*

A little on this side of Paris, there is the fairest gallows that ever I saw, built upon a little hillock called Mount Falcon, which consists of fourteen fair pillars of freestone: this gallows was made in the time of the Guisian massacre, to hang the admiral of France, Chatillion, who was a Protestant, in AD 1572....

This city is exceeding great, no less then ten miles in circuit, very populous and full of very goodly buildings, both public and private.... It is environed with very ancient stone walls that were built by Julius Caesar when he made his residence here in the midst of his French conquests, from whom some have not doubted in former times to call it the city of Julius.... As for her name of Paris, she hath it (as some write) from Paris, the 18th king of Gallia Celtica, whom some write to have been descended from Japhet, one of the three sons of Noah, and to have founded this city: but the name of Lutetia it doth well brook, being so called from the Latin word *Lutum*, which signifies dirt, because many of the streets are the dirtiest, and so consequently the most stinking, of all that ever I saw in any city in my life.

It is divided into three parts, the university, the city and the town, by the noble river the Seine.... The university, whereof I can speak very little (for to my great grief I omitted to observe those particulars in the same that it behoved an observative traveller, having seen but one of their principal colleges, which was their famous Sorbonne, that fruitful nursery of school-divines) was instituted in the year 796, by the good Emperor Charles the Great....

But to return again to the noble river Seine: there was building over it when I was in the city a goodly bridge of white freestone, which was almost ended....

The Cathedral Church is dedicated to Our Lady...I could see no notable matter in it, saving the statue of St Christopher on the right hand at the coming in of the great gate, which indeed is very exquisitely done, all the rest being but ordinary, as I have seen in other churches. The street which is called la rue de notre Dame...is very fair, being of a great length, though not so broad as our Cheapside in London: but in one thing it exceeds any street in London; for such is the uniformity of almost all the houses of the same street which stand upon the bridge, that they are made alike both in proportion of workmanship and matter: so that they make the neatest show of all the houses in Paris.

I went...to the King's Palace, which is called the Louvre. This was first built by Philip Augustus King of France, about the year 1214, and being afterward ruined by time, was most beautifully repaired by Henry II. Therein I observed these particulars: a fair quadrangular court, with goodly lodgings about it four storeys high, whose outside is exquisitely wrought with white free-stone, and decked with many stately pillars and beautiful images made of the same stone....

There is a goodly palace called the Tuileries, where the Queen Mother was wont to lie, and which was built by herself. This palace is called the Tuileries, because heretofore they used to burn tile there, before the palace was built. For this French word Tuilerie doth signify in French a place for burning of tile....

I observed in Paris a great abundance of mules, which are so highly esteemed among them, that the judges and councillors do usually ride on them with their foot clothes. Also I noted that gentlemen and great personages in Paris do more ride with foot-clothes, even four to one than our English gentlemen do.

1790 ARTHUR YOUNG

While undertaking a tour of France in which he commented on agricultural and social conditions, British economist Arthur Young (see page 99) saw Louis XVI and Queen Marie Antoinette in the Tuileries Palace under virtual house arrest at the hands of the revolutionary mob.

4 January After breakfast, walk in the gardens of the Tuileries, where there is the most extraordinary sight that either French or English eyes could ever behold at Paris. The king, walking with six grenadiers of the *milice bourgeoise* with an officer or two of his household, and a page. The doors of the gardens are kept shut in respect to him, in order to exclude everybody but deputies, or those who have admission tickets. When he entered the palace, the doors of the gardens were thrown open for all without distinction, though the queen was still walking with a lady of her court. She also was attended so closely by the *gardes bourgeoises*, that she could not speak, but in a low voice, without being heard by them. A mob followed her, talking very loud, and paying no other apparent respect than that of taking off their hats wherever she passed, which was indeed more than I expected. Her Majesty does not appear to be in health; she seems to be much affected, and shews it in her face; but the king is as plump as ease can render him. By his orders, there is a little garden railed off, for the Dauphin to amuse himself in, and a small room is built in it to retire to in case of rain; here he was at work with his little hoe and rake, but not without a guard of two grenadiers. He is a very pretty good-natured-looking boy, of five or six years old, with an agreeable countenance; wherever he goes, all hats are taken off to him, which I was glad to observe. All the family being kept thus close prisoners (for such they are in effect) afford, at first view, a shocking spectacle; and is really so, if the act were not absolutely necessary to effect the revolution; this I conceive to be impossible; but if it were necessary, no one can blame the people for taking every measure possible to secure that liberty they had seized in the violence of a revolution. At such a moment, nothing is to be condemned but what endangers the national freedom. I must, however, freely own, that I have my doubts whether this treatment of the royal family can be justly esteemed any security to liberty; or, on the contrary, whether it were not a very dangerous step, that exposes to hazard whatever had been gained.

I have spoken with several persons today, and have started objections to the present system, stronger even than they appear to me, in order to learn their sentiments; and it is evident, they are at the present moment under an apprehension of an attempt towards a counter revolution. The danger of it very much, if not absolutely, results from the violence which has been used towards the royal family.

1855 QUEEN VICTORIA

In 1855, Queen Victoria and Prince Albert paid a triumphant visit as guests of Emperor Napoleon III, the nephew of Napoleon I, who had been decisively defeated by Britain just forty years before. The Queen recounted the visit in detail in her diary.

20 **August** At ¼ p. 10 we started for Paris, with all our suite. The Emperor has pretty barouches, smaller than ours, & bay horses harnessed just like ours. The liveries are green, black & gold, with red & gold waistcoats. We drove by the Bois de Boulogne, the new Route de l'Impératrice, which is being planted & will be very fine, through that splendid Arc de Triomphe, finished in Louis Philippe's time – along the Champs-Elysées (our usual road every day) to the Exposition des Beaux Arts, which, together with the Palais de l'Industrie, with which it is connected, stands in it.... The Elysée is very pretty, but the decorations, excepting in one or two rooms are not nearly finished, & it is a small building. Here again, rooms were prepared for us, in which there were many souvenirs of Napoleon, la Reine Hortense, &c. Here, we took luncheon in a room, in which hung portraits of all the contemporary Sovereigns. Our quiet luncheon over, Albert went to put on his uniform, & the Emperor kindly took Bertie out in his Curricle, which he drove himself, with only two servants, taking him all over Paris. It was not the *least* interesting incident in this most eventful, interesting & delight-ful visit – showing the confidence that exists between us.... This over, the Emperor took us round the very pretty, shady little garden, & we reentered open carriages & drove along the beautiful Boulevards, the Rue de Rivoli, & quite new, the Emperor having cleared away many streets, making the new ones quite magnificent – by the new part of the Louvre, the whole of which is truly splendid – the Place de la Concorde, very fine, where poor Louis XVI, Marie-Antoinette & so many others were guillotined – past the Hotel de Ville – on to the Palais de Justice, from the steps of which the view of the richly decorated streets & enthusiastic assembled thousands was splendid. We visited the adjoining Sainte-Chapelle, which has been most exquisitely restored. It is small, of the purest early Gothic architecture & is celebrated for containing the heart of St Louis (the Chapel was built by him), & for many interesting ceremonies having taken place there. In passing the bridge from which one has a very fine view of the town, one sees the Conciergerie & the Emperor, pointing to it said: '*voilà ou j'étais en prison*'. What a *strange, incredible contrast*, to be *driving with us*, as *Emperor* through the streets – in triumph! We next went to the Cathedral of Notre Dame, the outside of which is magnificent, & were received by the Archbishop of Paris & Clergy. Except the beautiful carving of the Choir there is nothing particularly to admire in the interior. The Hotel de Ville is magnificent & the

street leading to it has been much widened & opened out. We passed along the Boulevards, by the Porte St Martin & Porte St Denis, along the Rue de la Paix, Rue Castiglione, full of shops & fine houses, by the Place Vendôme & the Place de la Bastille, where the Colonne de Juillet is placed. – The Fountains of the Château d'Eau, & then home, the usual way, by near 6. Everything, so gay, so bright, & though very hot, the air so clear & light. The absence of smoke keeps everything so white & bright, & this, in Paris, with much gilding about the shops, green shutters, &c. produces a brilliancy of effect, which is quite incredible. On getting home, we visited the dear Empress who received us upstairs for a short while, then we went back to our rooms. Nothing can be kinder, or more agreeable, than the Emperor is, & so quiet, which is such a comfort on occasions like this. – The view of Paris, from our rooms & balcony, lit up by the coming sun, the Arc de Triomphe rising so majestically & beautifully in the distance had a marvellous effect. I sat sketching on the balcony.

1869 MARK TWAIN

The American humourist Samuel Langhorne Clemens (1835–1910), who wrote under the pseudonym Mark Twain, was sent to Europe by a San Francisco newspaper; his record of this journey was published in The Innocents Abroad *(1869); he made a second trip to Europe in the late 1870s, which he published as* A Tramp Abroad *(1880).*

As nightfall approached we entered a wilderness of odorous flowers and shrubbery, sped through it, and then, excited, delighted and half persuaded that we were only the sport of a beautiful dream, lo, we stood in magnificent Paris!

What excellent order they kept about that vast depot! There was no frantic crowding and jostling, no shouting and swearing, and no swaggering intrusion of services by rowdy hackmen. These latter gentry stood outside – stood quietly by their long line of vehicles and said never a word. A kind of hackman general seemed to have the whole matter of transportation in his hands. He politely received the passengers and ushered them to the kind of conveyance they wanted, and told the driver where to deliver them. There was no 'talking back', no dissatisfaction about overcharging, no grumbling about anything. In a little while we were speeding through the streets of Paris and delightfully recognizing certain names and places with which books had long ago made us familiar. It was like meeting an old friend when we read Rue de Rivoli on the street corner; we knew the genuine vast palace of the Louvre as well as we knew its pictures; when we passed by the Column of July we needed no one to tell us what it was or to remind us that on its site once stood the grim Bastille, that grave of human hopes and happiness, that dismal prison house within whose dungeons so many young faces put on the wrinkles of age, so many proud spirits grew humble, so many brave hearts broke.

We secured rooms at the hotel, or rather, we had three beds put into one room, so that we might be together, and then we went out to a restaurant, just after lamplighting, and ate a comfortable, satisfactory, lingering dinner. It was a pleasure to eat where everything was so tidy, the food so well cooked, the waiters so polite, and the coming and departing company so moustached, so frisky, so affable, so fearfully and wonderfully Frenchy! All the surroundings were gay and enlivening. Two hundred people sat at little tables on the sidewalk, sipping wine and coffee; the streets were thronged with light vehicles and with joyous pleasure-seekers; there was music in the air, life and action all about us, and a conflagration of gaslight everywhere!

After dinner we felt like seeing such Parisian specialties as we might see without distressing exertion, and so we sauntered through the brilliant streets and looked at the dainty trifles in variety stores and jewelry shops. Occasionally, merely for the pleasure of being cruel, we put unoffending Frenchmen on the rack with questions framed in the incomprehensible jargon of their native language, and while they writhed we impaled them, we peppered them, we scarified them, with their own vile verbs and participles....

We adjourned to one of those pretty cafés and took supper and tested the wines of the country, as we had been instructed to do, and found them harmless and unexciting. They might have been exciting, however, if we had chosen to drink a sufficiency of them.

To close our first day in Paris cheerfully and pleasantly, we now sought our grand room in the Grand Hotel du Louvre and climbed into our sumptuous bed to read and smoke – but alas!

It was pitiful,
In a whole city-full,
Gas we had none.

No gas to read by – nothing but dismal candles. It was a shame. We tried to map out excursions for the morrow; we puzzled over French 'guides to Paris'; we talked disjointedly in a vain endeavor to make head or tail of the wild chaos of the day's sights and experiences; we subsided to indolent smoking; we gaped and yawned and stretched – then feebly wondered if we were really and truly in renowned Paris, and drifted drowsily away into that vast mysterious void which men call sleep.

1891 ANTON CHEKHOV

Russian playwright Anton Chekhov (1860–1904) travelled to Italy in 1891. On his return, he went to Paris and visited the site of the 1889 Exposition Universelle, held to commemorate the centenary of the storming of the Bastille, and for which the Eiffel Tower was the symbol. While enjoying 'Gay Paree' he also witnessed the political turmoil in the aftermath of a miners' strike that was put down by force, as he described in letters to his sister Maria Chekhova (1863–1957).

21 April Today is Easter. Very well, then. Christ is risen! This is the first Easter I've ever spent away from home.

I arrived in Paris on Friday morning and went straight to the Exposition. Yes, the Eiffel Tower is very, very high. The rest of the Exposition buildings I saw from the outside only, because the cavalry was stationed inside in case of disturbances. Riots are expected for Friday. Crowds of highly agitated people walked up and down the streets yelling and whistling, and the police kept dispersing them. About ten policemen are enough here to break up a big crowd. The police all attack together, and the crowd runs like crazy. I was deemed worthy of being caught in one of the attacks: a policeman grabbed me by the shoulder and began shoving me in front of him.

The city is very crowded. The streets swarm and seethe with people. Every street is like a torrent. The noise and hubbub are constant. The sidewalks are filled with tables; at every table there sit Frenchmen who feel completely at home on the street. They're wonderful people. But Paris is indescribable, so I'll put off describing it until I get home....

24 April Imagine how pleased I was to visit the Chamber of Deputies during the very session at which the Minister of Internal Affairs was being called to account for the violence the government resorted to while putting down the workers in revolt at Fourmies (many people killed and wounded). It was a stormy and highly interesting session.

People girding themselves in boa constrictors, ladies kicking their legs up to the ceiling, flying people, lions, *cafés chantants*, dinners and lunches are beginning to disgust me. It's time to go home, I feel like working.

1907 GERTRUDE STEIN

American novelist and art collector Gertrude Stein (1874–1946) made Paris her home from 1903. Her memoir of these years – including her long friendship with Picasso, in whose studio she saw his unfinished, seminal Les Demoiselles d'Avignon *– was written in the voice of her partner, Alice B. Toklas* (The Autobiography of Alice B. Toklas, *1933*).

Gertrude Stein and I about ten days later went to Montmartre, I for the first time. I have never ceased to love it. We go there every now and then and I always have the same tender expectant feeling that I had then. It is a place where you were always standing and sometimes waiting, not for anything to happen, but just standing. The inhabitants of Montmartre did not sit much, they mostly stood which was just as well as the chairs, the dining room chairs of France, did not tempt one to sit. So I went to Montmartre and I began my apprenticeship of standing. We first went to see Picasso and I then we went to see Fernande. Picasso now never likes to go to Montmartre, he does not like to think about it much less talk about it. Even to Gertrude Stein he is hesitant about talking of it, there were things that at that time cut deeply into his Spanish pride and the end of his Montmartre life was bitterness and disillusion, and there is nothing more bitter than Spanish disillusion.

But at this time he was in and of Montmartre and lived in the rue Ravignan.

We went to the Odeon and there got into an omnibus, that is we mounted on top of an omnibus, the nice old horse-pulled omnibuses that went pretty quickly and steadily across Paris and up the hill to the place Blanche. There we got out and climbed a steep street lined with shops with things to eat, the rue Lepic, and then turning we went around a corner and climbed even more steeply in fact almost straight up and came to the rue Ravignan, now place Emile-Goudeau but otherwise unchanged, with its steps leading up to the little flat square with its few but tender little trees, a man carpentering in the corner of it, the last time I was there not very long ago there was still a man carpentering in a corner of it, and a little café just before you went up the steps where they all used to eat, it is still there, and to the left the low wooden building of studios that is still there.

We went up the couple of steps and through the open door passing on our left the studio in which later Juan Gris was to live out his martyrdom but where then lived a certain Vaillant, a nondescript painter who was to lend his studio as a ladies dressing room at the famous banquet for Rousseau, and then we passed a steep flight of steps leading down where Max Jacob had a studio a little later, and we passed another steep little stairway which led to the studio where not long before a young fellow had committed suicide, Picasso painted one of the most wonderful of his early pictures of the friends gathered round the coffin, we passed all this to a larger door where Gertrude Stein knocked and Picasso opened the door and we went in.

He was dressed in what the French call the *singe* or monkey costume, overalls made of blue jean or brown, I think his was blue and it is called a *singe* or monkey because being all of one piece with a belt, if the belt is not fastened, and it very often is not, it hangs down behind and so makes a monkey. His eyes were more wonderful than even I remembered, so full and so brown, and his hands so dark and delicate and alert. We went further in. There was a couch in one corner, a very small stove that did for cooking and heating in the other corner, some chairs, the large broken one Gertrude Stein sat in when she was painted and a general smell of dog and paint and there was a big dog there and Picasso moved her about from one place to another exactly as if the dog had been a large piece of furniture. He asked us to sit down but as all the chairs were full we all stood up and stood until we left. It was my first experience of standing but afterwards I found that they all stood that way for hours. Against the wall was an enormous picture, a strange picture of light and dark colours, that is all I can say, of a group, an enormous group and next to it another in a sort of a red brown, of three women, square and posturing, all of it rather frightening. Picasso and Gertrude Stein stood together talking. I stood back and looked. I cannot say I realized anything but I felt that there was something painful and beautiful there and oppressive but imprisoned....

We left then and continued to climb higher up the hill. What did you think of what you saw, asked Miss Stein. Well I did see something. Sure you did, she said, but did you see what it had to do with those two pictures you sat in front of so long at the vernissage. Only that Picassos were rather awful and the others were not. Sure, she said, as Pablo once remarked, when you make a thing, it is so complicated making it that it is bound to be ugly, but those that do it after you they don't have to worry about making it and they can make it pretty, and so everybody can like it when the others make it.

PRAGUE

Built on an ancient crossing point of the Vltava River (Moldau in German), Prague developed around its castle (Hrad) in the 9th century. An early prince was Wenceslas, who was murdered in c. 939 but became the city's patron saint. It became the chief town of Bohemia and in the 14th century the Holy Roman Emperor Charles IV built the university and the Charles Bridge over the river. In the early 1400s Jan Hus led a movement of religious reform, and it was a centre of the Protestant Reformation in the 16th century.

After devastation in the Thirty Years War (1618–48), the now-Catholic city flourished and became a renowned centre for arts and music. In the 19th century Prague was still under Austrian rule and saw the development of industry, which complemented the city's cultural heritage.

Following the First World War, Prague became capital of the new republic of Czechoslovakia (described by British Prime Minister Neville Chamberlain in 1938 as 'a faraway country' of whose 'people we know nothing'.) It was under German occupation between 1940 and 1945, and under Soviet domination to 1989, despite the short-lived Prague Spring of 1968. It is now capital of the Czech Republic.

1591 FYNES MORYSON

English gentleman and traveller Fynes Moryson (see page 21) visited Prague in the 1590s, recording the sights and other curiosities.

In the afternoon we went three miles, for the most part through fruitful hills of corn, the rest through rocks and mountains planted with vines, and so came to Prague, through which the river Molda runneth, but is not navigable. On the west side of Molda is the emperor's castle, seated on a most high mountain, in the fall whereof is the suburb called Kleinseit, or little side. From this suburb to go into the city, a long stone bridge is to be passed over Molda, which runs from the south to the north, and divides the suburb from the city, to which as you go, on the left side is a little city of the Jews, compassed with walls, and before your eyes towards the east, is the city called new Prague, both which cities are compassed about with a third, called old Prague. So as Prague consists of three cities, all compassed with walls, yet is nothing less than strong, and except the stench of the streets drive back the Turks, or they meet them in open field, there is small hope in the fortifications thereof.

The streets are filthy, there be divers large marketplaces, the building of some houses is of freestone, but the most part are of timber and clay, and are built with little beauty or art, the walls being all of whole trees as they come out of the wood, the which with the bark are laid so rudely, as they may on both sides be seen. Molda in the winter used to be so frozen, as it bears carts, and the ice thereof being cut in great pieces, is laid up in cellars for the emperor and princes to mingle with their wine in summer, which me thinks can neither be savoury, nor healthful, since neither the heat of the clime, nor the strength of the Bohemian wines (being small and sharp) require any such cooling....

In public inns they demand some six Bohemian *grosh* for a meal, yet do they not commonly give meals at an ordinary rate, as they do through all Germany; but what meat you require, that they dress, and the servant buying all things out of doors (after the manner of Poland) makes a reckoning of the expenses. My self had my diet with a citizen very conveniently for a dollar and a half weekly. I did here eat English oysters pickled, and a young Bohemian coming in by chance and tasting them, but not knowing the price, desired the merchant to give him a dish at his charge, which contained some twenty oysters, and finding them very savoury, he called for five dishes one after another, for which the merchant demanded and had of him five dollars, the dearness no less displeasing his mind, then the meat had pleased his taste.

As you pass over Molda from the suburb Kleinseit, into the city, there is a hand of stone as it were cut off upon the gate of the city; signifying to strangers, that whosoever draws a sword there, or upon the bridge, loses his hand; and the like hand there is to the same purpose, on the Senate house in the town. The emperor hath two enclosures walled about, which they call gardens, one of which is called Stella, because the trees are planted in the figure of stars, and a little fair house therein is likewise built, with six corners in form of a star. And in this place he kept twelve camels, an Indian ox, yellow, all over rugged, and hairy upon the throat like a lion; and an Indian calf, and two leopards, which were said to be tame, if such wild beasts may be tamed. They were of a yellow colour spotted with black, the head partly like a lion, partly like a cat, the tail like a cat, the body like a greyhound, and when the hunts-man went abroad, at call they leaped up behind him, sitting upon the horse like a dog on the hinder parts; being so swift in running, as they would easily kill a hart....

In the church of the emperor's castle, these things are to be seen. A fair chapel named after the emperor's sister, married to the French king and crowned queen of the French. Another chapel belonging to the Barons, called Popelii (the greatest family of the kingdom, next to the Baron of Rosenberg) which chapel is proper to them for burial, and is dedicated to

St Andrew the Apostle. In the emperor's church is a monument of Rudolf II, then living emperor, built of white marble, and compassed with grates of iron. In the same place lie buried Charles IV in the year 1378. Wenceslaus in the year 1419, Ladislaus in the year 1459. Ferdinand IV in the year 1564. Maximillian II in the year 1577 (all being archdukes of Austria, and emperors) and George Pogiebrachius a Bohemian, and king of Bohemia. To all these is one monument erected, and that of small beauty....

In Old Prague towards the south, and upon the east side of Molda, there is an old palace, where they shew a trapdoor, by which the queen was wont to slide down into a bath, where she used to satisfy her unlawful lust. In the same place is graven the leap of a horse, no less wonderful then Bayard's fabulous leap. The house of Kelley, a famous English alchemist, was of old a sanctuary, and built for an order of friars...

I lived at Prague some two months.

1786 HESTER LYNCH PIOZZI

Hester Lynch Piozzi (1741–1821), an English woman of letters and – as Hester Lynch Thrale – friend of Samuel Johnson, visited Prague in 1786 and was struck by the quality of the food on offer. Written in conversational style, her two-volume Observations and Reflections Made in the Course of a Journey through France, Italy, and Germany *(1789) recorded her impressions and adventures on the Grand Tour.*

The eating here is incomparable; I never saw such poultry even at London or Bath, and there is a plenty of game that amazes one; no inn so wretched but you have a pheasant for your supper, and often partridge soup. The fish is carried about the streets in so elegant a style it tempts one; a very large round bathing-tub, as we should call it, set barrow-wife on two not very low wheels, is easily pushed along by one man, though full of the most pellucid water, in which the carp, tench and eels are all leaping alive, to a size and perfection I am ashamed to relate; but the tench of four and five pounds weight have a richness and flavour one had no notion of till we arrived at Vienna, and they are the same here.

How trade lands or moves in these countries I cannot tell; there is great rigour shewn at the customs house; but till the shopkeepers learn to keep their doors open at least for the whole of the short days, not shut them up so and go to sleep at one or two o'clock for a couple of hours, I think they do not deserve to be disturbed by customers who bring ready money. Tomorrow [30 November 1786] we set out, wrapped in good furs and flannels, for Dresden.

1936 ALBERT CAMUS

The young French philosopher and novelist Albert Camus (1913–1960) visited interwar Prague and recorded his feelings of isolation in his essay Death in the Soul.

I arrived in Prague at six in the evening.... I came out of the station, walked by some gardens and found myself suddenly thrown into the middle of the Avenue Wenceslas, swarming with people at that time in the evening. Around me were a million people who had been alive all this time and whose existence had never impinged upon mine. They were alive. I was thousands of kilometres away from a familiar country. I could not understand their language. They all walked quickly. And as they overtook me, they all cut themselves off from me. I felt lost.

I had little money. Enough to live for six days.... So I set out to look for a cheap hotel. I was in the new part of town, and all those that I could see were bursting with lights, laughter and women. I walked faster. Something in my rapid pace already seemed like flight. However, towards eight in the evening, exhausted, I reached the old town. There I was attracted by a modest-looking hotel, with a small doorway. I go in. I fill in the form, take my key. I have room number 34 on the third floor. I open the door and find myself in a most luxurious room. I look to see how much it costs – twice as expensive as I thought. The problem of money becomes really acute. I can live only poorly in this great city....

I washed, shaved, and methodically explored the town. I lost myself in the sumptuous baroque churches, trying to rediscover a homeland in them, but emerging emptier and in deeper despair after this disappointing encounter with myself. I wandered along the Vltava and saw the water swirling and foaming at its dams. I spent endless hours in the immense silent and empty district of the Hradchin. At sunset, in the shadow of its cathedral and palaces, my lonely step echoed along the streets.... Once, however, in a baroque cloister at the far end of town, the gentleness of the hour, the softly tinkling bells, the clusters of pigeons flying from the old tower, together with something like the scent of herbs and nothingness, gave birth in me to a silence full of tears, that almost delivered me.... And what other profit can we seek to draw from travel? Here I am stripped bare, in a town where the notices are written in strange, incomprehensible hieroglyphs, where I have no friends to talk to, in short where I have no distractions.

And I can now say that what I retain from Prague is the smell of cucumbers soaked in vinegar, which are sold at every street corner to eat between your fingers, and whose bitter and piquant flavour would awake and feed my anguish as soon as I had crossed the threshold of my hotel. That, and perhaps also a certain tune played on an accordion. Beneath my windows a blind, one-armed man, sitting on his instrument, kept it in place with one buttock while opening and shutting it with his one good hand. It was always the same childish and tender tune which woke me every morning and set me down brusquely in the unadorned reality where I was floundering.

RIO DE JANEIRO

Rio de Janeiro, often described as one of the most beautifully located cities in the world, set on a bay enclosed by soaring forested mountains, was founded in 1565 by the Portuguese, becoming capital of Brazil when the Portuguese royal family moved there in 1808. It remained the capital of the newly independent Empire of Brazil in 1822, and of the republic of Brazil from 1889. Its population, like that of the whole country, was strongly influenced by a high level of African slavery, a fact that many visitors noticed and commented upon, often with disquiet.

1788 JOHN WHITE

The Irish-born White (c. 1756–1832) sailed from Britain to New South Wales with Captain Arthur Phillips and the First Fleet of convicts (see page 298) as the principal naval surgeon; he became surgeon-general for the new colony until 1794, when he returned to Britain. In August 1788, on the way to Australia, the fleet was refitted at Rio, staying for a month. His journal was notionally written for a scholarly friend in England, but it was later published.

Rio de Janeiro is said to derive its name from being discovered on St Januarius's day. It is the capital of the Portuguese settlements in South America and is situated on the west side of a river, or, more properly (in my opinion), of a bay. Except that part which fronts the water, the city is surrounded by high mountains, of the most romantic form the imagination can fashion to itself any idea of....

The inhabitants in general are a pleasant, cheerful people, inclining more to corpulency than those of Portugal; and, as far as we could judge, very favourably inclined to the English. The men are strait and well-proportioned. They do not accustom themselves to high living, nor indulge much in the juice of the grape.

The women, when young, are remarkably thin, pale and delicately shaped; but after marriage they generally incline to be lusty, without losing that constitutional pale, or rather sallow, appearance. They have regular and better teeth than are usually observable in warm climates, where sweet productions are plentiful. They have likewise the most lovely, piercing, dark eyes, in the captivating use of which they are by no means unskilled. Upon the whole, the women of this country are very engaging; and rendered more so by their free, easy and unrestrained manner.

Both sexes are extremely fond of suffering their hair, which is black, to grow to a prodigious length. The ladies wear it plaited and tied up in a kind of club, or large lump, a mode of hair-dressing that does not seem to correspond with their delicate and feminine appearance. Custom, however, reconciles us to the most outré fashions; and what we thought unbecoming the Portuguese considered as highly ornamental. I was one day at a gentleman's house, to whom I expressed my wonder at the prodigious quantity of hair worn by the ladies, adding that I did not conceive it possible for it to be all of their own growth. The gentleman assured me that it was; and, in order to convince me that it was so, he called his wife and untied her hair, which, notwithstanding it was in plaits, dragged at least two inches upon the floor as she walked along. I offered my service to tie it up again, which was politely accepted, and considered as a compliment by both.

1821 MARIA GRAHAM

As a young British-born woman, Maria Graham (1785–1842) lived in India and – after the death of her husband in 1821 – Chile. In 1823 she visited the new Empire of Brazil and was appointed tutor to the princess Maria da Gloria. Later she moved to London and became the centre of a group of artists. She wrote of her experiences in India, Ceylon, Brazil and Chile.

15 December Nothing that I have ever seen is comparable in beauty to this bay. Naples, the Firth of Forth, Bombay harbour and Trincomalee, each of which I thought perfect in their beauty, all must yield to this, which surpasses each in its different way. Lofty mountains, rocks of clustered columns, luxuriant wood, bright flowery islands, green banks, all mixed with white buildings; each little eminence crowned with its church or fort; ships at anchor or in motion; and innumerable boats flitting about in such a delicious climate – combine to render Rio de Janeiro the most enchanting scene that imagination can conceive....

18 December I have begun housekeeping on shore. We find vegetables and poultry very good, but not cheap; fruit is very good and cheap; butcher's meat cheap, but very bad: there is a monopolist butcher, and no person may even kill an animal for his own use without permission paid for from that person; consequently, as there is no competition, he supplies the market as he pleases. The beef is so bad, that it can hardly be used even for soup meat, three days out of four; and that supplied to the ships is at least as bad: mutton is scarce and bad: pork very good and fine; it is fed principally on manioc and maize, near the town; that from a distance has the advantage of sugar cane. Fish is not so plentiful as it ought to be, considering the abundance that there is on the whole coast, but it is extremely good; oysters, prawns and crabs are as good as in any part of the world. The wheaten bread used in Rio is chiefly made of American flour, and is, generally speaking, exceedingly good. Neither the captaincy of Rio, nor those to the north, produce wheat; but in the high lands of St Paul's, and the Minas Gerais, and in the southern provinces, a good deal is cultivated, and with great success. The great article of food here is the manioc meal, or *farinha*; it is made into thin broad cakes as a delicacy, but the usual mode of eating it is dry: when at the tables of the rich, it is used with every dish of which they eat, as we take bread; with the poor, it has every form – porridge, brose, bread; and no meal is complete without it: next to manioc, the *feijao* or dry kidney bean, dressed in every possible way, but most frequently stewed with a small bit of pork, garlic, salt and pimento, is the favourite food; and for dainties, from the noble to the slave, sweetmeats of every description, from the most delicate preserves and candies to the coarsest preparations of treacle, are swallowed wholesale....

1 **May** I have this day seen the Val Longo; it is the slave-market of Rio. Almost every house in this very long street is a depot for slaves. On passing by the doors this evening, I saw in most of them long benches placed near the walls, on which rows of young creatures were sitting, their heads shaved, their bodies emaciated and the marks of recent itch upon their skins. In some places the poor creatures were lying on mats, evidently too sick to sit up. At one house the half-doors were shut, and a group of boys and girls, apparently not above fifteen years old, and some much under, were leaning over the hatches, and gazing into the street with wondering faces. They were evidently quite new negroes. As I approached them, it appears that something about me attracted their attention; they touched one another, to be sure that all saw me, and then chattered in their own African dialect with great eagerness. I went and stood near them, and though certainly more disposed to weep, I forced myself to smile to them, and look cheerfully, and kissed my hand to them, with all which they seemed delighted, and jumped about and danced, as if returning my civilities. Poor things! I would not, if I could, shorten their moments of glee, by awakening them to a sense of the sad things of slavery; but, if I could, I would appeal to their masters, to those who buy, and to those who sell, and implore them to think of the evils slavery brings, not only to the negroes but to themselves, not only to themselves but to their families and their posterity.

1842 PRINCE ADALBERT OF PRUSSIA

Prince Adalbert (1811–1873), grandson of King Frederick William III, helped establish the Prussian navy in the 1830s and 1840s. In 1842 he enjoyed an extended trip to Brazil, which he described in his Travels in the South of Europe and in Brazil *(1849).*

September All gazed with astonishment at the strange forms of the mountainous coast, which lay stretched out before us in wide extent from west to east. On the extreme left rose a small cone out of the sea, like an island, with which was connected on the right several small islands that looked like points. Then followed the wonderful mountain chain, the outlines of which resemble a giant lying on his back – a sure landmark to sailors at the entrance to the harbour of Rio – that king of harbours!...

I landed not far from the imperial castle at Rua Fresca, close to the Largo do Paço and opposite the Hotel Pharoux; the tall, obelisk fountain of Chafariz do Largo do Paço was on my right hand. A number of people had collected out of curiosity; the carriage was standing ready, and we quickly rolled off. Wherever I looked, negroes and mulattos were seen on all sides; they seem to constitute the greater part of the population; and although the features of the negroes were familiar to me from my Eastern travels, I had never before seen such a multitude of blacks collected; these, together with the mixed races, gave a peculiar appearance to the whole scene....

Scarcely had we taken luncheon, when the Minister of Foreign Affairs... waited on me with an invitation from his Majesty to an audience at ten o'clock the next morning, and also to attend the anniversary of the independence of Brazil, which was to take place the same day. When these gentlemen left me, I could no longer resist my impatience to go out into the open air and survey the wonderful objects in the vicinity: the little hill behind the house was ascended in quick time; I remarked that the mica in the granite rock which forms this acclivity appeared to be remarkably large-leaved.

The view from the top is even finer than that from the villa: on the terrace I could see every ship entering or leaving the bay, but at this point the eye follows the vessels further inland and observes their entrance still more distinctly.

1876 ANNIE ALLNUTT BRASSEY

Anna 'Annie' Allnutt Brassey (1839–1887) was a wealthy Englishwoman married to a Member of Parliament. In 1876–77 they toured the world on their yacht Sunbeam. *Her vivid account of the voyage was an international bestseller. She was also a prolific photographer.*

Monday, 21 August After an early breakfast, we started off to have a look at the market. The greatest bustle and animation prevailed, and there were people and things to see and observe in endless variety. The fish market was full of finny monsters of the deep, all new and strange to us, whose odd Brazilian names would convey to a stranger but little idea of the fish themselves. There was an enormous rockfish, weighing about 300 pounds, with hideous face and shiny back and fins; there were large ray, and skate, and cuttle-fish...besides baskets full of the large prawns for which the coast is famous, eight or ten inches long, and with antennae of twelve or fourteen inches in length. They make up in size for want of quality, for they are insipid and tasteless, though, being tender, they make excellent curry. The oysters, on the other hand, are particularly small, but of the most delicious flavour. They are brought from a park, higher up the bay, where, as I have said, they grow on posts and the branches of the mangrove tree, which hang down into the water. We also saw a large quantity of fine mackerel, a good many turtle and porpoises, and a few hammer-headed sharks. The latter are very curious creatures, not unlike an ordinary shark, but with a remarkable hammer-shaped projection on either side of their noses for which it is difficult to imagine a use.

In the fruit market were many familiar bright-coloured fruits; for it is now the depth of winter at Rio, and the various kinds that we saw were all such as would bear transport to England. Fat, jet-black negresses, wearing turbans on their heads, strings of coloured beads on their necks and arms, and single long white garments, which appeared to be continually slipping off their shoulders, here presided over brilliant-looking heaps of oranges, bananas, pineapples, passion fruit, tomatoes, apples, pears, capsicums and peppers, sugar-cane, cabbage-palms, cherimoyas and breadfruit.

In another part of the market all sorts of live birds were for sale, with a few live beasts, such as deer, monkeys, pigs, guinea-pigs in profusion, rats, cats, dogs, marmosets and a dear little lion-monkey, very small and rather red, with a beautiful head and mane, who roared exactly like a real lion in miniature. We saw also cages full of small flamingoes, snipe of various kinds and a great many birds of smaller size, with feathers of all shades of blue, red and green, and metallic hues of brilliant lustre, besides parrots, macaws, cockatoos innumerable, and *torchas*, on stands. The *torcha* is a bright-coloured black and yellow bird, about as big as a starling, which puts its little head on one side and takes flies from one's fingers in the prettiest and most enticing manner. Unfortunately, it is impossible to introduce it into England, as it cannot stand the change of climate. The other birds included guinea fowls, ducks, cocks and hens, pigeons, doves, quails, &c., and many other varieties less familiar or quite unknown to us. Altogether the visit was an extremely interesting one, and well repaid us for our early rising.

1933 PETER FLEMING

Peter Fleming (1907–1971), the elder brother of Ian, creator of the 007 novels (see page 135), was a prolific travel writer, whose volume Brazilian Adventure *described a hare-brained scheme that began with an advertisement in* The Times *to form an expedition to find the lost explorer Percy Fawcett.*

Looking back, I cannot remember very clearly what I expected from Rio, or why I was disappointed. It is, as they say, a fine city. Make no mistake about that. It is one of the places (for all I know, one of the several places) where Brazil's national motto, order and Progress, has not that rich flavour of irony which is too often, alas, the chief recommendation of public watchwords. Its streets are clean and wide and (when possible) straight. Its taxicabs purr majestically and go like the wind. Its tram service is indefatigable. Its cinemas are numerous, its gardens a delight, and all the male inhabitants wear collars. Its buildings boast – and in Brazil this is something to boast about – the usual offices. But above all I should like to praise its statuary.

I know nothing of sculpture. But there are plinths in some of Rio's public places before which even the Philistine must bow; he may even go back to his hotel and lie down for a bit. There really is something alarming about these turgid and pullulating groups. A great gout – a three-dimensional and lapidary gout – of legend, history, symbolism, religion and political history soars upwards and outwards from a base no bigger than your dining-table....

When you look down on Peking from the chipped and flaking terraces of the Winter Palace, you see as many treetops as roofs.... Rio has not this charm; in the tropics such a gentleman's agreement with nature is rarely possible. Looking down on the city from the Sugar Loaf, you are aware of conflict. Rio has edged in between the hills and the sea, and on that boldly chosen strip of land has met and trounced the jungle. She gleams up at you complacently, a successful opportunist.

But the jungle is still there. You can reach it easily by tram, or through suburban backdoors. It has been driven back into impregnable positions on the steep hillsides, and there it waits, conceding no more ground than it must. Somehow you feel that there ought to be a no-man's-land between the houses and trees, that there must be something embarrassing in having so old an enemy for so close a neighbour. But Rio is not embarrassed. I suspect her of relishing the stark and inescapable flavour of contrast, of flaunting her civic amenities rather provocatively at those glum and climbing walls of green.... On Rio's outskirts no bowler-hatted contractors carve Paradise into Desirable Building Sites; her inhabitants can enjoy a green thought in a green shade on the shores of that harbour which must surely have been described before now as God's gift to the picture-postcard industry.

ROME

The Eternal City has been the destination of innumerable visitors over the centuries. Founded, according to tradition, in 753 BC, it was at the heart of a hugely wealthy empire that covered the Mediterranean and much of the Middle East as well as Europe by the 1st century AD. When in the 4th century Christianity became the official religion of that empire, Rome became its head and has remained ever since as a site of pilgrimage and the dominant city of the Italian peninsula, the capital of Italy since unification in 1861.

By the late Middle Ages the grand remains of classical Rome were proving more attractive to visitors than the down-at-heel Christian city. In the following centuries, future popes were to vie with one another to beautify it and it became an unmissable destination for all those making cultural tours of Europe.

Under Fascist rule in the early 20th century, more improvements were made to the cityscape. Rome was bombed by the Allies in the Second World War before being liberated in 1944. It remains one of the world's most visited cities.

1143 ANON

The Marvels of Rome *was a guide for 12th-century pilgrims to the Holy City, setting out the sights. It was in common use to the 14th century, and placed as much emphasis on the sites of classical and pagan Rome as those with a Christian bent. The Egyptian obelisk now in St Peter's Square was thought, in medieval times, to contain the ashes of Julius Caesar.*

In the days of Pope Silvester, Constantine Augustus made the Lateran Basilica, the which he comely adorned. And he put there the Ark of the Covenant that Titus had carried away from Jerusalem with many thousands of Jews; and the golden candlestick having seven lamps with vessels for oil. In the which ark be these things, the golden emerods, the mice of gold, the Tables of the Covenant, the rod of Aaron, manna, the barley loaves, the golden urn, the coat without seam, the reed and garment of St John the Baptist, and the tongs that St John the Evangelist was shorn withal. Moreover he did put in the same basilica a civory [baldachin or canopy over the altar] with pillars of porphyry. And he set there four pillars of gilded brass which the consuls of old had brought into the Capitol from the Mars Field and set in the temple of Jupiter.

He made also, in the time of the said pope and after his prayer, a basilica for the Apostle Peter before Apollo's temple in the Vatican. Whereof the said emperor did himself first dig the foundation, and in reverence of the twelve Apostles did carry out twelve baskets full of earth. The said Apostle's body is thus bestowed. He made a chest closed on all sides with brass and copper, the which may not be moved, five feet of length at the head, five at the foot, on the right side five feet, on the left side five feet, five feet above and five feet below; and so he enclosed the body of the blessed Peter, and the altar above in the fashion of an arch he did adorn with bright gold. And he made a civory with pillars of porphyry and purest gold. And he set there before the altar twelve pillars of glass that he had brought out of Grecia and which were of Apollo's temple at Troy. Moreover he did set above the blessed Apostle Peter's body a cross of pure gold, having an hundred and fifty pounds of weight.

He also made a basilica for the blessed apostle Paul in the Ostian Way, and did bestow his body in brass and copper in the like fashion as the body of the blessed Peter.

The same emperor, after he was become a Christian and had made his churches, did also give to the blessed Silvester a Phrygium [marble statue] and white horses and all the imperialia that pertained to the dignity of the Roman Empire; and he went away to Byzantium; with whom the pope, decked in the same, did go so far forth as the Roman Arch, where they embraced and kissed the one the other, and so departed.

Within the palace of Nero is the temple of Apollo that is called St Parnel; before which is the basilica that is called the Vatican, adorned with marvellous mosaic and ceiled with gold and glass. It is therefore called the Vatican because in that place the *vates*, that is to say the priests, sang their offices before Apollo's temple, and therefore all that part of St Peter's church is called the Vatican. There is also another temple that was Nero's Wardrobe, which is now called St Andrew; nigh whereunto is the memorial of Caesar, that is the Needle, where his ashes nobly rest in his sarcophagus, to the intent that as in his lifetime the whole world lay subdued before him, even so in his death the same may lie beneath him for ever. The memorial was adorned in the lower part with tables of gilded brass, and fairly limned with Latin letters, and above at the ball, where he rests, it is decked with gold and precious stones, and there is it written:

Caesar who once was great as is the world
Now in how small a cavern art thou closed.

And this memorial was consecrated after their fashion, as still appears, and may be read thereon:

If one, tell how this stone was set on high
If many stones, show where their joints do lie.

1436 PERO TAFUR

Spaniard Pero Tafur (see page 141) visited Rome in the spring of 1436, finding it impressive but relatively inhospitable and with much damage done to the antiquities by visiting armies.

I stayed at Rome during the whole of Lent, visiting the sanctuaries and ancient buildings, which appeared to me to be very wonderfully made, but not only am I unable to describe them, but I doubt whether I could appreciate them as they deserved. Therefore I may be pardoned, such is the grandeur and magnificence of Rome, if I fall short in my account, for I am not equal to so great an undertaking in view of the extent to which these ancient buildings have been destroyed and changed, and are decayed. Nevertheless, to all who behold them it is clear that they were once very magnificent.... Pope St Gregory, seeing how the faithful flocked to Rome for the salvation of their souls, but that they were so astounded at the magnificence of the ancient buildings that they spent much time in admiring them, and neglected the sacred object of their visit, the Pope, I say, sent orders to destroy all or the majority of the antiquities which had survived from ancient times....

The church of St Peter is a notable church, the entrance is very magnificent, and one ascends to it by very high steps. The roof is richly worked in mosaic. Inside, the church is large, but very poor and in bad condition and dirty, and in many places in ruins. On the right hand is a pillar as high as a small tower, and in it is the holy Veronica [a veil with the image of Christ's face]. When it is to be exhibited an opening is made in the roof of the church and a wooden chest or cradle is let down, in which are two clerics, and when they have descended, the chest or cradle is drawn up, and they, with the greatest reverence, take out the Veronica and show it to the people. It happens often that the worshippers are in danger of their lives, so many are they and so great is the press....

The city is very sparsely populated considering its size. It is the opinion of many that now that it is thrown down and depopulated, there issues from the ruins of the great buildings, and from the cellars and cisterns and houses, and from the deep vaults, now uninhabited, such poisonous air that it affects human bodies, and therefore it is said that Rome is unhealthy. But when it was well populated it was the contrary. Even now it seems that in the places where it is most closely inhabited the people find better health, as in Campo dei Fiori, which is a large district, and Campidoglio, another large district, and in the Ghetto, which is like a great village. But all the rest of the city is but thinly scattered houses....

Close by is the Colosseum which was, so they say, unmatched in the whole world for size and magnificence, and although most of it is in ruins the greatness and the marvel of its building may well be seen. It would take long to tell how the Romans kept this Colosseum, and with what reverence, and of the statue they had there, which was so great that its feet stood on the ground and its head reached to the highest point of the roof.... They say that this statue was once surrounded by figures of all the kings and princes in the world, each having a chain round the neck fastened to the feet of that great statue, and when it was known that any king or prince was rising against Rome, they threw down his image and issued decrees commanding war to be made upon him. However this may be, the Colosseum shows that it was once a very magnificent and sumptuous building.

1580 MICHEL DE MONTAIGNE

French aristocrat and philosopher Michel de Montaigne (see page 108) visited Rome both in search of relief for his bladder stones and to visit the Vatican, where he was advised to make various changes to his Essais *to avoid heretical references.*

We set forth three hours before daybreak, so keenly was M. de Montaigne set on seeing the Roman plain by day. He found the cold air of morning as hurtful to his stomach as that of the evening, and was ill at ease till sunrise, though the night was fine. After the fifteenth milestone we caught sight of the city of Rome: then we lost it for some long time....

M. de Montaigne was annoyed to find such great number of Frenchmen in Rome, so great that almost every person he met in the streets addressed him in his own tongue. He found novelty in the sight of so mighty a court, thronged with prelates and churchmen, and declared that Rome was far fuller of rich men and coaches and horses than any other city he had ever seen, and that the seeming of the streets in various ways, and notably in the crowds of people, reminded him more of Paris than of any other place....

M. de Montaigne would not admit that liberty existed in Rome equal to that enjoyed in Venice, and would advance by way of arguments the facts that houses were so insecure against robbers that people who might bring home with them a large amount of property usually determined to give their purses in charge of the bankers of the city so as not to find their strongboxes rifled; that it was by no means safe to walk abroad by night; that in this month of December the General of the Cordeliers had been suddenly imprisoned because in his preaching, at which were present the Pope and the cardinals, he had censured the sloth and luxury of the prelates of the Church, and this without mentioning names and simply using commonplace remarks on the subject with a certain harshness of voice; that his own boxes had been searched by the tax officers on entering the city and turned over even to the smallest articles of apparel, while in the other towns of Italy the officers had been satisfied by the presentation of the boxes for search; that in addition they had seized all the books they found there with the view of inspecting them, over which task they spent so much time that any one in different case might well have given up the books as lost....

Touching the beauty of the Roman ladies, M. de Montaigne affirmed that this was not notable enough to raise the reputation of this city beyond all others; moreover that, as in Paris, the most remarkable beauty belonged to those who made a market of the same.

1764 EDWARD GIBBON

The British historian Edward Gibbon (1737–1794) famously wrote The History of the Decline and Fall of the Roman Empire in Six Volumes *(1776–88). In his* Memoirs *he described the moment at which, on a visit to Rome in 1764, he conceived the notion for his great work.*

My temper is not very susceptible of enthusiasm; and the enthusiasm which I do not feel, I have ever scorned to affect. But, at the distance of twenty-five years, I can neither forget nor express the strong emotions which agitated my mind as I first approached and entered the eternal city.

After a sleepless night, I trod, with a lofty step, the ruins of the Forum; each memorable spot where Romulus stood, or Tully spoke, or Caesar fell, was at once present to my eye; and several days of intoxication were lost or enjoyed before I could descend to a cool and minute investigation. My guide was Mr Byers, a Scotch antiquary of experience and taste; but, in the daily labour of eighteen weeks, the powers of attention were some times fatigued, till I was myself qualified, in a last review, to select and study the capital works of ancient and modern art....

It was at Rome, on 15 October 1764, as I sat musing amid the ruins of the Capitol, while the bare-footed fryars were singing vespers in the temple of Jupiter, that the idea of writing the decline and fall of the city first started to my mind. But my original plan was circumscribed to the decay of the city rather than of the empire: and though my reading and reflections began to point towards that object, some years elapsed, and several avocations intervened, before I was seriously engaged in the execution of that laborious work.

1844 CHARLES DICKENS

Dickens (see page 227) spent several months in Italy in 1844 after the triumph of A Christmas Carol *the previous year. His experience of Rome was much influenced by anti-clericalism and his preconceived notions of ancient grandeur.*

We entered the Eternal City, at about four o'clock in the afternoon, on the thirtieth of January, by the Porta del Popolo, and came immediately – it was a dark, muddy day, and there had been heavy rain – on the skirts of the Carnival. We did not, then, know that we were only looking at the fag end of the masks, who were driving slowly round and round the Piazza until they could find a promising opportunity for falling into the stream of carriages, and getting, in good time, into the thick of the festivity; and coming among them so abruptly, all travel-stained and weary, was not coming very well prepared to enjoy the scene.

We had crossed the Tiber by the Ponte Molle two or three miles before. It had looked as yellow as it ought to look, and hurrying on between its worn-away and miry banks, had a promising aspect of desolation and ruin. The masquerade dresses on the fringe of the Carnival, did great violence to this promise. There were no great ruins, no solemn tokens of antiquity, to be seen; they all lie on the other side of the city. There seemed to be long streets of commonplace shops and houses, such as are to be found in any European town; there were busy people, equipages, ordinary walkers to and fro; a multitude of chattering strangers. It was no more *my* Rome: the Rome of anybody's fancy, man or boy; degraded and fallen and lying asleep in the sun among a heap of ruins: than the Place de la Concorde in Paris is. A cloudy sky, a dull cold rain and muddy streets, I was prepared for, but not for this: and I confess to having gone to bed, that night, in a very indifferent humour, and with a very considerably quenched enthusiasm.

Immediately on going out next day, we hurried off to St Peter's. It looked immense in the distance, but distinctly and decidedly small, by comparison, on a near approach. The beauty of the Piazza, on which it stands, with its clusters of exquisite columns, and its gushing fountains – so fresh, so broad, and free, and beautiful – nothing can exaggerate. The first burst of the interior, in all its expansive majesty and glory and, most of all, the looking up into the Dome, is a sensation never to be forgotten. But, there were preparations for a Festa; the pillars of stately marble were swathed in some impertinent frippery of red and yellow; the altar, and entrance to the subterranean chapel: which is before it in the centre of the church: were like a goldsmith's shop, or one of the opening scenes in a very lavish pantomime. And though I had as high a sense of the beauty of the building (I hope) as it is possible to entertain, I felt no very strong emotion. I have been infinitely more affected in many English cathedrals when the organ has been playing, and in many English country churches when the congregation have been singing. I had a much greater sense of mystery and wonder, in the Cathedral of San Mark at Venice.

When we came out of the church again (we stood nearly an hour staring up into the dome: and would not have 'gone over' the Cathedral then, for any money), we said to the coachman, 'Go to the Coliseum.' In a quarter of an hour or so, he stopped at the gate, and we went in.

It is no fiction, but plain, sober, honest truth, to say: so suggestive and distinct is it at this hour: that, for a moment – actually in passing in – they who will, may have the whole great pile before them, as it used to be, with thousands of eager faces staring down into the arena, and such a whirl of strife, and blood, and dust going on there, as no language can describe. Its solitude, its awful beauty and its utter desolation, strike upon the stranger the next moment, like a softened sorrow; and never in his life, perhaps, will he be so moved and overcome by any sight, not immediately connected with his own affections and afflictions.

To see it crumbling there, an inch a year; its walls and arches over-grown with green; its corridors open to the day; the long grass growing in its porches; young trees of yesterday, springing up on its ragged par-apets, and bearing fruit: chance produce of the seeds dropped there by the birds who build their nests within its chinks and crannies; to see its Pit of Fight filled up with earth, and the peaceful Cross planted in the centre; to climb into its upper halls, and look down on ruin, ruin, ruin, all about it; the triumphal arches of Constantine, Septimus Severus and Titus; the Roman Forum; the Palace of the Caesars; the temples of the old religion, fallen down and gone; is to see the ghost of old Rome, wicked, wonderful old city, haunting the very ground on which its people trod. It is the most impressive, the most stately, the most solemn, grand, majestic, mournful sight, conceivable. Never, in its bloodiest prime, can the sight of the gigantic Coliseum, full and running over with the lustiest life, have moved one's heart, as it must move all who look upon it now, a ruin. God be thanked: a ruin!...

Here was Rome indeed at last; and such a Rome as no one can imagine in its full and awful grandeur! We wandered out upon the Appian Way, and then went on, through miles of ruined tombs and broken walls, with here and there a desolate and uninhabited house: past the Circus of Romulus, where the course of the chariots, the stations of the judges, competitors, and spectators, are yet as plainly to be seen as in old time: past the tomb of Cecilia Metella: past all inclosure, hedge, or stake, wall or fence: away upon the open Campagna, where on that side of Rome, nothing is to be beheld but Ruin. Except where the distant Apennines bound the view upon the left, the whole wide prospect is one field of ruin. Broken aqueducts, left in the most picturesque and beautiful clusters of arches; broken temples; broken tombs. A desert of decay, sombre and desolate beyond all expression; and with a history in every stone that strews the ground.

1900 OSCAR WILDE

Irish playwright Oscar Wilde (1854–1900), imprisoned 1895–97 for gross inde-cency, spent the final years of his life a broken man. Impoverished and in exile, he sought consolation in the Catholic church, visiting Rome and receiving the blessing of Pope Leo III. He died seven months later.

16 April We came to Rome on Holy Thursday. H.M. left on Saturday for Gland, and yesterday, to the terror of Grissell and all the Papal Court, I appeared in the front rank of the pilgrims in the Vatican, and got the blessing of the Holy Father – a blessing they would have denied me.

He was wonderful as he was carried past me on his throne, not of flesh and blood, but a white soul robed in white, and an artist as well as a saint – the only instance in history, if the papers are to be believed.

I have seen nothing like this extraordinary grace of his gesture, as he rose, from moment to moment, to bless – possibly the pilgrims, but certainly me....

I was deeply impressed, and my walking stick showed signs of budding; would have budded indeed only at the door of the chapel it was taken from me by the Knave of Spades. This strange prohibition is, of course, in honour of Tannhäuser.

How did I get the ticket? By a miracle of course. I thought it was hopeless, and made no effort of any kind. On Saturday afternoon at five o'clock Harold and I went to have tea at the Hotel de l'Europe. Suddenly, as I was eating buttered toast, a man, or what seemed to be one, dressed as a hotel porter, entered and asked me would I like to see the Pope on Easter Day. I bowed my head humbly and said, *'Non sum dignus'* [I am not worthy] or words to that effect. He at once produced a ticket!

When I tell you that his countenance was of supernatural ugliness, and that the price of the ticket was thirty pieces of silver, I need say no more.

1945 ELEANOR CLARK

Eleanor Clark (1913–1996) was an American poet and novelist, who visited Italy in 1945, and fell in love with Rome, although her pleasure was more in its historical legacy than in the actual modern city, marked as it was by Fascism, war and mass tourism.

The tourist or student or wandering intellectual, the poor seeker after something or other, comes in like a wisp of fog on a fog bank, with his angst and his foggy modern eye, and there are not many words that can help him even a little to find his identity and his way: history, surrealism, faith. The angst is going to get a lot worse: the eye, if he stays long enough, will be pried open week by week as if every lash has been glued down;

and meanwhile there are the mess and the blazing sun, the incongruities, the too-muchness of everything. The historian Taine said that really to profit from Rome you would have to be always in a gay mood, 'or at least a healthy one'; he would not have thought of using the word nowadays.

Ecco Roma.... Something is being presented to the glazed eyeball and paralysed sense of the worrying traveller, who came most often not looking for Rome at all but for love; whose distress about national responsibilities is painfully mixed up with anxiety about his baggage.

He sees a city of bells and hills and walls; of many trees Nordic and tropical together, pines, ilex and palm, and water and a disturbing depth of shadows; of acres of ruins, some handsome, some shabby lumps and dumps of useless masonry, sprinkled through acres of howling modernity – and impossible compounding of time, in which no century has respect for any other and all hit you in a jumble at every turn; of roaring motors and other dreadful noises, where some roaring festa with fireworks is always going on; whose churches are junk shops of idolatrous bric-a-brac; which calls on your awe and is absolutely lacking in any itself; where spaces open out or close up before you suddenly as in dreams, and a tormenting dream-like sexual gaiety seems to rise you cannot tell how from the streets; a place of no grandeur whatever of any kind you expected, ravaged by fascist vulgarities; in which the president's until recently the royal, palace looks from the outside like an old tobacco barn, and everything you came to revere turns up in a setting as of some huge practical joke; a place beautiful at certain points, at certain moments, but closed to you, repellent, where you are always being reminded of something, you cannot tell what, but it is like the fear of falling down a deep well....

Foreign visitors swirl in herds through the Vatican Museums, around the Colosseum – you would not think, as Dante said, that there could be so many; or sit in bars for two weeks 'getting the feel of the place'; or drag about in a dim melancholy of expectation and loneliness, often complicated by Roman stomach trouble; or take up with the variety of little sad fifth-rate adventurers always available along the Via Veneto, especially for homosexuals, because the city has become as much a world magnet in that respect as for Catholic converts or illuminated manuscript-worms.

ST PETERSBURG

St Petersburg was founded by Tsar Peter the Great in 1703, as his new capital city built at vast cost on the marshes of the Neva River on Russia's Baltic coast. Unique in 18th-century Europe as a great planned city, it attracted admiration from many visitors.

Renamed Petrograd in 1914, the city was the focus of the Bolshevik Revolution in 1917; it was renamed Leningrad in 1924. In 1941–44,

Leningrad was subject to a 900-day siege by the German army, which brought the city to the verge of starvation and destruction. After its relief, and Soviet victory in the Second World War, it was slowly rebuilt.

With the fall of the Soviet Union in 1991, the city reverted to its original name. In 2003 it lavishly celebrated the 300th anniversary of its foundation.

1774 NATHANIEL WRAXALL

Wealthy British traveller Nathaniel Wraxall (1751–1831) wrote an enthusiastic account of his visit to Catherine the Great's capital that was well received by the reading public.

I am struck with a pleasing astonishment, while I wander among havens, streets and public buildings, which have risen, as by enchantment, within the memory of men still alive, and have converted the marshy islands of the Neva into one of the most magnificent cities of the earth. The imagination, aided by so many visible objects, rises to the wondrous founder, and beholds in idea the tutelary genius of Peter, yet hovering over the child of his own production, and viewing with a parent's fondness its rising palaces and temples.

There is not only a magnificence and regal pomp in this court, which far exceed any I have beheld elsewhere, but everything is on a vast and colossal scale, resembling that of the empire itself. The public buildings, churches, monasteries and private palaces of the nobility are of an immense size, and seem as if designed for creatures of a superior height and dimensions to man; to 'a puny insect shivering at the breeze!'

The statue and pedestal which will soon be set up of Peter the Great, are of the same enormous and gigantic proportions, and may almost rank with the sphynxes and pyramids of Egyptian workmanship.... The palace which the present empress has begun, is designed to be two or three English miles in circumference; and in the mean time they have erected a temporary one of brick, for her reception....

The public buildings of different kinds are so prodigiously numerous in this city, that I am inclined to believe, they constitute a fifth or sixth part of the whole capital. Some of them are of stone, but the larger part are only brick, or wood plastered. The Winter Palace is composed of the former materials, and was erected by the late Empress Elizabeth.... It is not yet quite finished, like almost everything else in Russia. The situation is very lovely, on the banks of the Neva, and in the centre of the town. Contiguous to it is a small palace, built by the present empress, and called, why I know not, The Hermitage. It no more resembles our idea of a hermitage, than it does a temple; but when Her Majesty resides in this part of the building, she is in retreat, and there is no drawing room or court. I was admitted a few days ago to see these apartments, which are very elegant, and furnished with great taste.

There are two galleries of paintings, which have been lately purchased at an immense expense in Italy, and among which I would willingly, was it permitted, spend some hours every day during my residence here. The crown, which I saw in the palace itself, is perhaps the richest in Europe. It is shaped like a bonnet, and totally covered with diamonds. In the sceptre is the celebrated one, purchased by Prince Orlov for 500,000 rubles, and presented by him to his sovereign mistress only a few months ago....

I am more charmed with the river Neva itself, than with anything I see here. The Thames is not comparable to it in beauty; and as the stream sets constantly out of the Lake Ladoga into the Gulf of Finland, it is always full, clear and perfectly clean. Along its banks is beyond all doubt the finest walk in the world. It is not a quay, as vessels never come up to this part, but a parade, running a mile in length; the buildings on which are hardly to be exceeded in elegance. It is yet to be continued to double the length. Over the river in the narrowest part is a bridge on pontoons. From this noble river, canals are cut to all parts of the city; nor could any situation be more favourable to the genius of commerce, if the inclemency of the latitude did not keep it froze up, at least five months annually....

The police of Petersburgh is very good, and one may walk with great safety at any hour. Now and then a murder happens, but they are not frequent.

1805 ROBERT KER PORTER

Scottish historical painter Robert Ker Porter (1777–1842) was invited to Russia by Tsar Alexander I in 1805 to create a series of historical murals for the Admiralty,

and fell in love with a Russian princess whom he married in 1812. In 1817–20
he travelled in Central Asia, and in 1826 was appointed British ambassador
to Venezuela.

I am at a loss, my dear friend, where to commence a description of this
splendid city. Every object excites admiration and those objects are so
numerous, that I find it difficult to select what you might deem most interesting, from an assemblage of such, to me, equally prominent beauties.
I, who have come direct from London, may perhaps view St Petersburgh
with peculiar impressions. The plainness of our metropolis, the almost
total neglect of all architectural graces in the structure of even the best
houses, and the absolute deformity of many of the inferior sort; all these
things strike the eye as forcibly, though in an opposite direction, as mine
was with the magnificence of St Petersburgh. Such grandeur and symmetry
in building, I never before beheld in any of the different capitals to which
my fondness for travel has conducted me. Every house seems a palace, and
every palace a city....

I suppose no country can boast so long and uninterrupted a street as
the Great and English Quay; the granite front and pavement of which are
unparalleled. The canals are worthy of the same august hand; and the superb
bridges which clasp them from side to side, rear their colossi pillars in all
the majesty of immense magnificence....

Turn where you will, rise immense fabrics of granite: and did you not
know the history of the place, you might suppose that it had been founded
on a vast plain of that rocky production; whence had been derived the
stones of the buildings; and in the bosom of which had been dug the river
and canals that intersect its surface. But it is from the quarries of Finland
that the Russians dig these bodies of granite, and transport and place
them here in lasting monuments of their own unwearied industry. That
mass on which is erected the immortal statue of Peter the First, is one huge
instance of their indefatigable labour; and the forest of columns in the new
Metropolitan church, is not a less worthy proof of the vigour with which
they pursue so meritorious a toil....

Many of the labourers employed on these buildings come some thousand *versts* from the interior: and when the frost sets in, they retire thither
again, to await the more genial season which will allow them to recommence

their toil.... All difficulties connected with their business, are overcome by human exertions alone. What in England would easily be performed by one horse, with a little mechanical aid, is here achieved by the united strength of numbers of men.... Frequently we see a hundred men, with ropes and hand-spikes, busied in accomplishing no more than one quarter of that number, with a few of our assisting inventions, would easily finish in half the time. Setting aside utility, these groups add to the picturesque of the scene; which is considerably lightened by their long beards, rugged sheepskins and uncouth attitudes. How strange it is to look on these apparently savage beings, and think that from their hands arise such elegant and classical structures! Indeed I never saw, in all its parts, so regularly built a city; nor in any place, so much attention to keep all in due order. The present emperor who, like its illustrious founder, has the perfecting of this residence at heart, leaves no suggestion unexecuted, which can increase its ornament, or the people's convenience....

I am sorry to say that the spirit of extortion is very common at St Petersburgh. And as shopkeepers, and others of the lower orders, make a practice of demanding double the worth of their commodities, travellers, who know not that they will be content with half the sum, are liable either to be defrauded, and leave the place under the impression of its exorbitant expense; or, when they discover the cheat, conceive no very favourable opinion of Russian honesty. But alas! I fear the passion for a hasty accumulation of riches is not peculiar to our northern neighbours. In an ignorant people, just emerging to civilization, we see covetousness without a veil. Eager to share in the good things which are opened to them on every side, they consider not, because they do not yet understand, the superior advantages of character. But are the people who have long enjoyed the privileges of education and polished society, are they exempt from this degrading vice? I am afraid not.

1836 R. B. PAUL

A British clergyman and fellow of an Oxford college, R. B. Paul (1798–1877) wrote an account of an eight-week journey to Russia in 1836, when he was particularly struck by St Petersburg's 'white nights', and the Russian capacity for strong drink.

29 June Perhaps there is nothing that strikes a foreigner more, on his arrival at St Petersburg, than the silence of the streets, while the sun is yet high above the horizon. At first he is inclined to think that the inhabitants have all gone into the country, until looking at his watch he is reminded that it is actually the hour at which his own land shops are usually shut and the citizens retire to rest. I slept badly, or rather I believe not at all, the first night after my arrival, and amused myself with reading at the window a very closely printed book, which I found I could do without the least difficulty. There is in fact at this season of the year no night.

2 July Today is a fete. And 'universal Russia getteth drunk'. It is really no exaggeration to say that out of every ten serfs we have seen today, nine have been drunk. The Russian peasant is no soaker like the Swede or Norwegian: for days together he will abstain from spirits, but it appears to me that on certain solemn occasions every man proceeds in a systematic and business-like manner to deprive himself of his senses.

We have no bad opportunity of observing this as immediately under our windows is a shop where the fiery liquor they distil from corn is sold. Our London abominations, the gin-shops, are more magnificent and are probably more frequented on ordinary days, but I doubt much whether any district of London can make such a display of beastly intoxication as we saw at least once a week in the Molnoy Moskoi Street at St Petersburg.

1839 MARQUIS DE CUSTINE

The Marquis de Custine (see page 201) travelled in Russia to observe the interaction between a modern state and traditional religion. However, he was equally concerned by officious bureaucrats.

For three or four days in the year the sun of Petersburg is insupportable. I arrived on one of these days. Our persecutors commenced by impounding us (not the Russians, but myself and the other foreigners) on the deck of our vessel. We were there, for a long time, exposed without any shelter to the powerful heat of the morning sun....

At length I was summoned to appear before a new tribunal, assembled, like that of Kronstadt, in the cabin of our vessel. The same questions were addressed to me with the same politeness, and my answers were recorded with the same formalities.

'What is your object in Russia?'

'To see the country.'

'That is not here a motive for travelling.' (What humility in this objection!)

'I have no other.'

'Whom do you expect to see in Petersburg?'

'Everyone with whom I may have an opportunity of making acquaintance.'

'How long do you think of remaining in Russia?'

'I do not know.'

'But about how long?'

'A few months.'

'Have you a public diplomatic mission?'

'No.'

'A secret one?'

'No.'

'Any scientific object?

'No.'

'Are you employed by your government to examine the social and political state of this country?'

'No.'

'By any commercial association?'

'No.'

'You travel, then, from mere curiosity?'

'Yes.'

'What was it that induced you, under this motive, to select Russia?'

'I do not know,' &c., &c., &c.

'Have you letters of introduction to any people of this country?'

I had been forewarned of the inconvenience of replying too frankly to this question; I therefore spoke only of my banker.

At the termination of the session of this court of assize, I encountered several of my accomplices. These strangers had been sadly perplexed, owing to some irregularities that had been discovered in their passports.... The police permitted me to pass without searching my person; but when my baggage came to be unpacked before the custom-house officers, these new enemies instituted a most minute examination of my effects, more especially my books. The latter were seized *en masse*, and without any attention to my protestations, but an extraordinary politeness of manner was all the while maintained. A pair of pistols and an old portable clock were also taken from me, without my being able to ascertain the reason of the confiscation. All that I could get was the promise that they would be returned....

Between nine and ten o'clock I found myself, personally, released from the fangs of the custom house, and entered Petersburg under the kind care of a German traveller, whom I met by chance on the quay. If a spy, he was at least a useful one, speaking both French and Russian, and undertaking to procure me a *drowska* [open carriage].... The obliging stranger found even a guide for me who could speak German....

The too celebrated statue of Peter the Great, placed on its rock by the Empress Catherine, first attracted my attention. The equestrian figure is neither antique nor modern; it is a Roman of the time of Louis XV. To aid in supporting the horse, an enormous serpent has been placed at his feet; which is an ill-conceived idea, serving only to betray the impotence of the artist.

I stopped for one moment before the scaffolding of an edifice which, though not yet completed, is already famous in Europe, the church, namely, of St Isaac. I also saw the facade of the new Winter Palace; another mighty result of human will applying human physical powers in a struggle with the laws of nature. The end has been attained, for in one year this palace has risen from its ashes; and it is the largest, I believe, which exists, equalling the Louvre and the Tuileries together.

In order to complete the structure at the time appointed by the emperor, unheard-of efforts were necessary. The interior works were continued during the great frosts; 10,000 workmen were continually employed: of these a considerable number died daily, but the victims were instantly replaced by other champions brought forward to perish, in their turn, in this inglorious breach. And the sole end of all these sacrifices was to gratify the caprice of one man!

1902 CONSUELO VANDERBILT BALSAN

Consuelo Vanderbilt (1877–1964) was a wealthy American socialite married to the British 9th Duke of Marlborough, with whom she visited Russia in 1902. They divorced in 1921, after which she married the French aviator Jacques Balsan.

There were evenings when we drove in open sleighs to the islands on the frozen Neva and supped and danced to *tzigane* music. Russian days were short but their nights were endless and we rarely went to bed before the early hours of morning. At the opera the ballets were Tchaikovsky's; Diaghileff had not yet revolutionized the classic dance. The *danseuse-en-tête* had been the Czar's mistress, according to tradition, and others had been assigned to the Grand Dukes as part of their amorous education. As the intrigues and scandals of society became more familiar to us, we felt as if we had plunged into an eighteenth-century atmosphere, so different was it from the rigid Victorian morality of England.

We were privileged to attend three glorious court functions. For the first, a great ball of three thousand guests which was given at the Winter Palace, Milly Sutherland and I donned our finest dresses. Mine of white satin was draped in lines of classic simplicity and had a tulle train held by a belt of real diamonds. A tiara of the same stones lightened the dark waves of my hair and cascades of pearls fell from my neck. I looked very young and slight in that shimmering whiteness and my maid delightedly exclaimed, '*Comme Madame la Duchesse est belle.*'...

At the Winter Palace the stairs were adorned by a magnificent display of gold plate fixed to the walls. There were hundreds of footmen in scarlet liveries and Cossack guards in flowing robes, who gave an impression of barbaric splendour. In the great ballroom innumerable chandeliers threw a glittering radiance on the handsome men and graceful women assembled there....

With the entrance of the Imperial family to the inspiring air of the Russian anthem – the procession of Grand Dukes in splendid uniforms, the Grand Duchesses, lovely and bejewelled, the beautiful, remote Czarina and the Czar – the ball took on the aspect of a fairy tale. With the first strains of a mazurka, the Grand Duke Michael, the Czar's younger brother and heir since the Czarevitch had not yet been born, invited me to dance. It was a very different affair from the mazurkas I had learned at Mr Dodsworth's class. 'Never mind,' he said, when I demurred, 'I'll do the steps,' and he proceeded to cavort around me until I was reminded of the courtship of birds. But he was young and gay and, carried away by the increasing tempo, I found myself treading the Russian measure with the best. He was killed by the Bolsheviks in 1918.

1932 CORLISS LAMONT

The young Soviet Union was an object of fascination for many Westerners in the 1920s and early 1930s, who felt either horror at its destructiveness, or fascination at its attempt to forge a new, more just society. One of the latter was American social activist Corliss Lamont (1902–1995) who spent a year there in 1932 and praised everything he saw.

One of our first impressions of Leningrad is that a considerable amount of begging is going on. We pass a ragged woman sitting on a house-step with a tiny baby in her arms and holding out her hand for alms. Our interpreter says that most of these beggars are people who are too lazy to work, since *every* Russian can get a job if he wants to: or they are peasants of the kulak class who have drifted into the city and find themselves temporarily stranded. A few may actually be men or women workers trying to supplement their wages through begging. In any case it must be remembered that there existed in pre-war Russia a million professional beggars as a normal part of the scheme of things.

It is clear that the beggar problem, like a number of other difficulties bequeathed by the Tsarist regime, cannot be completely eliminated all at once. Another of our first impressions is the crumbling appearance of the buildings in Leningrad. It is evident that little has been done since the Revolution in the way of repairing the exteriors, at least, of the houses and apartments.

The streets of Leningrad are remarkably clean. Everywhere men and women with hoses are washing away dust and dirt. This is quite in accord with the Soviet insistence on sanitation. But the flies are very bad, even in our hotel, and apparently no serious attempts are being made to deal with them. A Soviet doctor tells us they are not so great a menace as they seem, because there is very little disease for them to carry about. The flies will be attended to in time, however. *In time:* whenever you bring such a problem to the attention of a Russian, the answer invariably is that the Soviet is well aware of the situation, that it is doing its best to cope with it, but that time and energy have not yet been available to fully rectify the situation.

SAMARKAND

The ancient Silk Road city of Samarkand, capital of the Transoxiana region, was visited by Alexander the Great, who is said to have commented: 'Everything I have heard about Samarkand is true, except that it is even more beautiful than I had imagined.' It was rebuilt by the Mongol warlord Timur from 1370 as his capital, making it one of the great cultural centres of the world. He was buried in the Gur-i Amir mausoleum.

Ancient Samarkand retains a place in the Western imagination thanks in part to the 1913 poem 'The Golden Road to Samarkand' by James Elroy Flecker (1884–1915).

It became part of the Russian Empire in 1868, and of an independent Uzbekistan in 1991.

c.1404 RUY GONZÁLEZ DE CLAVIJO

The Spanish nobleman Ruy González de Clavijo (d. 1412) spent several months in Samarkand (1404) as the ambassador of Henry III of Castile. He was seeking an alliance following Timur's recent victory over the Ottoman Turkish sultan Bayezid I at Ankara, but Timur's illness and impending death made the alliance impossible.

Now I must describe Samarkand and all that Timur has done to embellish his capital. Samarkand stands in a plain and is surrounded by a wall of earth, with a deep ditch. The city itself is larger than Seville, but beyond are extensive suburbs. The township is surrounded by orchards and vineyards, extending a league and a half or even more beyond Samarkand. Between these orchards pass streets with open squares which are densely populated, and where all kinds of goods are on sale. The population outside the city is more numerous than the population within the walls. Among these orchards are found the most noble and beautiful houses, and Timur has his many palaces and pleasure grounds. Here the great men of the government also have estates and country houses, each within its orchard: and a traveller approaching the city sees only a mountainous height of trees and the houses among them remain invisible. Through the streets of Samarkand, as through its gardens, pass many water-conduits, and in these gardens are the melon beds and fields of cotton.

The soil of the whole province is most fertile, producing great crops of wheat. There are abundant fruit trees also with rich vineyards: the livestock is magnificent, beasts and poultry all of a fine breed. The sheep are famous for having fat tails that weigh each some twenty pounds, in fact as much as a man can readily hold in the hand: and of these sheep the flocks are so abundant that even when Timur is in camp here with his armies, a couple

283

can be had in the market for the price of a ducat. Baked bread is plentiful and rice can be had cheap in any quantity.

The wonderful abundance of this great capital is why it bears the name of Samarkand: this name would be more exactly written Semiz-kent, two words which signify 'Rich-Town', for *Semiz* in Turkish is fat or rich and *Kent* means city. This land is also rich in manufactures, with factories of silk, also crapes, taffetas and the stuffs we call Tercenals in Spain, which are all produced in great numbers. Further they make special fur linings for silk garments, and manufacture stuffs in gold and blue with other colours of diverse dyes.

This trade has been fostered by Timur with the view of making his capital the noblest of cities: and during his conquests he carried off the best men of the population to people his capital. From Damascus he took weavers who work the silk looms; bow-makers who produce those famous crossbows; armourers; and craftsmen in glass and porcelain. From Turkey he brought gunsmiths who make the arquebus, silversmiths and masons. He also brought artillery men, both engineers and bombardiers, and those who make the ropes by which these engines work.

Here are to be seen Turks, Arabs and Moors of diverse sects, as well as Christians, both Greeks and Armenians, Catholics, Jacobites and Nestorians, besides those Indian folk who baptize with fire in the forehead, who are Christians of a faith peculiar to their nation. The markets further are stored with merchandise from distant and foreign countries. From Russia and Tartary [the steppes] come leathers and linens, from Cathay [northern China] silk stuffs that are the finest in the whole world. Thence too is brought musk which is unique to Cathay, with balas rubies and diamonds, also pearls, as well as rhubarb with many other spices. The goods imported from Cathay are the most precious of all those brought from foreign parts, for the craftsmen of Cathay are far more skilful than those of any other nation; and it is said that they alone have two eyes, while the Franks may have one, whereas the Muslims are blind.

From India come nutmegs, cloves and mace with cinnamon both in the flower and as bark, with ginger and manna; none of these are to be found in the markets of Alexandria. Throughout the city there are squares where meat ready-cooked – roasted or in stews – is sold, with fowls and game prepared for eating, also bread and fruit. All these are set out in a decent cleanly manner, in all those squares, and their traffic goes on all day and even through the night.

On the one part of Samarkand stands the castle which is protected by deep ravines on all its sides: and through these water flows which makes it impregnable. Here his Highness keeps his treasure, and none from the city without may enter save the governor of the castle and his men. Within its walls however Timur holds in captivity upwards of a thousand workmen; these labour at making plate-armour and helms, with bows and arrows.

1500 EMPEROR BABUR

As a descendant of Timur from Uzbekistan, Babur (1483–1530) conquered Samarkand in 1497 but was driven out a few years later. He moved to Kabul in Afghanistan, and then India, where he founded the Mughal Empire in 1520. A cultured man as well as a great soldier, he was particularly interested in architecture and gardens, especially those of his Timurid predecessor in Samarkand, Ulugh Beg Mirza (1394–1449).

Few towns in the world are so pleasant as Samarkand. Alexander the Great must have founded Samarkand, and it must have become Muslim in the time of the Commander of the Faithful, Uthman. Kusam ibn 'Abbas, one of the Companions of Muhammad, went there: his burial place is outside the Iron Gate. Samarkandis are all orthodox, pure in the Faith, law-abiding and religious. Timur made it his capital; no ruler so great ever made it a capital before. I ordered people to pace round the ramparts of the walled town; the distance measured 10,000 steps....

In the citadel, Timur Beg erected the great four-storeyed kiosk, known as the Kok Sarai. In the walled town, near the Iron Gate, he built a Friday Mosque of stone using the labour of many stone-cutters brought from Hindustan [India]. Round its frontal arch is inscribed in letters large enough to be read two miles away, the verse, *Wa az yerfa' Ibrahim al Qawa'id al akhara* ['And Abraham and Ismail raised the foundations of this house']. He also laid out two gardens, on the east of the town. From Dilkusha to the Turquoise Gate, he planted an avenue of white poplar, and in the garden itself erected a great kiosk, painted inside with pictures of his battles in Hindustan. He made another garden on the bank of the Kohik [Zeravshan

River]; it had gone to ruin when I saw it.... His own tomb and those of his descendants who have ruled in Samarkand are in a *madrasa*, built at the exit from the walled town.

Among Ulugh Beg Mirza's buildings inside the town are a college and a monastery. The dome of the monastery is vast; few so large can be seen anywhere in the world. Near these, he constructed an excellent hot bath known as the Mirza's Bath, with mosaic pavements; no other such bath is known in Samarkand or in all of Khurasan [now north-east Iran, Afghanistan and southern Turkmenistan]. To the south of the college is his mosque, known as the Carved Mosque because its ceiling and its walls are all covered with carved ornamentation and 'Chinese' pictures formed of segments of wood....

Another of Ulugh Beg Mirza's fine buildings is an observatory, that is, a building with instruments for writing astronomical tables. This stands three storeys high, on the edge of the Kohik upland.

Samarkand is a wonderfully beautified town. One of its specialities, perhaps found in few other places, is that the different trades are not mixed up together in it. Each has its own *bazar*, which makes a lot of sense. Its bakers and its cooks are good. The best paper in the world is made there; the water for the paper mortars all comes from Kan-i-gil, a meadow on the banks of the Kara-su (Blackwater) or Ab-i-rahmat (Water of Mercy). Another article of Samarkand trade, exported everywhere, is red velvet.

SAN FRANCISCO

Founded by the Spanish in the 18th century, San Francisco was ceded by Mexico to the United States in 1848 after the Mexican-American War, and became a boom town with the gold rush of the same year, the population growing twenty-five times in eighteen months. Many of the immigrants were Chinese, making it one of the most Chinese-influenced cities in North America. A major earthquake and subsequent fire in 1906 led to the rebuilding of the city; the Golden Gate Bridge opened in 1937.

In the 1960s the city became the epicentre of American counter-culture, and in the 21st century the nearby Silicon Valley attracted digital expertise from across the world.

1849 JOHN AUDUBON

American John W. Audubon (1812–1862), the son of ornithologist John James Audubon, travelled from New York to California in 1849 with a group of miners, intending to profit from the Gold Rush; when they arrived in San Francisco late in 1849, they realized they were too late. They moved on to Sacramento, but returned to New York shortly afterwards.

We reached San Francisco on Saturday night 21st December, and stayed in our blankets on the floor of the steamer until morning when we went off, on what is called 'the long dock' into mud half-leg deep. We paid fifty cents for a cup of coffee and a bit of bread, and I went for my letters, but found none, so went off to hunt up my men, found them all right, and returned to Henry Mallory, who having received letters was able to set my anxieties about my family at rest; but I alone of all the company had no home news. I sat on the deck of the steamer, the most quiet place I could find, re-read my old letters, and went about my business with a heavy heart.

25 December Christmas Day! Happy Christmas! Merry Christmas! Not that here, to me at any rate, in this pandemonium of a city. Not a lady to be seen, and the women, poor things, sad and silent, except when drunk or excited. The place full of gamblers, hundreds of them, and men of the lowest types, more blasphemous, and with less regard for God and his commands than all I have ever seen on the Mississippi, in New Orleans or Texas, which give us the same class to some extent, it is true; but instead of a few dozen, or a hundred, gaming at a time, here, there are thousands, and one house alone pays one hundred and fifty thousand dollars per annum for the rent of the 'Monte' tables.

Sunday makes no difference, certainly not Christmas, except for a little more drunkenness, and a little extra effort on the part of the hotel keepers to take in more money....

26 December I was not made more cheerful by finding that our agents had so conducted our affairs that instead of finding all our provisions and implements nicely stored, and in good order, waiting for us, I discovered that all that was most useful to us had been sold, and the balance lay about in the wet and mud, or was rotting, half dry for want of the requisite cover. The expenses had eaten up the money procured by the sales, or so we were told, and I found myself with forty men to take care of and in debt. I was on the point of breaking up the company, and letting every man shift for himself, but felt that it was neither brave nor honorable, so decided to make one more effort. I drew on my brother for one thousand dollars, borrowed all I could from the boys who had brought their own mules on with them, and concluded to take all who were not mechanics with me to the mines; the mechanics had, without exception, found work instantly at exorbitant prices. They were to keep half they made, and pay in the other half to the company. I have been offered thirty-five dollars a day to draw plans for houses, stores, etc., but though I never intended to go to the mines myself, I feel now for the sake of the men who stood by me, that I must stay by them.

1873 KUME KUNITAKE

Kume Kunitake (1839–1931) was a Japanese historian who in 1871–73 took part in a fact-finding mission to the West organized by the Japanese emperor to support Japan's modernization after the Meiji Restoration of 1868.

Westerners think trade is the most important business in life, and this is why Asians call their countries mercantile. Yet in fact a majority of their population are engaged in agriculture, the rest chiefly in industry, and only five or six out of one hundred in trade. It is simply inconceivable for the people of the East that not only merchants but also farmers and manufacturers are interested in the exchange of goods, and that big cities are eager to have merchants and trading vessels visit their ports. There are businesses that are indispensable to trade and taken for granted at commercial centres such as docks, markets, banking and exchange facilities, and chambers of commerce. These simply do not exist in the Orient.... In Japan there is, in contrast, general lack of interest in trade and ignorance of the fact that the essence of trade is to mediate between buying and selling and to transport goods to places which value them highly.

Possibilities for the further development of San Francisco seem limitless. It is a matter of fact that whenever one place flourishes in trade it brings forth prosperity in a corresponding place. London has been prosperous along with Paris, and these two cities have in turn brought forth the prosperity of New York and Philadelphia. Now geographically the ports that correspond to San Francisco in the East are Yokohama, Shanghai and Hong Kong.... But while San Francisco on the eastern shores of the Pacific has been thriving, what can we say of the situation at the Japanese and Chinese ports on the western shores? We Japanese must certainly reflect on these matters. San Francisco has taken advantage of its favourable location and safe conditions of the bay. At the same time, it should be noted that its land is vast and its population sparse, with the result that the demand for manpower is enormous, both in industry and agriculture. The cost of labour is exorbitant. As a result the manufacturing industry in San Francisco has been underdeveloped, and it has been very costly to process timber, wool, leather, gold and other kinds of metal. Glassware, chinaware, blankets, hats, shoes, silver and copper trinkets, leather instruments, lumber and even salted fish are so expensive that they have had to be imported from New York, Boston and Philadelphia. These goods are shipped through the Atlantic Ocean, the Gulf of Mexico and the Isthmus of Panama. It is obviously much more inconvenient to ship goods across such distances than to send them from Japan. Now it happens that Japan as well as other countries of the Orient are endowed with natural resources, where the population is large and labour cheap, in other words a situation the exact opposite of San Francisco.

1886 ELLEN G. HODGES

Ellen Hodges was a young woman from Boston when she undertook a journey around the United States in 1886. Her letters display a lively interest in the land and its people; in San Francisco she became involved with Christian missionaries working with the Chinese.

18 May, Palace Hotel, San Francisco We have driven about the city, and it is wonderful to see what has been made from the sand hills on which the city is built. Most of the best houses are built of wood. Mr Flood has one of stone, which is said to be magnificent in the interior. Driving out to the Cliff House, we passed the Golden Gate Park, which is still being enlarged and cultivated. A beautiful greenhouse stands in the park, with superb tropical plants and flowers growing profusely. The gardens around are prettily laid out....

The markets here are fascinating. The fruits, especially the cherries, are large, juicy and delicious. We are enjoying everything thus far, but we do object to the dust which sweeps the streets every afternoon. People who live in San Francisco seldom go out after one o'clock as it is so disagreeable after the wind comes up. I am looking forward to my visit to Chinatown where we are hoping to go in a day or two.

19 May There is so much to see and do here that I cannot keep quiet, and feel that I must be on the go the whole time.

A large party was made to visit Chinatown and one evening we set forth; when we reached a certain corner we were suddenly joined by a Chinaman. He was a fine-looking fellow, taller than most of them, and had a long pig-tail hanging almost to his heels with red silk braided in his hair. He had a very intelligent countenance and a lovely smile would spread over his face when we asked him questions. Of course he wore the usual costume of his country....

Our large party created quite an excitement; men peered out of doors and windows to see who and what we were, and we were glad to get out into the street again. We went to the theatre and were shown seats in the gallery.... The theatre was packed with these Mongolians, all with their hats on and all smoking. In a room full of Chinese you may imagine that the air was dreadful....

After spending twenty minutes here we were glad to get away from the pandemonium....

Next we visited a restaurant which was really beautiful; the walls of the rooms were panelled with carved teak wood; the table and stools were also carved and inlaid with marble. We were served tea and sweetmeats in true Celestial style.

A Chinaman waiter, clothed in spotless white, brought each of us a large teacup on a carved wooden stand, with a saucer covering it. He also brought a smaller cup without a saucer. The larger cup was filled with dry tea leaves; then the boiling hot water was poured over them. This was allowed to stand for a few seconds, then he dexterously poured the liquid off into the smaller cup, and it was ready for drinking. No milk or sugar is used....

We lingered at the restaurant a long time; then we wanted to visit the opium dens and were much disappointed when we were told there were too many of us. Very naturally Chin Jun did not want to expose his countrymen who probably would not have let him off easily for bringing us down to see them. We didn't blame him for not wanting to take us but we could not help being disappointed for we especially wanted to see these dens. But as it could not be done we said goodbye to our escorts and returned to the hotel where we had a late supper.

23 May The Chinese can live on six cents a day, and the company which imports them is responsible and has to look out that they don't starve; the consequence is that there are many idly lounging about the streets. There is no drunkenness among the Chinese as a rule, and but two men have been arrested for a long time for this cause; and these men learned the habit from miners with whom they had worked.

As you walk through the streets of Chinatown you would hardly realize yourself in America. The houses and shops are decorated with many coloured signs; lanterns hang from the balconies, which are painted Pompeian red, and it really looks quite Oriental....

It is said that the wife of Confucius had club feet and always had to be carried; it was she, being of high rank, who set the fashion for small feet. There are but three women here with small feet. I happened to see a little girl who was going through the street; she was laughing and chattering and seemed very happy with two companions who were supporting her as they walked along. There are so few women in Chinatown, and these are smuggled in, that they take great care in bringing up the girls.

1906 ENRICO CARUSO

The world-famous Italian tenor Enrico Caruso (1873–1921) was performing in San Francisco at the time of the great earthquake of April 1906, which reached

7.8 on the Richter scale and led to a devastating fire; four-fifths of the city was destroyed. Caruso vowed never to visit the city again.

You ask me to say what I saw and what I did during the terrible days which witnessed the destruction of San Francisco?...I was stopping at the Palace Hotel, where many of my fellow-artists were staying, and very comfortable it was. I had a room on the fifth floor, and on Tuesday evening, the night before the great catastrophe, I went to bed feeling very contented. I had sung in *Carmen* that night, and the opera had one with fine éclat. We were all pleased, and, as I said before, I went to bed that night feeling happy and contented.

But what an awakening! You must know that I am not a very heavy sleeper.... So on the Wednesday morning early I wake up about five o'clock, feeling my bed rocking as though I am in a ship on the ocean, and for a moment I think I am dreaming that I am crossing the water on my way to my beautiful country. And so I take no notice for the moment, and then, as the rocking continues, I get up and go to the window, raise the shade and look out. And what I see makes me tremble with fear. I see the buildings toppling over, big pieces of masonry falling, and from the street below I hear the cries and screams of men and women and children.

I remain speechless, thinking I am in some dreadful nightmare, and for something like forty seconds I stand there, while the buildings fall and my room still rocks like a boat on the sea. And during that forty seconds I think of forty thousand different things. All that I have ever done in my life passes before me, and I remember trivial things and important things. I think of my first appearance in grand opera, and I feel nervous as to my reception, and again I think I am going through last night's *Carmen*.

And then I gather my faculties together and call for my valet. He comes rushing in quite cool, and, without any tremor in his voice, says: 'It is nothing.' But all the same he advises me to dress quickly and go into the open, lest the hotel fall and crush us to powder. By this time the plaster on the ceiling has fallen in a great shower, covering the bed and the carpet and the furniture, and I begin to think it is time to 'get busy'. My valet gives me some clothes; I know not what the garments are but I get into a pair of trousers and into a coat and draw some socks on and my shoes, and every now and again the room trembles, so that I jump and feel very nervous.

I do not deny that I feel nervous, for I still think the building will fall to the ground and crush us. And all the time we hear the sound of crashing masonry and the cries of frightened people.

Then we run down the stairs and into the street, and my valet, brave fellow that he is, goes back and bundles all my things into trunks and drags them down six flights of stairs and out into the open one by one. While he is gone for another and another, I watch those that have already arrived, and presently someone comes and tries to take my trunks saying they are his. I say, 'No, they are mine'; but he does not go away....

Then I make my way to Union Square, where I see some of my friends, and one of them tells me he has lost everything except his voice, but he is thankful that he has still got that. And they tell me to come to a house that is still standing; but I say houses are not safe, nothing is safe but the open square, and I prefer to remain in a place where there is no fear of being buried by falling buildings. So I lie down in the square for a little rest, while my valet goes and looks after the luggage, and soon I begin to see the flames and all the city seems to be on fire. All the day I wander about, and I tell my valet we must try and get away, but the soldiers will not let us pass. We can find no vehicle to find our luggage, and this night we are forced to sleep on the hard ground in the open. My limbs ache yet from so rough a bed.

Then my valet succeeds in getting a man with a cart, who says he will take us to the Oakland Ferry for a certain sum, and we agree to his terms. We pile the luggage into the cart and climb in after it, and the man whips up his horse and we start.

1967 HELEN PERRY

The 'Summer of Love' saw the Haight-Ashbury district of San Francisco attracting visitors from across the world to explore a new 'hippie' way of being. One of these was New York psychiatrist Helen Perry (1911–2001), who described the inaugural Human Be-In in Golden Gate Park on 14 January 1967.

I knew I could attend the Human Be-In only as a potential initiate. The request for participation was very simple: if you feel sympathy, wear a flower, bring a musical instrument, wear bells. I went into a shop on Haight Street and purchased a silver chain with a bell at each end – from India, the young woman in the shop told me approvingly; and I had a sensation of having taken a monumental step, unknown in import to anyone but myself. When I got home and showed my husband the bells, he smiled and decided to go himself. I suggested that he wear a flower, and he found an old gray-green floppy Panama hat that made him look like a sheriff somehow and stuck a flower in it so that he did not look like a sheriff....

The Polo Field presented a new world. It was a medieval scene, with banners flying, bright and uncommitted; the day was miraculous, as days can be in San Francisco at their best, and the world was new and clean and pastoral. Children wandered around in the nude. People sat on the grass with nothing to do, sometimes moving up near to the small platform where a poetry-reading might be going on, or where a band might be playing. There was no program: it was a happening. Sights and sounds turned me on, so that I had a sensation of dreaming. The air seemed heady and mystical. Dogs and children pranced in blissful abandon, and I became aware of a phenomenon that still piques my curiosity: the dogs did not get into fights, and the children did not cry....

From time to time the loud-speaker on the platform would be turned up in volume and everyone would become quiet, while an important announcement was made. These announcements concerned lost children. 'The Hell's Angels have a little girl here behind the platform and she has curly hair. She says her name is Mary. She wants to see her mother.' For that particular tribe of young men on motorcycles had also appeared at the Be-In, replete with a station wagon, bearing apparently all kinds of refreshments, liquids and solids. They were well equipped for the task of serving as a clearing house for lost and strayed children since they had walkie-talkies and were well organized. Whether their services had been sought in advance or whether they were commandeered on the spot, no one seemed to know; in hippie language, it happened. When a call would go out for 'Timmie's mother', we all smiled and watched until finally from the huge throng a young woman would be seen moving serenely towards the Hell's Angels caravan, whereupon we would all settle back into our task of being....

It was difficult to sort out what happened. It was a religious rite in which nothing particular happened. And yet it was a day that marked for me at least the end of something and the beginning of something else. There was clearly a renewal of the spirit of man, unplanned, non-political. But then what do we mean by political? For at the end of the day, as the sun was sinking into the ocean beyond the Park, someone suggested from the loud-speaker that it would be nice to leave the Park clean, to practice kitchen yoga, and that is what happened. The litter of so many people, all the sandwich wrappings, the wine bottles, and the endless paper products so characteristic of the rubbish of our decade, disappeared, so that the police reported afterwards, with a sense of wonderment, that no other group of people of such a size in the memory of any living person had ever left an area so clean before, whether stadium or park....

Wine, incense, food and pot clearly intertwined that day; but none of these was necessary, as I can testify. We had not planned to stay so long, so we were without food; and we had no drugs. But it was the people that turned me on – the spectacle of people from so many walks of life, some come in curiosity, some in search of something, some in worship of the idea, some to be initiated into a new rite. It was people being together, unprogrammed, uncommitted, except to life itself and its celebration.

Afterwards, walking slowly toward the car, we did not have much to say.... Half the city seemed to be waiting at the bus stops.... Most of the people looked tired and droopy, but our eyes met in a secret delight. We had in common the sound of a different drummer.

SYDNEY

Sydney, in New South Wales, is the oldest European settlement in Australia, founded as Port Jackson by Arthur Phillip, commander of the First Fleet of convicts sent from Britain in 1788. It was initially the largest city in Australia until overtaken by Melbourne during the gold rush of the 1850s. Its remarkable setting on a large and protected sea inlet has always been admired, especially since the building of the iconic Harbour Bridge (opened 1932) and the Opera House (1973).

1788 JOHN WHITE

The journal of John White (see page 254) described both the voyage of Phillip's First Fleet and the new land, which he disliked despite taking a great interest in the unfamiliar flora and fauna. After setting up a hospital for the new colony, he returned to England in 1794.

Port Jackson I believe to be, without exception, the finest and most extensive harbour in the universe, and at the same time the most secure, being safe from all the winds that blow. It is divided into a great number of coves, to which his excellency has given different names. That on which the town is to be built, is called Sydney Cove. It is one of the smallest in the harbour, but the most convenient, as ships of the greatest burden can with ease go into it, and heave out close to the shore. Trincomalé [in Sri Lanka], acknowledged to be one of the best harbours in the world, is by no means to be compared to it. In a word, Port Jackson would afford sufficient and safe anchorage for all the navies of Europe.

1871 ANTHONY TROLLOPE

English novelist Anthony Trollope (1815-1882) wrote an account of a year he spent in Australia (1871-72), which the Australians themselves found unnecessarily critical even though his impressions of Sydney itself were favourable. By the time of his visit, transportation of convicts had ended thirty years earlier and the city comprised two hundred thousand people.

I despair of being able to convey to any reader my own idea of the beauty of Sydney Harbour. I have seen nothing equal to it in the way of land-locked sea scenery, nothing second to it....

The town itself, as a town, independently of its sea and its suburbs, was, to me, pleasant and interesting. In the first place, though it is the capital of an Australian colony, and therefore not yet a hundred years old, it has none of those worst signs of novelty which make the cities of the New World unpicturesque and distasteful. It is not parallelogrammic and rectangular. One may walk about it and lose the direction in which one is going. Streets running side by side occasionally converge – and they bend and go in and out, and wind themselves about, and are intricate....

The public gardens at Sydney deserve more than the passing mention just made of them. The people of Australia personally are laudably addicted to public gardens – as they are to other public institutions with which they are enabled to inaugurate the foundation of their towns, by the experience taught to them by our deficiencies. Parks for the people were not among the requirements of humanity when our cities were first built; and the grounds necessary for such purposes had become so valuable when the necessity was recognized, that it has been only with great difficulty, and occasionally by the munificence of individuals, that we have been able to create these artificial lungs for our artisans. In many of our large towns we have not created them at all. The Australian cities have had the advantage of our deficiencies. The land has been public property, and space for recreation has been taken without the payment of any cost price. In this way a taste for gardens, and, indeed, to some extent, a knowledge of flowers and shrubs, has been generated, and a humanizing influence in that direction has been produced.... For loveliness, and that beauty which can be appreciated by the ignorant as well as by the learned, the Sydney Gardens are unrivalled by any that I have seen.... A little beyond the gardens, almost equally near to the town, are the sea baths – not small, dark, sequestered spots in which, for want of a better place, men and women may wash themselves, but open sea spaces, guarded by palisades from the sharks which make bathing in the harbour impracticable, large enough for swimming and fitted up with all requisites. It is a great thing for a city to be so provided; and it is a luxury which, as far as I am aware, no other city possesses to the same degree....

I was much surprised at the fortifications of Sydney harbour. Fortifications, unless specially inspected, escape even a vigilant seer of sights, but I, luckily for myself, was enabled specially to inspect them. I had previously no idea that the people of New South Wales were either so suspicious of enemies, or so pugnacious in their nature. I found five separate fortresses, armed, or to be armed, to the teeth with numerous guns – four, five or six at each point – Armstrong guns, rifled guns, guns of eighteen tons weight, with loop-holed walls and pits for riflemen, as though Sydney were to become another Sebastopol. I was shown how the whole harbour and city were commanded by these guns. There were open batteries and casemated batteries, shell rooms and gunpowder magazines, barracks rising here and trenches dug there. There was a boom to be placed across the harbour, and a whole world of torpedoes ready to be sunk beneath the water, all of which were prepared and ready for use in an hour or two.... But, in viewing these fortifications, I was most specially struck by the loveliness of the sites chosen. One would almost wish to be a gunner for the sake of being at one of those forts.

Three different localities are combined to make Sydney. There is the old city...in which are George Street and Pitt Street, so called from George III and his minister, running parallel to each other, from the centre. The other chief streets are all named after the old governors – Macquarie Street, King Street, Bligh Street, Hunter Street and Phillip Street.... To the south of these rises the important town of Wooloomooloo – as to the remarkable spelling of which name the reader may take my assurance that I am right.... Then there is the 'North Shore', less fashionable, but almost as beautiful as the hills round the southern coves. The North Shore has to be reached by steam ferry from Sydney Cove, which now is better known as the Circular Quay, where is congregated the shipping of the port. When the wool ships from England are here, lying in a circle all round the margin, no port has a pleasanter appearance.... Crossing the main harbour from the Circular Quay, the inhabitants of the North Shore reach their side of the town in ten minutes.

1895 MARK TWAIN
Threatened with bankruptcy, the American writer known as Mark Twain (see page 241) undertook a long lecture tour of India and the Southern Hemisphere, which he turned into the book Following the Equator *(1897).*

We entered and cast anchor, and in the morning went oh-ing and ah-ing in admiration up through the crooks and turns of the spacious and beautiful harbor – a harbor which is the darling of Sydney and the wonder of the world. It is not surprising that the people are proud of it, nor that they put their enthusiasm into eloquent words. A returning citizen asked me what I thought of it, and I testified with a cordiality which I judged would be up to the market rate. I said it was beautiful – superbly beautiful. Then by a natural impulse I gave God the praise. The citizen did not seem altogether satisfied. He said:

It is beautiful, of course it's beautiful – the Harbor; but that isn't all of it, it's only half of it; Sydney's the other half, and it takes both of them together to ring the supremacy-bell. God made the Harbor, and that's all right; but Satan made Sydney.

Of course I made an apology; and asked him to convey it to his friend. He was right about Sydney being half of it. It would be beautiful without Sydney, but not above half as beautiful as it is now, with Sydney added. It is shaped somewhat like an oakleaf – a roomy sheet of lovely blue water, with narrow off-shoots of water running up into the country on both sides between long fingers of land, high wooden ridges with sides sloped like graves. Handsome villas are perched here and there on these ridges, snuggling among the foliage, and one catches alluring glimpses of them as the ship swims by toward the city. The city clothes a cluster of hills and a ruffle of neighboring ridges with its undulating masses of masonry, and out of these masses spring towers and spires and other architectural dignities and grandeurs that break the flowing lines and give picturesqueness to the general effect....

There are four specialties attainable in the way of social pleasure. If you enter your name on the Visitor's Book at Government House you will receive an invitation to the next ball that takes place there, if nothing can be proven against you. And it will be very pleasant; for you will see everybody except the Governor, and add a number of acquaintances and several friends to your list. The Governor will be in England. He always is. The continent has four or five governors, and I do not know how many it takes to govern the outlying archipelago; but anyway you will not see them....

Another of Sydney's social pleasures is the visit to the Admiralty House; which is nobly situated on high ground overlooking the water. The trim boats of the service convey the guests thither; and there, or on board the flagship, they have the duplicate of the hospitalities of Government House. The admiral commanding a station in British waters is a magnate of the first degree, and he is sumptuously housed, as becomes the dignity of his office.

Third in the list of special pleasures is the tour of the harbor in a fine steam pleasure-launch. Your richer friends own boats of this kind, and they will invite you, and the joys of the trip will make a long day seem short.

And finally comes the shark-fishing. Sydney harbor is populous with the finest breeds of man-eating sharks in the world. Some people make their living catching them; for the government pays a cash bounty on them. The larger the shark the larger the bounty, and some of the sharks are twenty feet long. You not only get the bounty, but everything that is in the shark belongs to you. Sometimes the contents are quite valuable.

1922 D. H. LAWRENCE
British novelist D. H. Lawrence (1885–1930) visited New South Wales with his wife Frieda in 1922, and his experiences fed into his novel Kangaroo, *published the following year.*

[In which state of mind] they jogged through the city, catching a glimpse from the top of a hill of the famous harbour spreading out with its many arms and legs. Or at least they saw one bay with warships and steamers lying between the houses and the wooded, bank-like shores, and they saw the centre of the harbour, and the opposite squat cliffs – the whole low wooded tableland reddened with suburbs and interrupted by the pale spaces of the many-lobed harbour. The sky had gone grey, and the low tableland into which the harbour intrudes squatted dark-looking and monotonous and sad, as if lost on the face of the earth: the same Australian atmosphere, even here within the area of huge, restless, modern Sydney, whose million inhabitants seem to slip like fishes from one side of the harbour to another.

Murdoch Street was an old sort of suburb, little squat bungalows with corrugated iron roofs, painted red. Each little bungalow was set in its own hand-breadth of ground, surrounded by a little wooden palisade fence. And there went the long street, like a child's drawing, the little square bungalows dot-dot-dot, close together and yet apart, like modern democracy, each one fenced round with a square rail fence. The street was wide, and strips of worn grass took the place of kerb-stones. The stretch of macadam in the middle seemed as forsaken as a desert, as the hansom clock-clocked along it.

TIMBUKTU

Timbuktu, in the West African state of Mali, was a significant centre for trade (especially gold and slaves) and Islamic learning in the 14th and 15th centuries. In 1468, it became part of the Songhai Empire. Although Timbuktu was in decline from the 16th century, it was remembered as a mythically wealthy place, unreachable by outsiders both because of its remoteness and the hostile Tuareg tribes of the region. The first European explorers reached it in the mid-19th century. It is now impoverished and threatened by desertification.

1510 LEO AFRICANUS

Leo Africanus (c. 1494–c. 1554) was a Spanish-born diplomat on behalf of the
sultan of Fez, who visited Timbuktu in 1510 and Constantinople in 1517, but later
moved to Rome, where he was baptized and wrote an account of his travels.

The name of this kingdom is a modern one, after a city which was built by
a king named Mansa Suleyman in the year 610 of the Hijra, around twelve
miles from a branch of the Niger River.

The houses of Timbuktu are huts made of clay-covered wattles with
thatched roofs. In the centre of the city is a temple built of stone and mortar,
built by an architect named Granata, and in addition there is a large palace,
constructed by the same architect, where the king lives. The shops of the
artisans, the merchants and especially weavers of cotton cloth are very
numerous. Fabrics are also imported from Europe to Timbuktu, borne by
Berber merchants.

The women maintain the custom of veiling their faces, except for the
slaves who sell all the foodstuffs. The inhabitants are very rich, especially
the strangers who have settled in the country; so much so that the current
king has given two of his daughters in marriage to two brothers, both
businessmen, on account of their wealth. There are many wells containing
sweet water; and in addition, when the Niger is in flood canals deliver the
water to the city. Grain and animals are abundant, so that the consumption
of milk and butter is considerable. But salt is in very short supply because
it is carried here from Tegaza, some 500 miles away. I happened to be in
this city at a time when a load of salt sold for eighty ducats. The king
has a rich treasure of coins and gold ingots. One of these ingots weighs
970 pounds.

The royal court is magnificent and very well organized. When the king
goes from one city to another with the people of his court, he rides a camel
and the horses are led by hand by servants. If fighting becomes necessary,
the servants mount the camels and all the soldiers mount on horseback.
When someone wishes to speak to the king, he must kneel before him and
bow down; but this is only required of those who have never before spoken
to the king, or of ambassadors. The king has about 3,000 horsemen and
infinity of foot-soldiers armed with bows made of wild fennel which they
use to shoot poisoned arrows. This king makes war only upon neighbouring

enemies and upon those who do not want to pay him tribute. When he has gained a victory, he has all of them – even the children – sold in the market at Timbuktu.

Only small, poor horses are born in this country. The merchants use them for their voyages and the courtiers to move about the city. But the good horses come from Barbary [the North African coast]. They arrive in a caravan and, ten or twelve days later, they are led to the ruler, who takes as many as he likes and pays appropriately for them.

The king is a declared enemy of the Jews. He will not allow any to live in the city. If he hears it said that a Berber merchant frequents them or does business with them, he confiscates his goods. There are in Timbuktu numerous judges, teachers and priests, all properly appointed by the king. He greatly honours learning. Many handwritten books imported from Barbary are also sold. There is more profit made from this commerce than from all other merchandise.

Instead of coined money, pure gold nuggets are used; and for small purchases, cowrie shells which have been carried from Persia, and of which 400 equal a ducat. Six and two-thirds of their ducats equal one Roman gold ounce.

The people of Timbuktu are of a peaceful nature. They have a custom of almost continuously walking about the city in the evening (except for those that sell gold), between 10 p.m. and 1 a.m., playing musical instruments and dancing. The citizens have at their service many slaves, both men and women.

The city is very much endangered by fire. At the time when I was there on my second voyage, half the city burned in the space of five hours. But the wind was violent and the inhabitants of the other half of the city began to move their belongings for fear that the other half would burn.

There are no gardens or orchards in the area surrounding Timbuktu.

1828 RENÉ CAILLIÉ

The first European to visit Timbuktu and return to Europe was French explorer René Caillié (1799–1838), in disguise as an Arab. On his return to France he won a prize of 10,000 francs offered by the Société de Géographie for the first man to reach Timbuktu.

At 3.30 a.m. on 28 April 1828, with the men of Sidi-Abdallahi-Chebir, we left the small town of Cabra, and set off northwards for Timbuktu. The slaves who were on the boat came too, so that together we made a fairly large caravan. The youngest slaves rode on donkeys, as the road was very sandy and wearisome....

At last we arrived at Timbuktu just as the sun touched the horizon. I could at last see this capital of Sudan [southern Sahara region], a place I had so long desired to set eyes upon. On entering this mysterious city, the object of research and fascination among the civilized nations of Europe, I was seized with a deep and inexpressible satisfaction; I had never felt the like, and my joy was extreme. But I had to hold it back; I confided my feeling to our Saviour alone; with such ardour did I give thanks for the success that had crowned my enterprise! What acts of grace had I performed that he had bestowed such marvellous protection upon me, amid such dangers and apparently insurmountable obstacles!

Coming out of my reveries I found a spectacle before my gaze that I must attend to, the grandeur and wealth of this town was a whole other idea. On first sight it was nothing but a heap of badly built mud houses. In every direction, all one could see were endless plains of moving sand, white and yellow, and the greatest aridity. On the horizon the sky was pale red, all nature looked sad, the deepest silence reigned, the song of not a single bird was to be heard.

Despite this it was somehow imposing to see this great city rising out of the sand, and one had to admire the efforts of those who had built it. I suspected that formerly the river had passed close to the town, though it was now eight miles to the north.

I went to lodge with Sidi-Abdallahi; he received me paternally. He was already indirectly aware of the events that had brought me here, and he invited me to dine with him. He served a very fine couscous and mutton. There were six of us at table; we ate with our hands, but as neatly as we could....

The following morning I greeted my host who welcomed me warmly, then I went for a walk around the town. It was neither as large nor as busy as I had expected, its commerce far less vigorous than by repute; there was no great market of strangers from all over Sudan, as at Jenne [Djenné]. I only saw camels from Cabra carrying goods brought on the flotilla, some groups of inhabitants deep in conversation on their mats, and many Moors sleeping in the shade of their porches. The whole town breathed a deep sorrow.

I was surprised at the lack of activity – I might even say inertia – that reigned in this town. Just a few nut-sellers cried their wares.

At four in the afternoon, when the heat dropped a little, I saw many well-dressed negro traders go off, mounted on finely caparisoned horses; but they took care not to go far from the town for fear of the Touregs.

The heat being excessive, the market was held in the evening, around three o'clock. Few visitors were in attendance, though the Moors of the neighbouring tribe of Zaouat often came there. But this market was virtually deserted in comparison to that of Jenne. Most of the goods on sale came from the riverboats, and some from Europe – such as the glassware, amber, coral, paper and other objects. I saw stalls laid out with European cloth.

1853 HEINRICH BARTH

German explorer Heinrich Barth (1821–1865) visited on his journey across the Sahara in 1853 and faced all the insecurities of being alone in an unknown city.

It had been arranged that, during the absence of the Sheikh el Bakay, whose special guest I professed to be, my house should be locked up and no one allowed to pay me a visit. However, while my luggage was being got in, numbers of people gained access to the house, and came to pay me their compliments, and while they scrutinized my luggage, part of which had rather a foreign appearance, some of them entertained a doubt as to my nationality.

But of course it could never have been my intention to have impressed these people with the belief of my being a Mohammedan; for, having been known as a Christian all along my road...the news of my real character could not fail soon to transpire.... I had been obliged to adopt the character of a Mohammedan in order to traverse with some degree of safety the country of the Tawarek, and to enter the town of Timbuktu, which was in the hands of the fanatical Fulbe of Hamda-Allahi....

Thus I had now reached the object of my arduous undertaking; but it was apparent from the very first that I should not enjoy the triumph of having overcome the difficulties of the journey in quiet and repose.

The continuous excitement of the protracted struggle, and the uncertainty whether I should succeed in my undertaking, had sustained my weakened frame till I actually reached this city; but as soon as I was there, and almost at the very moment when I entered my house, I was seized with a severe attack of fever. Yet never were presence of mind and bodily energy more required; for the first night which I passed in Timbuktu was disturbed by feelings of alarm and serious anxiety.

On the morning of 8th September, the first news I heard was that Hammadi...had informed the Fulbe that a Christian had entered the town, and that, in consequence, they had come to the determination of killing him. However, these rumours did not cause me any great alarm, as I entertained the false hope that I might rely on the person who, for the time, had undertaken to protect me; but my feeling of security was soon destroyed, this very man turning out my greatest tormentor. I had destined for him a very handsome gift, consisting of a fine cloth *bernús*, a cloth *kaftan*, and two robes, one of silk and the other of indigo-dyed cotton, besides some smaller articles; but he was by no means satisfied with these.... My host stated that as their house and their whole establishment were at my disposal, so my property ought to be at theirs. But even this amount of property did not satisfy him, nor were his pretensions limited to this; for the following day he exacted an almost equal amount of considerable presents from me, such as two cloth *kaftans*, two silk *hamail* or sword belts, three other silk *tobes* [kaftans], one of the species called *jellabi*, one of that called *harir*, and the third of the kind called *filfil*, one Nupe *tobe*, three *turkedis* [dresses], a small six-barrelled pistol, and many other things....

Thus my first day in Timbuktu passed away, preparing me for a great deal of trouble and anxiety which I should have to go through; even those who professed to be my friends treating me with so little consideration.

However, the second day of my residence here was more promising. I received visits from several respectable people, and I began to enter with spirit upon my new situation, and to endeavour by forbearance to accommodate myself to the circumstances under which I was placed. The state of my health also seemed to improve, and I felt a great deal better than on the preceding day.

I was not allowed to stir about, but was confined within the walls of my house. In order to obviate the effect of this want of exercise as much as possible, to enjoy fresh air, and at the same time to become familiar with the principal features of the town, I ascended as often as possible the terrace of my house. This afforded an excellent view over the northern quarters of the town. On the north was the massive mosque of Sankore, which had just been restored to all its former grandeur through the influence of the Sheikh el Bakay, and gave the whole place an imposing character.... The style of the buildings was various. I could see clay houses of different characters, some low and unseemly, others rising with a second story in front to greater elevation, and making even an attempt at architectural ornament, the whole being interrupted by a few round huts of matting....

But while the terrace of my house served to make me well acquainted with the character of the town, it had also the disadvantage of exposing me fully to the gaze of the passers-by, so that I could only slowly, and with many interruptions, succeed in making a sketch of the scene thus offered to my view. At the same time I became aware of the great inaccuracy which characterizes the view of the town as given by M. Caillié...in his representation the whole town seems to consist of scattered and quite isolated houses, while in reality the streets are entirely shut in, as the dwellings form continuous and uninterrupted rows. But Timbuktu at the time of Caillié's visit was not so well off as it is at present, having been overrun by the Fulbe the preceding year, and he had no opportunity of making a drawing.

Although I was greatly delighted at the pleasant place of retreat for refreshing my spirits and invigorating my body by a little exercise which the terrace afforded me, I was disgusted by the custom which prevails in the houses like that in which I was lodged, of using the terrace as a sort of closet; and I had great difficulty in preventing my guide, who still stayed with me and made the terrace his usual residence, from indulging in this filthy practice.

TOKYO
(EDO)

The small defended port of Edo or Yedo was chosen by Tokugawa Ieyasu as his headquarters; when he became shogun, or ruler, of Japan in 1603, it became capital of his government (the relatively powerless emperor resided at Kyoto).

Following the 'opening' of Japan by American naval commander Matthew Perry in 1853, Western missions were established in the capital Edo for the first time in 250 years. Following social unrest, in 1867 the last Tokugawa shogun was overthrown by supporters of the emperor, and the country opened fully to Western goods and fashions, as well as visitors. The first railway, between Tokyo and Yokohama, opened in 1872; the line to the old imperial capital of Kyoto followed five years later.

The city flourished in the 20th century despite a major earthquake in 1923, and heavy American bombing in 1945. Following Japan's defeat in the Second World War, there was a strong American influence in the city, which created a unique fusion of traditional Japanese and modern Western culture.

1613 JOHN SARIS

In 1611 Captain John Saris (1580–1643) of the British East India Company was sent to negotiate trading rights in Japan. He met the Tokugawa shogun (whom he called the king) and they exchanged gifts. The shogun gave the English trading rights on Kyushu island but these were never developed. The armour Saris was given became part of the Royal Collection that was dispersed after the execution of Charles I in 1649.

14 September I arrived at Edo, a city which made a very glorious appearance unto us; the ridge tiles and corner tiles richly gilded, the posts of their doors gilded and varnished. Glass windows they have none, but great windows of board, opening in leaves, well set out with painting as in Holland. There is a causeway which goes through the chief streets of the town; underneath this runs a river; at every fifty paces there is a well head fitted very substantially of freestone with buckets for neighbours to fetch water, and for danger of fire. This street is as broad as any of our streets in England.

The king kept his court in the castle of Edo which is much fairer and stronger than that of Surunga. He was better guarded and attended upon than the emperor his father....

My entertainment and access to the king here was much like to the former at Surunga with the emperor. He accepted very kindly our king's letters and presents, bidding me welcome and wishing me to refresh myself, and his letters and presents to our king should be made ready with all speed.

19 September I delivered the secretary his present. This day thirty-two men being commanded to a certain house for not paying their debts, and being in the stocks within the house, the house in the night-time by casualty fired and they were all burnt to death. Towards evening the king sent two varnished armours, a present to His Majesty the King of England. Also a *tachi* (a long sword which none wear but soldiers of the best rank) and a *wakizashi* (short sword) a present for myself.

1862 ERNEST MASON SATOW

Ernest Mason Satow (1843–1929) was a British diplomat and scholar of Japanese culture stationed in Japan from 1862 to 1869; his diaries for this period were published as A Diplomat in Japan *(1921). A mountaineer, he also wrote guidebooks to Japan.*

A couple of miles beyond the river we came to the well-known gardens called Ume Yashiki (the plum orchard), where we were waited on by some very pretty girls. Everybody who travelled along the Tokaido in those days, who had any respect for himself, used to stop here, in season or out of season, to drink a cup of straw-coloured tea, smoke a pipe and chaff the waiting-maids. Fish cooked in various ways and warm *sake* (rice beer) were also procurable, and red-faced native gentlemen might often be seen folding themselves up into their palanquins after a mild daylight debauch. Europeans usually brought picnic baskets and lunched there, but even if they started late were glad of any excuse for turning in to this charmingly picturesque tea-garden....

The building occupied as the legation was part of a Buddhist temple To-zen-ji, behind which lay a large cemetery. But our part of it had never been devoted to purposes of worship. Every large temple in Japan has attached to it a suite of what we might call state apartments, which are used only on ceremonial occasions once or twice in the year, but from time it has been the custom to accommodate foreign embassies in these buildings. A suitable residence for a foreign representative could not otherwise have been found in Yedo. As a general rule every Japanese, with the exception of the working classes, lives in his own house, instead of renting it as do most residents in an European capital. The only purely secular buildings large enough to lodge the British Minister and his staff were the *yashiki* or 'hotels' of daimyos but the idea of expropriating one of these nobles in order to accommodate a foreign official was probably never mooted....

The rooms were not spacious, and very little attempt had been made to convert them into comfortable apartments. I think there was an iron stove or two in the principal rooms, but elsewhere the only means of warming was a Japanese brazier piled up with red hot charcoal, the exhalations from which were very disagreeable to a novice. The native who wraps himself up in thick wadded clothes and squats on the floor has no difficulty in keeping himself warm with the aid of this arrangement, over which he holds the tips of his fingers. His legs being crumpled up under him, the superficies he presents to the cold air is much less than it would be if he sat in a chair with outstretched limbs in European fashion. To protect himself against draughts he has a screen standing behind him, and squats on a warm cushion stuffed with silk wool. These arrangements enable him even in winter to sit with the window open, so long as it has a southern aspect.... Underneath you there are thick straw mats laid upon thin and badly jointed hoarding, through which the cutting north-west wind rises all over the floor, while the keen draughts pierce through between the uprights and the shrunken lath-and-plaster walls.

1878 ISABELLA BIRD

The indefatigable British writer Isabella Bird (see page 119) visited Japan in 1878, arriving in Tokyo but mostly travelling in remote parts as she described in Unbeaten Tracks in Japan *(1880).*

24 May I have dated my letter Yedo, according to the usage of the British Legation, but popularly the new name of Tokiyo, or Eastern Capital, is used, Kiyoto, the Mikado's former residence, having received the name of Saikio, or Western Capital, though it has now no claim to be regarded as a capital at all. Yedo belongs to the old regime and the Shogunate, Tokiyo to the new regime and the Restoration, with their history of ten years. It would seem an incongruity to travel to Yedo by railway, but quite proper when the destination is Tokiyo.

The journey between the two cities is performed in an hour by an admirable, well-metalled, double-track railroad, 18 miles long, with iron bridges, neat stations and substantial roomy termini, built by English engineers at a cost known only to government, and opened by the Mikado in 1872. The Yokohama station is a handsome and suitable stone building, with a spacious approach, ticket offices on our plan, roomy waiting rooms for different classes – uncarpeted, however, in consideration of Japanese clogs – and supplied with the daily papers. There is a department for the weighing and labelling of luggage, and on the broad, covered, stone platform at both termini a barrier with turnstiles, through which, except by special favour, no ticketless person can pass. Except the ticket clerks, who are Chinese, and the guards and engine-drivers, who are English, the officials are Japanese in European dress. Outside the stations, instead of cabs, there are *kurumas* [carriages], which carry luggage as well as people....

The Japanese look most diminutive in European dress. Each garment is a misfit, and exaggerates the miserable physique and the national defects of concave chests and bow legs. The lack of a complexion and of hair upon the face makes it nearly impossible to judge of the ages of men. I supposed that all the railroad officials were striplings of 17 or 18, but they are men from 25 to 40 years old....

You don't take your ticket for Tokiyo, but for Shinagawa or Shinbashi, two of the many villages which have grown together into the capital. Yedo is hardly seen before Shinagawa is reached, for it has no smoke and no long chimneys; its temples and public buildings are seldom lofty; the former are often concealed among thick trees, and its ordinary houses seldom reach a height of 20 feet. On the right a blue sea with fortified islands upon it, wooded gardens with massive retaining walls, hundreds of fishing boats lying in creeks or drawn up on the beach; on the left a broad road on which *kurumas* are hurrying both ways, rows of low, grey houses, mostly teahouses and shops; and as I was asking 'Where is Yedo?' the train came to rest in the terminus, the Shinbashi railroad station, and disgorged its 200 Japanese passengers with a combined clatter of 400 clogs – a new sound to me.

These clogs add three inches to their height, but even with them few of the men attained 5 feet 7 inches, and few of the women 5 feet 2 inches; but they look far broader in the national costume, which also conceals the defects of their figures. So lean, so yellow, so ugly, yet so pleasant-looking, so wanting in colour and effectiveness; the women so very small and tottering in their walk; the children so formal-looking and such dignified burlesques on the adults, I feel as if I had seen them all before, so like are they to their pictures on trays, fans and teapots. The hair of the women is all drawn away from their faces, and is worn in chignons, and the men, when they don't shave the front of their heads and gather their back hair into a quaint queue drawn forward over the shaven patch, wear their coarse hair about three inches long in a refractory undivided mop....

Hundreds of *kurumas* and covered carts with four wheels drawn by one miserable horse, which are the omnibuses of certain districts of Tokiyo, were waiting outside the station, and an English brougham for me. The Legation stands in Kojimachi on very elevated ground above the inner moat of the historic 'Castle of Yedo', but I cannot tell you anything of what I saw on my way thither, except that there were miles of dark, silent, barrack-like buildings, with highly ornamental gateways and long rows of projecting windows with screens made of reeds – the feudal mansions of Yedo – and miles of moats with lofty grass embankments or walls of massive masonry 50 feet high, with kiosk-like towers at the corners, and curious, roofed gateways, and many bridges, and acres of lotus leaves. Turning along the inner moat, up a steep slope, there are, on the right, its deep green waters, the great grass embankment surmounted by a dismal wall overhung by the branches of coniferous trees which surrounded the palace of the shogun.... Besides these, barracks, parade-grounds, policemen, *kurumas*, carts pulled and pushed by coolies, packhorses in straw sandals and dwarfish, slatternly looking soldiers in European dress, made up the Tokiyo that I saw between Shinbashi and the Legation.

1889 MARY CRAWFORD FRASER

Tokyo, like all of Japan, is subject to frequent earthquakes, which visitors, such as Mary Crawford Fraser (1851–1922), American-born novelist and wife of a British diplomat, had to grow used to.

I am not new to earthquakes, and we have had no very alarming ones here as yet; but the Japanese papers are unkindly promising us a severe visitation shortly. It seems that the shocks are felt very strongly in Tokyo, as they are in all places where there is a large area of soft alluvial soil; and (consoling rider!) our house stands, so I am told, exactly where they all pass, no matter whence the current comes or whither it tends. It may be a distinction to live over a kind of Seismic Junction; but it is bad for the nerves – and the china!

25 May My daily drives in Tokyo are as full of fun and interest as was my first *jinriksha* ride in Nagasaki. The distances are enormous, and it often happens that I make a journey of three or four miles between one visit and another; but every step of the way brings me to some new picture or new question, reveals some unimagined poetry or bit of fresh fun in daily life. There are parties of little acrobats, children in charge of an older boy, who come tumbling after the carriage in contortions which would be terrible to see did one not feel convinced that Japanese limbs are made of India-rubber. Then there are the pedlars; the old-clothes sellers; the pipe-menders, who solemnly clean a pipe for one *rin* as they sit on the doorstep; the umbrella-makers, who fill a whole street with enormous yellow parasols drying in the sun. Here a juggler is swallowing a sword, to the delight and amazement of a group of children; there the seller of tofu, or bean-curd, cuts great slabs of the cheesy substance, and wraps it in green leaves for his customers to carry away. I love watching the life of the streets, its fullness and variety, its inconvenient candour and its inexplicable reticences. I am always sorry to come in, even to our lovely home with its green lawns and gardens in flower. It is like leaving a theatre before the piece is over, and one wonders if one will ever see it again.

1907 MARIE STOPES

Marie Stopes (1880–1958), a British botanist later better known as a birth-control advocate, spent eighteen months in Japan studying fossilized plants in coal mines. Her Journal from Japan *(1910) was her first book and only published piece of travel writing.*

10 August I am much surprised to find how like Venice Tokio is, with its numerous waterways. This hotel is on a very tiny island with six bridges, which connect it with the numerous other islands which seem to compose a large part of Tokio – there are waterways, lakes, docks or rivers everywhere.... At first I was a little disappointed in the streets, pretty and quaint though they were, but when we came to the broad roads outside the moats of the Imperial

Palace, I found far more of beauty and wonder than I had expected. Roads, grey sloping walls, green banks running up from the green water which shadowed the great trunks of fantastic trees – the heart of the city, and no sign of its life. In the grey sloping walls was a silent strength and majesty, in the beautiful trees a fantastic charm; the whole being one of the most impressive views I have ever seen in a city – a sight that brought tears to one's eyes....

In the afternoon I went to the Botanical Gardens and Institute.... The gardens are beautiful. The part with the little lakes and streams, distant views and wistaria arbours, more beautiful than anything of the kind I have yet seen. Some of the Gymnosperm trees are also very fine indeed. Parts of the garden are allowed to run wild, and there is a want of gardeners – the old story. The low, wooden-built, picturesque Institute, with palms growing almost into its windows, can show London and Manchester a good deal....

When returning in the rickshaw at night (it is an hour's drive to the hotel) the pretty Japanese lanterns decorated the dark streets. Our festival arrangements are here the daily custom. Alas, that there are now several red and white brick abominations of buildings in this low-built, grey wooden town. These brick buildings are quite new; but some of the older Europeanized buildings are beautiful, for example, the Japan Bank is dignified and graceful, of grey stone, set in brilliant green gardens.

11 August I had an exciting time going about Tokio; of course I could (and did until today) go in a rickshaw, but then one is simply a parcel of goods to be delivered. Today I sallied forth to a place three miles away, and to get there had to take three different tram-cars and walk a mile through little twisting streets. I took a map and got there without losing myself once until within a hundred yards of the place; then my guardian angel (in the shape of Professor F.) turned up and rescued me, though as I had planned this expedition without his knowledge, and spoken of it to no one, it was nothing short of a miracle. Tokio is enormous, for its two millions or so live in single-storeyed houses, and there are many parks and gardens, so that it is very easy to get thoroughly lost, and not one of the common people can speak English. In the afternoon I got one of my desires, and saw a real Japanese house. It was perfectly exquisite in snowy white, soft straw colour and grey. I took the shoes from off my feet. It belonged to the widow of an officer killed in the war and her daughter; and as a most exceptional favour

I am to be allowed to take part of the house and live with them as a kind of lodger. I could sing for joy. My rooms, of course, are small, but exquisite as a sea-shell; I shall live as nearly as possible in true Japanese style. The house is on rising ground, fifteen minutes from the Botanical Gardens, in a part that is almost country, near a great Buddhist temple; the air fresh and inspiring after that on the flats down here in Tsukiji.

12 August Glorious weather. I conveyed my luggage to my house and found that boxes look detestably out of place in such a dwelling, and appear more unutterably hideous than ever.

In the afternoon I had tea in the big summer house in the Botanical Gardens. The room is really a good-sized lecture hall, only flat and open after Japanese style; the three side walls had their screens taken out, and so we looked on to the lakes and streams of the landscape garden. At tea there was quite a party.

The *Stimmung* [mood] is strange and fascinating, and quite indescribable. Professor M. is in Japanese dress; real Japanese tea (totally unlike our tea) and real Japanese cakes, also as unlike cakes as possible. One is a kind of jelly, made of seaweed, and is very nice. I had my first lesson in eating with chopsticks, and have 'graduated'.

I had dinner with Dr M. and Professor F., and then returned for my first night in a true Japanese house.... They all kneel on the matting and touch the floor with their hands and foreheads, and I do a half-hearted imitation of the courtesy. It crushes my frocks, but otherwise does me no harm to be polite. The matting on the floor is delightful, so springy to walk on as well as pleasing to the eye.

My *futons* (soft, thick quilt-like mats) are beauties of silk and velvet and I feel ashamed to lie on them. The mosquito curtains are nearly as big as the room, and make a high, four-square tent when erected, but everything is put away in the day, and no sign of sleeping remains; hence everything gets aired and there is no possibility of dust collecting under beds. In many of the household arrangements we are far behind the Japanese. They have reduced simplicity to a fine art. The bath, where one sits upright instead of lying down, is most comfortable; but of course mine was too hot after a short time in it, as the fire is inside it, and I had to rush out and get help in Japanese!

At night the stillness was absolute, but the strangeness of the day kept sleep away.

1955 FOSCO MARAINI

Fosco Maraini (1912–2004) was an Italian anthropologist and photographer who taught in Japan from 1938 to 1943, but was interned with his family in 1943 until the end of the Second World War. His book Meeting with Japan *(1955) described his return to that country, which now combined traditional values and urgent Westernization.*

Now we were on terra firma. They opened the door, and we got out; and here were the first Japanese sounds, smells, voices. I felt very moved, though afraid of being disappointed. So many people had told me that Japan was spoilt, that the young had 'gone American' and chewed gum, and that the old were disillusioned and no longer thought about anything but money. Would this turn out to be true or false? I took deep breaths of the air of my second country, the country in which I had lived and suffered for so long, where my daughters were born, the air of this eastern Hellas which has the gift of putting those who have once loved her under a permanent spell.

I quickly completed the customs and passport formalities. How smoothly they went! Times seem to have changed greatly; in a few moments it was all over. Even my collection of photographic apparatus, my cine-camera, the many boxes of film I had brought with me, passed without question, almost without a glance. How different it was the first time I had arrived in Japan, in distant 1938! Then you were subjected to interminable inspections, interrogations, the most minute customs and medical examinations – even your faeces were examined; you had to give the name of all your close and distant relatives, and if it turned out that you had, or had had, a connection with any army or political party or international organization, it was just too bad. Finally you had to make a complete list of all the books and other printed matter you had with you....

Today I walked around Tokyo for the first time. As soon as I got out of the *shosen* [underground] I was surprised at the number of new houses and new concrete buildings, at the speed with which Japanese reconstruction had taken place, at the liveliness of the streets and, at any rate superficially and at first sight, the general impression of prosperity....

Nowhere else in the world can you see in the streets girls and women in kimonos, either vividly coloured or subdued according to their age, young women in Paris models, girls in jeans, or Indian saris, or neat Chinese dress; mothers leading their children by the hand, or carrying them on their back, or pushing them in prams; men in shirts, in work *happi* [coats], in the uniform of ten different armies, with their sons on their back, in straw sandals, gumboots, overalls, eighth-century costume, in shorts, rags, smart white suits, in *yukata* [informal kimonos], in *haori* [open jackets], *hakama* [pleated trousers] and bowler hats, or in *montsuki* [formal kimonos]; with black, red or fair hair; with almond-shaped eyes or blue eyes; men who drag their feet (Japanese), gesticulate (Latins), walk stiffly and inexorably (Teutons) or loosely and smilingly (Americans); Buddhist monks, Roman Catholic priests, orthodox archimandrites, protestant pastors, Shinto *kannushi* [priests], Indian sadhus, huge men with long hair knotted on top of their heads (*sumo* wrestlers), martial and agile Sikhs in pink turbans, human relics of Hiroshima or Nagasaki; white-shirted disabled ex-servicemen begging and pathetically playing some instrument while the victors pass by with girls on their arms; boys on bicycles demonstrating their virtuosity by threading their way through the traffic with one hand on the handlebar and the other holding aloft two or three layers of trays full of food; men-horses pulling perfumed, heavily made-up geishas, people terrified of infection wearing surgeon's masks over their faces, students in uniform, railwaymen in uniform, postmen in uniform, firemen in uniform, nurses in uniform; itinerant flute-layers who hide their heads on baskets; men disguised as insects or corpses who dance, cut capers or beat drums or do whatever else may be required to advertise some product or other; sellers of red-fish or of roasted sweet potatoes, or a special bean paste made up in beautiful wooden boxes; baseball players returned from a game; pipe-cleaners pushing carts on which a tiny kettle is permanently whistling; Coca-Cola sellers wearing the uniform and device of the firm; masseurs, who are generally blind; aged widows with their hair cut short; Buddhist nuns with shaved heads; scowling colonels of the reserve in kimono and bowler hat; and frivolous girls, often in wooden sandals, who probably belong to the reserve of another army, that of Tokyo's 80,000 prostitutes, for that is the number the city is said to muster.

VENICE

Arguably the most written-about city in the world, the unique situation and cityscape of Venice has fascinated travellers since the Middle Ages. Founded in the chaos of the last centuries of the Roman Empire when refugees from northern Italian cities hid from the Gothic invaders in the marshes of the Veneto, it used its impregnable situation to grow into a major maritime state. Its trading empire across the eastern Mediterranean challenged Byzantium, which it conquered during the Fourth Crusade in 1204, bringing many treasures back to Venice.

Although its trading wealth declined from the 16th century, Venice replaced this by projecting itself as a cultural centre on the Grand Tour, and more generally for tourists and other visitors from Europe and further afield. Many great writers have been tempted to describe this uniquely atmospheric playground full of architectural glories.

1438 PERO TAFUR

The Castilian Pero Tafur (see page 141) visited Venice as part of his three-year journey around the Mediterranean. His account of Venice combines descriptions of the familiar architectural glories with travellers' tales.

The city of Venice is very populous, and there is much country round about it. The houses are built very close together. They say that there are 70,000 inhabitants, but the strangers and serving people, mostly slaves, are very numerous. The city has no walls, nor any fortress, except those two castles which enclose the harbour, since its defence lies in the sea. They draw a chain across from one side to the other so that they may be secure, and if the whole world came up against the city, the Venetians could sink a ship between the two castles in the canal and be safe.

The city is built on the sea, and there are artificial canals along which the boats can pass, and in some parts there are streets where the people can go on foot. Elsewhere, in places where the canals are too narrow for ships, there are bridges, and as in Castile everyone has a beast to ride, so here they all have boats and pages to row and attend to them. And as we pride ourselves on a fine horse and a pretty well-dressed page, so they set great store by their boats, which are kept very properly. They are well hung and fitted with cabins and seats, so that one or two or more may travel in them....

There are many churches and monasteries in the city which are very rich and sumptuously built, among them the principal and greatest is the church of St Mark, which is the chief and head of all. It is built with domes in the Greek manner, covered with lead on the outside, with gilded cupolas. Inside, it is very finely decorated with rich golden mosaics. The floor also is decorated with similar mosaics, except that they are large and coloured. At the great door, high up over one of the arches, are four great horses of brass, thickly gilt. These the Venetians carried away and placed here in triumph when they took Constantinople. In front of this door is a great square, greater than the Medina del Campo, paved with bricks, and surrounded by many-storeyed houses with porticoes. They hold a market here every Thursday, which is greater than that of the Torre del Campo, a hamlet of Jaén in Castile. On one side of this square is a very high tower, as high as that in Seville, with a cross of fine gold on the top, a very beautiful thing to see. It can be seen in the sun at a distance of 80 miles away. In it are the bells which they ring, one for Mass, one for Vespers, one to summon the Council, which they call the Council Bell, and one when they arm the fleet, and each one is recognized by all. On another side of this square, facing the sea, are two very large and lofty columns. On the one is St George with the Dragon and on the other St Mark, the patron saint and the device of the city. These also were carried away from Constantinople. They say that no one could set them up, but a Castilian climbed up and raised and secured them, whereupon the Venetians ordered that he should have whatever he desired. He did not ask anything for himself, but round about the columns are certain steps, and he requested that if any criminal, whatever his offence, took refuge there, justice should not be executed upon him. And now rogues play there at dice and commit other knaveries, praising the man who secured them such immunity.

Between these columns and the church of St Mark is the Palace of the Signoria, and in one part of it the Doge is lodged with his family, and the rest is open for anyone to see, as well as that great hall. Here they hold the Council. There are other halls, also very rich, where they administer justice and have their prison, and beneath the arches, over against the great square, are certain marble stones. Three are coloured, and there they hang the nobles, and the others are for hanging the common people. In these porticoes strangers leave their arms, and there are also some skins of the beasts called crocodiles which the Sultan of Egypt sent as things most monstrous to the Signoria. This palace is indeed very noble....

In times past there were few weeks, or even days, when the fishermen did not take out dead babies from their nets, and this, they say, came from the fact that the merchants were so long separated from their wives. These, urged by their fleshly lusts, gave way to them and became pregnant, and with intent to save their reputations threw the offspring out of window into the sea as soon as they were delivered, the place being aptly disposed therefor.

The rulers, in view of such enormous crimes, took counsel together and founded a great and rich hospital, very finely built, and placed in it a hundred wet-nurses to suckle the babes, and now those who would hide their shame take their children there to be reared. The Venetians also obtained a Bull from the Pope that whosoever visited those children in hospital should gain certain pardons. Thus men and women can go there to visit their children, as if to gain pardons. Without doubt it was a very pious work, and it is held in great reverence.

1494 PIETRO CASOLA

Cleric Casola (see page 149) was held up in Venice while on pilgrimage to Jerusalem, waiting for a ship to take him to the Holy Land.

I must make my excuses to the readers of this my itinerary, if it should seem to them that I have overpraised this city of Venice. What I write is not written to win the goodwill of the Venetians, but to set down the truth. And I declare that it is impossible to tell or write fully of the beauty, the magnificence or the wealth of the city of Venice. Something indeed can be told and written to pass the time as I do, but it will be incredible to anyone who has not seen the city....

Indeed it seems as if all the world flocks there, and that human beings have concentrated there all their force for trading. I was taken to see various warehouses, beginning with that of the Germans – which it appears to me would suffice alone to supply all Italy with the goods that come and go – and so many others that it can be said they are innumerable. I see that the special products for which other cities are famous are all to be found there.... And who could count the many shops so well furnished that they also seem warehouses, with so many cloths of every make – tapestry, brocades and hangings of every design, carpets of every sort, camlets [fine woollen cloths] of every colour and texture, silks of every kind; and so many warehouses full of spices, groceries and drugs, and so much beautiful white wax! These things stupefy the beholder, and cannot be fully described to those who have not seen them....

As to the abundance of the victuals, I do not believe there is a city in Italy better supplied than this with every kind of victuals.... Whether it is due to the good order or other cause I do not know, but I never saw such a quantity of provisions elsewhere.

I went to the place where the flour is sold wholesale; the world at present does not contain such a remarkable thing. When I saw such abundance and beauty around me I was confused. The bakers' shops, which are to be found in one place specially, namely, the piazza of St Mark, and also throughout the city, are countless and of incredible beauty; there is bread the sight of which tempts even a man who is surfeited to eat again. In my judgment Venice has not its equal for this....

One thing only appears to me hard in this city; that is, that although the people are placed in the water up to the mouth they often suffer from thirst, and they have to beg good water for drinking and for cooking, especially in the summer time. It is true that there are many cisterns for collecting the rainwater, and also water is sold in large boatloads – water from the river called the Brenta, which flows near Padua. In this way indeed they provide for their needs, but with difficulty and expense, and the people cannot make such a business of washing clothes with fresh water as is done elsewhere.

1646 JOHN EVELYN

English diarist and horticulturalist Evelyn (1620–1706) left England to avoid embroilment in the Civil Wars, spending several years in Italy. He returned to England in 1647 and set up house at Deptford, where he created a famous garden and continued to write his famous diary of personal and public events.

In January, Signor Molino was chosen doge of Venice, but the extreme snow that fell, and the cold, hindered my going to see the solemnity, so as I stirred not from Padua till Shrovetide, when all the world repair to Venice, to see the folly and madness of the Carnival; the women, men and persons of all conditions disguising themselves in antique dresses, with extravagant music and a thousand gambols, traversing the streets from house to house, all places being then accessible and free to enter.

Abroad, they fling eggs filled with sweet water, but sometimes not over-sweet. They also have a barbarous custom of hunting bulls about the streets and piazzas, which is very dangerous, the passages being generally narrow. The youth of the several wards and parishes contend in other masteries and pastimes, so that it is impossible to recount the universal madness of this place during this time of license. The great banks are set up for those who will play at basset [a popular card game]; the comedians have liberty, and the operas are open; witty pasquils [satirical verses] are thrown about, and the mountebanks have their stages at every corner.

The diversions which chiefly took me up was three noble operas, where were excellent voices and music, the most celebrated of which was the famous Anna Rencia, whom we invited to a fish-dinner after four days in Lent, when they had given over at the theatre. Accompanied with an eunuch whom she brought with her, she entertained us with rare music, both of them singing to a harpsichord.

It growing late, a gentleman of Venice came for her, to show her the galleys, now ready to sail for Candia [Venetian colony on Crete]. This entertainment produced a second, given us by the English consul of the merchants, inviting us to his house, where he had the Genoese, the most celebrated base in Italy, who was one of the late opera-band. This diversion held us so late at night, that, conveying a gentlewoman who had supped with us to her gondola at the usual place of landing, we were shot at by two carbines from another gondola, in which were a noble Venetian and his courtesan unwilling to be disturbed, which made us run in and fetch other weapons, not knowing what the matter was, till we were informed of the danger we might incur by pursuing it farther.

1786 JOHANN VON GOETHE

The German poet, scientist and statesman Johann von Goethe (1749–1832) visited Italy aged thirty-seven in 1786–88, and published his diaries, as Italian Journey, *in 1816–17. In Venice he enjoyed acting as a typical tourist and used his scientific method to aid his understanding, although he also encountered great Renaissance art.*

28 September As the first of the gondoliers came up to the ship, I recollected an old plaything, of which, perhaps, I had not thought for twenty years. My father had a beautiful model of a gondola which he had brought with him from Italy; he set a great value upon it, and it was considered a great treat, when I was allowed to play with it. The first beaks of tinned iron-plate, the black gondola-cages, all greeted me like old acquaintances, and I experienced again dear emotions of my childhood which had been long unknown.

29 September The large canal, winding like a serpent, yields to no street in the world, and nothing can be put by the side of the space in front of St Mark's Square – I mean that great mirror of water, which is encompassed by Venice proper, in the form of a crescent. Across the watery surface you see to the left the island of St Georgio Maggiore, to the right a little further off the Giudecca and its canal, and still more distant the Custom House and the entrance into the Canal Grande where right before us two immense marble temples are glittering in the sunshine. All the views and prospects have been so often engraved that my friends will have no difficulty in forming a clear idea of them.

After dinner I hastened to fix my first impression of the whole, and without a guide, and merely observing the cardinal points, threw myself into the labyrinth of the city, which though everywhere intersected by larger or smaller canals, is again connected by bridges. The narrow and crowded appearance of the whole cannot be conceived by one who has not seen it. In most cases one can quite or nearly measure the breadth of the street, by stretching out one's arms, and in the narrowest, a person would scrape his elbows if he walked with his arms akimbo. Some streets, indeed, are wider, and here and there is a little square, but comparatively all may be called narrow....

6 October This evening I bespoke the celebrated song of the mariners, who chant Tasso and Ariosto to melodies of their own. This must actually be ordered, as it is not to be heard as a thing, of course, but rather belongs to the half-forgotten traditions of former times. I entered a gondola by moonlight, with one singer before and the other behind me. They sing their songs taking up the verses alternately....

Sitting on the shore of an island, on the bank of a canal, or by the side of a boat, a gondolier will sing away with a loud penetrating voice – the multitude admire force above everything – anxious only to be heard as far as possible. Over the silent mirror it travels far. Another in the distance, who is acquainted with the melody and knows the words, takes it up and answers with the next verse, and then the first replies, so that the one is as

327

it were the echo of the other. The song continues through whole nights and is kept up without fatigue. The further the singers are from each other, the more touching sounds the strain. The best place for the listener is halfway between the two.

To demonstrate this, my boatmen tied up the gondola on the shore of the Giudecca and walked along the canal in opposite directions. I walked back and forth, leaving the one who was just about to sing, and walking towards the other who had just stopped.

For the first time I felt the full effect of this singing. The sound of their voices far away was extraordinary, a lament without sadness, and I was moved to tears.

1825 THOMAS JEFFERSON HOGG

The English lawyer Thomas Jefferson Hogg (1792–1862) was friend and biographer of the poet Percy Bysshe Shelley. He made a long trip in continental Europe in 1825–26, the published journal of which (entitled Two Hundred and Nine Days, *1827) includes some dyspeptic descriptions of places and officialdom, interspersed with warm accounts of the ordinary people he met.*

Sunday, 15 January As I looked from the window upon the Canal Grande, I thought that, although it is handsome, yet too much has been said in its praise; it is not very wide; the houses are neither large nor lofty, nor of very noble architecture. The celebrated Rialto is a good bridge; high in the middle, like the roof of a house; to be ascended and descended by steps; and, as the guidebooks say, adorned – but I should say, disfigured – by a double row of shops: it has long been a wonder, because it is a bridge over the great canal; we now wonder that it is the only bridge.

After breakfast we sallied forth, crossed the Rialto, and wandered in a maze of courts and canals, in search of St Mark's Place; thinking the effect would be more striking, if we could contrive to stumble upon it by accident than after a regular and formal introduction by a guide.... The other canals and bridges are mean, insignificant and ugly; we came to some fine points of view; and at last from a promontory, saw the tower and cupolas of St Mark's on the opposite side of the Canal Grande; we puzzled out our way with difficulty to the Rialto and recrossing it we arrived at an arched gateway, on issuing from which we suddenly entered the Piazza S. Marco. The gaudy cathedral; the tall square brick tower; the columns, of which one is surmounted by the lion of St Mark; the three long masts, and the buildings and porticos; realized the paintings, engravings and panoramas which we had seen.

We entered St Mark's; it is chiefly remarkable for a certain air of barbaric and Eastern magnificence; the roof and the five cupolas are inlaid with gold mosaic; they seem as if they were lined with gilt leather; such at least is the ground, for there are figures upon it of all kinds, in bright gay colours. The pavement is also inlaid tastefully with coloured marbles, in various patterns; but by some accident it is very uneven, and as it were warped; and like everything else in this city, exceedingly slippery: the interior of the church is enriched with every kind of ornament.

We continued our walk to the public gardens, which it is said were made by the French, who delight in a promenade; in any other city they would seem poor, but in Venice they are a great acquisition: we met crowds of people there and on the road; many pretty girls and women; but not any, I think, of extraordinary beauty; they wore good clothes and were dressed neatly. I never found a great variety of colours; there was no fashionable, or prevailing colour; each wore what fancy, taste, or the want of taste, dictated.

1851 JOHN RUSKIN

English art critic Ruskin (1819–1900) is renowned as the greatest celebrant of Venice and its architecture. His finely wrought description of the exterior of St Mark's cathedral remains a classic of 19th-century artistic writing.

A yard or two farther, we pass the hostelry of the Black Eagle, and, glancing as we pass through the square door of marble, deeply moulded, in the outer wall, we see the shadows of its pergola of vines resting on an ancient well, with a pointed shield carved on its side; and so presently emerge on the bridge and Campo San Moisè, whence to the entrance into St Mark's Place, called the Bocca di Piazza (mouth of the square), the Venetian character is nearly destroyed, first by the frightful facade of San Moisè, which we will pause at another time to examine, and then by the modernizing of the shops as they near the piazza, and the mingling with the lower Venetian populace of lounging groups of English and Austrians.

We will push fast through them into the shadow of the pillars at the end of the 'Bocca di Piazza', and then we forget them all; for between those pillars there opens a great light, and, in the midst of it, as we advance slowly, the vast tower of St Mark seems to lift itself visibly forth from the level field of chequered stones; and, on each side, the countless arches prolong themselves into ranged symmetry, as if the rugged and irregular houses that pressed together above us in the dark alley had been struck back into sudden obedience and lovely order, and all their rude casements and broken walls had been transformed into arches charged with goodly sculpture, and fluted shafts of delicate stone.

And well may they fall back, for beyond those troops of ordered arches there rises a vision out of the earth, and all the great square seems to have opened from it in a kind of awe, that we may see it far away – a multitude of pillars and white domes, clustered into a long low pyramid of coloured light; a treasure-heap, it seems, partly of gold, and partly of opal and mother-of-pearl, hollowed beneath into five great vaulted porches, ceiled with fair mosaic, and beset with sculpture of alabaster, clear as amber and delicate as ivory – sculpture fantastic and involved, of palm leaves and lilies, and grapes and pomegranates, and birds clinging and fluttering among the branches, all twined together into an endless network of buds and plumes; and, in the midst of it, the solemn forms of angels, sceptred, and robed to the feet, and leaning to each other across the gates, their figures indistinct among the gleaming of the golden ground through the leaves beside them, interrupted and dim, like the morning light as it faded back among the branches of Eden, when first its gates were angel-guarded long ago. And round the walls of the porches there are set pillars of variegated stones, jasper and porphyry, and deep-green serpentine spotted with flakes of snow, and marbles, that half refuse and half yield to the sunshine, Cleopatra-like, 'their bluest veins to kiss' – the shadow, as it steals back from them, revealing line after line of azure undulation, as a receding tide leaves the waved sand; their capitals rich with interwoven tracery, rooted knots of herbage, and drifting leaves of acanthus and vine, and mystical signs, all beginning and ending in the Cross; and above them, in the broad archivolts, a continuous chain of language and of life – angels, and the signs of heaven, and the labours of men, each in its appointed season upon the earth; and above these, another range of glittering pinnacles, mixed with white arches edged with scarlet flowers – a confusion of delight, amid which the breasts of the Greek horses are seen blazing in their breadth of golden strength, and the St Mark's Lion, lifted on a blue field covered with stars, until at last, as if in ecstasy, the crests of the arches break into a marble foam, and toss themselves far into the blue sky in flashes and wreaths of sculptured spray, as if the breakers on the Lido shore had been frost-bound before they fell, and the sea-nymphs had inlaid them with coral and amethyst.

1883 HENRY JAMES

Several novels by American writer Henry James (1843–1916) concerned well-to-do Americans visiting in Europe. He lived much of his life in England and travelled widely in Europe, and his accounts of his travels appeared in several American magazines. They were collected in his Portraits of Places *(1883).*

The danger is that you will not linger enough – a danger of which the author of these lines had known something. It is possible to dislike Venice, and to entertain the sentiment in a responsible and intelligent manner. There are travellers who think the place odious, and those who are not of this opinion often find themselves wishing that the others were only more numerous. The sentimental tourist's only quarrel with his Venice is that he has too many competitors there. He likes to be alone; to be original; to have (to himself, at least) the air of making discoveries. The Venice of today is a vast museum where the little wicket that admits you is perpetually turning and creaking, and you march through the institution with a herd of fellow-gazers. There is nothing left to discover or describe, and originality of attitude is completely impossible. This is often very annoying; you can only turn your back on your impertinent playfellow and curse his want of delicacy. But this is not the fault of Venice; it is the fault of the rest of the world. The fault of Venice is that, though it is easy to admire it, it is not so easy to live in it. After you have been there a week, and the bloom of novelty has rubbed off, you wonder whether you can accommodate yourself to the peculiar conditions. Your old habits become impracticable, and you find yourself obliged to form new ones of an undesirable and unprofitable character. You are tired of your gondola (or you think you are), and you have seen all the principal pictures and heard the names of the palaces announced a dozen times by your gondolier, who brings them out almost as impressively as if he were an English butler bawling titles into a drawing room. You have walked several hundred times round the Piazza, and bought several bushels of photographs. You have visited the antiquity-mongers whose horrible sign boards dishonour some of the grandest vistas in the Grand Canal; you have tried the opera and found it very bad; you have bathed at the Lido and found the water flat. You have begun to have a shipboard-feeling to regard the Piazza as an enormous saloon and the Riva degli Schiavoni as a promenade deck. You are obstructed and encaged; your desire for space is unsatisfied; you miss your usual exercise....

The canals have a horrible smell, and the everlasting Piazza, where you have looked repeatedly at every article in every shop window and found them all rubbish, where the young Venetians who sell bead-bracelets and 'panoramas' are perpetually thrusting their wares at you, where the same tightly buttoned officers are for ever sucking the same black weeds, at the same empty tables, in front of the same cafés – the Piazza, as I say, has resolved itself into a sort of magnificent treadmill. This is the state of mind of those shallow inquirers who find Venice all very well for a week; and if in such a state of mind you take your departure, you act with fatal rashness. The loss is your own, moreover; it is not with all deference to your personal attractions that of your companions who remain behind; for though there are some disagreeable things in Venice, there is nothing so disagreeable as the visitors. The conditions are peculiar, but your intolerance of them evaporates before it has had time to become a prejudice. When you have called for the bill to go, pay it and remain, and you will find on the morrow that you are deeply attached to Venice.

VIENNA

Vienna, founded by the Celts and built by Romans, became capital of the Holy Roman Empire under the Habsburgs in the 15th century; after the dissolution of the empire in 1804, it remained capital of the Austro-Hungarian Empire, and then the Dual Monarchy of Austria-Hungary, to 1919. The city, with its strategic position on the Danube, was unsuccessfully besieged by the Ottomans twice — by Suleiman the Magnificent in 1529 and Mehmed IV in 1683.

It has been the cultural centre of Central Europe, with particularly strong musical heritage — it was Mozart's hometown in his final years. As capital of the republic of Austria in the 20th century, it became a frontline location of the Cold War.

1480 ANTONIO BONFINI

Bonfini (1434–1503) was an Italian poet and historian based at the court of the king of Hungary. In 1480, during the reign of Frederick III, he wrote 'In praise of Vienna', beginning with the words: 'Vienna is one of the most beautiful cities of the barbarians.'

The city proper seems like a royal palace amid the surrounding suburbs; and yet several of these vie with it for beauty and grandeur. Entering the city you might fancy yourself walking among the buildings of a huge royal castle, so perfect is the disposition of all the houses. Everything delights the eye of the observer: each house seems to stand more proudly than its neighbours. You have to pause constantly to enjoy so many beauties. The houses of the great, in particular, look like palaces. Almost every house has, in addition to its front portion, a rear building with vast peristyles covered or uncovered, offering protection from the cold winds that blow from the surrounding heights. The dining rooms are often splendidly panelled with pine and heated with great stoves. The windows are all glazed; some of them are beautifully painted and protected with an iron trellis. The houses have bathrooms and kitchen offices and bedrooms which can be rented. All of them are provided with cellars to store wine and provisions. The luxury of the windows and mirrors is almost equal to the splendour of olden days. So many birds sing in their cages that you fancy you are walking through a sylvan glade.

1665 EVLIYA ÇELEBI

Mehmed Zilli, known as Evliya Çelebi (1611–1682), was an Ottoman traveller and diplomat for Sultan Mehmed IV. His Book of Travels *covers much of Central Asia, the Middle East and eastern and Central Europe; his visit to Vienna was as part of a delegation to the emperor, and to assess the city's defences in the event of an Ottoman decision to attack.*

The fortifications have eight principal gates with several others along the banks of the Danube. Where the land is low, the ramparts are almond-shaped and with some 27 bastions are a formidable piece of construction, a powerful defence with high walls and extensive cover, a menacing fortress and a veritable temple of paganism. May Allah allow it to fall into our hands.

The shells which the Sultan Suleiman fired at the western fortifications still lie buried in the walls. Each year, though, monks come from other provinces and rebuild the damaged walls in accordance with their evil beliefs, and make them as strong as the castles of Alexander....

The air here is delightful, always evoking spring, so that everyone enjoys good health. The men, who live rather ascetically, may be thin but they live to a great age and are very fit.

These Germans all wear black coats and French shoes. Because of the delicious air, their skin is white like camphor and their well-formed bodies are soft, like the flesh of an ear-lobe. Often the exquisite German boys have such a light skin that they appear very pale.

In contrast to the young girls, the married women all display their bosoms which shine white as snow. They tie their dresses in a different way, towards the centre, which makes their ugly costumes appear even more out of shape. Thanks to Allah, the bosoms of their women are not like our ladies' and as large as wash-tubs, but small like apples.

The girls go everywhere with exposed skin and loose hair. Because the air and water are so fresh, they have a beauty and affection which is like a sun of gold.

1716 LADY MARY WORTLEY MONTAGU

Montagu (1689–1762) was the wife of the British ambassador to Turkey, and they passed through Vienna on the way to take up that post. Her letters show a great interest in the practicalities of life in the places she visited.

8 September This town, which has the honour of being the emperor's residence, did not at all answer to my ideas of it; the streets are very close, and so narrow one cannot observe the fine fronts of the palaces, though many of them very well deserve observation, being truly magnificent, all built of fine white stone, and excessive high, the town being so much too little for the number of people that desire to live in it, the builders seem to have projected to repair that misfortune by clapping one town on the top of another, most of the houses being of five, and some of them six, storeys. You may easily imagine that, the streets being so narrow, the upper rooms are extremely dark, and what is an inconveniency much more intolerable in my opinion, there is no house that has so few as five or six families in it. The apartments of the greatest ladies, and even of the ministers of state, are divided but by a partition from that of a tailor or a shoemaker, and I know of nobody that has above two floors in any house, one for their own use and one higher for their servants. Those that have houses of their own let out the rest of them to whoever will take them; thus the great stairs (which are all of stone) are as common and dirty as the street.

'Tis true, when you have travelled through them, nothing can be more surprisingly magnificent than the apartments. They are commonly a suite of eight or ten large rooms, all inlaid, the doors and windows richly carved and gilt, and the furniture such as is seldom seen in the palaces of sovereign prices in other countries – the hangings the finest tapestry of Brussels, prodigious large looking-glasses in silver frames, fine japan tables, beds, chairs, canopies and window curtains of the richest Genoa damask or velvet, almost covered with gold lace or embroidery. The whole made gay by pictures and vast jars of japan china, and in almost every room large lustres of rock crystal.

I have already had the honour of being invited to dinner by several of the first people of quality; and I must do them the justice to say, the good taste and magnificence of their tables very well answered to that of their furniture. I have been more than once entertained with fifty dishes of meat all served in silver, and well dressed; the dessert proportionable, served in the finest china. But the variety and richness of their wines is what appears the most surprising. The constant way is, to lay a list of their names upon the plates of the guests, along with the napkins; and I have counted several times to the number of eighteen different sorts, all exquisite in their kinds.

1836 FRANCES TROLLOPE

Frances Trollope (1779–1863) was a British writer who travelled in the United States in the early 1830s and wrote successfully about the life she found there.

She repeated the formula with books about Brussels, Paris and Vienna; she also wrote almost one hundred novels. Novelist Anthony Trollope (see page 298) was her son.

24 December A more than usual degree of animation has pervaded the whole town for some days past, occasioned by the preparations making to celebrate Christmas.

The shops are vying with each other which shall display the most tempting assortment of articles in their different lines; and though the more extensive elbow room of London and Paris permits of larger shops and showrooms, they can display nothing more brilliant and more beautiful that what may be seen here.

In the important matters of shawls, blonds [lace], velvets, silks, satins and so forth, it is quite impossible that they should be surpassed. The silversmiths and jewellers certainly exceed in their rich exhibitions those either of France or England, with the exception, perhaps, of the interior arcana of Rundel and Bridges, and of Hamlets. The show of ornamental glass is exquisitely and delicately beautiful, and might almost make one fancy oneself within the domain of some enchanter, so bright, so tasteful and so fanciful, in colour and in form, are the productions of the Bohemian manufactories.

The windows of the confectioners do not indeed exhibit, as with us, plum-cakes majestic in their grandiose proportions and splendid ornaments; but, in revenge, they become magazines of bon-bons that dazzle the eyes as you enter among them, for they sparkle like grottoes with a thousand crystals. The art of working in sugar was never carried, even in Paris, to greater perfection than it is here. You may find yourself eating all the fruits of the earth, whether in or out of season, while believing that you are only about to make your way through a sugar-plum.

They are, beyond all contradiction, the prettiest-looking comestibles in the world: nevertheless, were I a Vienna lady, I would never permit the elegant pyramidical tray charged with them to travel round and round at my parties; for as each one is enclosed in a little dainty dish of scolloped paper, that it may reach the mouth without soiling the gloves, the consequence is that the purity of the drawing-room carpets must inevitably suffer; for it is not uncommon, after two or three entries of refreshments, to see the floor perfectly strewed with these sugar-plum cases.

But all these extra preparations for enjoyment are by no means confined to the wealthier classes. At the corner of every street we see customers of quite the lower orders bargaining for trees, adorned with knots of many-coloured paper, in order to celebrate the Christmas. These trees, which, I believe, are always spruce-firs, are provided of every variety of degree, as to size and expense, by nearly every family in Vienna where there are young people. Nor is the custom peculiar to the capital; not a cottage in Austria, I am told, but has something of the same kind to solemnize this joyous season. The tree is called 'the tree of the little Jesus'; and on its branches are suspended all sorts of pretty toys, bijous and bon-bons, to be distributed among those who are present at the fete. On the trees that are offered for sale in the streets, the place of more costly presents is supplied with an apple or a raisin, a chestnut, or a bit of gingerbread: but still they all show a gay and gala aspect to the eye, with their floating paper ribbons; and I have watched as much happy interest in the countenance of a poor body, while balancing between boughs that waved with streamers of pink, and others where blue predominated, as the richest lady could have felt, while selecting the most elegant and costly offerings for her friends.

At some houses the tree is exhibited on Christmas Eve, which is tonight; and in others the fete is held tomorrow. For the first we are invited by the Princess Metternich, who means to make a set of little princes and princesses superlatively happy. From thence we go to a later party of the same kind given to children of a larger growth; and tomorrow we are engaged for a repetition of the tree fete at the house of another kind friend.

On New Year's Eve, too, a concert and supper are to welcome in the new year for us; and on the evening of New Year's Day there is to be a full-dress reception at Prince Metternich's, which is to be as splendid as diamonds and Hungarian costumes can make it.

All this, however, is but the foretaste of Vienna gaiety; the Carnival is to follow, and, if report say true, the dissipation that it brings will continue without interval or interruption till it is over.

1891 ANTON CHEKHOV

On Chekhov's two-month European tour by train from St Petersburg (see page 243), he was struck by the freedom of speech under the Dual Monarchy and in

France, in comparison with what he was used to in Russia. This letter was sent to his family (Chekhov is punning on the family name).

20 March

Dear Czech friends

I'm writing to you from Vienna. I arrived yesterday at four in the afternoon. The trip went very well. From Warsaw to Vienna I travelled like a railroad Nana in a luxurious car of the 'International Society of Sleeping Cars': beds, mirrors, gigantic windows, carpets and so on.

O my Tungus friends! If only you knew how lovely Vienna is! It is not to be compared with any city I have seen in my entire life. The streets are broad and elegantly paved, there are lots of boulevards and public gardens, six- and seven-storey houses, and stores – stores that are sheer vertigo, sheer mirage! The store windows have billions of neckties alone! And what amazing bronze, china and leather objects! The churches are gigantic, but their size is not oppressive; it caresses the eyes because it seems as though they are spun of lace. St Stephen's Cathedral and the Votiv-Kirche are especially lovely. They are more like pastries than buildings. The parliament, the town hall, the university are all magnificent. Everything is magnificent, and it wasn't until yesterday and today that I fully realized that architecture is indeed an art. And here that art is not scattered in bits and pieces as it is in our country; it extends for *verst* after *verst* [kilometre after kilometre]. There are many monuments. No side street is without its own bookshop. Some of the bookshops even display Russian books, but alas they are the works of all sorts of anonymous writers who write and publish abroad, not of Albov, Barantsevich or Chekhov. I've seen Renan, [Grimm's] *Secrets of the Winter Palace* etc. It's odd that here you may read anything you like and say whatever you please.

Harken, o ye nations, unto what the goddamn cabbies here are like. Instead of droshkies they have stunning, brand-new carriages with one, or more often two, horses. The horses are excellent. The drivers' seats are occupied by dandies in jackets and top hats, reading newspapers. They are courteous and obliging.

The dinners are fine. There's no vodka; they drink beer and fairly good wine instead. There's only one bad point: they charge for bread. When they bring you the check, they ask you *'Wieviel Brötchen?'*, that is, how many rolls did you polish off? And they charge you for each roll.

The woman are beautiful and elegant. When you get down to it, everything is pretty damn elegant.

I haven't completely forgotten my German. I understand them and they understand me.

It was snowing as we crossed the border, and though there's no snow in Vienna, it's cold all the same....

Your loving

A Chekhov

Everyone we meet recognizes us as Russians. No one looks me in the face; they all stare at my grizzled cap. Looking at my cap probably makes them think I'm a very rich Russian count.

1933 PATRICK LEIGH FERMOR

British travel writer Patrick ('Paddy') Leigh Fermor (1915–2011) is famous for having walked from the Hook of Holland to Istanbul as an eighteen-year-old, setting out in the winter of 1933, a journey he recounted in a three-volume memoir, starting with The Time of Gifts *(1977), which showcases his cultural sensitivity together with a special ability to make friends wherever he went. During the Second World War he was involved in Special Operations Executive (SOE) activities with partisans in occupied Crete.*

Meanwhile, there was Vienna....

Few delights could compare with these wintry days: the snow outside, the bare trees outlined by the frost, the muted light and, indoors, the rooms following each other filled with the spoils, the heirlooms and the dowries of a golden age. The galleries of the hibernating city retreated and grew smaller in the distance like vistas along dim rectangular telescopes. I had heard someone say that Vienna combined the splendour of a capital with the familiarity of a village. In the Inner City, where crooked lanes opened on gold and marble outbursts of Baroque, it was true and, in the Kärntnerstrasse or the Graben, after I had bumped into three brand-new acquaintances within a quarter of an hour, it seemed truer still, and parts of the town suggested an even narrower focus. There were squares as small and complete and as carefully furnished as rooms. Facades of broken pediment and tiered shutter enclosed hushed rectangles of cobble; the drip of icicles eroded gaps in the frozen scallops of the fountains; the statues of archdukes or composers presided with pensive nonchalance; and all at once as I loitered there, the silence would fly in pieces when the initial clang from a tower routed a hundred pigeons crowding a Palladian cornice and scattered avalanches of snow and filled the geometric sky with wings. Palace succeeded palace, casemented arches sailed across the streets, pillars lifted their statues; ice-fettered in their pools, tritons floundered beneath a cloudy heaven amid ribbed cupolas expanded by the score. The greatest of these, the dome of the Karlskirche, floated with a balloon's lightness in its enclosing hemisphere and the friezes that spiralled the shafts of the two statue-crowned guardian columns – free-standing and as heavily wrought as Trajan's – gained an added impromptu spin when they vanished halfway up in a gyre of flakes.

A hint of touchy Counter-Reformation aggression accompanies some ecclesiastical Baroque. There is a dash of it here and there in Vienna, and St Stephen's – steep and streamlined and Gothic – springs up unchallenged in the heart of it as though the balance needed redress. Bristling with finials and unloosing its gargoyles, the cathedral lifts a solitary and warning steeple which dominates every dome and cupola and bell-tower in the city.... In the rank of fiacres outside the south door of St Stephen's, cabbies in bowlers conversed in the Viennese dialect while they straightened the blankets on their horse's quarters and gave them their feed in buckets. Some of these were as heavily whiskered as their masters. They steamed and fidgeted between the shafts, scattering their oats over the caked snow and the cobbles and sending an agreeable stable-yard whiff across the fumes of the hot coffee and the fresh cakes in the pastry-cooks' shops. Joining in my memory with the cold edge of the frost, the combination of these scents conjure up the city in a second.

WASHINGTON D.C.

Washington D.C. was created as the seat of government of the United States of America from the 1790s, and was planned by engineer and designer Pierre Charles L'Enfant as a new city of grand vistas that would reflect the ambition of the young state. As the location of the White House and Congress, as well as many national monuments and museums, it has always attracted visitors from across the United States and the world.

1819 ADLARD WELBY

Adlard Welby (see page 226) visited Washington in 1819 while much of the city remained under construction, seven years after a British force had invaded and burned the White House (1812).

These American stages or caravans carry all the passengers withinside, an arrangement which renders travelling with servants expensive: we were eleven young and old, closely packed, and jumbled away at the rate of seven or eight miles an hour, without interest; for we could only catch a glimpse of the country now and then by lifting up the side leather. Soon after noon we came in sight of the Capitol, and were set down at a large tavern near to it.

The dirt, ill-arrangement and absence of common comforts in an American tavern or hotel have already been expatiated upon amply; but to meet with such things under the walls of the Capitol, at the very seat of government, I was not prepared. On entering the hotel, a poor lad, whose dishabille of dirt and rags defies description, came with a brush, which he was making less fit for use by rubbing its bristles upon his dirtier hand, to ask if he should brush our coats. We enquired for a room upstairs to shave, &c., and though past one o'clock not a bed had been made, or a breath of acceptable fresh air permitted to blow into these chambers of contamination! Having finished the toilette as well as we were able, our first visit was to the Capitol.

It stands finely upon the edge of a high commanding ridge, from whence with one sweeping glance one views the subjacent ground down to the Potomac River, and the elevated country beyond; to the right is seen George Town and the most populous part of Washington, the President's House, the Post Office, &c. but alas! excepting these and a few other mostly dispersed buildings, the horse, the cow and the swine still graze quietly around the Capitol of Washington. Viewing however the beautiful site of this city with the eye of its venerable founder, and with him letting imagination cover it with houses and 'the busy hum of men', if we then look round for the attractions of support for this multitude, the illusion vanishes. Commerce cannot but with difficulty flourish upon the shallow bed of the river, and agriculture may long strive for success in vain, with the surrounding sterility. Wherein then must the motive of the statesman be sought for founding a city in a place favourable alone to the eye? Could he make a mistake?

That is not probable. Could it be to favour his native State, or to gratify a whim? This is not consonant to the character of his great mind. A despot of Russia might build a city upon piles vainly to show posterity his power: Frederick of Prussia might have his Potsdam; but Washington ever kept utility in view, and never aimed to gratify a vain wish at the expense of his fellow creatures. It is then suggested, that, impressed with the importance of quiet deliberation, he fixed the seat of government upon a spot so unattractive to the multitude that their representatives might be unbiased by faction.

Of the Capitol the centre is yet to rear its head, the wings alone are finished; these contain the Hall of Representatives and that of the Senate – a Library – a Post Office for the Members – Committee Rooms, &c.

The Hall of Representatives is of semicircular form; a beautiful colonnade of native with capitals of Italian, marble, ranges along within the semicircle and its base, with rich crimson and fringed curtain drapery between the columns. The President's throne is placed on the centre of the base and fronting the semicircle, the seats and desks for the Members ranged so as to radiate from it; the whole area is covered with a rich and rather gaudy carpet.

The Hall of the Senate is as studiously plain as that of the Representatives is gaudy; in the same form, but upon a much smaller scale, and the gallery is only upon the base of the semicircle, so that a spectator here fronts the Members; the style of decoration throughout is far preferable to the other.

Of the debates on the tapis I can say but little, not having had time sufficient to give them much attention – they were apparently carried on however with more decorum than from report I had reason to expect, except that the exercise of spitting upon the beautiful carpet was continued as everywhere else; the walls of the stairs and the stairs themselves also were covered with the saliva of tobacco chewers.

It being an expected compliment from strangers coming to the Seat of Government to pay their respects to its head, we drove down to the President's house, at the hour appointed; it is a handsome stone building, which has now been restored and repaired since the shock given to it by the English; but the gardens and pleasure grounds, reaching down to the banks of the Potomac, and extending again up to the Capitol, are as yet only be seen upon paper; rude nature still rules absolute over the tract. Remains of the late snow yet lay in the shade, and negligence, studied or accidental, had left it upon the flight of steps to the President's house, an old plank being laid upon the landing that visitors might get dry to the door.

A servant, not a man of show, admitted us into a plain hall, and ushered us upstairs to the private apartment in which we found Mr Munroe [sic] seated alone at his bureau with various papers before him; he arose at our entrance, and himself placed chairs for us, which his independent servant had left the room without doing. Mr Munroe appeared a plain quiet man in dress and manners, the English country gentleman with a physiognomy which bore marks of deep reflection: a conversation of ten minutes on indifferent subjects terminated our visit, when, instead of formal etiquette he gave me a friendly shake of the hand with a 'God bless you', spoken in a pleasing tone, which left upon me a very favourable impression.

1848 THEODORE DWIGHT

Theodore Dwight (1796–1866) came from a prominent Connecticut family. He wrote several popular tourist guides to the United States, and in 1848 he undertook a journey down the East Coast, which he recorded in Travels in America *(1848).*

Some of the inhabitants of Washington have had intelligence and observation enough to afford much interesting information in relation to public men and national affairs. What we receive through the newspapers, or other channels little more correct, passes under their own eyes. And indeed, perhaps, no part of the country is left so much alone to form unbiased opinions. While speeches are made in Congress, written out, amended and published by thousands to influence some county, state or number of states, nobody tries to discover things to the Washingtonians, knowing that it would be in vain. Everything is therefore left to be seen by them without disguise; and the consequence is, they often form correct opinions, and speak with becoming frankness. It is gratifying also to reflect, that local interests and influences are not likely to engross and control the attention of the government in so great a degree as they have often done in large cities; and there is no mob to overawe or even to threaten their freedom.

To an American who has seen any of the capitals of Europe, the absence of military display is one of the most agreeable features in view, wherever he turns. There is not a soldier to guard gates or doors in Washington, with the single exception of those at the navy-yard, a mile or more from the capitol. The total want of every sign of military preparation is also very accordant with one's feelings. After the last war with England, a felon imprisoned for some crime confessed, as I recollect, that during his career of iniquity he had entered into a conspiracy to seize President Madison, and deliver him to the British ships then lying in the Potomac, while he was a sentinel to guard the President's house. As there was not even a wall of sufficient height to prevent an approach to the doors, and no other obstacle, such a plan might have been easily accomplished, I suppose, under favourable circumstances, by mere surprise. Though danger was thus in one instance incurred by the neglect to take military precautions, how much better it is than to have the display of paid soldiers at every turn, and to become familiar with the music and the weapons of death! From some acquaintance with the feelings and habits of foreigners, I can say with great confidence, that probably a large proportion of the intelligent men of Europe would learn with surprise that there is not a soldier on guard in the capital of the United States, even during the sessions of Congress, although the familiar fact excites not a thought in our minds....

With abundant materials for thought, I took my seat in a stage coach for Baltimore, and revived many a recollection of strolls through European palaces and prisons, and events in the history of courts. Washington, thought I, is a metropolis of nuisances, a capital of intrigues, and ever must be. But yet how different it is, in some respects, from the seat of an European court! The profession of a courtier requires a long apprenticeship, which it is almost impossible to obtain in this country, among the frequent changes to which our system subjects us. Though the growth of bad men may be rapid, their career must generally be short. But what results might not be produced, if such characters as may be conceived, were allowed to prosecute their operations for ten, twenty or thirty years, without fear of interruption, and under the shelter of an unchanging dynasty? Who would ever think of studying diplomacy in the United States, as it is regularly studied in some European countries? So preposterous a thing would be undertaken only by a madman. On the other side of the Atlantic, a man well trained in the forms of international business may expect to be gratified with the substantial rewards awaiting its performance: but here, selections of ministers, secretaries &c. may be next year on grounds which cannot now be conjectured:

and as for five or ten years hence, no one pretends to foresee who may be in a foreign embassy, or why. The only offices in Washington which can be looked on as permanent, are a few clerkships in the departments and the keepers of certain hotels; the very stage-horses must stare at the new faces they annually behold among the legislators, and wonder why there are so frequent changes in that line....

There was an elegant young Frenchman in the stage coach, who had arrived in Washington only the day before, but had become so much ennuyé, as he declared, at the sight of the city, that he had hurried away from it, intending never to return. Now, why was he disappointed? Washington certainly must be a very different city from what he had expected to find it. The seat of government, as such alone it appears, had not attracted him; for Congress, the Supreme Court, the President and all the machinery and accompaniments of it were there to be seen, but these he had not visited. He had missed the crowds and frivolities of Paris – I will not say the vices – and see how much we gain in having our capital in so great a degree as it is, divested of these. In Europe, courts corrupt capitals, and capitals courts and kingdoms.

1974 JAN MORRIS

By the later 20th century, in addition to being the seat of government, Washington had become a place to be venerated by American citizens and foreigners alike. Welsh travel writer Jan Morris (b. 1926) visited at the height of the Watergate scandal, 1974.

From the centre of that allegorical cemetery [Arlington] one may look out across the Potomac to the grand sweep of the capital beyond. Nothing could appear much less American, for while America is above all a country of verticals, artistic, economic, symbolic, phallic, imposed splendidly upon the passive landscape, Washington D.C. is all horizontal. Nowhere is much flatter than Washington. The ground is flat. The style is flat. The architecture is deliberately flat. From up there in the Arlington cemetery the whole city seems to lie in a single plane, without depth or perspective, its layered strips of blue, green and white broken only by the obelisk of the Washington Monument and the Capitol dome, as the massed ranks of Arlington are interrupted only by the graves of specially important corpses. It looks like a city of slabs, reverently disposed, and only the jets from the National Airport, straining themselves with difficulty out of the ambiance, throw a bold diagonal across the scene....

Sometimes I took the day off from politics, and did the tourist rounds: but for all the grandeur and meaning of the city, for all the endearing pride of my fellow visitors, still these experiences only heightened my sense of intrusion upon some immense private performance. Inorganic by origin, Washington is unnatural in behaviour; but far from heightening everything as New York does, it spreads everything out, memorializes it, puts it in a park and reflects it in an ornamental pool. In New York, I feel more myself than usual, in Washington much less, for when I look for my own reflection in this city, statues and symbols look back at me....

Nowhere in the world is so inexorably *improving*. Elevating texts and aphorisms, quotations from statesmen and philosophers, Thoughts for All Eternity nag one from every other downtown wall, and make one feel especially perhaps if one has come in a high-school excursion bus, awfully insignificant. What giants there were in those days! How grandly they expressed themselves! How thickly they stand about! Innocent III, Napoleon, Moses and St Louis supervise the Senate subway; clumps of heroes wrestle with their standards, horseback generals plan their strategies again on plinth and plaza across the capital. 'Where Law Ends,' booms the Department of Justice, 'Tyranny Begins.' 'Taxes Are What We Pay For a Civilized Society,' retorts the Department of Internal Revenue. 'Here Are the Ties That Bind the Life of Our People,' the National Archives cry; and across the Avenue the Mission responds, with an unctuous chime of the carillon: 'Come to me!'

When we came down from the top of the Washington Monument, even the elevator operator dismissed us with an injunction. 'Let's all work,' he said, 'to clean up our country for the 200th anniversary just coming up.' 'Yes sir,' we dutifully replied, 'you're darned right – you hear that, kids?' He had not, however, finished yet. 'And I'm talking,' he darkly added, 'about the mental aspects as well as the physical.' We had no answer to that.

The editor and publishers are grateful to the copyright holders and publishers who have given permission to reproduce extracts in this volume. Every attempt has been made to contact copyright holders and secure permission. The editor and publishers are happy to rectify any omissions in future editions. The editions cited are those from which extracts have been taken.

13–14 Strabo, *The Geography,* trans. H. C. Hamilton and W. Falconer, Book XXVII (London 1892–93)

14–15 Muhammad al-Idrisi, *Book of Pleasant Journeys into Faraway Lands,* in *Description de l'Afrique et de l'Espagne par Edrisi,* R. Dozy and M. J. de Goeje (Leyden 1866), trans. P. Furtado

16 Zhao Rugua, *Zhu Fan Zhi (A Description of Barbarian Nations),* trans. Frederick Hirth and W. W. Rockill (St Petersburg 1911)

16–17 Vivant Denon, *Travels in Upper and Lower Egypt,* trans. Arthur Aikin (New York 1803)

17–19 James Laird Patterson, *Journal of a Tour in Egypt, Palestine, Syria, and Greece* (London 1852)

21–22 Fynes Moryson, *An Itinerary Containing his Ten Yeeres Travell through the Twelve Dominions of Germany, Bohmerland, Sweitzerland, Netherland, Denmarke, Poland, Italy, Turky, France, England, Scotland & Ireland* (London 1617)

22–24 Peter Mundy, *The Travels of Peter Mundy in Europe and Asia,* ed. Richard Carnac Temple, Vol. IV (London 1925)

24–25 Samuel Ireland, *A picturesque tour through Holland, Brabant, and part of France, made in the autumn of 1789* (London 1795)

25–28 John Murray, *A Handbook for Travellers on the Continent: Being a Guide to Holland, Belgium, Prussia, Northern Germany and the Rhine from Holland to Switzerland* (ninth edition, London 1853)

28–29 J. D. Borenzstajn, *Dagboek 1943–1945,* published 1998 Uitgeverij Ambo, Amsterdam. © 1998 The Estate of Jozef Hilel Borensztajn. Reprinted by kind permission of Fred Borensztajn

31–32 Heracleides of Crete, quoted in *Pausanias and Other Greek Sketches,* J. C. Frazer (London, 1900)

32–33 Pausanias, *Description of Greece,* trans. W. H. S. Jones and H. A. Ormerod, Volume I (London 1918)

33 Synesius of Cyrene, Letter 136, quoted in *Barbarians and Politics at the Court of Arcadius,* Alan Cameron and Jacqueline Long (Los Angeles, 1993)

33–35 François-René, Viscount de Chateaubriand, *Travels to Jerusalem and the Holy Land,* trans. Frederic Schoberl, Vol. I (London 1835)

35–37 George Gordon Byron, 6th Baron Byron, *Childe Harold's Pilgrimage,* Canto the Second (London 1812–18)

37–39 James Laird Patterson, *Journal of a Tour in Egypt, Palestine, Syria, and Greece* (London 1852)

41–42 Benjamin of Tudela, *The Itinerary of Benjamin of Tudela,* trans. Marcus Nathan Adler (London 1907)

42–44 Yaqut al-Hamawi, *Geographical Encyclopedia,* from *Readings in Ancient History: Illustrative Extracts from the Sources,* ed. William Stearns Davis, Vol. II (Boston 1912–13)

44–46   Freya Stark, *Baghdad Sketches: Journeys through Iraq* (London 1937). © John Murray (Publishers) Ltd 1937

47–48   Robert Byron, *The Road to Oxiana* (London 1937)

50–51   Marco Polo, *The Travels of Marco Polo*, Book 2, trans. Henry Yule (London 1920)

51–53   Ferdinand Mendez Pinto [Fernão Mendes Pinto], *The Voyages and Adventures of Ferdinand Mendez Pinto, the Portuguese*, trans. Henry Cogan (London 1663)

53–54   John Nieuhoff, *An Embassy from the East-India Company of the United Provinces, to the Grand Tartar Cham Emperour of China, delivered by their excellencies Peter de Goyer and Jacob de Keyzer*, trans. John Ogilby (London 1669)

54–55   John Bell, *Travels from St Petersburg in Russia to Divers Parts of Asia*, Vol. II (Glasgow 1768)

55–57   Harry de Windt, *Pekin to Calais by Land* (London 1893)

57–59   Colin Thubron, *Behind The Wall* (London 1987), published by William Heinemann. Reprinted by permission of The Random House Group Limited. © 1987

61–62   Catherine Wilmot, *An Irish Peer on the Continent (1801–1803): Being a Narrative of the Tour of Stephen, 2nd Earl Mount Cashell, Through France, Italy, etc.* (London 1920)

62–64   Mary Shelley, *Rambles in Germany and Italy in 1840, 1842, and 1843*, Vol. I, Letter VI, ed. Edward Moxon (London 1844)

64–67   Thomas Wolfe, *You Can't Go Home Again* (New York 1940)

67–69   George Kennan, *Sketches from a Life* (New York 1989)

71–72   Nasir Khusraw, *Safarnama*, trans. W. M. Thackston, in *Nasir-i Khusraw's Book of Travels* (Costa Mesa, CA, 2010)

72–74   Ibn Battuta, *Travels in Asia and Africa 1325–1354*, trans. and ed. H. A. R. Gibb (London 1929)

74–75   Gustave Flaubert, *Gustave Flaubert as seen in his works and correspondence: Eastern Journey*, John Charles Tarver (New York 1905)

75–77   George Hoskins, *A Winter in Upper and Lower Egypt* (London 1863)

77–78   G. S. Fraser, *A Stranger and Afraid* (Manchester 1983). Reproduced by kind permission of the publishers, Carcarnet Press

80–81   John Walter, *First Impressions of America* (London 1867)

82–83   Mrs Howard Vincent, *Forty Thousand Miles over Land and Water: The Journal of a Tour Through the British Empire and America* (London 1886)

83–85   Rudyard Kipling, *American Notes*, in *Selected Works of Rudyard Kipling*, Vol. III (New York 1900)

85–87   Henry Miller, *The Air-Conditioned Nightmare* (New York 1945). Copyright © 1945 by New Directions Publishing Corp. Reprinted by permission of New Directions Publishing Corp

89–90   Ibn Battuta, *Travels in Asia and Africa 1325–1354*, trans. and ed. H. A. R. Gibb (London 1929)

90–92   James Laird Patterson, *Journal of a Tour in Egypt, Palestine, Syria, and Greece* (London 1852)

92–94   Isabel Burton, *The Inner Life of Syria, Palestine, and the Holy Land: From My Private Journal* (London 1876)

95–96 Freya Stark, *Letters from Syria* (London 1942). Copyright © Freya Stark. Reproduced by permission of John Murray Press, an imprint of Hodder and Stoughton Limited

98–99 François de La Boullaye Le Gouz, *The Tour of the French traveller M. de La Boullaye Le Gouz in Ireland, A.D. 1644* (London 1837)

99–101 Arthur Young, *Arthur Young's Tour in Ireland (1776–1779)*, ed. Arthur Wollaston Hutton (London 1892)

101–02 Jacques-Louis de Bourgrenet de la Tocnaye, *A Frenchman's Walk through Ireland 1796–97*, trans. John Stevenson (Dublin 1914)

102–05 Hermann von Pückler-Muskau, *Tour in England, Ireland, and France in the Years 1826, 1827, 1828, and 1829* (Philadelphia 1833)

105–06 Marie Anne de Bovet, *Three Months Tour of Ireland*, trans. Mrs Arthur Walter (London 1891)

108–09 Michel de Montaigne, *The Journal of Montaigne's Travels in Italy by way of Switzerland and Germany in 1580 and 1581*, trans. W. G. Walters, Vol. II (London 1903)

109–11 Richard Lassels, *The Voyage of Italy, or, A compleat journey through Italy: in two parts, with the characters of the people, and the description of the chief towns, churches, monasteries, tombs, libraries, palaces, villa's, gardens, pictures, statues, and antiquities: as also of the interest, government, riches, force, &c. of all the princes, with instructions concerning travel* (London 1686)

111–12 Anna Miller, *Letters from Italy : describing the manners, customs, antiquities, paintings, &c. of that country, in the years MDCCLXX and MDCCLXXI: to a friend residing in France*, Vol. I (London 1777)

112–13 T.Q. (Samuel Young), *A Wall-Street bear in Europe: with his familiar foreign journal of a tour through portions of England, Scotland, France and Italy* (New York 1855)

113–15 Mary McCarthy, *The Stones of Florence* (London 1959). Copyright © Mary McCarthy 1959

117–18 John Nieuhoff, *An Embassy from the East-India Company of the United Provinces, to the Grand Tartar Cham Emperour of China, delivered by their excellencies Peter de Goyer and Jacob de Keyzer*, trans. John Ogilby (London 1669)

118–19 Bayard Taylor, *A Visit to India, China and Japan in the Year 1853* (London 1855)

119–21 Isabella Bird, *The Golden Chersonese and The Way Thither* (New York 1892)

122–23 Simone de Beauvoir, *The Long March: An Account of Modern China*, trans. Austin Wainhouse (London 1958). *La Longue March* Copyright © Editions Gallimard 1958

125–26 Alexander von Humboldt, *The Island of Cuba*, trans. J. S. Thrasher (New York 1856)

126–27 Frances Calderón de la Barca, *Life in Mexico During a Residence of Two-Years in that Country* (London 1843)

128–29 Graham Greene, *Ways of Escape* (London 1980). Published by The Bodley Head publishers. Copyright © Graham Greene 1980

131–32 Bayard Taylor, *A Visit to India, China and Japan in the Year 1853* (London 1855)

132–35 Isabella Bird, *The Golden Chersonese and The Way Thither* (New York 1892)

135–36 Ian Fleming, *Thrilling Cities* (London 1963). Copyright © Glidrose

Productions 1962; Copyright © 1959, 1960 by Thomson Newspapers Ltd

138–39 *Chiu T'ang shu*, in *China and the Roman Orient: Researches into their Ancient and Mediaeval Relations as Represented in Old Chinese Records*, F. Hirth (Shanghai 1885)

139 Benjamin of Tudela, *The Itinerary of Benjamin of Tudela*, trans. Marcus Nathan Adler (London 1907)

139–41 Ibn Battuta, *Travels in Asia and Africa 1325–1354*, trans. and ed. H. A. R. Gibb (London 1929)

141–42 Pero Tafur, *Travels and Adventures of Pero Tafur 1435–1439*, ed. E. Denison Ross and Eileen Power (London 1926)

142–43 Jean Chesneau, *Le Voyage de Monsieur d'Aramon, ambassadeur pour le Roy en Levant* (Paris 1887)

143–45 Alexander Kinglake, *Eothen, or, Traces of Travel Brought Home from the East* (London 1898)

145 Steven Runciman, *A Traveller's Alphabet: Partial Memoirs* (London 1991). Published by Thames & Hudson Ltd. Copyright © Steven Runciman 1991

147–48 Bordeaux Pilgrim, *Itinerary from Bordeaux to Jerusalem in 333–334 CE* (London 1887)

148–49 Nasir Khusraw, *Safarnama*, trans. W. M. Thackston, in *Nasir-i Khusraw's Book of Travels* (Costa Mesa, CA, 2010)

149–52 Pietro Casola, *Canon Pietro Casola's Pilgrimage to Jerusalem in the Year 1494*, ed. Margaret Newett (Manchester 1907)

152–54 François-René, Viscount de Chateaubriand, *Travels to Jerusalem and the Holy Land*, trans. Frederic Schoberl, Vol. II (London 1835)

154–55 Elie Wiesel, in *Telling the Tale: A Tribute to Elie Wiesel* (St Louis, MO, 1993). First published in *Forverts* magazine. Trans. Irving Abrahamson (Tel Aviv 1967) Copyright © *Forverts* magazine 1967

157–58 Thomas Manning, *Narratives of the Mission of George Bogle to Tibet, and Thomas Manning to Lhasa*, ed. Clements Markham (London 1876)

158–59 Ekai Kawaguchi, *Three Years in Tibet*, The Shramana Ekai Kawaguchi (Madras 1909)

159–60 Francis Younghusband, *India and Tibet* (London 1920)

160–62 Heinrich Harrer, *Seven Years in Tibet* (London 1952). Reprinted by permission of HarperCollins Publishers Ltd Copyright © 1952 Heinrich Harrer

164–65 Thomas Platter, *Thomas Platter's Travels in England 1599*, trans. Clare Williams (London 1937)

165–66 César de Saussure, *A foreign view of England in the reigns of George I and George II: The letters of Monsieur César de Saussure to his family*, trans. Madame Van Muyden (London 1902)

166–66 Xia Qinggao, *The Hai-lu*, in *The Great Chinese Travelers*, ed. Jeanette Mirsky (New York 1964)

167–68 Louis Simond, *Journal of a Tour and Residence in Great Britain, During the Years 1810 and 1811*, Vol. I (Edinburgh 1815)

168–69 Hermann von Pückler-Muskau, *Tour in England, Ireland, and France in the Years 1826, 1827, 1828, and 1829* (Philadelphia 1833)

170 Harriet Beecher Stowe, *Sunny Memories of Foreign Lands*, Vol. I (Boston 1854)

171   Hippolyte Taine, *Notes on England*
       (New York 1885)

172–73 Samuel Selvon, *The Lonely Londoners*
       (London 1956). First published by
       Allan Wingate Ltd. Copyright ©
       Samuel Selvon 1956

175   Richard Wynn, *An Account of the
       Journey of the Prince's Servants into
       Spain, A.D. 1623*, in *The Autobiography
       & Correspondence of Sir Simonds D'Ewes,
       Bart., during the Reigns of James I and
       Charles I*, ed. J. O. Halliwell, Vol. II
       (London 1845)

176   Richard Ford, *Handbook for Travellers
       in Spain* (London 1855)

176–78 William Cullen Bryant, *Letters
       of a Traveller* (New York 1859)

178–79 Hans Christian Andersen, *In Spain
       and a Visit to Portugal* (Boston 1855)

180   Leon Trotsky, *My Life* (New York 1930)

182–83 Ibn Battuta, *Travels in Asia and Africa
       1325–1354*, trans. and ed. H. A. R.
       Gibb (London 1929)

183–84 Ludovico of Varthema *The Itinerary
       of Ludovico di Varthema of Bologna from
       1502 to 1508*, trans. John Winter Jones
       (London 1863)

184–86 Carsten Niebuhr, *Travels through
       Arabia, and other countries in the East*,
       trans. Robert Heron (Edinburgh 1792)

186–90 Richard Burton, *Personal Narrative
       of a Pilgrimage to Al Madinah and
       Meccah* (London 1855–56)

190–92 Hernán Cortés, *Cartas y relaciones de
       Hernan Cortés al emperador Carlos V*,
       ed. Pascual de Gayangos (Paris 1866)

192–94 Frances Calderón de la Barca,
       *Life in Mexico During a Residence
       of Two Years in that Country*
       (London 1843)

194–96 Graham Greene, *The Lawless Roads*
       (London 1939). Published by Longman
       Ltd. Copyright © Graham Greene 1939

198–200 Adam Olearius, *The Voyages and
       Travells of the Ambassadors sent
       by Frederick Duke of Holstein to
       the Grand Duke of Muscovy, and the
       King of Persia* (London 1669)

200–01 Eugène Labaume, quoted in *The
       Saturday Magazine Supplement for
       October 1833*, Vol. III (London 1833)

201–04 Marquis de Custine, *Russia*
       (New York 1854)

204–06 Bernard Pares, *Moscow Admits
       a Critic* (London 1936)

208–09 William Francklin, *Observations
       made on a Tour from Bengal to
       Persia* (Calcutta 1788)

209–11 Bayard Taylor, *A Visit to India,
       China and Japan in the Year 1853*
       (London 1855)

211–13 John H. MacCallum Scott, *Eastern
       Journey* (London 1939)

213–15 V. S. Naipaul, *An Area of Darkness*
       (London 1964). Copyright © 1964,
       1992, by V. S. Naipaul. Reprinted by
       Permission of Vintage Canada/Alfred
       A. Knopf Canada, a division of Penguin
       Random House Canada Limited.

217–18 William Beckford, *Italy Sketches*
       (Paris 1833)

218–19 James Fenimore Cooper, *Gleanings
       in Europe: Italy by An American*
       (Philadelphia 1838)

220–21 T.Q. (Samuel Young), *A Wall- Street
       bear in Europe: with his familiar foreign
       journal of a tour through portions of
       England, Scotland, France and Italy*
       (New York 1855)

222–23 Norman Lewis, *Naples '44* (London 1956). Copyright © 1978. Norman Lewis. Reprinted by permission of Da Capo Press, an imprint of the Hachette Book Group

225–26 Jasper and Peter Sluyter Danckaerts, *Journal of a Voyage to New York in 1679–80* (New York 1867)

226–27 Adlard Welby, *A visit to North America and the English settlements in Illinois*, in *Early Western Travels*, ed. Reuben Gold Thwaites, Vol. 12 (New York 1905)

227–29 Charles Dickens, *American Notes* (New York 1883)

229–31 John Walter, *First Impressions of America* (London 1867)

231–33 Simone de Beauvoir, *America Day by Day*, trans. Carol Cosman, Univ of California Press (Los Angeles 1996). First published as *L'Amérique au jour le jour*, 1947 © Editions Gallimard, Paris, 1954

235–36 Rabban Bar Sauma, in *The Monks of Kublai Khan*, trans Sir E. A. Wallis Budge (London 1928)

237–38 Thomas Coryat, *Coryat's Crudities: Hastily gobled up in five moneths travells in France, Savoy, Italy, Rhetia commonly called the Grisons country, Helvetia alias Switzerland, some parts of high Germany and the Netherlands*, Vol. I (Glasgow 1905)

238–39 Arthur Young, *Arthur Young's Travels in France during the Years 1787, 1788, 1789* (London 1906)

239–41 Queen Victoria, *Journal*. RA VIC/MAIN/QVJ (W) 20 August 1855 www.queenvictoriasjournals.org. © Her Majesty Queen Elizabeth II 2012

241–43 Mark Twain, *The Innocents Abroad* (New York 1869)

243–44 Anton Chekhov, *Letters of Anton Chekhov*, ed. Constance Garnett (London 1920)

244–46 Gertrude Stein, *The Autobiography of Alice B. Toklas* (New York 1933)

248–50 Fynes Moryson, *An Itinerary Containing his Ten Yeeres Travell through the Twelve Dominions of Germany, Bohmerland, Sweitzerland, Netherland, Denmarke, Poland, Italy, Turky, France, England, Scotland & Ireland* (London 1617)

250–51 Hester Lynch Piozzi, *Observations and Reflections Made in the Course of a Journey through France, Italy, and Germany*, Vol. II (London 1789)

251–52 Albert Camus, 'Death in the Soul' (1938), in *Lyrical and Critical Essays*, trans. Philip Thody (London 1968). Copyright © 1958, by Editions Gallimard. Reprinted by Permission of Vintage Books, a division of Penguin Random House Canada Limited

254–55 John White, *Journal of a Voyage to New South Wales* (London 1790)

255–56 Maria Graham, *Journal of a Voyage to Brazil, and Residence there during part of the years 1821, 1822, 1823* (London 1824)

257 Prince Adalbert of Prussia, *Travels in the South of Europe and in Brazil: with a voyage up the Amazon, and its tributary the Xingú* (London 1849)

258–59 Annie Allnutt Brassey, *Our Voyage in the Sunbeam: Our Home on the Ocean for Eleven Months* (London 1879)

259–60 Peter Fleming, *Brazilian Adventure* (London 1933). Published by the Alden Press. Copyright © Peter Fleming 1933

262–63 *Marvels of Rome, Or, A Picture of the Golden City*, trans. Francis Morgan Nichols (London 1889)

264–65 Pero Tafur, *Travels and Adventures of Pero Tafur 1435–1439*, ed. E. Denison Ross and Eileen Power (London 1926)

265–66 Michel de Montaigne, *The Journal of Montaigne's Travels in Italy by way of Switzerland and Germany in 1580 and 1581*, trans. W. G. Walters, Vol. II (London 1903)

266–67 Edward Gibbon, *Memoirs of My Life and Writings* (London 1796)

267–69 Charles Dickens, *Pictures from Italy* (London 1846)

269–70 Oscar Wilde, in *Letters of Oscar Wilde*, ed. Rupert Hart-Davis (London 1962)

270–71 Eleanor Clark, *Rome and a Villa* (London 1953), pp. 35–36. Copyright © 1992 by Eleanor Clark. Reprinted by HarperCollins Publishers

273–74 Nathaniel Wraxall, *A Tour through some of the northern parts of Europe, particularly Copenhagen, Stockholm and Petersburgh in a series of letters* (London 1776)

274–76 Robert Ker Porter, *Travelling Sketches in Russia and Sweden: During the Years 1805, 1806, 1807, 1808* (Philadelphia 1809)

276–77 R. B. Paul, *Journal of a Tour to Moscow, in the Summer of 1836* (London 1836)

277–79 Marquis de Custine, *Russia* (New York 1854)

279–80 Consuelo Vanderbilt Balsan, *The Glitter and the Gold* (London 1954)

281 Corliss Lamont, *Russia Day by Day* (New York 1933)

283–85 Ruy González de Clavijo, *Embassy to Tamerlane*, trans. Guy Le Strange (London 1928)

285–86 Emperor Babur, *The Babur-nama in English*, trans. Annette Beveridge (London 1921)

288–89 John Audubon, *Audubon's Western Journal, 1849–1850: Being the MS. record of a trip from New York to Texas, and an overland journey through Mexico and Arizona to the gold fields of California* (Cleveland 1906)

289–90 Kume Kunitake, *Records of My Visits to America and Europe 1871–1873* (Tokyo 1876)

290–92 Ellen G. Hodges, *Surprise Land: A Girl's Letters from the West* (Boston 1887)

292–94 Enrico Caruso, *The Sketch* magazine (London 1906)

294–96 Helen Perry, *The Human Be-In* (New York 1970). Published by Basic Books. Copyright © Helen Perry 1970

298 John White, *Journal of a Voyage to New South Wales* (London 1790)

298–300 Anthony Trollope, *Australia and New Zealand* (London 1876)

300–02 Mark Twain, *Following the Equator* (New York 1897)

302 D. H. Lawrence, *Kangaroo* (London 1923)

304–05 Leo Africanus, *The History and Description of Africa,* trans. Robert Brown, Vol. I (London 1896)

305–07 René Caillié, *Revue des deux mondes. Journal des Voyages*, Series II, Vol. I (Paris 1830)

307–09 Heinrich Barth, *Travels and Discoveries in North and Central Africa* (New York 1857)

311–12 John Saris, *The Voyage of Captain John Saris to Japan, 1613*, ed. Ernest M. Satow (London 1900)

312–13 Ernest Mason Satow, *A Diplomat in Japan* (Philadelphia 1921)

313–15 Isabella Bird, *Unbeaten Tracks in Japan* (London 1880)

315–16 Mrs Hugh [Mary Crawford] Fraser, *Letters from Japan: A Record of Modern Life in the Island Empire* (London 1899)

316–19 Marie Stopes, *Journal from Japan* (London 1910)

319–20 Fosco Maraini, *Meeting with Japan*, trans. Eric Mosbacher (London 1959). Published by Hutchinson Ltd. Copyright © Fosco Maraini 1959

322–24 Pero Tafur, *Travels and Adventures of Pero Tafur 1435–1439*, ed. E. Denison Ross and Eileen Power (London 1926)

324–25 Pietro Casola, *Canon Pietro Casola's Pilgrimage to Jerusalem in the year 1494*, ed. Margaret Newett (Manchester 1907)

325–26 John Evelyn, *The Diary of John Evelyn*, Vol. I (London 1818)

326–28 Johann von Goethe, *Italian Journey*, in *The Works of J. W. von Goethe*, Vol. 12, trans. A. J. W. Morrison (London 1892)

328–29 Thomas Jefferson Hogg, *Two Hundred and Nine Days; or, The journal of a traveller on the continent*, Vol. II (London 1827)

329–31 John Ruskin, *The Stones of Venice* (London 1851–53)

331–32 Henry James, *Portraits of Places* (London 1883)

334 Antonio Bonfini, in *Daily Life in the Vienna of Mozart and Schubert*, by Marcel Brion (London 1961)

334–35 Evliya Çelebi, *In the Empire of the Golden Apple*, trans. Richard Bassett, quoted in *Vienna, A Travellers' Companion*, edited by John Lehmann and Richard Bassett (London 1988)

335–36 Lady Mary Wortley Montagu, *Letters* (London 1789)

336–38 Frances Trollope, *Vienna and the Austrians: with some account of a journey through Swabia, Bavaria, the Tyrol, and the Salzbourg*, Vol. II (London 1838)

338–40 Anton Chekhov, *Letters of Anton Chekhov*, ed. Constance Garnett (London 1920)

340–41 Patrick Leigh Fermor, *The Time of Gifts* (London 1977). Copyright © 1977 Patrick Leigh Fermor. Reproduced by permission of John Murray Press, an imprint of Hodder and Stoughton Limited

343–45 Adlard Welby, *A visit to North America and the English settlements in Illinois*, in *Early Western Travels*, ed. Reuben Gold Thwaites, Vol. 12 (New York 1905)

345–47 Theodore Dwight, *Travels in America* (Glasgow 1848)

347–48 Jan Morris, 'The Morning After: Washington D.C. 1974'. First published in *Travels*, by Faber & Faber (New York 1980). Copyright © 1974 Jan Morris